FALKLANDS HERO

FALKLANDS HERO

Ian McKay – The Last VC of the 20th Century

JON COOKSEY

Pen & Sword
MILITARY

First published in Great Britain in 2012 by
Pen & Sword Military
An imprint of
Pen & Sword Books Ltd
47 Church Street
Barnsley
South Yorkshire
S70 2AS

ISBN 978 1 84415 493 7

A CIP catalogue record for this book is available from the British Library.

Typeset in 11pt Bembo by Mac Style, Beverley, East Yorkshire
Printed and bound in the UK by CPI Group (UK) Ltd, Croydon, CRO 4YY

Pen & Sword Books Ltd incorporates the imprints of Pen & Sword Aviation, Pen
& Sword Maritime, Pen & Sword Military, Wharncliffe Local History, Pen
& Sword Select, Pen & Sword Military Classics, Leo Cooper,
Remember When, Seaforth Publishing and Frontline Publishing

For a complete list of Pen & Sword titles please contact
PEN & SWORD BOOKS LIMITED
47 Church Street, Barnsley, South Yorkshire, S70 2AS, England
E-mail: enquiries@pen-and-sword.co.uk
Website: www.pen-and-sword.co.uk

Contents

Foreword

By eminent historian Andrew Roberts

The word 'hero' is used all too easily and often nowadays, even to describe sportsmen and entertainers. This fine book is about a genuine hero, someone who at the age of only 29 quite deliberately sacrificed his own life in battle so that others – his comrades in the 3rd Battalion, The Parachute Regiment – might live.

No-one could be better qualified to tell the, by turns, appalling and thrilling story of what happened on the night of 11/12 June 1982 on Mount Longdon in the Falkland Islands than Jon Cooksey, who has several first-class works of military history to his credit, including a history of the battle of Mount Longdon itself, and who is a former editor of the magazine *Battlefields Review*.

Cooksey draws a superb word-picture of the grand strategy of the Falklands War, why Mount Longdon was such a key tactical objective in the struggle to recapture the Falklands' capital Port Stanley, the personality of the Yorkshire-born sergeant of 4 Platoon, B Company Ian McKay, and his truly inspiring act of valour. Jon Cooksey has also broken significant new ground in our knowledge of the period, both in his devastating castigations of Intelligence and communications failures on the Falklands, and in identifying beyond doubt Ian McKay as one of the paratroopers who fired two live rounds on Bloody Sunday in Londonderry, both of which he carefully and conscientiously places in their proper historical context.

Cooksey's spare, direct prose puts us right there with B Company that night on Mount Longdon, 'among the rocks in the dark', facing Argentine snipers armed with night-sighted rifles, with two protected machine guns pouring fire into the British lines. Their officer was down, the danger of delay was potentially lethal, and the cries of the wounded were ringing in McKay's ears when he gathered his small group of men around him. Then they did what they did. Readers will agree that in the long and impossibly glorious history of the ultimate award for personal courage, none has deserved the Victoria Cross more than Sergeant McKay. (Today his medal can be seen in the splendid Lord Ashcroft Gallery at the Imperial War Museum.)

The Falkland Islands, at the eastern entrance to the Magellan Straits in the South Atlantic east of the Argentine province of Patagonia, were a strange place for Britain finally to shrug off her post-imperial decline. For more than a quarter of a century since the Suez Crisis of 1956, Britain had seen a gradual, seemingly-inexorable lessening of her power and influence in the world. She had, in the American Secretary of State Dean Acheson's cruelly perceptive words, 'lost an empire but failed to find a role'. Then, without warning, Britain was suddenly tested in the South Atlantic in such a way that shook her out of her post-Suez torpor. The Falklands Crisis gave her the will to re-discover her capacity for greatness, and the sacrifices made by men like Sergeant Ian McKay VC were integral to that sense of national recrudescence.

The sudden capture of British Crown territories by an Argentine dictatorship (or *Junta*) in March 1982 presented Britain with a stark dilemma. All the experience of the post-Suez world told the British Government that it should negotiate with Buenos Aires in the hope that something might be salvaged from the disaster. The scuttle from Empire, deep defence cuts, Soviet incursions in Africa and Asia, the withdrawal of all military commitments east of Suez, the IRA bombing campaign, ever-deeper European integration: all played a part in setting the political DNA of the British governing class towards negotiation, and, if it seemed necessary, appeasement.

Standing starkly opposed to that defensive, apologetic reaction by then so deeply ingrained in the mind-set of British policy-makers were the instincts of the then prime minister, Margaret Thatcher. She had come to power in 1979 determined to effect fundamental reform in Britain, and one of the things she most wanted to change was the negative assumptions that many in the government and civil service made about Britain's future potential overseas. Never was her 'can-do' approach to governance more vividly demonstrated than in her decision, from the very start of the crisis, to liberate the Falklands, come what may.

The 1,813-strong population of the Islands of only 4,618 square miles were 97 per cent British, but since the Islands had been taken and held principally by *force majeure*, there was technically a legal question over who legitimately owned them. Although Britain could claim the first recorded landing on the Islands in January 1690, they had also belonged to both France and Spain in the meantime. Even though they were 250 miles away from the Argentine coastline, they were fully 8,000 miles from Britain.

So the decision to send a large naval and military Task Force that distance through some of the roughest seas on any oceans, and then to assault larger forces, in order to free a small population of British citizens, flew directly in the face of all post-Suez experience. To many people in the Foreign Office, parliament, press and even some in the Tory government – brought up on the assumption of British retreat and defeat – it beggared belief. Yet that is exactly what Mrs Thatcher and her small, hand-picked war cabinet proposed to do.

Yet however much moral and political courage Mrs Thatcher might show, victory in the Falklands campaign would come down to the sheer physical courage of men like Ian McKay. They had trained ceaselessly for this moment, but would they be able to deliver what the nation craved? Jon Cooksey is particularly good in this book at getting deep into the psychology of the ordinary 'squaddie', into what makes him tick. For as Wellington said of his men before Waterloo: that is the article upon which everything depends.

'I've no intention of taking any risks and getting killed,' McKay had told a friend on his way down to the Falklands. 'If I do… then it will be to protect my men, to save lives.' The Falklands War took place thirty years ago, yet heroic statements like that cross the ages without paying regard to time and place, and could have been made by NCOs of the British Army at the time of El Alamein, or in the trenches of the Western Front, or during the Napoleonic Wars, or further back to the wars of the Duke of Marlborough. Today, in the harsh and unforgiving hills of Helmand province in Afghanistan, such sentiments still actuate senior non-commissioned officers like Sergeant Ian McKay VC. The day they no longer do will be the day that we must give up any hope of making the world a better place. Yet so long as Britain continues to produce men of his calibre, we will always have a fighting chance of making a positive contribution to the history of Mankind.

I cannot recommend this book more highly.

Andrew Roberts (www.andrew-roberts.net)
March 2012

Acknowledgements

Researching military history is one thing but researching the entire life of someone who is remembered by the majority of people for one single act in a military context, albeit an act of extraordinary courage which resulted in the award of the Victoria Cross, is quite another. Whilst I a felt at least competent to research the military aspects of Ian McKay's life by doing what most researchers, when pressed, enjoy most – delving into various military records and archives and talking to fellow historians and archivists – I confess to having been moved beyond my comfort zone with this study of Ian's life.

Of course I have done a good deal of 'grubbing' around in various archives and rummaging through documents from the period which coincided with Ian's almost twelve years of service in the Parachute Regiment, but the work has taken me into realms which have been unfamiliar territory. Family, institutional and sporting history – including sifting through a mass of football statistics and results of the old English First Division and lower leagues as far back as the late 1920s and 1930s – have all been trawled in the cause of attempting to get to know what shaped Ian McKay the man.

A book like this, therefore, is impossible to complete without the support, help, advice, enthusiasm and encouragement of a great many people, many of whom have a deep knowledge of and expertise in their particular field. In particular I must thank members of Ian McKay's family, particularly his mother Freda who has given her wholehearted support to the project from the start. I visited her on several occasions and spoke to her often throughout the period of research and realize how painful some of my more prying questioning might have been. I certainly could not have completed the book without her support.

My thanks also go to Ian's wife Marica who agreed to talk to me and read some of the early drafts. I hope that both she and Freda feel that the final result was worthy of their support.

I am particularly indebted to Peter Harper, an ex-pupil of Rotherham Grammar School and more recently of Bath University who had the diligence and foresight in the mid-1980s to produce a substantial memoir on Ian McKay. He collated many personal accounts and cuttings and was kind enough to allow me to use it in my research. It proved to be a huge help as did the material which Mark Adkin had found useful for his research into the 'Last Eleven' VC recipients since 1945 and to which he kindly pointed me.

The help and assistance I received from many others who knew Ian during his formative years was at all times prompt, courteous and unfailingly supportive and I must record my gratitude to his boyhood friend Philip Leeson and to Phil Toft and

Steve Beevers of Rotherham Grammar School Old Boys Association. Peterborough United Football Club historian Peter Lane was able to confirm the service of Ian McKay's grandfather at the club, for which I am most grateful. Peter Bower, the Local Studies Supervisor at Rotherham Archives, fielded several queries regarding local examination results.

In terms of understanding Ian's military life and his service with the Parachute Regiment since August 1970 many have given of their time and knowledge to help clarify various issues. Special mention must be made of those with whom Ian had served in the Parachute Regiment and who went out of their way to meet me and to speak about their memories of him. Sir Hew and Lady Jean Pike have been enthusiastic supporters of the project from the start – Sir Hew loaning many valuable documents – as has Bob Darby, who was a wonderful source of contacts and acted as a critical sounding board for my theories both in the UK and whilst in the Falkland Islands.

Ian Bailey and Andrew Bickerdike – not forgetting their wives Tracey and Mo – and Brian Faulkner have always been willing to help as have, in alphabetical order: Lawrie Ashbridge; 'Baz' Barrett; Laurie Bland; Tony Bojko; Dave Brown; Roy Butler; Kevin Capon; David Collet; Sammy Dougherty; Bob Hilton; Giles Orpen-Smellie; Kevin McGimpsey; the late Roger Patton; Harry Randall; Nick Rose; Mick Southall; Steve Tuffen; John Weeks; John Wood and Mick Whattam.

Rod and Jan Hutchings, who lived at Teal Inlet at the time of the Argentine invasion in 1982, also agreed to speak with me and loaned precious photographs. It was Rod who made the crosses for those men originally buried at Teal Inlet, including that of Ian McKay, and who later built and erected the memorial which still stands on the site of the original burial plot.

Others to whom I am indebted for their studied comments on drafts, the loan of documents, maps and photographs or the results of their own research are Julian Thompson, Nick van der Bijl, Tim Lynch and Mark Higgitt. BBC radio producer Graham McKechnie is always a trusted point of reference. He has once again taken seriously the invaluable role as 'ever critical friend' in reading and commenting honestly on extensive sections of the book in draft form.

Accessing a battlefield or material half a world away is always a challenging prospect and I owe a particular debt of gratitude to those on the Falkland Islands who threw their weight behind my work without even setting eyes on me. Falkland Islanders are a determined, hardy, industrious and busy breed and retain a fierce sense of pride in being British, which many of us who live in Britain seem to have somehow forgotten. Ailsa and Tony Heathman visited Mount Longdon on my behalf armed only with an email and photographs from a complete stranger, as did Tony Smith. Later, when I visited the Falklands on my research trips, all of them took care of me and, with Nobby Clarke, ferried me around. Ailsa and Tony fed me royally at Estancia House and it was my privilege to walk the Mount Longdon battlefield with Vernon Steen on which he had fought with Ian and members of Patrols Company of the 3rd Battalion, the Parachute Regiment (3 Para) on 11/12 June 1982.

It was a chance remark over lunch with author Nigel West which led to him putting me in touch with Colonel Carlos Doglioli in Argentina. Carlos had served as an ADC to Military Governor General Mario Menendez on the Falkland Islands in 1982 and his wholehearted support for my cause when he heard about it was much appreciated. It was Carlos who put me in touch with Colonel Carlos Eduardo Carrizo Salvadores who was in command of the Argentine unit which faced Ian's 3rd Battalion of the Parachute Regiment on Mount Longdon during the battle in which Ian won his VC. Their insight into the arrangement of the defences of Mount Longdon and the weaponry employed was valuable indeed, as was information supplied by Anibal Grillo who fought with the Argentines that night.

Ian McKay's VC was purchased by Lord Ashcroft in 1989 for the Ashcroft Collection which has now found a home in the Ashcroft Gallery at the Imperial War Museum in London where Ian's VC is on permanent display. I am grateful to Michael Naxton, Curator of the Ashcroft Collection, for clarifying several points relating to the display of Ian's VC. Thanks also to my copy editor Lynne Maxwell, who has looked over the text with a detached eye and has made several improvements and probably spared a few blushes in the process, and to Jon Wilkinson and Dominic Allen for their ideas for the art work, maps and jacket design.

Simon Watson and Nicolas Avrillon helped with the translation of text from Spanish to English.

My family often bear the burden of maintaining 'normal life' and do so marvellously in spite of my often irregular and anti-social working habits and research trips. Grateful thanks go to my wife Heather and daughter Georgia for their seemingly limitless patience and understanding in continuing to support me in my work.

If anyone who has been kind enough to help in any way has been missed out please be assured that it has not been intentional. To those so affected please accept my sincere apologies.

In all instances every effort has been made to seek appropriate permissions where necessary but if, inadvertently, these have been overlooked then I or the publishers should be pleased to hear from copyright holders. If any errors or omissions remain, then they are entirely due to oversights on my part.

Introduction

I never met Ian McKay but I knew him. Or rather I knew his world. Not the world he chose to make his life after 1970 when he joined the Airborne Brotherhood of the Parachute Regiment and made the army his life, but the world into which he was born and grew up. I know of some of the formative experiences and forces which shaped him for I am of his generation and I grew up in very similar circumstances, in a very similar environment and in the same period in history as he did.

He lived in Rotherham, I lived just outside another South Yorkshire town, fifteen miles away as the crow flies and in those days – in those far off heady days before the collapse of most of the British manufacturing and production base – you could really count the number of industries in South Yorkshire, apart from agriculture, on two fingers of one hand. There was coal and there was iron and steel. Ian's father was in steel; my father was in coal. In the mid-1960s I used to visit relatives who, like Ian at the time, lived on the huge Kimberworth Park Estate. It may sound strange today but a journey to Kimberworth Park to visit an aunt and uncle was something of an adventure requiring three buses and several hours.

My uncle worked in the steel industry as did Ian's parents, Ken and Freda McKay, Freda in administration. And my relatives lived almost at the end of Leybourne Road, just under a mile from the house in which Ian used to live on Shearman Avenue; a brisk ten minutes on foot or about three minutes by car.

We both grew up in communities of like-minded people with similar interests. Ian's early life was punctuated by events and vignettes remarkably similar to those which sprang up in mine and the *dramatis personae* who moved and interacted with the young Ian McKay in his story bore a remarkable resemblance to many of the characters who moved in mine.

Here there were hard-working and honest fathers who toiled for long hours in heavy, often dirty and always exhausting jobs; doughty women who looked after the children and the pennies, who cooked, cleaned and often held down part-time jobs to earn a little extra for luxuries. There were numerous aunts and uncles who 'popped round' regularly for cups of tea and a chin wag. There were working men's clubs where the men played snooker or cards on weekday evenings and then got dressed up in shirt and tie and took their wives to watch the 'turn' on a Saturday evening.

At weekends and during school holidays entire days would be spent roaming over hill and dale on bikes or out in the woods, splashing in streams, 'scrimming' up trees and hurtling through the undergrowth playing soldiers with best friends. There were family holidays – a week in August – mostly taken on the east coast at Scarborough, Bridlington or Filey, with donkey rides, beach cricket, windbreaks, cold seas and goosebumps galore.

One of Ian's friends, perhaps his best friend from his early childhood and through into secondary school, was Philip Leeson. He remembers how, even when playing 'war', Ian would impose certain rules and a very strict code of conduct. The young 'soldiers' could not 'kill' someone if trees or bushes were in the line of fire – it could only be done out in the open – which led to heated disagreements, almost invariably when Ian was 'shot', because some bough or twig had got in the way.

Philip Leeson grew up with Ian McKay and spent countless hours in his company, not only at school, but in and out of each other's houses and out in the semi-urban 'playground' that was their small patch of industrial South Yorkshire.

Although they drifted apart when they were 15-years–old in 1969 and rarely saw each other after that, Ian's friendship during those early years had, nevertheless, left a deep impression on his boyhood friend. Ask yourself the question: how many of your boyhood friends would drive up to the house you lived in during your childhood – a house in which you last set foot more than forty years ago – park their car outside and sit in silence, in spite of the fact that they had not seen you in more than three decades? Philip Leeson did, on Remembrance Day 2011 at 11.00am. That simple act of remembrance of someone special who had touched his life speaks more eloquently of the impact Ian McKay had on those he came into contact with than thousands of my words ever will.

Ian's family, although far from poor, was not materially well off. Whatever the bank balance lacked it was more than amply offset by the incalculable riches of love, warmth and security which came from belonging to a close-knit family in which both parents gave of their best for their children, instilling within them a confidence and a code of values which they hoped would improve their lives.

This then was Ian McKay's world and his life until he joined the Parachute Regiment at the age of 17 in August 1970, a decision which caused his parents, and his father particularly, a good deal of anxiety for Ian was not a youth faced with an 'either or' choice of the army or the dole queue. He was an intelligent, bright and enthusiastic boy and passed the 11-plus examination to attend the local grammar school. That he was more interested in the lure of the playing field than the classroom was immaterial. Thousands of working class boys and youths, deemed by the education system to have some modicum of above average intelligence, would sooner don games strip and chase a ball around a muddy field or hit it with a bat or racquet than stick their noses inside a text book.

The number of GCE O-Level passes Ian achieved was perhaps limited but he nevertheless had choices when his compulsory schooling approached its end. He could have done re-sits and could have gone on to do A Levels, followed by further or higher education.

Such a route was quite within his capabilities and many of his contemporaries did just that, securing for themselves professional qualifications, good jobs with career development prospects followed by senior positions with commensurate salaries and comfortable lives. Ken McKay was dead set against the army as a career for his son. He wanted him to be a PE teacher.

I have no doubt that had he followed his father's wishes and gone on to become a PE teacher Ian would have become an outstanding member of the profession and one of the best in terms of setting and expecting high standards of dress, manner and approach, and developing his skills to become an excellent teacher and coach. This is not pure speculation on my part. That he had these skills and qualities in abundance we know from those who can testify to his pride in his own appearance whilst in the army – Ian did all the ironing at home as he wanted everything to be just so and his kit was always immaculate. He had a quick and logical mind, excellent co-ordination, dexterity, strength and cardiovascular endurance, and a deep well of patience when dealing with youngsters in his role as an instructor of recruits which never, it seemed, ran dry.

He would have become an outstanding role model in the teaching profession as indeed he did in the army and would inevitably have progressed through the profession to a position in senior management, having a healthy disdain for some of the more outlandish schemes hatched by those of his superiors along the way.

But it was the army which benefitted from Ian McKay's skills and personal qualities and what was a loss to the nation's schoolchildren was the army's – and specifically the Parachute Regiment's – gain. Ian was everything that every Parachute soldier aspired to be: very fit, honest, hard-working and skilful, quick-witted, intelligent, adaptable, solid and reliable.

Within seven month of joining up Ian was in Northern Ireland at a time of cataclysmic social and political upheaval in the province. Within a week of his arrival three young Scottish soldiers were murdered by the IRA near Belfast and the dreadful news caused much anguish in the McKay household as they feared for their son's safety. That gnawing anguish never diminished throughout Ian's long months of service over two separate tours of duty and in fact was heightened when, on Sunday, 30 January 1972, his company of the 1st Battalion, The Parachute Regiment, was ordered into the Bogside in Derry to conduct an arrest operation during a civil rights march. Ian McKay found himself in the car park of the Rossville Flats with acid bombs being thrown down on him from the balconies above. His sergeant ordered him to fire at his assailants and Ian fired two aimed shots at a man he thought was responsible, although he believed he had not hit his intended target. Ian was not the only soldier who fired that day and by the time he and the rest of his company had been pulled out thirteen civilians lay dead in the Bogside, with a similar number wounded. The day became known as Bloody Sunday, a day which history would mark out as the most pivotal day in the long agony of Northern Ireland during the time known as The Troubles. Its repercussions were monumental and were felt around the globe; there was an increase in support for the IRA and a boost in volunteers to its cause; there followed the abolition of the Northern Ireland Government and Direct Rule from Westminster and the dawning of the grim realization on the part of the British that a purely military solution was now no longer possible.

The 18-year–old paratrooper Ian McKay was one of those at the centre of the storm which characterized one of the most momentous events in recent British history. The resulting public inquiry called him as a witness and he duly gave his evidence under oath in front of the then Lord Chief Justice of England, Lord Widgery. To preserve his anonymity he became 'Soldier T'.

Yet Widgery's report only served to inflame the Nationalist community who claimed it was a Westminster government-backed whitewash. The wounds – physical, emotional and political – of Bloody Sunday simply festered and it was not until the publication, in 2010, of the report of a second inquiry, instigated in 1998 at enormous expense by then Prime Minister Tony Blair and chaired by Lord Saville, that the relatives of the dead felt justice had at last been done.

Ian was also involved in that second inquiry, albeit posthumously, when his original evidence was looked at afresh and 'Soldier T' appeared once more in the conclusions of a landmark official report of a public inquiry.

In a little more than ten years after Bloody Sunday, Ian would yet again be in the vanguard of those who were shaping history as he faced the greatest test of any soldier – to be committed against an organized enemy on the battlefield. One wonders whether he ever questioned, as many soldiers do on the eve of their first battle, that he would pass that test.

I spoke with many, many people who served with Ian McKay at different times in his army career during the research for this book. There was absolutely no link between many of them, save for the fact that they, like him, had also worn the coveted Red Beret. I noted in their recollections that the same types of illustrations, often using the same words, would surface again and again. I almost came to hope that someone, somewhere would tell me how he had, at some point, say, let them down, had said or done something cruel, or had simply 'messed up'. I can honestly say that no such incidents were ever reported to me.

There were flaws, of course there were – which man doesn't have them – but these were more to do with his frustration at the overweening pettifogging of quasi-officialdom or the sheer stupidity (in his eyes at least) of some of the orders he was expected to carry out and which he felt were simply not logical or practical. Stubbornness was another trait which could surface at times and an occasional unwillingness to become fully involved in a sport or activity if he sensed that he could not be the best.

Some of those who knew him referred to him as being 'old fashioned' or 'conventional'. This was not meant as an insult, rather that he did not care for fads and trends and preferred to plough his own furrow, a feature of his behaviour that continued in the army to a certain extent. One colleague related how Ian, although always friendly and accepted by his peers, would often join his mates for a drink in the bar. As others got into the swing of the evening and hunkered down for a boozy session he would 'have a couple of pints and then quietly slip away'. Ian McKay could never be accused of being boastful, a show-off or a crowd pleaser.

As a young soldier Ian certainly took advantage of many of the opportunities for rest and relaxation offered but perhaps he didn't always feel the need to be the life and soul of the party or to follow the crowd. Being his own man, Ian didn't recognize that the generally accepted customs and traditions usually associated with male bonding in a male-dominated environment were the be-all-and-end-all of being able to fit in. After all he had had some strong role models in his life and many of them had been women. His mother Freda, his maternal grandmother and several aunts were all strong women in their own ways. His grandmother – or 'Jamjar' as Ian had called her since childhood – had followed his professional footballer grandfather around the country during the economically depressed 1930s and had later run several public houses.

After Ian's birth his mother had two more sons, Graham and Neal, both of whom suffered with cystic fibrosis which, at the time they were born in the 1950s, almost always proved fatal in childhood. Caring for them took up a great deal of her time and energy and there were times when Ian simply had to get on and do things for himself when he was still quite young. He was most certainly not unloved or neglected but by necessity was left to his own devices whilst his father was at work and his mother worked through her daily cycle of exhausting physical treatment of his brothers. This helped to foster traits of independence, resourcefulness, self-reliance and assertiveness in Ian, traits which had been developed, albeit in different circumstances, in the young Winston Churchill through a lack of parental contact. 'Solitary trees, if they grow at all, grow strong…' the future British Prime Minster and war leader had reflected when writing of his childhood in 1899.[1]

Although he acknowledged it, Ian seemed to accept that caring for his brothers took up much of his parents' time. That he loved his brothers was never in question and, as their older, fitter, stronger and healthier brother, he was extremely protective of them.

It was during a posting to Germany in the mid-1970s that Ian met Marica, another woman with a strong personality, whom he later married and with whom he had a daughter Melanie. Marica already had a son by a previous marriage to another paratrooper and Ian viewed his new role of family man very seriously. With the arrival of Melanie he took to fatherhood with even greater relish and was absolutely besotted with his daughter, so much so that there was talk of him leaving the army and changing tack in terms of his future career. A few years later, however, a man called Constantino Davidoff stepped on to an island called South Georgia in the South Atlantic half a world away and sparked a war which would rob Ian of his future.

Out on an unforgiving battlefield, in a desperate situation and facing fearsome Argentine resistance, Ian McKay found somewhere within himself a vital wellspring of extraordinary courage and self-sacrifice which inspired the men around him and helped his battalion to victory, a victory which exacted a heavy price and for which he paid with his life. It is for his part in that war and, more specifically, for receiving the Victoria Cross for that one crucial action that Ian McKay is now best remembered.

There has always existed a special aura around the Victoria Cross and the few men who have received it since its institution in 1856 at the behest of Queen Victoria. At the time of writing it has been awarded 1,356 times to 1,353 recipients. Three men have received it twice. The VC takes precedence over all other British and Commonwealth honours and it is this, when coupled with the paucity of its bestowal, which gives it a cachet which no other award in the world can match.

The men – for it has only ever been awarded to a man, although women are eligible – who have received this most prestigious and pre-eminent of gallantry awards and have survived, have truly earned the right to wear that 'little bit' of crimson ribbon.

When, on 11 October 1982, the name of Ian McKay entered into the pantheon of that select band who have been granted the Victoria Cross he at once became cocooned by the aura which emanates from that elegantly simple bronze cross which bears his name, but the story of Ian McKay is so much more than that of his association with the VC, albeit the most highly prized award 'for valour' in the world. His is a story of service and duty to his family, to the army and the Parachute Regiment and to the men he trained and led. Those men would follow him anywhere.

After Ian's death his close family chose to deal with it in different ways.

The immediate impact of Ian's loss was perhaps felt less overtly but no less keenly, having lost her father, by his young daughter Melanie. Ian had just five precious years with his daughter. He never saw her grow up into the talented and dedicated teacher she became. For her part Melanie was initially told that her father was very ill and that he would not be coming home. She has only fleeting scraps of memories of the man who, for the nation, was and will always remain a Falklands hero but to her was simply 'Daddy'.

From the moment they heard the news of Ian's death, tragedy, it seemed, was intent on stalking the McKay family, paying close attention to Freda in particular. Ken McKay did not want to talk about Ian's death but that was all Freda wanted to do. These polar opposite approaches to bereavement and the grieving process eventually drove a wedge between them which could not be bridged and they separated eighteen months later after more than thirty years of marriage. Although Freda McKay went on to find happiness and some comfort over the next ten years with a new partner, she and Ken eventually worked through their differences and found a way to become friends again until they were united in grief once more with the death of their youngest son, Neal, in 1989.

Freda lost her partner Jeff Agar to cancer in 1994 and the following year, in 1995, her third and last surviving son, Graham, lost his battle against cystic fibrosis. All three of the McKay boys were now dead. It is ironic that Ian, strong, healthy and fit as he was and their protector for so many years, should die at the age of 29 whilst his brothers outlived him; Neal reaching the age of 32 and Graham 39. Had he lived, Ian would have been extremely proud of the way both his brothers had epitomized the McKay family's grit and determination to battle against overwhelming odds to survive much, much longer than the medical profession expected and that they, too, had lead fulfilling lives, albeit lives cut tragically short.

In 1998, three years after Graham's death, Freda was waiting at the Cenotaph near the entrance to Clifton Park in Rotherham on Remembrance Sunday. Ken was due to join her and other members of the family in their annual act of remembrance during which they always laid a wreath in Ian's memory. He did not turn up. Ken McKay died – on that most sadly poignant of days – of a massive heart attack whilst getting ready. Perhaps the strain of being reminded of his loss, yet again and so publicly, was too much for his already ailing heart to bear.

As the widow of one of only two men who had been awarded the Victoria Cross in almost seventeen years and only the eleventh since the end of the Second World War, Marica McKay became 'hot news' and found herself at the epicentre of a firestorm of publicity. As a recipient of the VC Ian McKay now belonged to the nation and Marica was fully expected to play the role of grieving widow in full view of the harsh glare of the media spotlight. Reporters, photographers and television cameras contacted her for words, more words and pictures, and everyone wanted a piece of her.

But in the autumn of 1982 one newspaper stepped way over the mark. *The Sun* ran a 'World Exclusive' with Marica which would have been a fair 'scoop' if any of its reporters had spoken to her at all. Instead, the resulting piece could have won a prize for best new work of fiction, for Marica had agreed to talk to another paper and was at a London hotel with its representatives at the time *The Sun* claimed she was talking to them.

The Sun was censured by the Press Council and apologized but the damage was done and Marica, already reserved, was now bruised and ultra-suspicious of the motives of those who wanted to use her for their own ends. She turned away from both the papers and the publicity and instead relied on her own inner reserves of strength to protect herself and her children, especially her five-year-old daughter Melanie from possible further damage. Her name later cropped up in a debate in the House of Commons on privacy and remains on record in *Hansard* for posterity.

Marica was the daughter of an army father and had married two soldiers. She knew how the army worked and had lived all her life with its vicissitudes, the constant coming and goings, relocations, periods of enforced separation and the 'hurry up and wait' culture of some of its logistical operations. She kept her own council and made a conscious decision not to become involved in many of the events which, over the years, have been held either to commemorate Ian's VC or the Falklands War. That her silence or absence from these events has been read by some as indifference rather than a personal coping mechanism is a harsh judgment given her history with and suspicions of the media.

Only Marica McKay knows how she felt when her husband was killed and how she feels now as, at the time of writing, the thirtieth anniversary of the Falklands War approaches. Only she knows what it means to lose *her* husband and to be robbed of the ability to look back over a long, successful and happy family life at a time when many of her contemporaries are beginning to contemplate retirement together with their spouses. Instead she looks back over the last thirty years to a time when she had to cope as best she could. Bereft of Ian's love, friendship and support she has had to live with the memory that her husband's last breath was expended in flinging his battered body at an Argentine machine-gun pit on a night when the freezing air was filled with fear and blood and the sounds and screams of battle amongst the rocks of a far distant mountain.

Much has been written on 3 Para's battle for Mount Longdon on the night of 11/12 June 1982 at the height of the Falklands War and the deeds of its B Company during that battle. Thousands of words have sought to describe and analyze the fighting in which B Company was engaged, and the manner in which Sergeant Ian McKay of 4 Platoon earned his VC has been the subject of much discussion and speculation.

The bare bones of that attack have been well-rehearsed in the pages of several books and magazines, including some under my name: how they came in from the west, in line with the axis of Mount Longdon and assaulted it 'end on'; how they traversed a minefield on the way and then fought their way doggedly through a series of sheer-sided and virtually parallel rock channels – some men clawing their way ever higher towards the western summit whilst others grappled with a series of Argentine sangars many feet below on the northern face of the mountain. After bitter gutter fighting of the most vicious and personal nature – bunker by bunker and often hand-to hand – somewhere in the region of that first summit, either around it or below it, Argentine resistance stiffened around a series of sangars centred on a well-sited heavy machine-gun complex. At this point Andrew Bickerdike, 4 Platoon's commander was seriously wounded along with several others and the attack stalled.

Enter 24210031 Sergeant Ian John McKay, aged 29 and with a wealth of experience accrued during eleven years and ten months of service in two of the three battalions of the Parachute Regiment. Assuming command of 4 Platoon, it is an accepted fact that Ian McKay gathered a small group of young men around him, organized them and led them in a charge against the machine-gun position which was pinning his men down. The gun was silenced and the attack was resumed but Ian was killed in the process, an act which was recognized with the posthumous award of the VC.

It was assumed that no-one would ever know the exact spot at which Ian McKay had died. A small cross has since been erected on the north face of Longdon, in the middle of a patch of open ground and directly below the sheer wall of the western summit which purports to mark that site.

This was an orthodoxy to which I also subscribed until I began the research for this book and met and spoke at length with men of 3 Para who had been with Ian McKay on Mount Longdon and had seen him in the minutes and, in some cases, seconds, before he died. I met Ian Bailey – the last man to have seen Ian McKay alive – several times, as I did Andrew Bickerdike, Ian's immediate superior who devolved command to his platoon sergeant after he himself was wounded.

Others who had had contact with Ian prior to, during, or in the immediate aftermath of the battle – men like Bob Darby, Brian Faulkner, John Weeks, Sammy Dougherty and Tony Bojko to name a few – were kind enough to talk to me.

These men have gone their separate ways in the thirty years since 1982 and rarely see each other, except for meeting up with the odd ex-comrade here or attending an infrequent reunion there. Many have lost touch altogether, even those who were very close friends in 1982. Although there is an immense sense of pride in their individual and collective achievements and a deep well of shared respect for Ian's memory, most do not meet to discuss the events of 11/12 June 1982 on Mount Longdon on a regular basis. As 'Baz' Barret, a trained, qualified and serving teacher when I spoke to him, put it to me so succinctly twenty-five years after the battle in which he was wounded, 'funnily enough Jon, we don't sit around all day and talk about Longdon and Ian McKay!' Time and lives may have moved on but that is not to say they do not still remember.

Some men, like Ian Bailey and Andrew Bickerdike, told me that for all the words written about them since 1982, no-one had spoken to them at length about their experiences in all that time save for a flurry of comment in late 1982. I had not set out to question the orthodoxy or to court controversy but as I listened to what these men had to say, independently and without prompting, I sensed an underlying unease with the accepted version of events regarding the battle fought on Mount Longdon by 4 and 5 Platoons in particular. On several occasions I was informed that the platoons had fought their way a great deal further along the mountain that night before their attack was held up than the published works would have us believe.

The legacy of what Ian McKay did that night lives on. Ian Bailey was amongst a few others who happened to be there and if Ian McKay had picked up anything from his time as an instructor he knew quality and talent in a junior non-commissioned officer when he saw it. He was not about to let Corporal Ian Bailey scuttle off to another part of the battlefield just because he was in another platoon when the entire attack was in danger of grinding to a halt at that very point.

When Ian organized the attack and his small party broke cover to attack the Argentine bunkers the rest of Ian's party were either killed or wounded within a few seconds. Ian Bailey was shot in the hip – one of three wounds he received – and fell but he saw Ian McKay charging on as he did so. He was the last man to see Ian alive, had received a Military Medal in October 1982 for his part in the VC action and it was essential that I heard his first-hand account.

My curiosity was aroused as I sat with Ian Bailey in his front room near Aldershot one day in November 2006 on the first of my two visits to see him. A speculative question regarding his location that night, to which I admit I was not really expecting a firm answer, was met with an astounding admission. 'I know exactly where I was,' he said with absolute conviction:

In January 1983 I was at the Depot and was called in one day by Lieutenant Colonel Brewis. Royal Engineers had been clearing up on Mount Longdon and had found my dog tags. One of the three rounds which hit me went straight across the back of my neck and I didn't know it then but it severed the cord on my dog tags. When I was recovered later the dog tags were left where they had fallen. The engineers had taken a photograph of the position and sent the dog tags and the photograph back to the Parachute Regiment HQ and they were handed back to me. When I was posted back to the Falklands in 1998–99 I went back up [Longdon] and I went straight to the place. I followed the route up, where we'd gone. We were far in advance of anybody else; we were nearly at our objectives at the far end of the mountain and had to withdraw afterwards because there were so few of us up there.[2]

He went upstairs and returned with the dog tags, cord severed just as he had said and he showed me the horizontal scar across the nape of his neck. But that was not all, he had further photographs. These were of his return visit to Longdon during his posting in the late 1990s. In one he is pictured crossing rising ground towards a jumble of rocks further up the slope, in another he is pictured 'standing on the spot where my dog tags were found'.[3] In both there was a distinctively-shaped rock.

I now had photographs but out of context they meant nothing. Distinctive or not there are thousands of rocks on Mount Longdon and Longdon is a very large mountain. It is also a very long way away. A visit to check for myself was out of the question for the time being. At this point I had the good fortune to be put in touch with Ailsa and Tony Heathman at Estancia House on the Falkland Islands. Well known to many soldiers of 3 Para, Ailsa and Tony had welcomed the battalion in 1982 when it had been making its epic cross-country TAB (Tactical Advance to Battle) across East Falklands towards Port Stanley.[4] It was from positions around the Heathman farm and Mount Vernet that Ian McKay and 3 Para had begun their final advance on the night of the battle.

Ailsa and Tony had visited Mount Longdon many times in the past and kindly agreed to help find the position as had Tony Smith, another islander with whom I was put in touch. I sent the photographs and found it humbling that these people should give up valuable spare time in their very busy lives to help a complete stranger on the other side of the world by taking several blurred photographs up on to Mount Longdon and to look for a single rock amongst thousands. On 24 April 2007 I received an email from Ailsa:

> At long last, Tony and I and a few others ventured up to Longdon yesterday in a bitterly cold wind that turned to driving rain as we were about to leave. To cut a long story short, we found the rock in Ian Bailey's photos fairly easily. It is definitely east of the bowl by 100yds or a little more. The ridge of rocks runs along the north face of Longdon and then there is a gap of open ground before you go on to Full Back [3 Para's second and final objective]. Ian B's rock is less than 100yds from the east end of the long rocky ridge. The mark showing on the rock in the photos you sent is caused by a shadow as the bottom, right corner of the rock is missing… Very recently I heard something about Vernon Steen [another Falkland Islander] being with Ian McKay that night too so I rang him this morning to see if he could throw any light on the matter. If I understood him correctly, he last saw Ian in about the same place as Ian B's photos were taken. He said he was only with Ian [McKay] for about an hour and there were four or five in the group but Ian McKay was the only one named to him. He described seeing Ian below a rock face, in a gulley, which seemed to fit the position we were at yesterday.

This was news indeed; Ian Bailey's position had been found but even more encouraging was the fact that there was another who had seen Ian McKay in roughly the same place.

Towards the end of 2007 and again in early 2008 I was able to make three research trips to the Falkland Islands. I met Ailsa and Tony Heathman and Tony Smith and spent a total of some 14 hours over a period of three days walking Mount Longdon. I was introduced to Vernon Steen who had seen Ian just before he had set out on his mission to destroy the Argentine machine-gun position.

We spoke at length and he and Tony Smith accompanied me onto the mountain during one of my research trips. Vernon had never met or discussed the battle with Ian Bailey, in fact Vernon Steen, the quiet, unassuming man that he is, chooses not to discuss the battle or his part in it with many people but on 11/12 June 1982 he was one of two civilians who fought with 3 Para on Mount Longdon and, like Ian Bailey, he too knew exactly where he had been on the night of the battle and where he had set eyes on Ian McKay.

He had first set foot on Longdon's steep slopes and crags as a boy in the early 1950s, helping out on the sheep farm which included its jagged spurs and boulder-strewn heights in its acreage. He had played on Mount Longdon, worked on Mount Longdon, trained with the Falkland Islands Defence Force on Mount Longdon and, at one time, had even been responsible for maintaining the telephone line across Mount Longdon. If nothing else, Vernon Steen knows Mount Longdon.

We were standing at the stainless steel memorial cross on the western summit – B Company's first objective called 'Fly Half' – after working our way up the mountain from the northwest. We studied the memorials and the cans of Boddington's beer and the bottle of Lamb's Navy Rum placed there by 3 Para veterans for their dead comrades. I asked Vernon where he had seen Ian: 'I'll show you,' he said and gestured with his hand for me to follow. He set off at pace, striding out purposefully past the squat, granite memorial adorned with poppies of bronze and down the incline from Fly Half into a hollow in the ground beyond. Forging ahead, up and over the hollow and on to the saddle of the ridge, he passed another significant gap in the rocks to the left and pushed on even further towards the jagged fingers of another outcrop which formed the snout of the positions held by the 2nd Platoon of B Company of the Argentine 7th Mechanized Infantry Regiment under Staff Sergeant González. Passing this outcrop he now veered left and dropped away down the rocks – half-walking, half-sliding on the coarse green ferns which sprouted from them and came to rest in a sheltered spot which described a roughly rectangular-shaped depression surrounded on three sides by rising rock walls. It was like a narrow room but with no roof and with one wall open to the elements to the north. Grey rocks, which could have passed for flagstones on the floor, peeped through a carpet of green and yellow vegetation. It was perfectly sheltered. It was here, he said, that he had seen Ian McKay just before he set off to attack the Argentine machine-gun post.

We set off in the direction Vernon said Ian had taken and followed a sheep track at a much lower level. Hugging a high rock wall to our right we came to a gap in the rocks. Thirty metres away, across open ground, was the rock in Ian Bailey's photograph and above it were two Argentine sangars, the second of which bore the characteristics described to me by Company Sergeant Major Sammy Dougherty who had found Ian's body. So this was where Ian McKay died; 100m or more beyond what has been accepted as the furthest point of penetration by any members of B Company and based on the testimony and evidence of those who were in a position to know. Ian's achievement that night on Mount Longdon was a staggering effort but given the advanced position of the location at which we were now standing the award of the VC appears all the more significant.

Standing and gazing around the position, the decaying yet distinctive remains of the Argentine sangars at my feet and up ahead, not too far distant, the secondary peak which marked 3 Para's final objective, I marvelled at how far Ian McKay had come, not just on that night but during the course of his life. It was a life which had begun in a small South Yorkshire town and had for its first seventeen years traced a path very much like my own but Ian McKay chose a more difficult route. That it should have lead us both ultimately to this bleak and lonely place and for him to lose his life in the very act of saving the lives of his fellow paratroopers was a truly sobering experience.

A sentence once uttered by Marica McKay soon after Ian's Victoria Cross had been awarded came back to me. Her fear, she said, was that the VC and what Ian had done 'would all be forgotten in twenty years time'. At the time of writing we are now ten years beyond the time of Marica's prediction and, as the thirtieth anniversary of the Falklands War approaches, the question of ownership of the islands is very much headline news once again.

Almost thirty years after the bestowal of the rare honour of the Victoria Cross upon my fellow Yorkshireman I salute him as a man whom I feel I have come to know at least a little through my research, and yet despite the similarities in our origins, my role in the story of Ian McKay's short yet remarkable life is simply to have had the privilege of researching and recording it so that others may learn of his story. Ian McKay has deserved his place in history. He has not and will never be forgotten. He is and will always be remembered as a man who cherished his family, who lived, breathed and was shaped by the Parachute Regiment. Ian McKay, Falklands VC, the last British hero of the Twentieth Century.

Jon Cooksey
Warwickshire, 2012

CHAPTER ONE

Forebears, Flour and Football

It was Rotherham-based journalist Mark Whiting who scooped both his local rivals on other newspapers in South Yorkshire and those employed by the 'nationals' – red top tabloids and august broadsheets alike – when his Falklands War article was splashed on the front page of the *Rotherham and South Yorkshire Advertiser* on Friday, 18 June 1982:

Bravest of the Brave
Para Ian Dies in Final Battle of Falklands
A Rotherham soldier was killed in one of the last major clashes between British and Argentine troops on the Falkland Islands.

The tragic news reached his family on Monday, just a few hours before it was known the Argentine forces had surrendered and the fighting was over.

Sgt Ian McKay, aged 29, was killed in action with the 3rd Battalion Parachute Regiment, in what was believed to be an operation against a strong enemy position. There were other British casualties.

Ian lived with his wife, Marica, and his step-son and young daughter in army accommodation at Aldershot, Hampshire.

His parents, Kenneth and Freda McKay, live at Briery Walk, Munsborough. Ian had two brothers, Graham, aged 26, and Neal, 25.

Mrs McKay went to Aldershot to be with her daughter-in-law after receiving the news. They were comforted, she said, by the wife of a major serving with the Regiment on the Falklands.

'The day that we knew was the day the surrender came. It seemed so pointless,' said Mrs McKay. 'But the major's wife, a Mrs Patton, said if it had not been for the courage of Ian, and the men who died in the attack, there probably wouldn't have been peace at that time and a lot more deaths on both sides would have resulted from it.

'My daughter-in-law won't break. She's tremendously brave. We both know Ian died bravely. We are sure he did, it was his nature. What we both want is public recognition for what they've done.'

In a letter from Mrs Patton to Mrs McKay, Ian was said to be 'the bravest of the brave'.

A number of other soldiers died and more were wounded in the attack on Saturday in which Ian was killed.

Ian was a soldier for 12 years. He joined up after leaving Rotherham Grammar School and at 17 was serving in Northern Ireland. He also had postings in West Germany.

At school he was an outstanding all-round sportsman. He was later in Sheffield United boys' team.

Said brother Neal: 'If ever there was a military type it was Ian. He was incredibly fit, and a physical sort of person.'

Ian was buried on the Falklands in a military ceremony.

A special memorial service will be held on Sunday at Rotherham Parish Church.

A full military ceremony will be held when the battalion return home.

It was, by necessity perhaps, rather a sketchy piece given that the staff at the *Rotherham Advertiser* were keen to break their story; for here was a local boy – one of their own – who had been killed fighting for Queen and country in a war against the forces of Argentina, half a world away in the Falkland Islands. That war – a war which some had said just could not be waged given the vast distances involved – had ended just four days earlier, indeed the paper went to press with the story less than a week after the battle which had claimed the life of Sergeant Ian McKay. It is hardly surprising then that the details of the fighting and the manner in which Ian McKay had been killed were vague to say the least.

The *Sheffield Star* had also been in touch with the McKays but by then, after speaking to Mark Whiting, their grief had naturally overwhelmed them. A relative had had to act as a spokesperson.

That evening the editor of the *Sheffield Star* chose to put the following rather brief piece by Mark Skipworth and Ray Parkin on page 13.

Heartbreak Goes On

Sheffield-born Sgt Ian McKay, a 29-year-old paratrooper and father of two, was in the battle forefront as British forces launched their final offensive on the Falklands' tiny capital.

His parents, Kenneth and Freda McKay, of Briery Walk, Munsborough, Rotherham, were informed of his death on the day of the ceasefire.

They were too upset to speak but according to his uncle, Gordon McKay, it is believed Ian was killed by enemy mortar fire bombarding the high ground surrounding the beleaguered town.

The former Rotherham Grammar schoolboy joined the paratroopers at 17 and spent two years in Northern Ireland. His last years were in Aldershot, training recruits.

He leaves a widow, Marica, a daughter, Melanie, aged four, and a step-son, Donny, aged 14. A service will be held in memory of Ian at Rotherham Parish Church on Sunday, June 20, at two o'clock.

Ian's death was indeed a tragedy for the McKay family but Mark Whiting had at least managed to speak to members of his immediate family and had begun the process of painting a picture, of fleshing out facts, and, even more importantly, revealing tantalizing glimpses of the character of this local man who had paid the ultimate price in helping to secure a British victory.

To his family Ian McKay was a much-loved husband, a gentle and caring father, a fine son and a respected older brother, yet, even then, just days after the Argentine surrender and at the very nadir of their own deep shock, grief and despair, there were hints that Ian's family knew that the manner of his death had been somehow courageous; that he had 'died bravely' and that there should be some 'public recognition' of what had been achieved. They could not know it then but when the full details emerged of what Ian had done on the night of 11–12 June 1982, amid the sharp, stabbing crags of an inhospitable mountain on a remote island deep in the South Atlantic, some 8,000 miles from Rotherham, they would indeed lead to 'public recognition' and the name of Ian McKay would forever be marked in the annals of British military history. His name would become forever linked with the discipline, professionalism, dogged tenacity and extraordinary acts of selfless courage of that select band who have been awarded Britain's highest military honour 'For Valour' – the Victoria Cross. Ian McKay fought – and died – in that short but bitter struggle in the teeth of a southern hemisphere winter against determined opposition in what was Britain's last war of 'Empire', late in the twentieth century. His was the very last VC of that turbulent and bloody epoch.

And yet his origins – normal, humble – were the lot of hundreds of thousands of 'baby boom' children born into working-class families living in the ever-expanding heavy industrial sprawls of large cities such as Sheffield, less than a decade after the end of the Second World War, and were far removed from what would come to pass 29 years later. Just as a local paper had been the first to break the news of Ian's death in action to his local community in 1982 so it had been a local rival that had first broken the news of his arrival into this world.

Provincial newspapers are strange and curious creatures, always looking for the local angle in often earth-shattering world events – indeed Mark Whiting and the Rotherham Advertiser had done just that on 18 June 1982 – whilst at the same time appealing to the seemingly unquenchable thirst on the part of its readership for the minutiae of local life. Even today – after a cursory glance at the headlines, which might deal with anything from spats involving local councillors, planning problems or renegade monster cats – most readers quickly turn to the letters page and then go on to scan the births, marriages and deaths columns (otherwise known as the 'hatched, matched and despatched' notices). And so anyone running their finger down the 'births' column on page twelve of *The Sheffield Star* on the evening of Tuesday, 12 May 1953, would have read the following:

McKay – To Freda (Hargreaves) and Kenneth, a son (Ian John), on May 7, at Hallamshire Maternity Home. Thanking all concerned.

Family and friends reading the above notice would have been well aware that the McKay family name is pronounced in South Yorkshire to rhyme with 'day' and not with 'sky' as is usual in Scotland – or indeed in military circles throughout Ian's twelve years of service, for the Scottish pronunciation of Ian's surname was, and still is, used by the army. The subject of the pronunciation of the McKay name would be a topic of conversation between Ian's parents and the queen during the VC investiture ceremony on Tuesday, 9 November 1982.

At the time of Ian's birth Kenneth John – always Ken – and Freda McKay (née Hargreaves) were living with Ken's sister in the suburb of Blackburn in Rotherham; the McKay family doctor being based in another suburb which delighted in the name of Wincobank. When the time of Freda's due date neared the doctor secured for her a bed in Wharncliffe hospital and she was duly admitted for observation. She was not to stay there for long. At the time of Freda McKay's pregnancy in late 1952 and early 1953, the mantra being handed down to expectant mothers from the health department was that the majority of babies had to be born in maternity homes. So she was transferred to what was known to all as the 'Hallamshire', not to be confused with the hospital of the same name which, at the time of writing, is still admitting patients in Sheffield. Ian John McKay was born on 7 May 1953 in the Hallamshire Maternity Home in the borough of Wortley on the edge of the village of Chapeltown, which is, some would say, well on the road towards Barnsley.

Even though Ian was her first child, his birth was, to use Freda McKay's own words, 'relatively normal'. Neither had there been any hint of complications prior to delivery. In fact, the day before she gave birth to Ian at 7.30am on 7 May, she had spent the entire morning down on hands and knees scrubbing the linoleum clean in the back bedroom of their house.

Freda McKay's 'confinement' was ten days which, for a relatively uncomplicated birth, is unheard of today. Freda stayed in bed and the babies were with the new mothers all day in cots.

When 'finally' Freda was allowed to leave the maternity home she found that she could not escape hospitals or the name 'Hallamshire'. It was decided that, in order to provide the new mother with the support of the extended family, she and Ian would move in with her mother and father who just so happened to be running a pub – one of two named 'Hallamshire' – situated behind the Royal Infirmary. Ian's father Ken was then working for Firth Brown, one of the oldest, established steel manufacturers in the world. Freda's parents were overjoyed to be able to help out, especially as there had been so few boys born into the family, at least in its recent history.

Ian's father, the fourth child and the second son of the twelve offspring of Angus Fergus and Sabina Evelyn McKay, had been born in Sheffield in 1929. He was 'a Sheffielder born and bred', as he was always at pains to point out, but with a surname like McKay it is no surprise that his family had distinctly Scottish roots.

The birth certificate of Ken McKay's grandfather (Ian's great-grandfather) John Nathaniel McKay, records that the occupation of his father, William Welsh Forbes McKay (Ian's great, great, grandfather) was 'baker/journeyman'. The year was 1874 and the McKays were then living at 4, Gentle's Close at 122, Canongate in Edinburgh. William McKay, born in Inverness in 1845, had married a girl called Jane Cochrane less than three years earlier and it is interesting to note, in the light of Ian McKay's later connections with Ireland, that his great, great grandmother Jane was an Irish lass who had been born in Dublin.

By the time of the Census of 1881 records show that William Welsh Forbes McKay had moved his growing family – three boys and a girl aged 10 and under – to the settlement of Lochinver at the mouth of the river Inver in the parish of Assynt in Sutherland, on the far north-west coast of the Scottish Highlands.

Lochinver had then, and still has today, some of the most spectacular coastal and mountain scenery in the British Isles on its doorstep and William McKay's time would have been well spent providing the locals with their daily bread, for he was still baking for a living and had even added the title 'confectioner' to that of his occupation.

For some reason now lost in the mists of time, sometime during the decade between 1881 and 1891 the family had moved south, making the long, 500-mile journey from the salt-laced coastal air of Sutherland in the north of Scotland to the smoke and smog of Sheffield in South Yorkshire. Here the now middle-aged William and his wife Jane squeezed into four rooms at 14 Court, 3 Woodside Lane in the north eastern suburb of Brightside Bierlow, along with their five sons, two of whom, William junior and John Nathaniel, were aged 20 and 16 respectively. There is no record of their daughter Elizabeth, who would have been aged 2 in 1881 and 12 in 1891.

The family were just seven of about 400,000 souls living in Sheffield by 1891, almost a four-fold increase on the population figure of forty years previously and most of them had come to Sheffield seeking work; drawn to the opportunities offered in the heavy industries based on the raw materials of coal, iron, millstone grit and ganister for the lining of furnaces, like iron filings drawn to a magnet.

Just as his surroundings had changed dramatically, so too had William McKay's trade and calling. One could be forgiven for thinking that, as Sheffield was widely regarded as a town associated with the production of iron and steel, cutlery or silver-plate, he too would have been involved in such work but his job revolved around none of these. Instead, it appears he had forsaken baking bread and cakes for a living and had exchanged his pastry brushes for paint brushes, now spending his working hours painting houses.

Even though he had no direct contact with the traditional, heavier industries for which Sheffield was becoming world-renowned, nonetheless the living and working conditions for the working classes in the area of the city into which William McKay had brought his family had been grim for many decades and they had not improved much as the nineteenth century drew to a close.

Forests of chimneys belched out noxious fumes round the clock, whilst the metal forgers forged and the grinders ground day and night as Sheffield stamped its authority on the global iron, steel and cutlery markets. Health and safety considerations were vague or non-existent, working hours long, life expectancies short. Numerous large families living cheek-by-jowl in the cramped, two-up-two-down, back-to-back dwellings in the 'courts' in Brightside tested the residents' health, patience and privacy to the limit.

John Nathaniel McKay was then working as a porter but it was not long before he followed in his father's footsteps. The certificate of his marriage three years later, on 10 June 1894 to the 19-year-old Mary Wear at St Matthew's parish church reveals that he had also taken up house painting for a living.

After almost exactly two years of married life Ian McKay's paternal grandfather, Angus Fergus McKay, was born in Sheffield on 25 June 1896. His birth certificate records that his parents were then living at 4 Court, 5 Bailey Lane and that his father – simply recorded as 'John McKay' – still gave his occupation as 'house painter/journeyman'. The birth certificate makes for amusing reading in one respect. One can only assume that the registrar, one Percy Sykes by name, initially struggled with Ian's great-grandmother's pronunciation of the infant Angus' name. In the columns 'Name' and 'Sex' he quite clearly first wrote 'Agnes' and 'Girl' only to cross these through later and replace them with 'Angus Fergus' and 'Boy'.

By the time of the 1901 Census five years later the McKays had moved; John taking his wife Mary along with 4-year-old Fergus to Martin Street in Nether Hallam, in the parish of St Philip's. Nether Hallam only exists as a historical area today but then it was one of several townships which together formed the Municipal Borough of Sheffield and which later became the City of Sheffield in 1893.

Ten years, and another house move, later Ian McKay's paternal grandfather Angus had left school and, at the age of 14 was running errands for a grocer near his home in Blackburn Street. But, as in the case of his grandson almost seventy years later, war was on the horizon for the young Angus McKay. Three years on, in 1914, Britain declared war on Germany and on 7 June 1915, just eighteen days shy of his nineteenth birthday, Angus Fergus McKay signed his name, swore an oath of allegiance to King George V and became Number 2376, Driver McKay in the 2/3 West Riding Brigade of the Royal Field Artillery (RFA) to do his bit for king and country.

The 2/3 West Riding Brigade of the RFA was a Second Line Territorial Force unit made up of part-time, volunteer soldiers and which, along with its associated infantry units, was then part of the West Riding Division. Its role, as a second line unit, was to act as a feeder to replenish numbers in the first line unit of the same brigade, in this case the 1/3 West Riding Brigade, RFA.

The Territorial Force had originally been created for home defence but as the small, regular British Expeditionary Force, which had been sent to war in August 1914, had almost been wiped out by the end of that year due to some very hard fighting, the call had gone out for the part-timers to sign up for service overseas to fill the gaps. Many had done so and Angus McKay's Service Record shows that he too signed the Imperial Service Obligation 'with respect to service outside the United Kingdom'.

After eight months in training Angus, now transferred to the First Line, 1/3 West Riding Brigade, RFA, sailed from Southampton on 10 February 1916 and arrived at Le Havre the next day. He served on the Western Front almost continuously until the Armistice in November 1918, with stints in the 49th West Riding Divisional Ammunition Column, the X Corps Heavy Artillery Working Party prior to and during the Somme offensive from May to November 1916, and then, finally, with 246 Brigade of the RFA when the West Riding Royal Field Artillery units were renumbered. In all that time he had seen much action and had received just twenty days leave. Remarkably there are no records of any wounds or illness in his service papers. He came home for good in February 1919 and was finally demobilized in April 1919. Angus McKay had undoubtedly served his country well and after the war he worked on the trams in Sheffield.

Ian's father Ken was born ten years after Angus McKay had returned from the Western Front to get on with his life and make the best of a 'Land Fit For Heroes', which he had fought so long to secure. The economic reality for many returning 'heroes' and their families during the immediate post-war years and well into the 1930s proved somewhat different as the lean years of the Depression made their mark.

Ken McKay recalled growing up in 'very cramped conditions' in the Fir Vale area of Sheffield. There were, he recalled, 'at least twelve' shoehorned into a two-bedroom house before the family moved into a much larger four-bedroom house sometime about 1941. Like his father before him, Ken left school at the age of 14 in 1943 to work in the steel industry at nearby Firth Brown, 'doing anything you're asked to and quick'. Except for a period of national service in the Royal Army Pay Corps, between 1948–50, during which time he rose to the rank of sergeant, he remained in the steel industry until ill-health, brought on by eight years of chronic heart problems, angina and the stress of losing his eldest son in the Falklands War, forced him into early retirement in 1985. A triple heart bypass operation followed in 1987. Ken McKay died of a massive heart attack on the night of 7–8 November 1998.[1]

Ian's mother was born Freda Hargreaves in Sunderland in 1933 and, although the Hargreaves' were a Rotherham family through and through, the geography of Freda's birth was due entirely to the trade of her father who, like the male ancestors on Ian's paternal side, was also a 'journeyman' in his own way.

Freda's father, Leonard (Len) Hargreaves (Ian's maternal grandfather) was born in Kimberworth, Rotherham on 7 March 1906 and became a professional footballer who played for, amongst others, Sunderland and Sheffield Wednesday when those teams were in their English League Division 1 pomp in the late 1920s. Just turned 19, and then living at 104, Blackburn in Wincobank, Len Hargreaves' first step on the road to almost every young boy's dream career began when he agreed and signed professional terms with English League Division 3 North club, Doncaster Rovers, on 25 April 1925. Richard Ray, acting on behalf of the club, agreed to pay 'said Player the sum of £1-5-0 per week from August 8th 1925 to May 1st 1926' with the agreement ceasing on 1 May 1926. Poached from under the very noses of Division 3 North local rivals, and arguably his 'home team', Rotherham United, Len Hargreaves signed what was at the time a standard professional footballer's contract and in return for his weekly wages he had to agree to 'play in an efficient manner and to the best of his ability…', 'do everything necessary to get and keep himself in the best possible condition so as to render the most efficient service to the club' and not 'engage in any business or live in any place which the Directors…may deem unsuitable'. There was a hand written addendum to the provisions which held out the promise that if he was eventually 'brought into full training' that he was 'to be paid £4 per week' – not quite the quarter of a million a week some of our rather tarnished 'golden generation' of present day (at the time of writing) footballers can fritter away on Baby Bentleys and soulless country estates, but in 1925 a not inconsequential sum for a 19-year-old lad from Rotherham!

As has been the lot of professional footballers down the ages, moving from club to club due to transfers was not an unusual occurrence and during his season at Doncaster, although he was not a first team regular, his performances as an attacking left-half back obviously attracted the attention of scouts for Sunderland AFC, then playing in the English first division alongside the likes of Manchester United, Arsenal and Liverpool. On 20 April 1927 Len signed forms for Sunderland in return for £6-0-0 a week plus the usual bonuses for a win, with his wages being increased to £7-0-0 if and when he played in the first team. And play in the first team he did; his debut coming on 1 September 1927 in a 4–2 away victory over West Ham United in front of a crowd of 19,000.

Ironically it would be West Ham United's Upton Park ground which his grandson Ian would later visit on a school football trip to the capital in the 1960s to see a game involving the great 1966 World Cup winning legends of Bobby Moore, Geoff Hurst and Martin Peters.

In all, Len Hargreaves played in twenty-eight league games and three FA Cup ties that season and scored eight league goals – including strikes against Liverpool home and away – and one FA Cup goal against Northampton Town at home on 14 January 1928. Len must have been playing so well that just a few days earlier the Board of Directors had agreed to increase his wages to £8-0-0 per week whenever he turned out for the first team.[2] In his first season for the Wearsiders Len helped Sunderland to finish fifteenth out of twenty-two teams.

He played again the following season but only appeared in nine league and cup games, scoring three goals before he returned to South Yorkshire to sign for Sheffield Wednesday on 15 March 1929 for a transfer fee of £2,000 – roughly equivalent to £90,000 in 2010. He was drafted straight into the Wednesday first team squad, studded with present or future England internationals such as Alf Strange, Ernie Blenkinsopp, Billy Marsden and Ellis Rimmer, and played the next day in the 1–0 home win against eventual Division 1 runners-up Leicester City, watched by 30,000 fans. His second and last game of the 1928–1929 season came the following week when he scored the only goal in Wednesday's 2–1 defeat at the hands of Manchester United at Old Trafford in front of 27,000 people. Although he played in only two games that season he had nevertheless done his bit in helping Sheffield Wednesday to win the first of two consecutive English League Division 1 Championship titles between 1929–1930.

Everything seemed rosy for the young professional footballer. Len had by now fallen in love and had struck up a steady relationship with Sunderland girl Winifred Housam, the daughter of the family with which he was lodging at 14 'Zion Terrace. He was also earning a straight £8-0-0 a week during the playing season, plus bonuses for wins and draws, and was set to receive £6-0-0 during the summer break. This seemed an incredible income for a working class lad in the inter-war period, so much so that the parents of Winnie Housam thought their daughter was 'stepping out' with a millionaire!

Unfortunatley, Len Hargreaves' period of playing in the top drawer of English professional football was short-lived due to injury and he moved in quick succession to play for Workington Town (1931), Doncaster Rovers for a second stint (1932) and Luton Town (1933). This rather swift movement in and out of the turnstiles of four different clubs in as many years is the lot of many 'journeyman' footballers, even today, plying their trade for whichever club is willing to pay a fee for their services.

Given that many of them – and Luton especially – were a good distance from Wearside may have caused something of a problem for the young Len Hargreaves, especially as he had persuaded Winnie Housam to be his wife in the interim. The couple were married at St Bede's Church in Sunderland on 4 August 1931 and as Len was often 'playing away' in the strict, literal sense of the term for a professional footballer, and new bride Winnie had a job in ladies' fashion at Binns department store in Sunderland, they continued to live at the parental home.

Len was still at Luton when his first child, Freda, Ian McKay's mother, was born on 4 December 1933.

A little more than seven months after Freda was born her father signed for Peterborough United on a one-year contract at £3-10-0 a week. These were not the heady days of £8-0-0 a week but, then again, Peterborough United was a relative non-league minnow compared to the mid 1930s first division footballing superpowers of teams like Sheffield Wednesday or Sunderland. In fact, the club had only been in existence for two months when Len had signed for them.

Peterborough United Football Club – known as 'The Posh' since a previous manager had said he was looking for 'Posh players for a Posh team' – had risen, Phoenix like, from the ashes of the demise of the Peterborough and Fletton United Club and, hiring the London Road ground from Peterborough City Council, had gained a place in the Midland League under William 'Jock' Porter, their sometime innkeeper manager. For a man who had played in front of 30,000–40,000 people week in week out in the first division just a few years before, the 4,000 souls who lined the terraces at London Road as he ran out for his league debut (he had played in a friendly against Westwood Works the week before) on 1 September 1934 must have seemed very sparse indeed. That said, Len Hargreaves treated the 'The Posh' faithful to a goal; the first strike in a 4–0 thumping of Gainsborough Trinity and so carved for himself a niche in both the annals of Peterborough United FC in particular and Association Football history in general, as the man who scored the club's first ever goal. As such his name will be remembered forever by anyone who is, has been, or ever will be, passionate about 'The Posh'.

Len moved his family down to Peterborough during his first season with the club; first into a boarding house and then, when he had saved enough money, into a house he'd bought in the northern suburb of Paston. He stayed with the Posh for three seasons; his final game, celebrating 102 appearance for the club, being against Barnsley Reserves at Oakwell on 14 April 1937.[3]

In the final few seasons before the outbreak of the Second World War Len played for Stamford Town in 1937 and Wisbech Town in 1938 but now, with a second daughter Jean, who had been born in 1937, he had also to think about his family's financial security and so had taken a job with the Peterborough engineering firm of Peter Brotherhood.[4]

Immediately after the war and in addition to the engineering job Len became, in effect, Peterborough United's unpaid manager and trainer. Indeed, at this time, the practicalities of running the club were very much a family concern. Len was a very quiet man who never talked or boasted about his past successes but simply got on with the job at hand with the help of his family, and help they did. His wife Winnie and daughters Freda and Jean washed the players' kit, and Freda also helped by blowing up the footballs and putting dubbing on the players' boots. Players who were still in the forces were put up overnight. These things were not a chore for the Hargreaves family for football and sport was in their blood. Winnie Hargreaves had been a reasonable athlete in her youth and had won prizes for running and eldest daughter Freda showed signs of being physically able. It had been her father who had taught her how to dance – old-time ballroom dancing – at weekly church socials in Peterborough; her first ever dance with her father being the quick-step to *Tiptoe through the Tulips*. She also developed into a talented schoolgirl hockey player whilst the family lived in Peterborough.

Freda's childhood dream was to be a PE teacher. It was all she ever wanted to do. When the family moved north from Peterborough and she went to school at Rotherham Girls' High School, she played hockey for the school with some fixtures being held at the Lady Mabel College at Wentworth Woodhouse, later to become known for its association with the training of teachers of girls' PE. It is hardly surprising then, given the sporting background of his parents and grandparents, that sport would become a significant part of Ian McKay's life as he grew up; one could perhaps say that a desire to strive for sporting excellence was hard wired into his DNA.

In 1948, however, Len Hargreaves took the family 'home' – his home at least – and they returned to the Blackburn area of Rotherham with the encouragement of Len's mother, initially to help run her shop and later to manage a couple of pubs in Sheffield.

Freda Hargreaves met Ken McKay at the local swimming baths sometime after Ken's return from National Service. Ken was working as a metallurgist at the Firth Brown works and Freda – who had sadly not realised her dream to teach PE – had also managed to get a job with the firm. For two hours every Friday evening Firth Brown Sports and Social Club hired the local swimming baths for the recreational use of their employees. It was also an opportunity for groups of girls to meet and mix with the younger male employees socially in a safe environment and, eventually, Freda and Ken's eyes met over a crowded pool.

On 22 November 1952 the bells of St Philip's and St Anne's church in the Upperthorpe area of Sheffield rang out to proclaim the joyful tidings of the marriage of Ken McKay and Freda Hargreaves. The following year the McKay clan was enlarged with the arrival of their first child, a boy, and they were quite certain what they wanted to call him. That had all been decided by the time the announcement of his birth appeared in the Rotherham Advertiser five days after his arrival. They had chosen strong, uncomplicated names. He was, after all, their gift from God. They would name him Ian John.

CHAPTER TWO

My Scruffy Little Kid

The newly wed McKays had moved in with one of Ken's sisters before the birth of Ian in May 1953 and had then lived with Freda's parents for a short period before obtaining their first home as a couple at 112, Blackburn Road in the Blackburn area, a mixed residential and industrial village on a steep site between Rotherham and Sheffield.

When the northerly stretch of the M1 was constructed in the late 1960s, half of the original village of Blackburn, which Len Hargreaves would have known, was lost and today Blackburn Road runs just below and roughly parallel to the west of the MI motorway, close to very busy Meadowhall shopping complex interchange.

Here, at their new home, they could embark on family life proper and one of their first tasks was to have the young infant McKay christened. Ken and Freda chose St Philip's and St Anne's church in Upperthorpe for the simple reason that this was the church where they had been married. It seemed a perfect choice. What's more, Freda's sister, Marie, had never been christened and so she was going to be christened at the same time.

The venue and time were fixed and on the appointed day family and friends duly turned up at the church. It was while they were waiting that the vicar approached the proud parents. Freda recalled the moment when what should have been a joyful family gathering turned into a family crisis.

> The vicar came to see us and told us that he would not christen our baby 'Ian John'; his reason being that 'Ian' was the Scots form of 'John' and that in effect he was being asked to christen the baby 'John John'. The vicar flatly refused to do it; he just would not change his mind no matter what we said. He was absolutely adamant that he was not going to perform the ceremony for Ian. We had to think very quickly and the only thing we could think of was to go ahead with the baptism and christen him 'Ian Kenneth'. So he had 'Ian John' on his birth certificate but 'Ian Kenneth' on his baptism certificate. It was a very hurried decision. We didn't have the chance to think properly. The church was demolished not long afterwards.[1]

Freda had stopped working at Firth Brown to devote her time to her new baby and even during Ian's formative early years, footballing legends and the professional footballing career of his maternal grandfather loomed large in his life. Ian McKay never witnessed his grandfather play football when he was at the peak of his powers but he did see him play. At about the age of 1 Ian was wheeled in his pushchair to

Hillsborough Park to watch his grandfather Len play in a benefit match between Sheffield Wednesday and ex- Sheffield United professionals. The match was for a gritty, gifted footballer who, despite a personal tragedy which changed the course of his career, went on to be associated in several capacities with both Sheffield Wednesday and Sheffield United and as such become a true, all- Sheffield football legend.

On 14 February 1953, three months before Ian had been born, the popular and free-scoring Sheffield -born, Sheffield Wednesday forward Derek Dooley had collided heavily with Preston North End goalkeeper George Thompson at Preston's home ground of Deepdale. Dooley had not got up; X-rays later confirmed that he had broken a leg in two places but worse was still to come. Taken into hospital Dooley had had his broken leg re-set and placed in a plaster cast but during his discharge examination the following Monday an observant nurse noticed that there was no reaction when she had touched his toes. The plaster cast was removed and it was found that a scratch on the back of Dooley's leg had become badly infected; so bad, in fact, that gangrene had set in and it was already too late for treatment. The leg could not be saved. Amputation was the only option. A rumour was abroad at the time that chemicals from the white touchline markings had penetrated his injury. It was all over for Dooley. At the age of 24 his professional career as a player – full of promise and with possible international honours on the horizon – lay in ruins.

Decades later he revealed that he thought his whole world had collapsed at that moment: 'I'd been married for just six months, I'd got no house, no money and football was my life. I thought, "Well, I might as well snuff it because I've not got a lot to live for".' But the people of Sheffield in general and the footballing community in particular rallied around their local hero. A benefit fund was begun and local newspapers promised to donate money. The football match at Hillsborough Park, in which Len Hargreaves took part, was just one way that ex-professionals could show their solidarity and provide real practical and financial support for one of their own. By that time Len Hargreaves, like many old pros, was suffering with arthritis in his joints, in his case in both hips. Freda recalled that 'he could hardly move' but move he did that day in Hillsborough Park to show his support of a fellow professional who had lost his livelihood in an instant. Freda had worked with Derek Dooley's brother when she had first started in the labs at Firth Brown and so her support too had a personal dimension.

The size of the McKay family was increased considerably within five years of Ian's birth as he was followed by two more children: brothers Graham Roy, born on 11 February 1956 and Neal Andrew, a little over a year later. In contrast to the sturdy frame and robust health exhibited by their firstborn it was clear to Ken and Freda almost as soon as he had been born that Graham was not a healthy baby. His breathing difficulties and almost constant lung, upper respiratory tract and chest infections, digestion problems, and weight loss alarmed and worried his parents in equal measure, but he was not diagnosed as having cystic fibrosis (CF) until Freda was already pregnant with third son Neal.

First identified less than 30 years earlier, CF is caused by a defective, recessive gene which a child must inherit as a 'double dose' – one defective gene from each parent – before any outward signs or symptoms become apparent. Any child of parents both carrying the defective gene has a roughly one in four chance of inheriting them and so being born with CF. Although treatments based on effective antibiotic drugs had improved by the mid-to-late 1950s, when Graham and Neal were born, many children with CF died during childhood and for those few who survived into adulthood the outlook was relatively bleak, with ill-health a constant drain on their quality of life. Despite tremendous progress in diagnostic techniques and new treatments in recent years it remains a very serious and potentially fatal disorder.

In 1956 the prognosis for Graham McKay hit the family hard at a vulnerable time. While expecting their third child Freda and her husband were told in no uncertain terms that the life expectancy of their second child was three years.

That said, as the time approached for Neal's birth the McKay's looked to their eldest son as a wellspring of hope. If the dice of destiny could roll and land so favourably that he had won in the chromosomal lottery so parental hopes soared that their third child had also somehow ducked his potentially lethal genetic ineritance, for Neal appeared to be a perfectly healthy baby for the first few months. But then he too began to show similar symptoms to Graham and in due course he too was diagnosed as having CF.

In an eloquent and intensely moving recollection written in June 1988, Ian's youngest brother Neal McKay conceded that it was 'strange trying to piece together thoughts upon someone who, although a very close brother, I saw all too little of.' He went on to record that 9 March 1987 was a sadly ironic day for the McKay family:

It was the day of my 30th birthday – nothing special in that itself but if we had turned the clock back 30 years to when I was born – the youngest of three boys – and someone had predicted that of the three boys only the two younger ones would live to reach the ripe old age of 30, it would have been taken as a bad joke bordering on the ridiculous. For whilst the eldest son Ian John had been granted the gift of good health, both of the other two sons – Graham Roy and myself, Neal Andrew – were born with the disease Cystic Fibrosis which in those days was nearly always fatal either at birth or in early childhood. However the facts are that Graham was 30 in February 1986, myself a year later, whilst Ian was killed in the Falklands in 1982 aged 29 years.[2]

Neal McKay died on 25 June 1989 at the age of 32, a year after writing the above and eight months after having undergone a heart and lung transplant at Papworth Hospital. Graham, the second eldest of the three McKay boys, who also underwent a heart–lung transplant at Papworth in 1991, died six years later, in 1995, at the age of 39.[3]

Freda McKay readily admits that times were tough with the youngest two being ill. She had made the decision to stop work to look after Ian but now, with her two younger boys having CF, there was no question of going back even on a part-time basis. She would not work full-time again until after Neal went to school.

Bringing up three boys born within five years of each other is hard enough but with two having serious health difficulties the pressure of the routine which had to be followed to keep them in some semblance of health, and at the same time keeping a home afloat while her husband was out at work, was unrelenting and exhausting:

I had to do a form of 'postural drainage', which I had learned from the staff of the hospital, on them both, three times a day; what they used to call giving them a 'bashing'. They had first to lie on the bed and then push themselves forward so that their upper bodies were over the side of the bed and their heads were on a pillow which was on the floor. They would stay like that for a while then get back on the bed and I would then have to cup my hands and beat them on the chest – just like playing a drum – to make them cough so that they would physically eject the excess fluid from their lungs. I had to do this as their condition meant their bodies couldn't do it naturally. In fact I was once reported to the authorities – someone saw me doing this 'bashing' through the window and thought I was abusing them! It became better when Graham and Neal went to school because at least one of the sessions could be done at lunch time but we were forever at the hospital and doing this, that and the other with them.

As Ian got older and then again when he got married I asked him outright if he felt as if he'd been neglected and he told me that, yes, he had because Neal and Graham took up so much of our time and energy as parents. But when he got into the grammar school it opened up a whole new life for him. He got into all the sports – tennis, badminton, athletics – and Ken had taught him how to play chess. He soon gave that up though as they were all better at it than he was and if he couldn't be top he didn't want to know.[4]

Neal recalled how it had amused him to read, in the post-Falklands newspaper stories, of their family life and how Ian was invariably portrayed as the 'big, kind, loving brother' to his two sickly younger brothers. He didn't doubt the fact that it probably made for a good story but his own recollections were slightly at odds with the musings of the popular press given that the McKay household had witnessed its fair share of brotherly 'rough housing', which countless parents of brothers born within a few years of each other would recognize:

My father worked in the steelworks in Sheffield and, once I had started school, my mother got a job in a carpet shop in the town. I guess we grew up in a fairly traditional working class situation with money, or the lack of it, always a problem. We were very fortunate though, insofar as due to the many sacrifices made by mum and dad – and the long hours they worked – we seldom went short of anything. It must have been a struggle, especially as Graham and myself were so demanding of time and resources to keep our illness under control. My own recollections, however, are of the constant bickering, arguing and fighting the two of us did as kids, Graham keeping well out of it! Nothing too bruising or unusual, just the normal, brotherly scrapes that happen between growing kids. This went on throughout our teens although usually Ian used to take much of the blame – and punishment – for all the troubles. I guess with me being very small and not very strong it was 'safer' to mete the discipline out to him than to me – a factor I probably played on until one day when I'd be about 12 or 13 and we were at it again, only on this occasion the blame was very definitely Ian's, yet he blamed me and although Mum wasn't fooled by his accusations it was me that got a right pasting. Now whether it was a guilty conscience or whether we just grew up I'm not sure, but after that I can't remember us seriously falling out again and in time we became the closest of brothers.[5]

Freda remembers the childhood incident vividly. Exhausted and frayed with the constant care of the two younger boys and sick and tired of the continuous squabbling between the eldest and youngest brothers, at her wits' end she had slapped Neal's legs smartly whilst Ian looked on after yet another bout of rowing.

> I had just had enough! After I had done it, I got Neal to one side of me and stood Ian at the other and I told them both that if they fell out again, no matter who started it, I would hit Neal. Well it might not have been the right thing to do and I probably wasn't thinking straight but we seemed to have a lot more peace in the house after that. Neal daren't start anything for fear of getting hit and Ian daren't start because he didn't really want Neal to get smacked. So I suppose it worked.'[6]

Ian would not have wanted to see his younger brother punished unduly and although undoubtedly there were family squabbles that was 'family business'; woe betide any outsider if they tried to interfere or treat members of his family unfairly. Some of his army pals would later feel the full force of this fierce family loyalty and his instinct to protect his own. Neal recalled an incident during their teenage years which illustrated this perfectly:

> Though we might have fought among ourselves, Ian was, however, very protective towards [us] against others. There was an occasion (when Ian would be about 16 or 17) which reveals this 'big-brotherly' role and also – perhaps oddly in view of the army life he chose – the irritation and dislike he had for 'jumped up little Hitlers' as he would describe anyone wearing a uniform who usurped his authority. The three of us were going to Sheffield by foot and bus (our Dad was a great believer in walking anywhere and everywhere). We walked down Droppingwell and got on a bus to Firth Park with Graham and myself eating a lollipop. When we came to get off the bus the conductor refused to let us off until me and Graham had picked up the discarded lolly sticks from amongst all the other rubbish on the floor of the bus; this was very silly and unnecessary and Ian would have none of it, so he made his way to get off the bus, at this the conductor put his arms across the exit point so Ian just 'leant' on him without using any violence and his sheer force of strength sent the poor conductor flying out of the back of the bus, whereupon all his pennies rolled all over Firth Park![7]

And so after being 'the only child' for just short of the first four years of his life, the home situation for the infant Ian McKay had changed dramatically and irrevocably with the birth of his brothers and their constant attendant medical needs. Not only that, he had also to contend with a new chapter in his life – starting school.

Ian began his education at the Blackburn County Primary School, a spacious, state-of-the-art school built as recently as 1951, but the family were keen to move to escape the atmospheric pollution of Blackburn, deep in the Don Valley, and the harmful effects this might have on the damaged lungs of the younger brothers.

Close by was a factory, from whose chimneys there belched thick, black smoke and noxious fumes which smelled strongly of ammonia and coated everything with a layer of 'muck'. It was a standing joke amongst the residents of Blackburn that there was little point in them washing their curtains – they simply threw them away!

In 1959 the family moved into a house on Shearman Avenue, a road on one of the then modern, newly-raised estates of the Kimberworth Park area to the northwest of the town centre and Ian transferred to the brand new Roughwood Junior School. Situated on the slopes to the north of the River Don, with the Wortley Road running behind it, Kimberworth Park was surrounded on its three other sides by a horseshoe of open fields, lanes, copses and woodland to the north, east and southeast. This landscape, along with the labyrinth of streets which made up the estate on which he lived, became Ian McKay's playground in a more innocent time when children, on summer weekends, provisioned only with a bottle of 'pop' and a bag of crisps, went out to play from dawn until dusk. Here he inhabited a world in which adults did not exist, save for the distant plaintive cries of mothers calling the boys home by name as the gloom gathered around the end of another long day of running, whooping, sweating and screaming, skinning knees and snagging clothes climbing trees, playing at Soldiers, Cowboys and Indians, Kick out Can or hide and seek chasing games like Relevo.

And when Ian was finally retrieved there was always the task of trying to get him clean.

I remember once getting him in the bath and getting the pumice stone out on the back of his neck and giving it a rub because I thought it was so dirty but it wasn't – he had just been playing outside so much that his skin was weathered a deep shade of brown. He always looked scruffy, no matter how hard I tried to keep him tidy because he was so active. I know he's become a hero to a lot of people now but then he was just a scruffy kid, and he'll always be my scruffy little kid.[8]

The Leeson family lived next-door-but-one to the McKays and their son, Philip, was five months older than Ian. He was in the same class at school and also enjoyed sports and the outdoor life. It was perhaps natural that the two boys became friends and Philip Leeson paints a vivid picture of what made Ian tick even at an early age when he recalls his memories of their shared Kimberworth childhood:

My recollection of the war games we used to play was that half-a-dozen of us would play in the woods when we were about 9 or 10. Ian made the rules as usual, one of which was that you couldn't shoot the enemy if any trees or bushes were in the line of fire. Playing the game in the woods obviously gave rise to many arguments on this matter – about 99 per cent of which involved Ian being 'shot' and him being insistent that a branch or a twig had obstructed the line of fire. It used to develop into a proper war just arguing with him but thinking about it, I don't think I or any of the lads who befriended him at that time ever had a fight with him. It's not that we were scared of him, even though he was extremely well-built for his age, in fact Ian would shy away from any physical combat with us, and I can't believe that that was because he was scared of us either. [There were] six of us that used to play just about every type of sport (Ian, his two brothers, Pete Lockwood, Greg Artel and myself). Pete, Greg, Ian and myself were roughly the same age with Ian's two brothers being a lot younger, but whenever sides were picked at football or cricket, Ian always chose to be on the same side as his two brothers even though he knew they would be the weaker team. Looking back, his caring and thoughtfulness towards Neal and Graham was quite touching especially as he was physically strong and athletic and they were quite frail in comparison. I think this may have helped Neal and Graham throughout their childhood – they looked up to Ian and, in a way, tried to live up to him. Obviously there were times when they had quite heated arguments but their closeness was never in question. Ian was also close to his parents, especially his father. He had a lot of respect for Ken and always looked for his approval. Ken used to spend a lot of time with us in the fields playing cricket and although Ian was head and shoulders above everyone else in terms of ability (a fact that must have brought a great deal of satisfaction to his dad), Ken would always encourage the rest of us to do well rather than Ian – but I think this only stirred Ian up to be even more competitive. I think that word 'competitive' was a key word to Ian during the time I knew him. He always wanted to do well in everything. Winning was important to him, although if it was a team game, his own personal performance was what mattered. He was supremely confident, almost to the point of arrogance, a fact that was to rebound on him later during secondary school. I remember when he played for the junior school football team for the first time. Our school played Herringthorpe School – we beat them about 9–0 and Ian scored about seven. For one of those goals he beat just about every player in the opponent's team, dribbled past the goalkeeper, stopped the ball on the goal line and bent down and headed the ball in! Great showmanship but guaranteed to annoy his opponents and even some of his own team.[9]

The move to Kimberworth Park also coincided with the first time the McKays went on holiday to Bridlington. Ian was 6 years old. Like hundreds of other honest, hard-working, working-class families from the heavy industrial areas of Yorkshire during the late 1950s and 1960s, the McKays annual holiday to 'Brid' was something to look forward to. Neal McKay had fond memories of those precious annual pilgrimages to enjoy the sea, sand and fresh air of the coast together and remembered how Ian felt about them:

Bridlington itself held a special place, not only in Ian's heart but for the rest of the family… Our annual holidays were *always* taken during [the factories'] shutdown fortnight at this popular east coast resort. I think like all of us he enjoyed the simple pleasures of the place – long walks on the beach, ball games, swimming, fishing in the harbour, the 'slots', lots of wonderful home cooking at the lodgings, where we invariably returned year after year to such places as Mrs Dench's [at 42,

Marshall Avenue], and just generally whiling away the days among honest down-to-earth people mostly from South and West Yorkshire. Sunshine – occasionally. Wind traps – essential! Not only was this an occasion when the five of us would be together, which was rare enough with mum and dad working so much and me and Graham going to a different school to Ian but it was an opportunity to get together with other relatives who joined us there either for a day or the week. My dad has twelve brothers and sisters and my mum has two sisters, and many of these would turn up occasionally. On a good turnout by friends and family we could have a cricket match on the beach with up to 20–25 taking part, with Ian usually the one most intent on hitting the ball across the North Sea. We were, at this time, a very close family – aunts, uncles, grandparents, cousins etc. The extent to which Ian's death touched all these people so much reflects not only his popularity but the depth and warmth of feeling that existed throughout the family. Even after Ian joined the Army he would make every effort to try and get to Bridlington to join us even if only for two or three days. Going back there [since] I can't think for the life of me what we found to keep us occupied and amused for much more than a long weekend, but they were very happy days and probably remained as much a part of Ian's image of us as a close family as it does with us all now. A great deal has happened since those days and inevitably I think there is an air of sadness around whenever any of us return to 'Brid'.[10]

On one occasion, when Ian was very young and they had yet to discover the warm welcome of Mrs Dench's boarding house, the family had trooped to the beach and parked themselves next to a tunnel which the donkeys were led through to access the sands. There was a reason for this specific positioning. Freda had given the boys strict instructions in case they wandered off and became lost, that they must ask someone where the tunnel was and that there they would find their parents. It was not long before Ian disappeared. There one minute and gone the next he had simply vanished and after a frantic search of the immediate area with no success panic set in. The fear of that moment has stayed with Freda:

Ken had to stay and look after the rest of the kids while I went off in search of Ian, calling in vain at the lost children's office. Why I don't know but I decided to go back to our boarding house which was quite a few streets back from the 'prom'. When I arrived I went straight upstairs to find Ian sitting on the bed reading a comic dressed only in his trunks. I asked him, 'how on earth did you find your way back here?' and he said 'I remembered it was North Street, so I asked a policeman who was standing in the middle of a crossing and he told me how to get to North Street and I knew the house had a great big yellow basket of flowers near the door and I found it.' I wasn't angry, I was just so relieved. He had wanted to read his comic and had just decided he would go back and do it.[11]

Many years later, with all three boys either in their late teens or early twenties and just a few years before Ian went to war in 1982, the family were still visiting Bridlington and Ian had managed to join them.

Ian would have been about 22 [and] we had started to kick a ball about on the cliff top near Sewerby when someone miskicked and sent the ball (worth approximately 37p) rolling towards the cliff edge. Ian ignored our warnings and set off after the ball, he dived [at it] about ten yards from the edge, flicked the ball back with his outstretched arm and came to a stop with his head and arms dangling over the edge! It could have been incidents like this that sowed the seeds for the heart attack that Dad was to have some years later.[12]

After five years at junior school Ian sat and passed his 11-plus examination in 1964 and started at Rotherham Grammar School that September. Ian's Headteacher at Roughwood Junior had expressed some surprise at his success in a conversation with Freda and thought that he might have done better as a 'big fish in a little pond rather than a little fish in a big pond', the latter of which she felt he would certainly be, academically speaking, at the grammar school. Nevertheless, grammar school it was to be and the fact was marked in the school magazine of 1964 with an official '*Salvete*' on page eleven as I. J. McKay became one of exactly 100 first form pupils in the new intake Class of 1964. He was placed in Bishop's House, with another twenty-two of his peers; Bishop's being the smallest House, in terms of raw numbers alone, of the four houses then in existence.[13]

The school which Ian joined in September 1964 – motto: *ne ingrate videamur* ('lest we seem ungrateful') – could trace its origins back some 500 years to the foundation of the College of Jesus by Thomas Rotherham, Archbishop of York, in 1483. Sitting in a commanding position on Moorgate it was a solid, stone-built structure in the Collegiate Gothic style, consisting of a central, four-square, crenellated tower flanked by wings on either side with numerous gables, chimneys and tall windows with further crenellations crowning various ground floor window bays and extremities. The main building had originally been built as a theological college to educate students for ministry in Congregational churches. Purchased for £3,200 in 1870, the original 8½ acre plot had initially lain dormant due to delays in building owing to the commercial uncertainties arising from the outbreak of the Franco-Prussian War. Construction eventually commenced, however, and the building was officially opened on 20 September 1876 at a final cost of £23,000.

But the new Rotherham Congregational College was only used in the capacity for which it was intended for twelve years and in 1888 it amalgamated with the Congregational College at Bradford and the newly-merged college operated from the Bradford premises. Superfluous to requirements, the fine building in Rotherham was sold to become the premises of the Rotherham Grammar School and the school finally moved in and began operation in 1890.

By September 1964 things had changed a good deal but the school could never lay claim to being a hotbed of progressive methods. Ironically for a man who would become a paratrooper, Ian's Headmaster went by the name of Mr G. E. Gunner, known universally to the boys as 'GEG'. GEG was a huge man who taught poetry to the young Ian McKay. For homework he would give out poems which the boys had to learn off by heart then, during the next lesson, he would pick on individuals to recite selected lines. Sanctions for any boys who hadn't learned – or had simply forgotten – the poem were severe and they lived in fear of being called on to recite a few lines.

Mr Gunner oversaw an all-male Senior Common Room of predominantly late middle-aged, white male teachers who still wore gowns and taught their lessons in a very traditional way. The balding, bespectacled Richard 'Dickie' Pyle – a shorter, more stout version of the poet Philip Larkin – taught solid grammar in English lessons for example, and the year before Ian arrived one pupil, Lol Middleton, remembered the English set text as being *The White Company*, an historical novel recounting the exploits of a company of mercenary archers set in the Hundred Years War and one of the less well known works of Sir Arthur Conan Doyle. 'Dry and dusty' was the universal pupil verdict on this offering from the man who had bequeathed the legendary Sherlock Holmes to the world.

Ian's first 'home' became Woodhurst, a large stone building detached from the main school which had once been a private house and which had become the base for the first and second year boys. Before that, however, he had to get through the first day and for new arrivals at Rotherham Grammar, as in so many other schools of a similar ilk, that meant an induction ceremony. As the three new boys from Shearman Avenue who had passed the 11-plus approached the school gates for the first time, a hostile force was lying in wait to ambush them. There could be no escape; Ian, Philip Leeson and Steve Akid simply had to run the gauntlet.

> On our first day at the Grammar School, the three lads who had passed the 11-plus exam from our street all walked up Moorgate together. We all knew about the First Year 'clip' tradition and were a little apprehensive as we approached the school, except for Ian who just strolled up the drive and didn't bat an eyelid as we were being clipped [around the head] left, right and centre.[14]

The new boys viewed the grammar school with both a sense of pride and a sense of fear. Coming from the smaller sphere of education at a relatively new primary school the grammar seemed immense and school traditions were rammed into them from the outset. Ian and his schoolmates were taught all about the school's history and how this was reflected in the Four Houses – Bishop's (green), Snell's (blue), Hoole's (red) and Founder's (yellow). Ian and next-door-but-one neighbour Philip Leeson were pleased when they were told they were both in the same house. Each house had its own tie which had to be worn at all times, as did their school cap. Every teacher had to be called 'Sir' and the more senior teachers always wore gowns and, to the boys, looked like they'd taught there since the place was built! Ian's first year was spent getting used to the place and discovering which teachers you could push and which ones you couldn't. Corporal punishment was still allowed and meted out on a regular basis to transgressors. Mr Standeven taught science and, using his knowledge of speed, time and distance, once took a run-up in the gym to slipper Ian's friend Philip. Mr King – another senior teacher – once slippered about twenty boys for playing football in the Woodhurst playground having been told not to.

At that time senior school prefects were still charged with maintaining discipline and keeping good order amongst the lower school pupils and could even administer a good deal of low level, but often quite painful, punishment armed with a 'slipper', which they were allowed to carry. 'The hardest thing to comprehend' said Philip Leeson, 'was the authority given to prefects – who all, it seemed, walked around as if they owned the place. I think we all paid them respect initially but from the second year onwards it was a different matter'. In Ian's eyes, some of the prefects undoubtedly allowed this power to go to their heads and they became the very embodiment of the 'jumped-up little Hitlers' he so railed against throughout his life.

In the second year Ian was placed in the bottom class, 2 Beta, with Philip Leeson. Still based in Woodhurst, something of a 'class' divide began to open up, with the top set having a classroom on the first floor to the front of the building whilst the lower set was housed on the ground floor at the back. Philip Leeson is adamant that the setting created a certain 'us and them' attitude which, together with an increasing self-confidence on the part of the boys, gave rise to a sort of rebellion.

> Some of the teachers, particularly our maths teacher, were crucified. He had no control over us and everybody just took the mickey out of him. I don't think he lasted very long. We were a very boisterous class, always misbehaving and I don't think there were many of us – including Ian – who didn't get the cane or slipper at one time or another. Being a grammar school, other schools used to think we were elitist and a bunch of posh boys, especially Oakwood School pupils. Oakwood was a secondary school just up the road from the grammar. Buses used to drive past our bus stop full of Oakwood pupils waving and jeering at us, but when a bus stopped and it had Oakwood pupils on it we exacted our revenge. Nearly every morning assembly saw Gunner expressing his disgust about the behaviour of boys at the bus stop.

Ian had certainly shown his mettle when he had braved the 'clipping' initiation ceremony on his first day and it was during his time in Woodhurst that he became the ringleader in several schoolboy pranks, at one point rallying his fellow oppressed lower school pupils in a daring snowball assault on an unpopular senior prefect.

Philip Leeson remembers:

> Once [Ian] and a few more of us broke into the old attic at Woodhurst and stole some stuffed birds that were stored there. There was also another time when a guy called Foster (a school prefect who was only small but used to revel in the authority he'd got) was giving our class a hard time for no apparent reason and reported our unruly behaviour to our form master. Nobody in our class liked Foster and one afternoon as we were walking down towards the bus stop on our way home, Foster drove past on his motor scooter (prefects were allowed to come to school on motor scooters at that time). Anyway, Ian picked up a snowball and threw it at him – Ian was the school record holder for throwing the cricket ball so this snowball hit Foster with some force. Foster stopped and looked round to see who the culprit was only to be bombarded with literally hundreds of snowballs from Ian and about thirty more of us. We were willing to carry on what Ian had started but I don't think any of us would have had the nerve to start

it ourselves. My mother also remembers an incident where I'd been caned at school for something I wasn't actually involved in. Ian got home before me on that day and told her what had happened and that I'd been caned unjustly, thus proving that although he was sometimes a bit of a rogue he was also very fair.[15]

Ian spent the next six years in secondary education, staying on at school an extra year beyond his five years of compulsory schooling, by which time the grammar school that he had joined passed into history and became reincarnated, in 1967, as the Thomas Rotherham College.

After Ian's death in 1982, several national newspapers credited him with anything from four to six passes in the General Certificate of Education (GCE) 'Ordinary' or 'O' Level' subjects. However, every August, at the end of the examinations season, Rotherham Grammar School – and later Thomas Rotherham College – proudly proclaimed, in banner headlines, its pupils' examination successes by furnishing the local newspaper with a full list of names all those who had gained GCE 'O' Level passes. A detailed trawl through the archives for the relevant years, 1968–1970, reveals that Ian's name appeared in the *Rotherham Advertiser* under the heading 'Joint Matriculation Board:- Lower Sixth Boys' with four passes to his name.[16]

The uncertain details of his 'O' Level subjects do not, however, obscure the fact that Ian, bright and alert lad that he was, was no text book scholar. Stuart Metcalfe, one of his teachers and one of the few younger members of staff, recalled that for a 'young, very raw new teacher Ian McKay was in different ways the best and the worst of boys to encounter':

> The classroom was not his natural environment; quiet study and contemplation not his temperament. He was not a lad to sit still, let alone sit silently and in many a lesson his concentration span was short. Outside the classroom, however, the same personality traits made him a straightforward, endlessly enthusiastic and irrepressible youngster who was refreshing to deal with. He loved sport, especially football and seemed to have boundless energy. He was very friendly and outgoing – almost a compulsive talker – and fully involved himself with unbridled, innocent enthusiasm and cheerfulness. No introvert, gloomy adolescent![17]

Neither of his brothers could testify to what exactly Ian got up to at any of the schools he attended because, unlike all the other families on their estate in which younger brothers and sisters followed their older siblings into the same infant, junior and secondary schoolyards Neal and Graham never followed in their elder brother's footsteps due to their ill health. They attended the Newman Open-Air Special School on the opposite side of town. The only two things that Neal could later state with any certainty was that, 'he was no fool academically, although I don't think he ever enjoyed his studies, and his priority was sport'.

Neal believed that Ian had adopted a personal philosophy 'that if an object was round then it was there to be hit and hit hard – either into a net, between posts, on a court, into a hole or, on occasion, as far as possible'. This was a philosophy which, when combined with his natural Ian Botham-like physique, brought him much success and enjoyment at numerous sports and pastimes.

> From early infant school onwards he loved competitive sport. I'm not sure whether the emphasis should be on the word 'competitive' – he was always someone who played to win and hated losing – or sport for sport's sake. I think possibly the older he grew there was a change from the former to the latter. His school, college and army records will show that he was very good at rounders, cricket, tennis, badminton, squash, golf and football: add to this list skiing and snooker and a Wilson of *The Wizard* character emerges (reading adventure comics was one of his main teenage hobbies – *The Victor, The Wizard, Hotspur*).[18]

His brothers always felt that in sports where stamina and strength mattered, Ian's success was almost entirely due to a 60:40 ratio of strength over skill. Golf in particular was a good example. If struck correctly he could fire a ball 300yds-plus off the tee and it didn't really matter which club he had in his hands. He once related a story of how he nearly got himself thrown out of an army golf club at one point during his service. Not renowned for his limitless patience – which, when playing golf, can be a problem – he became so exasperated waiting to tee-off at one hole whilst waiting for the players in front to hole-out some 300yds ahead on the green that he decided to take his tee shot. Although Ian could hit the ball a long way this was a relatively infrequent occurrence. On this occasion, however, he found the ball's sweet spot and sent it whistling past the ears of the players on the green up ahead. These players – senior officers as it turned out – were none too impressed at this feat of quality, long-distance driving and duly warned the 'other rank' McKay of the proper golfing etiquette and the likely consequences should such a breach of the code happen again.

Sport then was the abiding passion of his schooldays. Every break was spent playing football or when it was wet playing 'snobs' or '7 or 11' (a gambling game with dice).

He also played a variety of games and represented the school at football, cricket, badminton and tennis, usually with great success, as well as competing with distinction in the school's annual athletics championship. The school magazine and the local newspaper record his sporting achievements.

In the Rotherham Grammar School Athletics Championships – the last of which, due to the change of name to Thomas Rotherham College and the transition to being a comprehensive school, was held at the end of his third year – Ian distinguished himself in field events, especially throwing events where his ability to generate power came to the fore; he was never a sprinter or long distance runner.

Competing in the first year championship as a junior in July 1965 he won both the cricket ball throw and the long jump. In the next year's junior championship (for second year boys only) he won both the cricket ball and discus and took second place in the shot. His winning throw of 189ft 10in in the cricket ball broke the school record by more than ten feet – the championship's only record – and as no records were broken in the next and what proved to be the final championship under the name of Rotherham Grammar School, Ian McKay's record still stands. And in that final grammar school athletics championship in July 1967 Ian, a third year pupil competing with fourth years in addition to his own year, won the javelin.

He also enjoyed considerable success at racquet sports and competed for the school at badminton and tennis. In the former sport Ian and his partner Stuart Forrest won the Rotherham Schools' Under 16 Doubles knock-out competition two years in succession in 1968 and 1969. In tennis Ian, partnered with Christopher Gibson, won the Rotherham Schools' Over 16 Doubles Tournament in 1970. Ian's prowess at cricket and football are less well documented in the school magazines, although Ian played for school teams with great success from junior school onwards.

In 1969 he was one of the youngest members of a First XI football squad which visited London during the Easter holidays to play several comprehensive schools. The trip was organized by teacher Stuart Metcalfe, a tremendously enthusiastic teacher of history and economics at Thomas Rotherham College. Stuart Metcalfe had given up the best part of his two-week school holiday that April in order to take his squad – a group of sixth formers and a few fifth form boys like Ian – on the tour to the capital. His plan was that he would enrol the squad as members of the Youth Hostel Association and then transport them to London by coach on Wednesday, 9 April. Once there they would spend a week staying in pre-booked cheap and cheerful accommodation, alternating between two youth hostels in Holland Park and Blackfriars, before returning to Rotherham on 16 April. The week would be spent playing four football matches against London comprehensive school opposition, attending the West Ham v Chelsea game, and visiting some of London's more famous tourist attractions, museums and landmarks on the way.

Stuart Metcalfe remembered that 'in a mixed group of sixth formers and fifth year boys Ian was one of the younger lads and was full of all he saw and heard but by no means overawed: he was himself... He played football for the school team throughout his school career, his main attributes being considerable pace and a strong stocky physique... He played mainly on the right wing, where his speed could take him beyond the full back and he was strong enough to shrug off all but the most solid of challenges. He was confident on the ball and always wanted to be involved, being sometimes rightly and sometimes wrongly criticized as a 'greedy player'. He certainly did not let the game pass him by for too long.[19]

And so it was that on Saturday, 12 April 1969, the 15-year-old Ian McKay came to be standing on the terraces at Upton Park, home of the East End 'Hammers' of West Ham United, amid the babbling cacophony, the swirling blue clouds of cigarette smoke and beefy waftings of hot Bovril and meat pies. It was a long way from his home and family in South Yorkshire but that wouldn't have bothered him. He would have been far too excited. After all he was there to watch football, the game he adored, with one of his favourite schoolteachers and thirteen of his footballing pals, the pick of the footballers in his school, along with 32,307 other football fans, all eagerly anticipating the London Derby between West Ham and the fashionable 'Blues' of Chelsea.

For a boy who loved and lived for football and was the grandson of a talented and successful professional footballer of his day, the prospect of seeing some of the finest players ever to grace the British game in action in the flesh was a mouth-watering prospect. As the minutes ticked by towards the three o'clock kick off he would have cheered as loudly as the rest of the watching host as the home team trotted out, led by Bobby Moore, England's World Cup winning captain of less than three years earlier, followed by the rest of the men in claret and blue, including the scorers of all four of England's goals in that 1966 victory against West Germany at Wembley – hat-trick hero Geoff Hurst and Martin Peters.

And there were stars too in the ranks of the Chelsea team as they took to the field; England reserve goalkeeper Peter Bonetti, star-striker Peter Osgood, the formidable and much feared Ron 'Chopper' Harris, and the long-haired, long-sideburned Ian Hutchinson – arguably the best exponent of the tactical long throw-in which he would launch deep into his opponents' penalty box on a regular basis.

Who can say whether that young and excited South Yorkshire lad on the Upton Park terraces studied Hutchinson's technique that afternoon and decided to emulate him but what is not in doubt is that Ian would become well known for his ability to employ a similar tactic, to the joy of his team mates and the chagrin of the opposition, in years to come.

That game at Upton Park was in fact the youngsters' second match of the day. That very morning they had played the third game of their London football trip. Childhood friend Philip Leeson was another member of the squad:

Ian and I were the best of friends up until years three or four of the grammar school. Up until then we shared a passion for football and cricket. We were both in Bishop's and Ian played a huge role in our house becoming the best in terms of sporting achievement. [Ian's] self-assurance caused a few lads at school to dislike him and although he recognized this he didn't change his ways, though I think it hurt him not to be liked. It was his nature and there was nothing he could do about it. He wasn't actually becoming a loner but more and more of the gang were moving on to different things and leaving Ian behind and, I must admit, I was one of them. Although I left school in 1969, I really lost touch with Ian about two years before that. It was about this time that the hippie era started and for a bunch of us our interests moved from sport to music and girls. Ian never showed any interest in either topic. About 90 per cent of our class grew long hair, listened to what was then called 'progressive music', and spent most of our spare time going out with girls. Ian seemed to carry on in the same old way and preferred to retain what we'd have referred to at the time as old-fashioned values and so, as our new social group became so wrapped up in ourselves, I lost touch with Ian and don't really have any memories of him after this.

He never seemed to come to terms with our new ways and didn't want anything to do with us. I can't really remember how he spent his leisure time during those days – the only real contact I had with him at that time was on Saturday mornings at the school football team's fixture.

One event surprised me during those last few years at school. Ian and myself were both in Bishop's. Before each term the house would meet to choose the various team captains and it was always the same situation whereby the best player was chosen. Ian was far and away the best player we had and probably the main reason why we won the championship that year, but the house chose me as captain and Ian was never even considered. I suppose it was a bit like the Geoff Boycott syndrome – he's recognized as the best player and always the first name on the team sheet but his team mates didn't want him as leader. It wasn't Ian's leadership capabilities that they were taking into account – they were, in effect, registering their views on his character. I do remember the football trip to London though. We stayed in youth hostels and just about made it back every night before the doors were locked. We were given two brand new strips to play in rather than the traditional amber and black strip we always wore which I think was a replica of the 1960 Wolverhampton Wanderers team kit. I remember that almost every school we played [in London] was made up of players who had signed schoolboy terms with one or other of the top London clubs. God knows what they thought about playing a bunch of yobbos from Rotherham.[20]

South Yorkshire yobbos or not, all things considered the tour had gone well so far, although the football results had been a little disappointing. The result of the game that Saturday morning had been especially galling – the team slumping to its second defeat of the tour, losing 2–1 to the Cardinal Vaughan School – following, as it did, a solid 3–2 victory over Holloway School the day before.

Recording the results for posterity after that game Mr Metcalfe had jotted down the names of the three goal scorers – McKay, Harrison and Hill – and it had been Ian McKay, one of his three fifth formers, who had scored the first goal.

Now, no doubt buoyed by the expectant hubbub amongst the crowd as they waited eagerly for the kick off at Upton Park, the 15–year-old Ian McKay might have felt proud that he had already got his name on the Thomas Rotherham tour scoresheet and, who knows, might have dreamed that he would one day pull on some legendary coloured kit, take part in a contest watched by millions on TV around the world, and hope that his name would go down in history by winning the highest honours his profession could bestow.

All these events would eventually come to pass but the legendary kit would not be a football shirt, it would be the uniform and red beret of the elite Parachute Regiment; the contest not a 90-minute match but a short and bloody war 8,000 miles from his South Yorkshire home, and the highest honour not league championship or world cup medals but the Victoria Cross for valour in the face of the enemy. Ian McKay's name and his deeds would indeed be remembered forever when, in a little over thirteen years after watching his English football heroes on the Upton Park turf, the lad from Rotherham would exchange his own dreams of sporting glory on the playing fields for the grim realities of combat in the darkness and destruction of a South Atlantic battlefield.

Philip Leeson also remembered that Stuart Metcalfe took the boys to see the film *If*, 'even though we weren't old enough to get in because of the nudity in it'. That afternoon, as the adult punters looked on and waited patiently in the queue behind him, Mr Metcalfe was earnestly engaged in deep discussion with the staff of the box office at a central London cinema and appeared to be having a spot of bother.

There he was with a restless group of fourteen boys on his hands on a dull and damp afternoon and with several hours to kill, trying to convince the cinema staff that the boys from Rotherham, mumbling and shuffling around awkwardly in the foyer behind him, were all over 18 so that they could get in to watch the recently released and highly controversial X-rated film.

Negotiations had reached a crucial stage when a rhythmic 'thump, thump, thump' began to echo around the foyer to accompany Stuart Metcalfe's final pleadings. It didn't help his cause. Turning around his eyes were drawn to the source of the noise and fell on the perpetrator; it was one of his charges. Standing there, absent-mindedly bouncing a football up and down, was the 15-year-old fresh-faced new recruit to the Youth Hostel Association; Junior Member No. 483545 Ian John McKay looking, according to Stuart Metcalfe, who recalled the incident more than twenty years later, 'for all the world the fifth-year boy that he was' – a true innocent abroad!

Despite this, Mr Metcalfe managed to buy tickets for the entire group and they duly shuffled off towards the flickering darkness of the inner sanctum of the big screen. And what a film was in store for these non-metropolitan northern boys. Directed by Lindsay Anderson, *If* (the title is taken from Kipling's famous poem of the same name) stars Malcolm McDowell as Mick Travers, a brooding schoolboy intent on bringing down the established order in his hierarchical English public boarding school populated by begowned white, male, middle class masters and prefects administering humiliating and ritual punishments as a matter of course.

McDowell's character declares war on the school and the film's narrative moves inexorably towards a surreal and violent finale as Travers and his fellow rebels break into the school's cadet force armoury and mount a Founders' Day massacre from their positions on the rooftops; furiously firing Bren and Sten guns and mortaring the panic-stricken crowd below. Deeply rooted in the late 1960s anti-Vietnam, anti-establishment, counter-cultural movement, the film's sentiments and themes may have had some resonance and raised a cheer amongst boys who, like Philip Leeson, had grown their hair, were listening to prog rock, and had been beaten on several occasions by masters at Rotherham Grammar, some of whom had taken a run up in the gym in order to 'slipper' them more forcefully. Ian McKay's verdict on the film was not recorded but as he had retained his traditional values – as perceived by some of his contemporaries – then the sight of young men in uniform attempting to bring down the established order with extreme violence may not have chimed so well with a lad who, just a year later, would swear an oath of allegiance to the Crown and don uniform to serve his country. As Stuart Metcalfe later remarked, 'we did get in to see the film and returned home and soon Ian was to be leaving school – a straightforward, uncomplicated and normal young man.'

In the late 1980s Philip Leeson spoke to several schoolmates who were in the same class as him and Ian at Rotherham Grammar School and he came to the conclusion that they all seemed to highlight the same sort of characteristic features of Ian that he had noted:

But when I asked them if they really knew Ian, they all said they didn't. The classes we were in tended to have the same pupils year after year which formed into four or five different groups of friends, and when you look at the old school photographs I can remember which people belonged to each group – but I couldn't say which group Ian belonged to because I don't think he belonged to any. He was a very misunderstood person who was always likely to suffer in an all-boys school which, to be honest, could be quite cruel to someone who was openly confident or equally, to someone who was weak-minded. But, on the outside, Ian never let it show, he never seemed to alter right throughout secondary school. Reading back on what I've written, especially about Ian's secondary school life, it doesn't paint a very rosy picture of him but that's how I remember it. I'd known him for a few years before we started at the grammar school and so I suppose I accepted his ways better than the rest. There was no malice in him; he was exceptional at most sports and proud of the fact. I'm sure that if people had taken the time to get to know him he would have been as thoughtful with them as he was towards his brothers – he was certainly a good friend to me and never did me any harm whatsoever. Ian is always the one I think about during the Remembrance Day silence.[21]

On Sunday, 13 November 2011 – Remembrance Sunday – Philip Leeson eschewed the crowds at a formal and organized Remembrance Service. Instead he drove up to Kimberworth Park in Rotherham and parked outside Ian McKay's old house on Shearman Avenue at 11.00am. As he sat in his car he remembered the endless games of football he had played with Ian on the street outside his house and tried to relate this to the brave hero he became. 'It just made me think that any success his other friends and I may have achieved just pales into insignificance compared to what Ian achieved.'

Of all the sports with which Ian was involved – and squash, golf and cricket, which he played for the Scholes village team in his last years at school, could be added to the list of those already mentioned – it was, of course, football which was and remained his greatest love. Perhaps this was part of his inheritance from his grandfather Len Hargreaves. Certainly the possibility of Ian stepping into his grandfather's professional footballer's boots was seriously considered for a time and as a career choice professional football would have been very welcome to his father, Ken.

Ian had trials with Sheffield United, training with the boys' team, although never playing for them and, according to the newspapers in 1982, was approached by another local club, Doncaster Rovers, appropriately his grandfather's first club, to sign on as a professional. Newspaper accounts also related that he was 'dissuaded from becoming a professional by Billy Bingham, a former manager of the Northern Ireland national team, who was married to Freda McKay's cousin. "Billy told him that you have to be exceptional to make the grade and Ian was the sort of boy who, if he couldn't be No. 1 didn't want to know," said Mrs McKay.'[22] Those familiar with Ian's game at school and later, during his army career, have differing views as to whether he could have made the grade and established himself as a professional footballer.

Ian had stayed on at school after the fifth form, ostensibly to gain further 'O' Levels but speculation about his future career, which included other possible openings for his sporting talents, such as attempting to study to become a PE and games teacher as his mother had always longed to be, was cut short when he returned one day from a visit to the Army Careers Information Office in Sheffield. He was joining the army, he announced to his family, and not only that but he had set his sights on joining the elite Parachute Regiment. Although Ian's mother thought the army a suitable career, his father Ken was not keen, drawing in part on his own national service experience and in part on his knowledge of his son, asking, amongst other things, how Ian could expect to make the grade jumping out of aeroplanes when even the shortest car journey made him as sick as a dog.

Ken initially refused to sign Ian's papers but like many before him his opposition was futile. Beaten down by his son's insistence that Ken could refuse all he liked but he would simply wait until his eighteenth birthday and then join up anyway, without his father's permission. Ian reasoned with his father that he might as well sign the papers there and then and let him get on with it.

The careers teacher at school raised the question of Sandhurst; Ian had, after all, been a bright, albeit more physically inclined, grammar school boy and already secured several 'O' Level qualifications. Why not wait until he had gained more? If successful in those and by buckling down to some further, sustained study, there might be the possibility of a commission. But Ian, who had no appetite for the time and effort this course of action would require, was impatient for the business of soldiering, and enlisted as an 'Infantry Soldier Class One' in the Parachute Regiment on 3 August 1970, three months after his seventeenth birthday.

Against his better judgement Ken McKay signed his name on the forms and they were returned by Ian with alacrity. It was done. Ian McKay had joined the 'Airborne Brotherhood'. Blood, sweat and countless tears lay ahead. The army would become his life – and would ultimately prove to be his death.

CHAPTER THREE

Crow

Ian set out from the family home, by now a little further northeast of Shearman Avenue, at 132, Ochre Dike Walk in Rockingham, at the beginning of September 1970 for his journey into the unknown. Armed with a pass from the Sheffield Army Careers Information Office in his wallet and a very large suitcase he caught the train from Rotherham and changed at Sheffield, bound for the brand new Browning Barracks in Aldershot and the depot of the Parachute Regiment and Airborne Forces.

What awaited him was a life quite apart from that which he had known before. The front cover of the Parachute Regiment recruiting brochure of the time featured a recently dropped Para in the foreground charging towards the camera, with twelve further canopies dangling behind him and the simple legend 'THE PARACHUTE REGIMENT – CHALLENGE' picked out in block capitals above and below. On page 12 there was another image, this time in full colour, of a soldier of the 1970s – captioned 'a parachute regimental soldier in operational free fall kit' – fully kitted out with Para smock, helmet, goggles, gas mask, personal weapon and both main and reserve chutes. Ian, who had first seen such literature at the Army Careers Information Office in Sheffield, could not but have been impressed by the Parachute Regiment's bold claim that this was 'The Infantry of the Future'. 'THE PARACHUTE SOLDIER MUST BE OF HIGH QUALITY BOTH IN MIND AND BODY,' it proclaimed in block letters, 'FIT TO FIGHT AND FIGHTING FIT.' It went on: 'Training is hard and only the best is good enough. Parachute soldiers need intelligence, common sense, determination and willpower: these qualities are not rare. Men in the Regiment in all probability claim that they are no different to anybody else, yet the fact remains that a special spirit, an integral, all embracing confidence exists between men of the Parachute Regiment. Perhaps this emanates from the shared confidence of jumping out of a hole in the side of an aircraft or the fact that they are truly professional soldiers who usually go into battle first – and alone.'[1]

This last sentence was stirring stuff. Essentially the Paras – a regiment that only 30 years previously had been no more than an idea of wartime Prime Minster Winston Churchill – were being portrayed as the same but different from other regiments in the British Army, chosen men linked by a common bond which stemmed from the knowledge that they were the army's 'spearhead'; its shock troops. 'Their duty lies in the van of battle,' Field Marshal Viscount Montgomery of Alamein had famously set down in the Parachute Regiment Charter, 'They are, in fact, men apart – every man an Emperor.'

From now on Ian McKay would devote himself to becoming one of those emperors; he would become part of a tribe which saw itself as one of the more elite of the many and varied tribes which made up the British Army. From now on he would live the tribal life, internalize the tribal traditions, absorb the tribal history and learn the tribal lore. For the next twenty-one weeks he would be organized, drilled, disciplined carried, ferried and airlifted and he in turn would run, jump, hump, carry and crawl to the best of his ability in the cause of earning the right to wear the coveted red beret and the much sought after parachute 'wings' which went with it.

The Depot had only moved across to Browning Barracks from Maida Barracks, also in Aldershot, two years previously and Ian found himself posted to 359 Recruit Platoon, one of several of that particular cohort which made up the Recruit Company intake. Under the care and guidance of Lieutenant Thursby and Sergeant Downes and several junior non-commissioned officers, Ian and the rest of 359 Platoon would begin to learn their craft and be put through their paces; the weak would be weeded out, the physically and mentally strong would survive to face the rigorous regimes of field training at the Brecon Battle School in Wales and 'P' Pegasus Company – the Pre-Parachute Selection phase. If he survived that he would go on to spend the best part of a month learning how to jump out of aeroplanes; it may have been a daunting prospect for a young man who had a tendency to throw up after a few miles as a passenger in a car.

Ian's family, particularly his mother, wrote almost weekly letters filled with family news and soothing advice for a young man far away from home for the first time and coping with the novelties of barrack room life and the intricacies of pay slips, income tax and 'stoppages'. In a letter still addressed to 'Mr I. J. McKay c/o PSO, The Depot, Browning Barracks, Parachute Regiment and Airborne Barracks, Aldershot, Hampshire' and posted on 6 September with a 5d stamp, Freda wrote: 'We were so pleased and relieved to hear that you eventually arrived there safely. You certainly had a high time. We are also very proud and pleased with the results of your first tests. After a few rounds of that assault course you should begin to lose a bit of that excess weight. I hope the food is good enough to keep up your strength. Have you got your uniform yet and are you in with a good set of lads? Are you in a large barrack room or what?... Make sure you show that captain and the corporal how badminton is played in Yorkshire. All the fun has gone out of hoovering now that you are not here to grumble about it. Take care of yourself love and we are all looking forward to seeing you as soon as you can get home.'

In so far as his busy timetable allowed Ian attempted to reply in kind but as Neal later observed:

> Obviously once Ian joined the army we saw little of him. I think the original doubts my mum and dad may have had when he first talked of joining up were soon replaced by feelings of pride when Ian proved himself equal to the very demanding requirements of the Parachute Regiment training course... He would write one or two letters but until the Falklands I don't think he'd seriously put pen to paper – he much preferred to keep in touch via the telephone. We received calls from all over the place: never very long calls as neither caller nor receiver could afford to chat for too long.[2]

Nonetheless, any letter or phone call, however brief, was eagerly anticipated back in Rotherham.

By late September, although they were not using a regimental number, his family was getting used to the fact that the private citizen Mr Ian McKay had now been transformed into Private McKay and were addressing his letters accordingly. As a raw Para recruit he was officially now a 'Crow' – the standard term of endearment for those new to the regiment. Everyone had expected to see him home for his uncle Keith's wedding to future wife Sue on 3 October but as he had begun his training he could not make it. It was far too early for Ian to be given leave and those first few weeks of training were crucial in terms of him being able to bond with his new comrades and to carve himself a niche. As busy as he was he was thoughtful enough to remember to send a telegram though, which was greatly appreciated by all.

When young men from different backgrounds are thrown together and are forced to live cheek by jowl difficulties can sometimes arise. In Ian's case he had more than a strong suspicion that one or more of his fellow recruits were involved in some petty pilfering. He wrote that his wallet had gone missing and that although it had turned up, some of what little cash he had had gone missing. Ian hit upon the bright idea that he would write down the numbers of his bank notes and spread the word in the hope that others might do the same and the culprit would be sufficiently deterred.

On hearing the news his parents suggested a course of action. Although they knew he wouldn't have much left out of his pay, his father Ken suggested that he make an allowance to Freda so that she could pay it straight into Ian's bank to let it accumulate and thus save it from being pinched.

Being the target of an unknown thief may have unnerved Ian in his first few weeks of army life but all was not doom and gloom. Certainly there were disadvantages of being lumped together with lots of other young men but there were also high spots, and as the bonding process developed Ian began to make friends; one new pal simply being referred to as Jock. Freda wrote dryly that he 'must be one of the Scots lads you mentioned. (Great deduction)'. In fact the family never got to know Jock's full name. The army loves nicknames; often the more obvious and hackneyed the better. Jock was the name he had been christened by his army pals and as far as Ian and the army was concerned, Jock he would stay.

By early October Ian had started training in earnest, and this was one of the reasons he had missed the family wedding. In addition to spending hours on the parade ground learning drill he had also ventured out of the barracks and had already spent a week outdoors under canvas. Freda wrote: 'I expect you will be pleased to get back to your nice warm barracks after this last week in the rough.'

Ian did manage to get home for the first time on the weekend of 9–11 October 1970, some six weeks into his ten-week basic training and selection course, and the family were overjoyed. Freda noted later that it had been really marvellous to see him and he told them that he had had to race across London from St Pancras to Waterloo on his return to get back to barracks on time. He had been in such a rush to pack that on that occasion he had left his ring in the bathroom. It was returned to him later.

In a letter dated 19 October 1970 Freda wrote: 'Did the passing out go OK? Was it hard getting back into training after your break? Did the rest of the boys enjoy themselves?' This was a reference to the new recruit's rite of passage known as 'Passing Off the Square' which took place after the first six weeks of basic training in drill whilst absorbing some of the Parachute Regiment's relatively short but action-packed history. There was also some concern over an ankle injury which had been troubling Ian and which coincided with 359 Platoon's first foray into the wilds of the Brecon Beacons in Wales. Anyone who has ever been a member of a new group knows that being fully involved in all group activities during the first few weeks is a vital step to becoming accepted, adopting a position in the group and thus helping to shape group norms and behaviours. Everyone has a role to play. In an elite group like the Paras the desire to belong, to co-operate and work as a team, to succeed and to demonstrate personal physical and mental fortitude is even more accentuated, indeed the Parachute Regiment training regime is founded on and demands these qualities of its recruits. The scrutiny of behaviour – from both superiors and equals – is intense. To miss out on Wales due to a physical problem would have put Ian at a crucial disadvantage. He simply could not miss this key element of his training. Ian's brothers had been urged to write to him by Freda and Graham expressed the hope that Ian's ankle would hold up so that he could continue his induction with, as Graham put it, his normal squad. Whether the injury healed or was simply masked and endured is not known but Ian went to Wales anyway and completed all that was asked of him. After all he wanted to be the best.

It was in making preparations for the phase of his training in the wild, open spaces of Wales that Ian wrote and made an unusual request of his mother. They had been told, he said, to buy several pairs of women's tights as an aid to keeping their legs warm on cold, winter nights outdoors. Freda went out and did as she had been asked and posted them off: 'Would love to see you all in your nylons,' she teased gently. 'Will know what to put in your Xmas stocking.'

Ian's siblings' letters were posted to Wales on 19 October 1970 in the same envelope. Neal wrote: 'Glad to hear that your ankle improved in time and that you are now in Wales, also that your passing out parade came off successfully. So keep them 'thar' pit boots spick and span and keep the good work up in Wales.' He signed off with a warning to his elder brother not to get 'drunk on the pint the sergeant offered to buy'. For her part Freda was glad that Ian had seemed to enjoy himself. 'It made me exhausted just to read your letter… Hope the ankle is much better now (after what it went through last week it must be).'

Even with this worry uppermost in his mind his respect for his father shone through as he still found time to shop and buy a card and post it off in time for his father's birthday – one of very few that his father received that year as most of the extended McKay family appeared to forget!

Towards the end of October Ian was becoming confused and worried about his pay. He had never had to concern himself with bodies such as the Inland Revenue and the intricacies of deciphering a pay slip but now he was struggling to work it out, and the fact that he was away from home and endlessly busy in training made it more difficult.

His friend Jock was battling with figures for pay and deductions too. It was becoming a millstone around Ian's neck and he asked for his parents' help. Freda suggested he make an appointment to see the 'pay people' and ask them to explain all the stoppages. She did a little detective work on his behalf and cast around for advice in Rotherham. As far as she could discern Ian – in those far off days of pre-decimal currency – should have been deducted £3.1s for board and food and 11s.5d for his insurance stamp. She ventured that as he did not pay any graduated contributions and that he was under 18 and had joined straight from school then he should not be subject to income tax deductions for several months yet. There may have been a sports fund and a platoon fund to which Ian had to contribute but as she was unaware of these she advised him to find out. She didn't know if there was any superannuation scheme but felt that such schemes didn't usually apply until a person reached 21. 'Try and get this sorted out with the pay people,' she soothed, 'but let me know if you have any trouble or doubts. Don't get despondent love, it will all sort itself out, especially if you are beginning to settle into the life. It sounds as if you should be one of the selected few that pass through the tests. We are very proud of you, love. Let me know if there is anything you are wanting (cakes, biscuits, sweets etc.). We miss you a lot love but only want that you should be happy doing what you like best. Write back soon. All our Love, Mum and Dad. XXX.'

On 4 November 1970 Freda wrote and told Ian what the family had planned for Bonfire Night. He had let them know that he was due to have an interview with his superiors regarding his performance and when Freda wrote back she was keen to know the results: 'Do you know what they decided?' As she wrote they were all sitting watching the experimental, professional five-a-side football on TV – Manchester United v Crystal Palace. With Ian's passionate love of football Freda knew that he would be interested and so she punctuated her comments on everyday family events which would only be of interest to the McKays, with frequent updates as the game on the screen progressed. 'I think we will paper [the room] straight away and emulsion over the top (Best has just scored for Man U)... I now have another trouser suit (Man U 3, CP 0)... Hope you are keeping well love. It can't be much fun marching and doing the obstacle course in this weather. It has been shocking up here. High winds and lots of rain.'

By mid-November 1970 Ian had been allocated his regimental number – 24210031 – his problems with pay appeared to have been resolved for the time being and he had even written with the cheering news that he had received a slight pay rise. His interviews had gone well and he was pushing on with his recruit training. He also told his parents that he had had a 'forty-eight' – a forty-eight hour pass – which he had spent in London and which had involved much drinking of beer, a relatively new pastime for him.

If Ian's love of football came top of his list of passions, then most of the people who knew him well will confirm that eating, and particularly eating hefty helpings of good, honest-to-goodness home cooking, came a close second. It was a well known fact – and one never lost on Ian himself, even when writing letters from the Falklands – that he had a tendency to put on weight if he ate and, after he joined the army, drank more than usual at a time which coincided with periods when he was not active or in training. It would be a perennial problem and one which brother Neal recognised only too well.

Throughout his sporting days he was always fighting a battle with his legs and his weight: he liked his food and, in later years, beer, and if he was not careful he would soon become overweight. His legs must have been under constant strain and this led to many problems with his knees in particular.[3]

Freda warned him that 'you will end up with a real beer belly just like your father's at this rate… Look after yourself love and slow down on the booze, [kit] models will do you more good as well as your pocket.' Just for good measure she emphasized her last point; 'for goodness sake look after your money'. He had also picked up another skill which could have been seen as a money saver, although it was one which was not particularly good for his health – he had learned to roll his own 'tabs'!

By now the relentless grind of training was weeding out the wheat from the chaff amongst the recruits. Ian remarked that some had dropped by the wayside but he and his friend Jock marched on. 'It certainly sounds rough and tough' was the verdict of his mother and towards the end of November Ian learned that he had passed his physical with flying colours.

Having successfully completed his basic training Ian and his fellow recruits travelled to Hythe, six miles west of Folkestone, for a fortnight of skill-at-arms weapons training and handling, and live-fire exercises. During this phase of his training Ian was taught the intricacies of all infantry weapons and how to fire them in anger. There was a shock in store for the family whilst he was at Hythe, however, and his parents were reminded with a jolt of the dangerous nature of their son's chosen profession when news of the accidental shooting of a young soldier on the ranges at Hythe hit the front page of the *Daily Express*. The young soldier in question was named and, so the report said, lay critically ill in hospital. The family were understandably relieved that it was not Ian.

As the festive season approached thoughts turned to whether Ian would be home for Christmas. A dutiful son, Ian always tried to get home on leave whenever he could, even if that meant just for a short weekend; sometimes knocking on the door in the early hours of a Saturday morning having hitched his way from Aldershot, Brecon, Salisbury or some other far-flung outpost of the British Army in the UK. The family always told him that as long as he let them know what time he was due to arrive then there would be someone waiting up for him but on at least one occasion he pitched up in the early hours to find the household asleep and had to bed down in what the family called 'the concrete mixer'; the old banger of a car which sat on the McKay's drive. There he would snooze until the family woke and let him in.

During those first few months of his army career, Ian's absence certainly appeared to make all hearts grow fonder and the entire family enjoyed his homecomings but, as brother Neal observed, none more so than Freda and Ken. According to Neal those treasured homecomings were 'never grand affairs though, just lots of home cooking which Ian could not resist, despite the problems he knew his excess weight would give him, going out for walks, watching TV and time spent with friends and relatives at the Wingfield Social Club'.

Father Ken was not as frequent a correspondent as Freda yet his letters reveal a dry wit and a humorous turn of phrase which would have no doubt amused Ian reading them sitting on his bed in his barrack room. Having put his initial objections regarding Ian's chosen career firmly to one side, his musings also exuded a degree of warmth towards his eldest son which Ian could not fail to have picked up on. Heading one letter 'The Ochre Dike Institute for the Cripples and the Toothless' this was a humorous 'in joke' referring to an ongoing family saga in which Ian's uncle Stuart, who had broken his leg in a car crash, had subsequently had to have all his teeth removed '… the dentist, being a trade unionist, immediately said "All Out",' observed Ken wryly. It was a good one-liner but the state of labour relations in the country at the time was certainly no joke, as Ken went on to describe how tensions between the government and some trade unions were affecting the family in Rotherham.

'All out' was precisely what was happening in some parts of the economy – Ken informed Ian that the McKay household had been plunged into darkness along with most of the rest of Britain as employees in the electricity supply industry had embarked on an overtime ban and had staged 'work to rule' strikes from 8 December 1970. It had been thought that any disruptions to supply would take several weeks to bite but the power cuts came within hours of the strikers' action and chaos reigned. Ken commented that Ochre Dike Walk in Rockingham had experienced power cuts and that he had written his letter by candlelight. The family had also eaten their evening meal in the same fashion although it was hardly romantic; Ken complaining to his eldest son that he had struggled to see what he was picking up with his fork. What's more the McKays were unable to heat water for baths.

On 9 December 1970, the day after Ken wrote his letter, power cuts nationwide averaged 31 per cent and reached 40 per cent in some areas, with hospitals being hardest hit; staff struggling to maintain both essential and non-emergency services using candles, battery power and standby generators supplied by army units mobilized specifically for that purpose. The country was almost brought to a standstill. Even amongst the turmoil Ian's father managed to sound upbeat and supportive as he signed off 'with love from all at home and from everybody in *Sheffield* and surrounding districts. Your loving Dad'.

But where Ian and the rest of his platoon of would-be Paras were going, power cuts would not be a problem. In any event, power cuts and blackouts would have been the least of their worries, for 359 Platoon were about to embark on what was perhaps the most challenging, gruelling and, for those who were still not quite in the best of physical and mental shape, spirit-sapping phase of their training.

In the final few weeks leading up to the Christmas of 1970 Ian was going back to Wales, back to the Parachute Regiment Battle School, which some Para officers had dubbed the 'University of the Parachute Regiment'. During this, their second visit to the Battle School at Brecon, the recruits of 359 Platoon would be introduced to the lung-bursting, muscle-wrenching misery of the ten-mile route march up and over the 866m high Pen-y-Fan – the highest peak in southern Wales – in full battle order. For many paratroopers of Ian's generation the word 'fan' was synonymous with the contraption used for jump simulation during parachute training at Abingdon but for others 'The Fan' conjures up the sheer physical strain of that ten-mile slog over the pinnacle of the Brecon Beacons in what was christened by the SAS as 'The Fan Dance'.

By the end of the first week of December Ian was getting used to being out in the field, developing his skills of field craft, map reading, and section tactics using fire and movement manoeuvres. In attempting to put all that he had learned so far into practice it was as close to real soldiering as he had come.

Ian had let the family know that they could expect him home on the weekend of 20 December for Christmas leave. On Monday, 14 December his mother wrote that she was 'keeping her fingers crossed that you will get this letter before you leave Brecon... I hope everything has gone well for you love... I bet you are pretty exhausted by now. Everyone is looking forward to seeing you and keep asking about you. Take care of yourself love. Roll on this weekend.' Freda expressed the hope that the fun and games they had experienced with the electricity 'go slow' would have cleared itself up for Christmas, and told Ian of his impending itinerary: the family going over to The Alma as usual on Christmas morning to stay with Ian's Grandma and Granddad Hargreaves at their pub, then home on Boxing Day and 'having own turkey on the Sunday'.

Fresh from his successes at Brecon and nursing his aching limbs, Ian duly arrived home and ate heartily as usual. Although he had told his mother that the food was good in the army, in a letter written in early January 1970 Freda joked that 'I would have thought with what you managed to put away while you were home you would have had to have gone on a diet for a couple of weeks. You will be thinking next you should have joined the RAF.'

The New Year of 1971 saw Ian packing his kit bag and travelling to RAF Abingdon – then in Berkshire but after the 1974 boundary change 'moved' into Oxfordshire – to join Regular Basic Parachute Course No. 736 for parachute training at No. 1 Parachute Training School. The school had come into existence as a self-contained unit on 9 July 1941 under Squadron Leader Maurice Newnham and had moved to Abingdon in 1950 from RAF Upper Heyford in Oxfordshire. It had marked its one millionth parachute descent as recently as 1969 when Private Norman Bunn, another recruit from the Parachute Regiment and Airborne Forces Depot, had jumped on Regular Basic Parachute Course 701 at Abingdon.

Freda had written a letter addressed to Ian at 'Course 736 PCAU (Parachute Course Administration Unit) RAF Abingdon which was eventually posted on 12 January 1971. In it she told Ian that she was entitled to four days for her spring holiday in late January but that she was only taking two mornings off in order to save her other days so that she could attend his passing out parade.

Her letter was already sealed and ready to be posted when she received one from Ian. He told her he had suffered 'bangs and bruises' and explained how he had been introduced for the second time to 'the fan' – not the infamous Pen-y-Fan this time but what he referred to as a 'fan contraption'; the parachute jump training aid whereby part of the descent could be simulated from a scaffold tower some thirty feet high. He also mentioned drinking again and so, concerned mother that she was, Freda felt it her duty to respond with a word of advice. She re-opened her letter and fashioned an addendum. 'Do try and save a bit, even if it is a bit and I'm not preaching Ian but watch the booze. It can't be very good for you and you also risk being convicted of drinking under age.'

Ian's course – he was, by turn, bumped, banged and bruised – lasted for most of January 1971; the first part consisting of ground parachute training, practising landings from various heights of apparatus onto mats and using free-flight trainers, swings and trapezes which simulate flight drills. The free-flight trainer would have been the 'fan contraption' he spoke of. Ian practised exiting from a plane, descents and landings building to eight drops proper, with and without equipment and then again by night.[4]

On completion of his course on 29 January 1971 Ian received his 'wings' and returned to the Depot as a qualified parachutist entitled to additional Para pay of £136.00 per year or 7s.6d a day. Any lingering doubts Ken may still have harboured regarding his son joining the Paras were soon replaced by feelings of pride when Ian proved to himself and the world that he was equal to the very demanding requirements of the Parachute Regiment's training course.

A few weeks after completing his parachute training and receiving his wings, Ian's mother and father travelled down to Aldershot with Ian's uncle Keith and his wife Sue in their car for his passing out parade on 12 February 1971. They stayed overnight at the White House near Farnham. The weather on the day of the parade was dreadful, with heavy rain and high winds. The families of the forty-five young soldiers were drawn up on a slope to one side of the parade ground and Freda remembered an amusing incident when one father's 'pork pie' hat blew off and he scuttled to retrieve it. On his return Keith McKay pulled a 6in nail from his pocket and offered it to the man to help keep his hat on. All the spectators were absolutely soaked but it could not dampen Ken and Freda's pride as their son, who had proved he had made the grade and was now set to become one of those 'emperors' of which Montgomery had spoken, swung past with a smart 'eyes right'. 'The day of his passing-out ceremony, when he became a full member of the Parachute Regiment, was a very memorable and proud day for all of us,' noted Neal many years later.

The only blot on the day was that Ken and Freda had arranged to meet Ian after the parade but there had been a mix-up in times and meeting points and somehow it did not happen. His parents drove all the way back to South Yorkshire, having retrieved dry clothes from their suitcase, without being able to tell him in person how proud they were of him.

It was after he had earned his wings and he had passed out that 'that' photograph of Ian – perhaps the most famous of all images of Ian McKay; the one of the smiling, relaxed, moon-faced teenager in a red beret with the dog – was taken. After his death in 1982 and the announcement of his Victoria Cross it was the one which was emblazoned across the front pages of the national and local press and even the Parachute Regiment's own journal. The image has been used on postage stamps, first day covers, commemorative postcards and numerous other documents.[5] It is the one image above all others, which even those who have but a fleeting interest in the Victoria Cross, the Parachute Regiment and all things military, will probably associate with Ian McKay. Although it is a much overused word, that one photograph has indeed become 'iconic' as the enduring image of Ian McKay in the minds of the British people. But it was only ever meant to be akin to a family snap, even though it was to feature as a local news item in *The Rotherham Advertiser* and the events surrounding its creation were more luck than judgement. Even the dog, which looked for all the world like Ian's faithful canine companion in that image, didn't belong to the McKays!

John Bates, a young photographer who had just started working for *The Rotherham Advertiser*, had met Freda previously and was aware of the McKay family through various local news items and Freda's connection with the Newman Special School, which Graham and Neal McKay attended. Word had come into the *Advertiser* newsroom that a local lad had joined the Parachute Regiment, had earned his wings and had passed out. 'This was a big deal for a town like Rotherham then' said John, 'we had heard that Ian was home on leave and I was sent up to take a photograph.' Grabbing his old Rolleiflex twin lens reflex camera he made his way up to the McKay family home in Rockingham.

Ian was not really dressed for a photo shoot and was certainly not in full regulation Para uniform. He did, however, have his tunic with him, now with the proud addition of his hard-won Parachute wings, stitched to his upper right sleeve, and his red beret, bought at his own expense from Victor's in Aldershot. The standard issue red berets made by Kangol simply could not be shaped and were more akin to a 'huge saggy bag', to quote Bob Hilton, an ex-member of the 2nd Battalion of the Parachute Regiment (2 Para) who, at the time of writing, works voluntarily for the Parachute Regiment and Airborne Forces Museum at Duxford. Men were only allowed to wear the non-standard 'Victor's' after successfully completing the course known as Advanced Wales, and the lanyard over his left shoulder is another clue to the date of the photograph as the lanyard was only issued after recruits had passed out.

He had not been in uniform when he had arrived home and Freda had never seen him in it. She would like the photograph as a keepsake, she said, and with her urging Ian had agreed:

He'd got a normal shirt on with a borrowed tie and he just put his uniform jacket on. If you look at the photograph he has ordinary light-coloured trousers on as well. The dog from next door had come around – it was called Spot as it had a white patch on its head. John had his camera and took it. When [Ian] got the VC and [the press] wanted a picture that was the only one I could find. I hated that photograph; he doesn't even look 16 on it but I'm glad John [Bates] made his name out of that photograph.

When John Bates arrived he and Ian had a brief chat and John decided that he would photograph Ian sitting on the doorstep.

Ian just put the beret and jacket on, that's all. When I got there my intention was to take a portrait – just a head and shoulders shot – but when the dog wandered across and sat with him I thought I would keep the dog in. I came to know Freda, Ken and the family very well afterwards and particularly after Ian had been killed and won the VC in 1982 when I would say I saw Freda almost on a weekly basis, but that was the only time I ever met Ian. We didn't talk much but I remember clearly I said to him, 'the Paras eh?' to which he replied 'Yes, only the best'.[6]

But his time at home, deep in the bosom of his family – enjoying his mother's cooking, playing football with his brothers, meeting friends and playing snooker in the various clubs which his family had frequented before he joined up – would be all too brief. There would be no honeymoon period for Ian McKay with the service to which he had pledged his oath of allegiance; no exotic foreign posting where he could hone his skills and learn his trade at his leisure. The British Government and the army had a more urgent and pressing need for his services much closer to home.

Decades of deep-seated discrimination, distrust, division, resentment and rage had served to fill a simmering cauldron of sectarian hatred which had finally boiled over on 12 August 1969, pouring its terrifying poison onto the streets of what was then called Londonderry in Northern Ireland in what became known as the three day Battle of the Bogside.

Vicious and sustained rioting broke out, civil authority was undermined, the police lost control and took heavy casualties, law and order broke down. Worse still for the British and Northern Irish Governments, these were not the dusty streets of some colonial outpost like Aden or Cyprus, these were the streets of a modern city just across the Irish Sea. This was the United Kingdom. The situation was so serious that water cannon were employed and the historic decision was made to use CS gas for the first time on UK soil. More significantly, British troops were called in to help the beleaguered and exhausted police and to try and re-establish some semblance of normality. But even as the rioting in Londonderry had begun to subside and the embers of the smouldering buildings and burnt-out cars begun to cool on the third day, the sparks from the Battle of the Bogside had simply served to ignite another fuse seventy miles away in Belfast.

If the people of Londonderry felt that they had just lived through a battle then the residents of Belfast must have felt that they were caught up in the onset of a war, and so they were. Tensions flared along the volatile junctions – the so-called 'Orange-Green Line' – which separated the Protestant Shankill Road from the Catholic Falls Road to the south and the Catholic Ardoyne to the north.

On 13 August 1969 shots were fired by members of the Irish Republican Army (IRA) and a hand grenade was thrown. The following night, Herbert Roy, a 26-year-old Protestant, was struck in the chest and killed by an IRA bullet at the same time as three policemen were wounded. The police responded by deploying armoured cars mounted with 0.30mm machine guns; a tracer round from one of them penetrating two walls and killing 9-year-old Catholic boy Patrick Rooney as he lay in his bed in the Divis Flats. With passions inflamed by the killings on both sides of the sectarian divide the violence escalated. On 15 August five more people – four Catholics and one Protestant – were shot dead and Catholic families were forced to flee in fear of heir lives as loyalist hordes descended on their houses in shared streets and torched their homes. Belfast burned. With the last vestiges of control slipping through his government's fingers the Northern Ireland Prime Minister, Major James Chichester Clark, formally contacted Labour Home Secretary James Callaghan shortly after mid-day on 15 August, with a direct request for military assistance. Less than three hours later the British Government took the momentous decision to deploy British soldiers on to the streets of Belfast to bolster the civil authorities. The British Army were 'in'. It was the start of a military commitment to Northern Ireland which would last more than 30 years.[7]

For the beaming youngster in the red beret, proudly sporting his parachute wings on his upper right sleeve and stroking next door's dog in John Bates' now famous photograph, the rioting, the bombings, the killings and the social and political ramifications of that fateful decision taken by the British Government 18 months earlier seemed a far cry from the peace and quiet of the back step of his parents' home in Rotherham. Despite his tender years and relative inexperience, however, Ian was now a member of that same British Army which was fully engaged in what was to be a long and gruelling war against the IRA; a young man deemed to be a fully-trained and fully-qualified Para – no longer a 'crow'. As such the British Army in general and the Parachute Regiment in particular would post him wherever it saw fit and, just two months shy of his eighteenth birthday, the regiment saw fit to post him to its 1st Battalion (1 Para), and 1 Para was already stationed in Belfast. Ian McKay was bound for active service.

As John Bates' shutter clicked and fixed the image of Ian McKay for a general public eleven years in the future, little did the subject of the picture know that within the year he would become embroiled in events in Northern Ireland so serious and far reaching that the reverberations would shock the world, striking at the very heart of British Government policy towards the province and the methods employed by its army and Ian's beloved Parachute Regiment.

CHAPTER FOUR

1 Para

By the time Ian received concrete news of his posting to the Parachute Regiment's 1st Battalion, the unit was already some six months into a twenty-month residential tour of duty in Northern Ireland with 39 Infantry Brigade, commanded by Brigadier Frank Kitson who had, coincidentally, arrived in the Province at the same time in September 1970.

Kitson's 39 Airportable Brigade had originally consisted of six battalions, four of which were deployed in Belfast, and 1 Para, at that time commanded by Lieutenant Colonel Michael Gray, was one of two units which made up Kitson's Brigade Reserve, stationed at Palace Barracks in the suburb of Holywood in County Down, just two miles northeast of Belfast city centre.[1] In order to join his battalion in Belfast Ian had first to cross the Irish Sea.

Given that, at the time of writing, Northern Ireland has enjoyed a decade of relative peace and returned prosperity since the IRA's historic statement in late October 2001 that it would put its arms 'beyond use', it is difficult for modern audiences to imagine that 30 years earlier, individual reinforcements like Ian, when posted for duty to a battalion already serving in Northern Ireland, travelled together in small groups, in uniform on public transport (train and ferry) and carried their personal weapons with them. Although one MOD source on the history of the army's deployment to Northern Ireland clearly states that troops travelling by those means were issued with five rounds of ammunition for their personal protection, 'Tom', one of Ian's more experienced colleagues at the time he joined the battalion, is adamant that young, green soldiers such as Ian, embarking for duty for the first time to Northern Ireland, would never have been allowed to travel on public transport with live ammunition.[2]

Live rounds or not, Ian did take the ferry from Liverpool to Belfast and reported to Palace Barracks to be formally entered on the nominal roll of 1 Para on 2 March 1971. He was now officially on duty in what the army called Operation Banner, the codename for its operations throughout Northern Ireland.[3]

The surroundings of Palace Barracks, situated a short distance from the waterfront of Belfast Lough on the approaches to Belfast harbour, might have been a novel and unfamiliar environment for Ian McKay but for the more experienced men of the battalion the streets of Belfast were, by March 1971, all too familiar, for many were on their second operational tour of the province.

Ian's battalion, 1 Para, held the distinction of being the first of the Parachute Regiment's three regular battalions to serve an emergency *roulement* tour in Northern Ireland when an advance party of A Company and elements of D (Patrol) and Support

Companies had flown in from training on the Isle of Man at midnight on 12 October 1969, two months after what is now generally accepted as being the start of 'The Troubles'. Battalion HQ and C Company had arrived in the small hours of 13 October and in less than twelve hours the men had been out on the streets, relieving the hard-pressed soldiers of the 3rd Battalion the Light Infantry on the Shankill Road in the aftermath of serious rioting, during which the light infantrymen had been 'bricked', petrol bombed and shot at, resulting in sixteen casualties.[4]

Tensions had been running high in the wake of the rioting and the men of 1 Para had initially endured a torrent of abuse, aggression and hostility from both sides – Catholics fearing that the army had come in to finish the burning of their homes started by the Protestants, and Protestants angered by the fact that the army had prevented them razing those same Catholic houses to the ground. But the atmosphere gradually calmed over the following few days as Lieutenant Colonel Gray, under orders from his superiors to return the area to at least some degree of normality for both Catholics and Protestants, insisted that his men make every effort to establish good relations with the communities on either side of the Orange-Green Line in the Falls and Shankill Roads.

Tom was a corporal in 1 Para's Mortar Platoon, part of the battalion's Support Company, during that first emergency tour and came to know the newly-joined Ian McKay well

> I went from private soldier to full corporal in about nine months. We were training all of '68 and then, of course, in October '69 we got called out to do our first emergency tour of Northern Ireland when it all 'kicked off' over there. At first it was a 'softly softly' approach – all hearts and minds stuff – with the odd riot here and there. It wasn't as serious as it became later on. We came back home later on in '69 then we got posted on a residential two-year tour over there; the married men taking their wives and kids with them into quarters. I had a 'quarter' while we were at Palace Barracks. We had obviously done too well the first time round!

As part of Lieutenant Colonel Gray's community relations campaign during that first tour, Tom and the rest of 1 Para, including Ian, had climbed ladders to fix broken street lights, unblocked sewers, organized old people's parties and had played football with the local children, whilst at the same time going about their military business of vigorous patrolling in order to pick up vital intelligence and establish a highly visible presence.[5] It was not unknown, after the initial surge of animosity on the part of the locals had been stemmed, for members of the Catholic community to supply the soldiers of 1 Para with 'endless cups of tea and biscuits'.[6]

But the honeymoon period would not last beyond that first emergency tour. The mutual enmity which existed between the Republicans and the Loyalists was never far from the surface and this was only exacerbated at the end of 1969 as the IRA tore itself asunder due to internal differences, resulting in the birth of the more hard line Provisional IRA with its avowed policy of an all-out military offensive against the British Army. Add to that the realization on the part of the Paras that the tactics they had employed so successfully on internal security operations in the fading outposts of Empire were of little use when faced with, as ex-1 Para officer and later Brigadier Hamish McGregor put it, 'our own people, British people on the streets of the United Kingdom'.[7]

Tom remembers standing at the bottom of the Shankill Road facing a baying mob of some of these British people and 'getting into a box-formation like we had used in Aden and then someone getting placards out with "disperse or we fire" written on them. It had worked in Aden but we quickly realised that in Belfast this was just silly. It wasn't working. These people were smarter than the crowds we had faced in Aden. We had to adapt and we changed the way we operated to do the job.'

It was clear to all – from other ranks through to officers – that the politicians in Westminster would not authorize opening fire on rioting British citizens. Battalions had to find new ways of handling the crowds and quelling trouble, and this inevitably meant adopting a different approach to riot control. The battalion faced a very steep learning curve and although there would be no overnight solutions it gradually developed and refined its tactics based on speed of deployment and momentum; driving hard into a crowd to wrest the initiative from the mob, to minimize the opportunities for rioters to throw stones, bricks and bottles, and to make arrests.

Over many weeks and months the developments and refinements resulted in an even harder edge for a battalion well-known for its muscular approach and forceful efficiency in getting the job done. The Paras' penchant for dominating the ground and, as one ex-Para told me, 'never backing down from a punch-up', in spite of a policy of attempting to win hearts and minds, eventually chafed on the Catholic community as they began to view the British Army as an occupying force. Hard line army curfews, 'lockdowns' and 'cordon and searches' to find concealed IRA weapons resulted in losing friends in the Catholic areas of Ulster. The evolution of a no-nonsense approach to crowd and riot control of the men in the red berets even rankled with sections of the community loyal to the union with the UK.

'Dick', another member of Support Company, tells how attitudes to 1 Para eventually began to harden on both sides: 'A man once told me "you know we hate you but at least you're even-handed. You lot hate both 'Prods' and Catholics. You're just bastards to everybody".'[8]

By the time Ian joined the battalion in Northern Ireland, men like Tom and Dick had notched up a total of some eleven months in the province spread over two tours. In that time they had seen a great deal and learned much but they had also noticed a sea change both in the attitudes of the local Catholic community towards them and the tempo and intensity of the violence on the streets which had changed beyond all recognition since they had first arrived in Northern Ireland in mid-October 1969; the communal and civil disorder of 1969–70 giving way to what some commentators have called a 'full-scale guerrilla war striking indiscriminately at civilian and military targets.'[9]

The tragic statistic of being the first British soldier to be killed in the Troubles was claimed by 20-year-old Gunner Robert Curtis; hit by a single bullet in the chest when shots were fired at British troops during rioting in Belfast less than four weeks before Ian arrived in Northern Ireland. He had died almost immediately. In the following three weeks two more British soldiers had been killed – Lance Bombardier John 'Jock' Laurie, 22, who died a week after being shot by a sniper during an ambush on the Crumlin Road in Belfast, and Corporal William Joliffe, 18, of the Royal Military Police, who died in hospital of burns and chemical inhalation from a fire extinguisher the day after the armoured personnel carrier in which he was a passenger came under petrol bomb attack in Londonderry on 28 February. William Joliffe had succumbed even as Ian had been journeying towards his first posting.[10]

This then was the atmosphere in Northern Ireland at the time Ian McKay joined 1 Para. Plunged feet first into a real war on the streets of the United Kingdom, at 17 years and 10 months he was not much younger than those first three British military victims of the Troubles.

The streets of Belfast and Londonderry were now very dangerous places to be for a man in a British soldier's uniform. Ian had much ground to make up and if he wanted to stay alive he would have to listen and learn quickly; picking up the essential skills, hints, tips and tricks of his chosen trade on the job from the more experienced 'Toms' who now surrounded him. His own learning curve would be sheer indeed, yet the savagery of the events which unfolded in Belfast just over a week after Ian arrived at Palace Barracks would overshadow his own settling-in period.

Only days after his posting three young Scottish soldiers of B Company of the 1st Battalion, The Royal Highland Fusiliers – John McCaig, 17, from Ayr; his brother Joseph, 18, and friend Dougald McCaughey, 23, from Glasgow – were off duty, unarmed and dressed in civilian clothes in Mooney's bar in the Cornmarket area of Belfast on 10 March 1971. The exact details of what happened next are hazy but it appears certain that they were approached by three men, including a former British soldier, who invited them to a party. Relaxed, with a few drinks inside them and completely off guard, they were driven north and eventually taken down a quiet country lane off the Ligoniel Road at the White Brae, Squire's Hill, on the outskirts of North Belfast, oblivious to the fact that their new-found, ex-army 'friend' was the leader of an IRA group from Ardoyne. When the car pulled up to allow the three young squaddies out to relieve themselves the IRA men executed them at close range and left their heaped bodies by the roadside, one of them reportedly propped up and with a half-empty beer glass still in his hand.[11] Their bodies were found by children at 9.30pm that night. They became the fourth, fifth and sixth British soldiers respectively to die in the province since the shooting of Gunner Robert Curtis on 6 February, but crucially were the first three to be killed whilst dressed in civilian clothes and off duty.[12]

The first inkling of the killings had been beamed directly into the sitting rooms and kitchens of the UK mainland via radio initially then, the following morning, television news and the newspapers too had screamed their outrage. In Rotherham, the McKay family had not been immune to the coverage and were worried sick. Freda still recalls the heart-stopping moment she and Ken heard the news.

[Ian] went to Belfast and he hadn't been there two weeks when some young soldiers were killed. First reports just said they were Scottish soldiers and two of them were brothers. We knew that Ian had become friends with a couple of

Scottish lads and with a name like McKay we feared the worst and were just waiting for the knock on the door. We sat up all night just listening to the radio, waiting and dreading getting the call. It was only at about six o'clock in the morning when the news said that the soldiers had belonged to a Scottish regiment that we could finally stop worrying. All I felt was a terrific relief. It was only later that I realised a mother would have had to have gone through what I went through later. That was when the army said that young soldiers could not go to Northern Ireland until they were 18.

When at last the phone rang and Freda heard Ian's voice on the other end of the line her relief was palpable. Several more calls did much to calm her nerves. Later, in a letter which betrayed her worries, substituting her usual 'Dear Ian' salutation with the more fond 'Dearest Ian', she was even able to muster a joke about a comment he had made in an earlier telephone call, doubtless to buoy her son's spirits at such a grim period: 'We were so shocked and upset over what happened in Belfast last Wednesday and so worried for you that it was marvellous to hear your voice,' Freda wrote on 17 March, just a week after the atrocity. 'I can't tell you how much your telephone calls have cheered me up this last week... We watch television very carefully in case there is a chance of seeing you when anything comes on from Ireland but to tell you the truth love, you all look the same. Lots of people have come up to me and said they were sure they had seen you... I do hope everything calms down over there and that you will be able to enjoy your stay in Ireland... Anyhow take good care of yourself love. When you first said "Mortar" on the phone I thought you were learning to drive.'

Under the circumstances the word 'enjoy' was not perhaps the word which sprang readily to mind when men of the British Army thought about tours of duty in the province. The time for enjoying that particular posting had well and truly passed.

As it percolated through the media, news of the murders caused widespread revulsion on all sides. In a statement to the House of Commons of the UK Parliament the following day, Home Secretary Reginald Maudling utterly condemned the killings as 'an appalling crime', whilst his Labour predecessor at the Home Office, Jim Callaghan, chose to use the word 'barbarous'.[13] Officially the IRA did not claim responsibility and amongst ordinary members of the nationalist community there were those who agreed with the politicians in believing that the murders had plumbed new depths of depravity.

The ensuing public outcry resulted in calls from all sides – not least in the UK Parliament – for restrictions on the service of soldiers under the age of 18 in Northern Ireland. In his prepared statement Reginald Maudling informed the House that security arrangements for off-duty soldiers were being reviewed. Calling for calm and restraint on the part of the British troops on the ground in Northern Ireland, he suggested that the aim of the killers was to provoke the security forces into reprisals.

Nevertheless, he made it clear that the British Government felt that the IRA, despite its official denials of responsibility, had crossed the line and that battle had now been joined against the terrorists. It was a battle which, he assured the House, would be 'fought with the utmost vigour and determination. It is a battle against a small minority of armed and ruthless men whose strength lies not so much in their numbers as in their wickedness'.[14]

Towards 7.30pm that same evening, during a debate on the Defence Estimates for the coming year, Ian Gilmour, the Under Secretary for Defence, prefaced his statement with the following remarks:

> In view of the tragic events of last night, I hope that the House will think it appropriate that I should begin by talking about the army in Northern Ireland and postpone until later a brief review of the army's activities throughout the world. My Right Hon. Friend and the whole House have already expressed their abhorrence at the cowardly assassinations which took place last night and have expressed their sympathy with the relations of the murdered soldiers. So I will pass on to a more general survey of the army's role in Ulster. But just how arduous and thankless that role is has been underlined by the appalling events of last night.

Echoing the sentiments of Reginald Maudling earlier that day and in words that were to become sadly prophetic just less than a year later, Gilmour went on:

> Unfortunately, it is a regrettable but unavoidable fact that in a situation like the present some innocent people will suffer… We are anxious to do all that we can to keep the inconvenience or the damage suffered by innocent people to the barest minimum. But, at the same time, we shall be relentless in our actions against gunmen and we will be as tough with them as we have to be in order to stamp out terrorism. The army will not hesitate to open fire when they or others are shot at by gunmen or attacked by petrol bombers. But they will not be indiscriminate in their fire—nor would anyone in the House want them to be.[15]

The MP for Mansfield, Don Concannon, urged that the Select Committee then working on the Armed Forces Bill look at an amendment to prevent some of the more unpleasant consequences of having 17-year-old servicemen in Northern Ireland. 'I well understand how it has happened,' he went on, 'due to the wording of the active service clause in the army's disciplinary code, but what it comes to is that there can be *de facto* active service in the United Kingdom, and we cannot declare a whole area in the United Kingdom as an active service area. We have had serious discussions on this point in the Select Committee, and I am sure I am right in saying that an Amendment may well come out which will delete the two words 'United Kingdom' and probably save such a situation in the United Kingdom, with soldiers serving in Northern Ireland at the age of 17… I should like to see a change made to save that possibility in Northern Ireland.'

Ian Gilmour returned to Don Concannon's point at the end of the debate and revealed that although the government conceded that one of the young soldiers 'so tragically killed in Northern Ireland yesterday' was only 17, he was, in fact, 17 years and 5 months and that under the existing rules 'it was in order for Fusilier McCaig to have served in Northern Ireland'. That said, Gilmour could tell the House that, 'in view of the recently changed circumstances there, the government were considering whether a change in these rules should be made'.

The change to the rules did come to pass and the army raised the minimum age for service in Northern Ireland to 18 as a direct consequence of the murder of 17-year-old John McCaig. It has always been thought that Ian McKay – four months older than John McCaig at the time McCaig was killed – was ordered back to the UK immediately on leave until he turned 18 on 7 May 1971 but the dates of the letters written to Ian by his parents do not appear to bear that out. Freda's letter of 17 March 1971, in which she referred to her shock and upset at the news of the murders, was franked in Sheffield on 19 March and there was a further letter which was written on 30 March and franked on 1 April, a full thirty-seven days before Ian's eighteenth birthday, in which his mother expressed her relief that, 'at least according to the telly things seem to have quietened down over there. I hope you enjoyed yourself on your 72hr break. Did you play football last Sunday?'

In spite of the horrific events so fresh in everyone's memory Freda did her best to ensure she hit a positive note in the letter and filled it with chit-chat and family gossip in the hope that she could maintain a veneer of normality which would mask her obvious concern for her son's safety. She also revealed that she had another bit of good news, whilst looking forward to a time in the summer when the family could get together again on holiday.

'We had a letter for you last week from that Save and Prosper Group. I opened it for you & inside was a cheque for £10 which I have banked for you. I see from today's Budget that you can get even more from your money with that Save as You Serve scheme so I would advise you love to try and get in it as soon as possible. See your paymaster about it. Take great care of yourself and enjoy yourself. Take special care of them 'Mortars' whatever they are. We are all arranging our holidays for when you have yours. If you have any other suggestions than 'Brid' you had better send them quick… But it really doesn't matter where we go we will have a good time.'

Tom recalls that everyone in 1 Para was well aware of the killings of the young soldiers: 'You couldn't escape it. It was all over the papers over there. When we were fighting on our streets and our young soldiers were being killed it was a political hot potato and I can see why the politicians felt that they had to change it. But the situation didn't change overnight. The young soldiers under 18 were not taken off the streets straight away and I certainly can't remember any young soldiers being sent home until they were 18.'

Freda remains convinced, however, that at some point during those five weeks until his eighteenth birthday, Ian did manage to get home and it is certainly true that after the letter written by Freda on 30 March and posted to Northern Ireland on 1 April there is a gap in the sequence of letters written from home until a letter franked on 15 June 1971 – an unusual hiatus given the frequency with which the family wrote to Ian prior to the end of March. A 'PS' to another letter written by Ian's Aunt Marie and dated Monday 7 June 1971, appears to support the theory that Ian was at home around the time of his birthday: 'Hope the cake is alright – just a taster. Get yourself something with the money as I forgot to give you your birthday present when you were home.'

Freda's conviction, that Ian came home for a period after the murders of John and

Joseph McCaig and Dougald McCaughey, is unshakeable as she tells of a serious 'sit down' conversation that she and Ken had with him in the wake of the atrocity. Ken McKay had never wanted Ian to join the army in the first instance and so, citing the murders of the three young soldiers, his parents tried once again to talk him out of his decision. 'I said to him, "will you please come home now" but he would have none of it. He said: "no, no, no; I could walk out of here today and get knocked over by a bus. If your name's on the bullet that's it. It's what I want to do and I'm going back".'

And go back is exactly what he did. It is clear from the contents of Freda's letter of mid-June 1971 that Ian was most definitely back in Northern Ireland and had been on duty in addition to keeping up with some of the athletic activities in which he had excelled at Rotherham Grammar School.

Dear Ian,

Hope you didn't have much trouble last week. We saw that 1st Para regiment were on duty at the Orange Men's Parade on Sunday. Were you in that scuffle on the river? We were watching it on the new TV. Your dad was very undecided whether to get a colour TV or not, anyhow we have put it off for this year and are going to reconsider it again next year... Hope you enjoyed your athletics last Wednesday & that the javelin is travelling far... Keep your pecker up love, it won't be long until the holidays. Let's hear from you soon.[16]

Perhaps her mind was fixed on her eldest son's safety as she signed off with:

'All our love Mum, Dad, *Ian* and Graham', (author's emphasis).

His family also sent him a belated birthday present in June – a fountain pen.

'Here at last love is your belated birthday present with all our love. There are some cartridges in the bottom of the box.' Ian obviously tried out the pen for size and on the back of one envelope practised writing his signature, I. J. McKay, the capital 'J' resembling a capital 'T' which sometimes happened when he signed his name – finished off with a final flourish beneath.

It was unusual for one so young and relatively inexperienced to be posted from the Depot into a battalion which revelled in its reputation as a tough, experienced and elite unit and to find a berth, almost immediately, in the Mortar Platoon of its Support Company which, in turn, saw itself as the *crème de la crème* of the battalion. Yet the addresses on his mother's letters quite clearly state 'Mortar Platoon, Support Company'. Ian quickly carved himself a niche in the Mortar Platoon and in the process acquired a new nickname or two.

Tom remembers the time Ian McKay pitched up in Palace Barracks, Belfast, for a second time in the summer of 1971 and joined the Mortars:

Mac came into the battalion around the time I went to the junior NCOs cadre in 1971 while we were in Ireland. Mac's path would have been the same as mine I should think. He wasn't out of the Depot very long. I remember talking to him and him telling me he was from Rotherham and somebody else told me a story that he had played for Rotherham United. That's when he first came into focus because he was quite a talented footballer and he played for the battalion. Like most lads, when they first came from the Depot he was a bit wary. He was very aware of everything that was going on. Nobody talks to you for the first few days until they get to know you and learn to trust you and Mac was no different. It's exactly the same when you transfer over to Support Company. Usually you had to have had at least three years experience and then you could apply to join Support Company. Although by then you've got a bit more 'wool on your back', nevertheless people might not talk to you until you've done the course and passed and if you pass the course you're then in the Mortars and you're accepted. I think when I first met him and we got talking I remember thinking, 'should he be a Tom [Parachute Regiment term for soldier], him? Shouldn't he be an officer?' Not that he was arrogant or stand-offish, he was just that bit different from the rest of us who were a bit rough and ready. I wouldn't say he wasn't streetwise because he was as streetwise as the rest of us but he just seemed to have a bit more... what can I say ...decorum. People used to say 'you ought to be an officer young Mac'. Now whether they were taking the piss or not I don't know but still, I used to think he was a canny lad and had been well educated. When I say educated I knew he hadn't been to university but certainly he'd been to grammar school. Mac was very likeable; a very friendly lad who always had a smile on his face. In fact I can see Mac smiling now in my mind's eye.

Tom remembered that, even as a young man in what could have been an intimidating environment, as he became more established in the platoon Ian demonstrated a strength of character beyond his years:

He was quite strong willed. If he'd got something to say he'd say it; not at first obviously but when he settled in. You could see him and sometimes he'd keep things in until he couldn't [keep them in] any more. But he wasn't one of those who would mouth off from a distance; he would come up to you and have his say. I can remember him coming up to me once and he had that face on and I remember thinking 'what the hell's up with you?' We had a little chat and he was upset about the way something was being done. I told him 'yeah Mac but it's still got to be done' and he went on about 'what if this?' and 'what if that?' I said it didn't matter 'why' or 'how' it still had to be done so let's do it and then sort out any problems later. So he was quite prepared to say 'I don't agree with that'. He'd have his say and he might not like what he had to do but he would always get on and do it.[17]

The following anecdote, an occasion which really tested Ian's patience to the limit, illustrates perfectly his incredulity as a combat soldier at some of the things the army occasionally asked him to do. At the time, as is the case at the time of writing, the army was subject to cuts in defence spending and significant pressure was coming down from on high to make 'efficiency savings'. The Mortar Platoon of 1 Para was not immune in being ordered to find ways of cutting back. Tom takes up the story:

Every time you wanted to fire a mortar you would put the base plate on the ground and then fire two rounds just to bed it in, so that was two rounds just going down the range and being wasted. Our platoon commander was given an instruction that he had to find ways of saving ammunition and one of those ways was to try and find another way of bedding in to save those two rounds. Now the amount of pressure it takes to bed a mortar base plate in properly could only come from an explosion. Well, the captain had us driving Land Rovers over the base plates and digging out the hole. We used to prepare the surface but not dig the hole as only the bedding in could make it firm. Our captain even went to the pioneer platoon and asked them if they could work out a device that we could fasten to the side of a Land Rover, put the base plate down on the ground, pull this device and somehow drive the base plate in. Well, like most of us Mac just couldn't believe it. When we were told that we were going out on exercise and instead of firing the two rounds to bed in as we had been trained, we were going to have run over it with a Land Rover, Mac just looked at me as if to say, 'tell me you're joking'. I said to Mac, 'look, let's get on with it' and he looked at me quizzically with his hands on his hips and started to say 'but Tom...' but I cut him short and said 'Mac, just fucking do it', but he didn't move. He just stood there with his hands on his hips, looking at me as if to say, 'what is he asking me to do?'[18]

Those who served with Ian McKay in Northern Ireland in 1971–72 stress how few troops there were in the province to deal with the situation successfully and how 1 Para – as resident battalion and, therefore, force reserve – could be deployed anywhere in the province as reinforcements. One member of Ian's platoon commented in May 1988 that it was more like a war in those days and Tom admits that in Northern Ireland 1 Para were 'certainly in a difficult situation – counter-terrorism, call it what you like. We, Support Company, seemed to be called in often to do all sorts of jobs,' yet he also maintains that the biggest battle the men had to fight was boredom:

If the balloon went up you knew the blokes would be there doing their jobs, it was filling the hours while you were waiting that sometimes became a problem. Most of the Northern Ireland tours consisted of boring, mundane jobs – patrol, patrol, yet another patrol, VCPs [vehicle check points] and the like. On one occasion we'd been out on patrol for more than three days and you get very tired – you catch your sleep where you can. We were out one night and I said to the lads 'park the 'pig' [a four-wheel drive armoured 1-ton Humber truck used as a personnel carrier] up against the wall.' I put some sentries out and told the lads inside to get an hour's kip and then we'd change over. It was just a way of re-charging the batteries. I was sitting in the front of the 'pig' nodding, and I heard this 'pssst, pssst' and thought 'what the hell's that?' I looked and couldn't see anything and nodded again. Then I heard it again: 'pssst, pssst'. I noticed that every time a vehicle went past I heard this 'psst' sound. I woke some of the others up and asked them, 'what's that noise?' 'Dunno'. Then we looked out and we noticed one of the lads had a can of silver spray paint and every time a vehicle went past he was spraying it so that he knew it had been through the checkpoint before.

When I asked 'Dick', another member of the Mortar Platoon during 1971–1972, what the men did to combat the boredom whilst sitting in the back of a stuffy Humber 'pig' for hours on end waiting for something to happen, he told me that there was very little the men could do but that inevitably a pack of cards would be produced. The reason for getting the deck of cards out was simple, 'it was about the only thing you could play using the back of a riot shield in the back of a 'pig'.' With his sharp wits and quick reactions Ian, who had been used to playing cards at home with his family, became quite competent at most games and, according to Dick, was especially adept at games such as Chase the Ace and Partner Nomination.

Like Tom, Ian's comrades at the time often remember the young soldier for his cheery disposition, always appearing to look on the bright side of any situation. Dick recalls that 'we all started to call him 'Sunshine' as he always seemed to have a smile on his face.' They also remember his technical proficiency, his application and his competitive streak in whatever he was doing in order to become the best he could. He became the No. 1 in a three-man mortar team immediately after completing training on the weapon, which was quite unusual. 'He had good technical skills,' said Dick, 'the No. 1 actually lays the mortar and adjusts it. He was wise – and fast.'

Most importantly, perhaps, his comrades remember Ian McKay as a 'good man to have at your side' when confronting rioters or going in amongst them to make arrests and take the ringleaders into custody. Dick simply recalled that 'he was reliable – a good man to have at your back', whilst Tom was of the opinion that:

> If you'd got Mac by your side you knew he'd be there doing his job. Most of the blokes were like that of course and Mac was no different in that respect except that he was that little bit more educated than most of the lads and there was that bit more thought went into whatever he was doing and why he was doing it. I never heard Mac raise his voice – never, ever. If Mac disagreed with you he never spoke loudly. He might be a bit surly with you at times but he never, ever raised his voice. He wasn't someone who would just be 'gobbing off' for the sake of it. If he had something to say he had a reason behind it and he'd put that across. It's hard to describe it really because he wasn't any different from the rest of the lads but at the same time he was. He had that little bit of reserve that the others didn't have. That's not to say he didn't get up to some of the things young soldiers got up to. I'm sure there are photographs of Mac doing silly things. Mac was just another lad in the 'pig' but then again, he wasn't just another lad; he was one of the Mortars – he was special. I'm sure that every other platoon thinks they're special but we used to fancy ourselves as special. We had a good bunch, fantastic characters and every one of us depended on each other. Mac just expressed everything that everybody else [in the Mortar Platoon] was. It doesn't surprise me one iota what Mac did in the Falklands.

By now 1 Para had a new commanding officer. Lieutenant Colonel Gray had departed Northern Ireland to take up a position as GSO 1 on the directing staff at the Staff College in Camberley and Lieutenant Colonel Derek Wilford had arrived to take up his post on 21 July 1971.

Lieutenant Colonel Wilford's arrival coincided with the British Army putting the finishing touches to its plans for the execution of Operation Demetrius; the arrest and internment without trail of those suspected of any act which threatened the maintenance of peace and law and order in the province. In the wake of the killing of the Scottish soldiers on 10 March the Northern Ireland Government had come under increasing pressure from unionists to get tough in order to restore order. They wanted to see the army adopt a harder line and there were yet other voices which called for dangerous men to be taken off the streets. Internment had worked before, they reasoned – against the IRA in the late 1950s and early 1960s – surely it could work again. This time, however, there was no appetite on the part of the Irish Government to support such a policy. The Stormont Government was on its own.

After several dry runs in late July 1971, during which the British Army visibly and noisily gave the game away, enabling key members of the IRA to melt away, the 'Knock' finally came on 9 August, when 3,000 troops crashed into nationalist areas throughout the province and hauled out 342 'suspects' – not a single Protestant amongst them.

Peter Taylor, one of the leading commentators on the history of the Troubles, is convinced that 'any credible claim the 'Brits' still had to being even-handed was shattered in the small hours of that morning'.[19] The list of detainees provided by the RUC was hopelessly out of date. The majority of the men 'lifted' by the army were old – even retired – IRA activists. The young bloods of the Provisional IRA were little known then and escaped.

The implementation of Operation Demetrius effectively derailed any work already done by battalions such as 1 Para in attempting to win nationalist hearts and minds and, in fact, unleashed a hurricane of violence, burning and bloodshed, not least on the streets of Belfast which Ian McKay and 1 Para were ordered to try and contain.[20] The green light for Demetrius had been given whilst Brigadier Frank Kitson had been away from the province on holiday and although he had railed against its cack-handed implementation and warned of the possibility that the entire nationalist community of Belfast would turn its collective back on the British Army as a result, he had nevertheless resolved to get a grip of the incendiary situation on his return.[21]

Little by little and using a deliberate policy of early and vigorous action, the soldiers of Brigadier Kitson's 39 Brigade, with Support Company of 1 Para – euphemistically known as Kitson's Private Army – to the fore, had begun to re-assert their authority on the streets of Belfast.

Despite the spate of rioting, burning, bombing and bloodshed which fired Belfast in the wake of Operation Demetrius, the concept of IRA 'no-go' areas on his patch, on his watch, was unthinkable to Brigadier Kitson. The very idea that the IRA could erect, hold and defend barricades of rubble and burnt-out vehicles, behind which it could establish no-go areas in order to control, organize and foment further violence, largely unmolested by the army, was something that Kitson would not contemplate. It was not that the IRA hadn't tried. Although violence continued to flare as the late summer of 1971 gave way to autumn and into the darker days of winter, although roads had been blocked and barricades had gone up, Kitson was having none of it. He reasoned that there was not a street in the United Kingdom that the British Army should not be able to enter, be it Belfast or Bradford. His policy, filtering down the chain of command and understood at the level of even the lowliest of Toms in 1 Para, was that law and order would be restored, that barricades would be removed before they could solidify, and that there would be no half-measures in its implementation.

Time and again Support Company and the Mortar Platoon were called out, often at very short notice, to restore order and clear up the mess after confrontations had got out of hand. There is a photograph of a group of seven members of the Mortar Platoon taken at about this time; four of them looking on whilst three more play cards around a table in a barrack room which, at best, can only be described as basic. Ian, sitting shoulders hunched on a stool and gazing intently over a comrade's shoulder at the hand held by one of the players, has his face daubed in 'cam' cream, as are all the other men's faces. One of them wears an SAS windproof smock. A map of Belfast adorns the side of a locker whilst suitcases are piled on top of other lockers to right and left. The one red beret which is being worn has its Parachute Regiment badge 'blacked' to prevent light reflecting from it and thus saving its wearer from the unwanted attentions of a sniper. Torches are in evidence. In all probability Ian and his colleagues in the Mortar Platoon were on 'one-hour standby'– in other words all set, ready and waiting, vehicles outside, to get out and reach any trouble spot within an hour of getting the call to go.

Corporal Tom recalled that time as a period of tough soldiering, with everyone knowing exactly what they were doing. 'We were on standby at various levels, from one hour – where we were basically on call to go at the drop of a hat – through four hour, twelve hour and twenty-four hour. On one hour standby we napped in the barracks; even those of us who had a married quarter. You knew what your tasks were and if you were on standby you were given up-to-date intelligence. If there was anything going on you would be made aware of that and of course you were told that there would be a good chance of being sent out at a particular time.'

The soldiers of Support Company were tough (they had to be), highly motivated and, it is fair to say, viewed themselves as a cut above the rest of the British Army in Northern Ireland at the time. Some authors have gone so far as to say that 1 Para was 'arguably the most aggressive unit in the British army'.[22] This mindset did not win them many friends as they set about their tasks of barricade busting and riot control with a single-minded professionalism which, as 1971 drew to a close, inevitably brought some members of the battalion into contact with investigators of the Royal Military Police. Warrant Officer 1, John Wood, one of the investigators who was later to conduct interviews with men of Support Company of 1 Para in the immediate aftermath of Bloody Sunday in January 1972, recalled that his team 'did major business with 1 Para'.[23]

Ian may have been part of a tough unit but in talking through his experiences of Northern Ireland with his parents and brothers, they always remembered how he was at pains to emphasize the great natural beauty of the country beyond the ravaged streets of Belfast, the friendliness of many of its people and the embarrassment of those who approached him to assure him that not all Irishmen and women were rioters, bombers or gunmen. He was also at pains to explain, however, that he could not let his guard drop for one moment and that even the most innocuous of situations could conceal hidden dangers. The semi-humorous anecdote he always related was of certain Belfast housewives attacking the Paras by swinging shopping bags weighted with house bricks or tins of baked beans at them. And so in the end the only people he said he could really trust were his mates in red berets.

In early December Freda McKay wrote: 'Lovely to hear from you this morning love and many thanks for the cheque. We are all keeping our fingers crossed that you will win the raffle. It would be marvellous to see you and be the best Xmas present we all could have. Things seem to be hotting up again over there. I am pleased to see though that all you soldiers are to be allowed double time for your money in phone calls… Take good care of yourself love. Till we hear from you again please be careful and think of us often. All my love Mum. XXXXX.'

Three weeks earlier she had sent Ian what can only be described as a lucky charm. This had been pressed on to her by a friend who had obviously been aware of the escalation of violence in Northern Ireland and who had Ian's safety at heart:

> For a start I had better explain about the coin you will find enclosed [it was sellotaped to the top of the letter]. Joy gave it to me the other week. She was most insistent that I send it to you. It was given to her before the last war and she carried it with her all the time she was in the services (WACS) and she says it was her good luck charm. It was an old Irish lady who gave it to her and as I said she was most insistent that you have it. If it wasn't for the hole in it I guess it could be pretty valuable. So here you are…. I hope you are keeping very well love and managing to catch up on your lost sleep. Just got your phone call love, so pleased to hear from you. You sound very well.

Ian had also had yet another mix up over his pay and Freda hoped that it would once again sort itself out and that he would receive a nice big payment. Not that he was spending much money on pubs, clubs and discos due to his commitments and the fact that it was not now safe for young, off-duty soldiers to frequent the bars of Belfast. Towards the end of November 1971 he had, though, treated himself to a portable cassette player; a new gadget at the time which his mother knew that he had always wanted and felt sure would bring him hours of pleasure even if she was unsure about the type of cassettes to buy! It would help to while away the time in his barrack room when not on duty. In one of her letters she also included a small note which provides a snapshot of the young Para's assets towards the end of 1971:

> 'I thought you might like to have a statement of all your accounts love and see how much you are now worth.'

HALIFAX SHARE DEPT. –		£72.00
"	SAYE (1)	£72.00
"	SAYE (2)	£12.00
TRUSTEE SAVINGS BANK		£70.58
"	" INTEREST	£2.16

As it became clear that Freda's hopes of getting her son home for Christmas would be dashed Ian's family started to look beyond the New Year of 1972 to February when he had told them he would be home. Three days before Christmas it was his father's turn to write: 'It won't be too long before you are home. Once we get Xmas over the days, weeks etc will fly and February will be here in no time… So cheerio Ian. All at home sincerely hope that you have as good a Xmas as you possibly can and what you miss out on we will try and put right when you come home. With lots of love and very best wishes from all at the Ochre Dike Institution.'

As the Christmas of 1971 approached, Ian sent a specially designed Christmas card to his family bearing the legend 'Christmas Greetings' on the cover and depicting a paratrooper in uniform, wearing a red beret and holding his rifle. Inside were printed the words:

'Christmas Greetings,
1st Battalion The Parachute Regiment,
Belfast 1971'

and underneath Ian had written,
'To Mum, Dad, Neal & Graham.
Have a good Christmas.
& a Merry New Year.
All my love
Ian.'

As the McKays prepared to spend their second Christmas at home in Rotherham without their soldier son, in his absence they fervently hoped that he too would make the best of his Belfast Christmas. They hoped too, for his sake and the sake of all those, soldiers and civilians alike, who were embroiled in the seemingly endless agony and tragedy of the Troubles, that 1972 would bring at least some semblance of peace to the province. But peace, as was so often the case in the conflict in Northern Ireland, would be in short supply. Although in Belfast, from where Ian had written his seasonal greeting, the killings and bombings went on, the streets had at least been brought under some measure of control thanks to Brigadier Kitson's policy of barricade busting, backed up by the hard edge of Support Company of 1 Para. But the situation in the city of Londonderry, seventy miles to the west, was an entirely different matter. There the IRA held sway and taunted the security forces from behind a profusion of barricades, through many of which the army simply dared not venture. In what had been proclaimed by the IRA as 'Free Derry' there were most definitely 'no go' areas for the army and the best that it could hope to do was to secure and hold a containment line in order to protect the commercial heart of the city from attack. There were those in authority who felt that this state of affairs should not be allowed to continue but in order to effect a change, tough action would have to be taken. For tough action the army would require a tough battalion.

Ian's battalion had never been to Londonderry but its time would come and when it did 1 Para, and more specifically Support Company, would become embroiled in what was, and arguably remains, the most controversial episode in the history of the Troubles. Worse still for the McKays, their son would be heavily involved. Bloody Sunday was just weeks away.

CHAPTER FIVE

Bloody Sunday

For Ian McKay the New Year of 1972 had opened with a surprise. On duty in Belfast on Sunday, 2 January, he had been sitting in the back of a parked 'pig' listening to a radio which, in addition to another set being tuned into the military networks, had been tuned into Two-Way Family Favourites, a very popular programme, whose tried and tested format was based on playing records requested by families in the United Kingdom for their relatives serving in British Forces Posted Overseas. The programme had become somewhat of a fixture on Sunday lunchtimes – even in non-military households – as it was devoted to playing records not chosen by the presenters but selected by members of its audience especially for their kin abroad. As such it was seen not only as a vital means of maintaining links between service personnel and their families but also a high profile way of boosting morale.

Towards the end of 1971 Freda McKay had hit upon the idea of requesting a record for her son in Belfast as a way of cheering him up as he had not been able to get home for Christmas. Without telling Ken she had written in to the programme with Ian's details but, unable to decide on a suitable record for him, she had indicated that, should her request be successful, then the choice should be left to the producer. Having sent the request off, she duly forgot all about it.

When Ian's name was announced over the radio in the 'pig' that Sunday lunchtime there was a buzz of excitement as his mates wondered what the record would be. The Christmas Number One had been the novelty song *Ernie* (*The Fastest Milkman in the West*) by Benny Hill but 'Ernie' was just about to be knocked off his stop slot of four weeks by The New Seekers with *I'd Like to Teach the World to Sing*. When the dulcet tones of Olivia Newton-John delivering the opening line of the lyric – 'I asked my love to take a walk' – drifted from the radio, the other Paras in the back of the 'pig' collapsed in a fit of mutual mirth. As good an old country song as it was, *The Banks of the Ohio* was not exactly a hip and happening song for an 18-year-old Para and, despite Ian's protestations that he had had nothing to do with its selection, he later admitted to his family that he had been ribbed mercilessly for a good while after its transmission.

In a letter posted on 10 January 1972 Ken McKay had written, 'Well Ian, I hope you did have as good a Xmas as was possible...We were pleased to hear that you heard the record last Sunday. I bet you were as much surprised as I was. Apparently neither of us knew about it. Pity we were the only ones in both families that heard it although most people in the club heard it.'

Ian could take the ribbing. After all, he was looking forward to a change of scenery and to visiting warmer climes in a couple of weeks and then, after another month or so, he had a good chunk of leave and getting home to the family to look forward to.

He was itching to visit Cyprus where he could chalk up a few more parachute jumps and get a little winter sunshine and rest and recreation at the same time with a small group of his mates. It was just the tonic he needed after a grim autumn and winter on the streets of Belfast and it would be a bit of a change from 'Brid'. He couldn't wait. He was due to leave on 23 January and return on the morning of Sunday, 30 January 1972, when doubtless his superiors would see fit to put him straight back on duty. Just another bloody Sunday spent in the back of a 'pig'!

His father duly reminded him of his upcoming schedule and how keen everyone at home was to see him in the flesh: 'As I said in my last letter, two weeks this Saturday and Cyprus here you come (lucky) then four weeks and leave. I must say I have never known a leave more eagerly awaited by so many. Probably because most people here are rather short after their festivities and are awaiting to re-line their pockets on the snooker table. Have informed everybody that the Belfast snooker champ goes under the *nom-de-plume* of 'Hurricane Ian' but it doesn't seem to deter. Before I forget, many thanks from all of us for the wonderful presents. The cigars were the best. I have smoked them all myself, buying rolled old socks to hand out to the un-initiated.'

But unlike the prospects for Ian and his family, the dawning of a New Year in Northern Ireland held very little to look forward to with any optimism for any of the parties involved in the province's recent slide into disorder, division and death. Belfast and Londonderry, the main centres of population, were troubled cities with deeply fractured societies, in a troubled and deeply fractured country. In Londonderry, where the nationalist community had largely turned its collective back on the security forces, many believing that the army and the RUC were simply the paid enforcers of an oppressive regime, the situation was very serious and in danger of spiralling out of control. Parts of the city which lay to the west of the River Foyle beyond the containment line resembled a rubble-strewn wasteland; the result of serious and chronic rioting, most of which seemed to take place every day at tea time at the junction of William Street, Little James Street and Rossville Street. This spot had come to be known euphemistically as 'Aggro Corner' – fomented by a group of young men known to the army as the 'Derry Young Hooligans' (DYH).[1]

Large parts of the nationalist areas of the city were still barricaded and, under the organization and control of the IRA, were resistant to any semblance of normal civil order which the RUC and the Army hoped to enforce. Any hopes that the New Year might yet bring a peaceful settlement for the people of Londonderry were in woefully short supply and the views of those in senior positions in the army in Northern Ireland only added to the gloom.

The grim scenario outlined by Major General Robert Ford, Commander Land Forces, Northern Ireland, in a secret memorandum titled *Future Military Policy for Londonderry. An Appreciation of the Situation by CLF* sent to his direct superior, Lieutenant General Sir Harry Tuzo two weeks before Christmas 1971, acknowledged that the security forces faced 'an entirely hostile Catholic community numbering 33,000' in the Bogside and Creggan areas of the city alone and that 'the hate, fear and distrust felt… is deeper now than at any time during the current campaign.'

According to Major General Ford the only way to wrest control of the Bogside and Creggan areas from the DYH and the IRA would be by military action and he outlined three options as to as to how such military action might be prosecuted. It is important to stress that these were not agreed strategies or policy decisions but proposals as to how control and stability could be brought to the streets of Derry so that the political process could be allowed to breath. By far the most drastic of the three options he proposed – a surge beyond the existing containment line into the no-go areas of Free Derry in enough numbers to establish a visible and permanent army presence – was not without serious risks. Ford himself realized that such a bold move could well be seen as an invasion of Londonderry and would inevitably stir up such a hornet's nest that casualties might be the consequence, not only amongst gunmen or bombers but amongst the 'so-called unarmed rioters, possibly teenagers… certain to be shot in the initial phases'.[2] Ford was unequivocal in stating that this course of action could only be approved by his political masters and it is evident that he himself believed that the political fallout from such a 'nuclear' option would be so grave that he ruled it out.

It is a fair assessment then to say that as the New Year turned, the outlook was bleak in the extreme and the continuing repercussions of the Northern Ireland Government's introduction of internment without trial the previous August only added fuel to an already inflamed situation as the year progressed.

At the same time as internment had been introduced, the Stormont Government – with the backing of the British – had also imposed a ban on marches and processions by groups from both sides of the sectarian divide, stating that such a ban would, at a stroke, strip out the many opportunities such gatherings provided for those intent on using them as cover for acts of violence and confrontation. The ban itself caused much anger and resentment and was seen by some organized groups as no less than a clear breach of a basic democratic right. One such group was the non-violent, Northern Ireland Civil Rights Association (NICRA) whose leadership was considering openly defying the ban by organizing an anti–internment march in Londonderry – starting in the Creggan estate and routed eventually to the Guildhall Square, where it would be addressed by several speakers – on a Sunday in mid-January.

The army got wind of the plans and Brigadier Patrick MacLellan, the commander of 8 Brigade in Londonderry, was tasked with developing a plan to counter the possibility that, despite its best efforts, NICRA's march would be hijacked by hardcore elements of the DYH, possibly backed up by Provisional IRA gunmen intent on taking control and using it for their own purposes. As part of the proposed plan for dealing with such a march Lieutenant Colonel Derek Wilford was put on notice that 1 Para might be needed in Londonderry.

Although the march scheduled for mid-January was called off another took place on Saturday, 22 January when some 3,000 people marched towards the recently opened interment camp at Magilligan Point on the shore of Lough Foyle, twenty miles west of the city. Defying the urgings of soldiers of the Royal Green Jackets to stick to an agreed route, the marchers broke ranks and made for the camp along the sandy beach. Stopped by barbed wire behind which were also soldiers of C Company of 1 Para armed with batons, drafted in from Belfast to support the Green Jackets in case of trouble, some of the marchers rushed for a gap which had opened up between the end of the wire and the waterline as the tide had receded. The Paras moved immediately to plug the gap and ugly scenes developed in which some nationalist demonstrators were roughly handled on the ground and baton rounds – rubber bullets – were fired. Television cameras were on hand to capture the unedifying scenes for posterity.

As he was not in C Company, Ian McKay was not involved in the events at Magilligan and, in any case, he had already left the province the previous Thursday bound for training in sunny Cyprus along with his Mortar Platoon sergeant. During Ian's absence fateful decisions were made by several parties which would significantly shape events the following week; events that would plunge the province still deeper into chaos and crisis and open a deep wound which would fester for almost forty years.

On 25 January, five days after Ian had left Northern Ireland and hard on the heels of the Battle of Magilligan Strand, NICRA urged its supporters to turn out in numbers the following Sunday, 30 January 1972, for another anti-internment march, intended to maintain pressure on the Northern Ireland Government to re-think its decision. As had been the case with the march which had been postponed earlier that month, the organizers were planning a route which would see the procession leave the Creggan Estate during the early afternoon and wend its way down, into and through the Bogside towards Guildhall Square in the city centre, where prominent speakers would address the throng outside the Guildhall, the marchers' final destination.

Again the security forces knew of the proposed march and looked at how best to manage it. Once again the prevailing view – apart from the lone voice of Chief Superintendent Frank Lagan in charge of policing the Londonderry area, who advised that the march should be allowed unhindered with photographs taken of anyone causing trouble – was that it should not be allowed to proceed in case it undermined law and order and provoked a violent reaction from unionists. With the expectation of a large turnout, the army was to take the lead role ahead of the RUC. The specifics of the plan which finally emerged was to allow the marchers to gather and process through the nationalist areas of the city, but then prevent them from moving east towards the River Foyle and reaching their intended terminus in Guildhall Square by barricading all access roads leading to the square and city centre.

Channelling them down William Street after the procession had descended from the Creggan and had snaked its way through the Bogside area, the aim of the security forces was to ensure the marchers were stopped from making further progress towards Guildhall Square by re-routing them south along Rossville Street and back beyond the containment line into the Bogside when they reached Aggro Corner. Once on Rossville Street it was hoped that the procession would proceed peacefully past Block 1 of the Rossville Flats, and move beyond a rubble barricade to an open patch of waste ground called Free Derry Corner where, it was hoped, they would hold their rally and listen to their speakers before dispersing.

Violence flared and tensions rose on the Thursday before the march when the IRA shot dead two policemen in Londonderry – the first to die in the city since August 1969 – and two bombs went off inside the perimeter fence of 1 Para's base at Palace Barracks in Holywood, Belfast the same afternoon.

Given the increasing levels of violence it was a forlorn hope that any march would pass off peacefully and the authorities fully expected a riot to break out at some point.

The flash point, as had been so often the case in the past, was expected to be Aggro Corner; the point at which the march was to be funnelled down Rossville Street. The very sight of army barricades – wooden 'knife rests' festooned with barbed wire – blocking their path with soldiers standing behind them would, so the army's logic ran, attract the attentions of the DYH and a rain of missiles would be directed towards them. Although any rioting would undoubtedly cause problems for the army it also threw up possibilities; if ringleaders could be identified amongst the stone and bottle throwers as they menaced the barricades then they could be tackled, arrested and taken off the streets; perhaps significantly curtailing the activities of the DYH in the process.

To that end, and although the detailed planning for the operation was down to Brigadier MacLellan, Major General Ford had called in 1 Para from Belfast to act as the arresting force in support of the local units. Lieutenant Colonel Wilford's men would be held behind the soldiers of the Royal Green Jackets and 22/Light Air Defence Regiment (22/LAD) manning the barricades and when rioting duly broke out, as everyone expected, and only if the rioters crossed the containment line and attempted to rush the soldiers at the barricades, 1 Para would be sent forward to scoop up the rioters on foot. Brigadier MacLellan's Operation Order made it perfectly clear, however, that an arrest operation 'either in whole or in part' was only to be mounted on his express orders.[3]

Kitson's Private Army, 1 Para's Support Company – consisting of the Mortar, Anti-Tank, and Machine-Gun Platoons in the infantry role – were handed the lead role in this scoop up and arrest operation which was now given a name, Operation Forecast. The men of Support Company may have been well-versed in the geography of Belfast but it is crucial to note that, well-briefed though they may have been, most of them had never set foot in Londonderry before and had certainly never been into the sacrosanct (to the IRA at least) no-go area of the Bogside. And given the inevitable confusion which would probably accompany such an arrest operation, an incursion into the Bogside was almost a certainty. The only question was: how far they would go? If Support Company breached the containment line in the pursuit of rioters who had done the very same in the other direction, their actions would be seen as both a physical and symbolic penetration into the heart of Free Derry. In such circumstances they were told by Lieutenant Colonel Wilford that they could be going into a potentially dangerous situation and that they had to be prepared to face gunmen – possibly snipers firing from the Rossville Flats – petrol bombers and nail bombers who, enraged at the violation of their territory, might use the rioters as cover to exact their revenge.[4]

The die was cast for the tragedy which was to follow but as the morning of Sunday 30 January dawned clear and bright in Northern Ireland, Ian McKay and his platoon sergeant were unaware of the briefings already held and their imminent role in Operation Forecast for they were still on the last leg of their journey back to Northern Ireland; memories of their early morning jumps in the warmth of Cyprus fading fast with every mile the ferry made across the Irish Sea. The ferry was not due to dock in Belfast until 10.00 am that morning when trucks and Land Rovers would be waiting to whisk the men back to Palace Barracks with just enough time for them to pick up their combat gear, rejoin their platoon and be filled in on the details of the operation during the seventy-mile drive in Mortar Platoon's 'pigs' to their assembly area at a disused factory at Drumahoe, being used as the HQ of 22/LAD.[5]

Ian's Platoon Sergeant 'O' recalled their arrival that morning; '[We were] taken straight up to the camp. Drove past my house. You know, that's my house, why aren't we stopping? No. Was driven round a corner, there was [redacted] various people, flack jacket on, helmet on my head, weapon in my hand, ammunition, get in the 'pig' you're moving... About half way [to Londonderry] there's a real steep grade up over the mountains, [the Glenshane Pass] at the top of that we stopped to rest the 'pigs', and I was briefed then by the Platoon Commander about exactly what's happening. Arrest operations going in. If the march goes ahead.'[6]

The details of the sequence of events and the movements of civilians and soldiers on 30 January 1972, a day which has now become known as Bloody Sunday – are complex in the extreme. The bald facts are that on that day thirteen men were shot and killed by members of the Mortar and Anti-Tank Platoons of Support Company, eleven men and one woman were wounded by shots fired by members of the Mortar, Anti-Tank and Machine-Gun Platoons, whilst a further three men were injured by flying debris as a result of Support Company's fire. Two people, a man and a woman, were injured when they were struck by a 'pig' of mortar platoon, a 'pig' in which Ian McKay was a passenger, as it turned in to the car park of the Rossville Flats.

Those may be the hard facts but during the forty years which have passed since that day millions of words have been spoken and written on the subject by those who took part in, witnessed or reported on the events at the time. Memories have failed, participants have died, confusion has arisen and distortions have occurred. The waters have undeniably been muddied and myths have most certainly been generated. There have been claims, counter-claims and much rancour and recrimination. What has sometimes seemed like an industry has sprung up as articles and books have appeared in print, television documentaries and a feature film have been produced, websites built and two official inquiries launched – all of them aiming to shine light into the darkest recesses of what really happened that day and discover 'the truth'.

The first official inquiry, that conducted by Lord Chief Justice Lord Widgery, published its report eleven weeks after the day and, although critical of some of the firing by members of Support Company of 1 Para that Sunday – the oft quoted phrase being that some of the firing 'bordered on the reckless' – it was seen by many in nationalist circles as rushed and fundamentally flawed. The summary of its conclusions included statements such as 'there would have been no deaths in Londonderry on 30 January if those who organised the illegal march had not... created a highly dangerous situation in which a clash between demonstrators and the security forces was almost inevitable' and, with regard to the firing on the part of Support Company, 'there was no general breakdown in discipline', ensured that the report was seen as pro-army and pro-Para in the eyes of nationalists, and as such it was dismissed as a 'whitewash'.[7]

The second judicial inquiry, instigated by the then Prime Minister Tony Blair in a statement to the House of Commons on 29 January 1998 and subsequently chaired by the English Law Lord, Lord Saville of Newdigate, was again tasked with establishing and telling the truth in the light of new evidence which had emerged during the intervening years. Lord Saville and his team formally opened their inquiry, which they named The Bloody Sunday Inquiry, in the symbolic surroundings of the Guildhall in Derry on 3 April 1998 and published their long awaited report – 196 chapters and appendices in ten volumes – a little more than 12 years later on 15 June 2010 at a cost approaching £200 million.

The Saville Report is a dense document indeed; its scope is staggering and the depth of its detail almost overwhelming. Its examination of the available evidence and of witness testimony goes far beyond the scope of this book which is not and was never intended to be a study of Bloody Sunday beyond the part played in the events of that day by Ian McKay, and for which we have his evidence in his own words submitted to both the Widgery and Saville inquiries. The evidence Ian provided to the former was also reviewed by the latter, albeit posthumously in Ian's case. Ian McKay's initial statement was made in the small hours of the night following Bloody Sunday and in one of those strange quirks of fate the man who interviewed the 18-year-old private from the Mortar Platoon and began the process of obtaining his evidence was the most experienced Royal Military Police (RMP) Special Investigations Branch (SIB) investigator in the province at the time.

It was 1.30am on the morning of Monday, 31 January 1972 by the time Warrant Officer 1 (WO1) John Wood of the SIB had finished taking the eighth consecutive statement from soldiers who had been involved in firing shots in Londonderry the previous afternoon – five members of 1 Para, three soldiers of 1st Battalion the Royal Anglian Regiment (1/Royal Anglian) and one from 22/LAD – but even at that hour he was not quite finished. He and his team of SIB corporals, acting as statement takers, had operated what they called a 'cab rank' system of selecting interviewees all evening; that is to say that each member of the team took whichever soldier was next in line to be interviewed once they had finished taking a particular statement. As John Wood emerged from the confines of the small room he had been using as an interview room, one of several which clustered around a larger central hall, he looked around for his next interviewee. It had been dark when he had arrived so he did not have much recollection of the exterior but he remembered that 'the main internal feature was a large hall with individual rooms around the perimeter, brightly lit with fluorescent lamps. There was a large (for those days) TV on a wall. The main hall was furnished with tables as one might expect in a canteen. We [the RMP] each grabbed an individual office. These in general contained a table and number of chairs and were lit with incandescent lamps. I explained the 'cab rank' system to my guys and, I think, Major Loden of 1 Para. The soldiers were already *in situ* when we arrived. The chaps we wanted were in the central hall watching TV, drinking tea or eating their ration packs. As an interview ended, the interviewer called someone from the hall in no particular order. When finished, the interviewee was told he could report back to his boss.' When John Wood had finished interviewing the 1 Para soldier who became known as 'Private 017', Ian McKay was next in line.

By January 1972 John Wood was a vastly experienced Warrant Officer holding the rank of RSM in 178 Provost Company, a specialist company consisting of a nucleus of SIB trained senior NCOs augmented by RMP corporals who were regarded as 'statement takers'.[8] As such RSM Wood was responsible for the work of a team of investigators some sixty strong. Based at Thiepval Barracks, the Northern Ireland HQ in Lisburn, the majority of 178 Provost Company's work was centred on Belfast but it nevertheless had jurisdiction over the entire province and had a small detachment in Londonderry under a Sergeant Major detached to 176 Provost Company.[9]

Posted to HQ Northern Ireland for a two-year tour in late July 1970, RSM Wood's CV already boasted an impressive catalogue of involvement in internal security operations which mirrored almost exactly the major operational commitments of the British Army from the 1950s onwards. An eighteen-year career as a military investigator had seen him dealing with what were termed internal security (IS) incidents – incidents in which British soldiers on duty had opened fire and had either killed or wounded another person – in locations as far afield as Egypt, Malaya, Aden and Cyprus. In addition he had spent time during training, studying the investigative methods of the CID in the Metropolitan Police. Indeed, such was his wealth of expertise in dealing with internal security incidents, that immediately upon his arrival in Northern Ireland he took up a position as Staff Assistant to the Provost Branch; the headquarters department which dealt with military policing matters. At the time he thought that his appointment – an SIB-trained serviceman acting in the role of Staff Assistant and answering directly to the Assistant Provost Marshal, Northern Ireland – was highly unusual and felt certain that he would be engaged more on organizational matters rather than as an operational investigator. Indeed it was John Wood who drew up the two-page document *Brief for Investigators Engaged on Enquiries into IS Matters in Northern Ireland* on 14 July 1971, along with a seven-page aide memoire designed to assist investigators with their task.

Although WO1 Wood might have been forgiven for thinking that he had seen, heard and done it all in terms of his investigative duties, the sheer magnitude of the task which confronted him and his team in the aftermath of the events that had occurred nine hours earlier on the streets of Londonderry the previous afternoon was unlike anything he had ever witnessed before.

John Wood had actually been in the city the previous afternoon. Dressed in plain clothes, as is the norm for SIB investigators, he had heard of the proposed NICRA organized march and had driven his newly-arrived commanding officer over from Belfast in the unit's Austin 1800 so that the new man might understand what the army had to face if a riot broke out. He knew the Paras were there as he saw their red berets and he introduced his new CO to Major Loden, the Officer Commanding Support Company, whom he had known from previous meetings.

John Wood had seen the Paras enter the Bogside and had even followed them for a short distance but had retreated to an army observation post (OP) on top of the Embassy Ballroom when he had heard shots being fired. On reaching the OP he had been told by a staff officer that five people had been shot and he had then heard more firing which he felt was 'from the military'. He had looked down onto the Bogside to see 'clusters of civilians carrying people by their arms and legs'. Acutely aware now that he and his team had work to do he had called in to the RMP HQ at Ebrington Barracks and had phoned the duty officer in Lisburn to tell him to send a team of SIB investigators over to Londonderry immediately. Scooping up a map of the city which could be photocopied and then distributed to his colleagues to be marked up and then attached to the soldiers' statements, he prepared for a long night. He left, determined to find out where 1 Para would be withdrawing to in order to follow them there and get to work taking statements in accordance with the procedures he had drawn up in the summer of the previous year. Although the deliberations of the Saville Inquiry point to Ebrington Barracks as the main location for the taking of statements, WO1 Wood is convinced that he eventually travelled to Drumahoe, the location at which 1 Para had assembled that morning and to where they withdrew that evening.

John Wood called Ian into his office and the interview got under way. He recalled the process:

> We had formalized the content and scope of these IS interviews. We would tell the witness our names and ask if they felt OK to be interviewed. Under normal [non-IS circumstances] the statement-taking procedure would be to ask the witness what happened and make notes as to his answer. The written statement would then be prepared from the notes, amplified with detail and leaving out hearsay. The IS statements were not made like that. The statement taker knew what had to be ascertained and questioned the soldier as he wrote. The soldier would read the statement, be asked if there was anything missed and reminded that his statement could be used in legal proceedings. We did major business with 1 Para and we were either known personally to those we interviewed from other events or they knew us by reputation. Units such as Para normally feel indisposed to speak with RMP and covering-up was not unusual. I was well aware of this and, at an early stage, had made it clear to a previous CO and the Adjutant and RSM that that situation might continue in routine matters but where IS was concerned, we had to know the full truth, unvarnished, right from the start. We invariably 'broke' the false information in routine matters but to have to do this in IS matters was unproductive. The soldiers knew this and seemed to appreciate it. The interviews were simplified and more relaxed because of it.[10]

As the questioning began and Ian McKay, bright and articulate ex-grammar school pupil that he was, began to answer, John Wood began to write:

> I am a member of 1 Para. On the afternoon of 30 Jan 72 I was on duty with the regiment at Londonderry, Northern Ireland.
> About 16.10hrs on 30 Jan 72 I was amongst troops who deployed against rioters in the Rossville St/William St area. We moved in in vehicles and debussed so as to make arrests of the rioters.
> My APC halted to the east of the northernmost block of Rossville Flats. We had outflanked a large proportion of the rioters and I assisted in making two arrests. I then moved back to my APC in the forecourt of Rossville Flats.
> When I re-joined the troops there they were under a heavy stoning attack from all the three blocks of flats. As I was in cover I became aware of people on the balconies of the flats dropping bottles and other missiles from the verandahs (sic) onto our position.

I noticed that the bottles contained a liquid and thought they were petrol bombs. However, none of the bottles was alight and none went on fire when they smashed. After a couple had broken as they fell I smelt a strong acid smell and realised that the bottles contained acid.

Sgt. O was behind me and told me to fire at whoever was dropping the acid bombs if I saw him about to throw any more. One of the bottles landed very close to me and broke. I was splashed with the liquid in the bottle. It covered the front of my trousers from the waist to the knee. I saw that it had been dropped from a balcony almost directly above me. This balcony was some 20 to 30ft above me. I saw a man step back from the edge of the balcony as I looked up.

I continued to watch the balcony and saw the man again come to the front edge of the balcony. I could see that he had a white shirt on with a blue tie and jacket. I saw that he had a bottle in his hand and, as I watched, the man threw the bottle at me.

I then fired one round from my Self-Leading Rifle at the man. I came to the aim after he drew his arm back and fired as he let go of the bottle. I did not see the result of the shot. The man seemed to freeze and I then fired a second shot at him. This did not hit him.

The man went away from the balcony and no more acid bombs were thrown at us. Also after I fired, there were no more bottles or stones dropped or thrown at us from the balconys (sic) of the Flats.

I felt a tingling on my legs very soon after my trousers were splashed. Other soldiers poured water onto my legs and I changed my trousers. I soaked the trousers in water. I have today passed the trousers to WO1 Wood SIB and seen them marked [redacted] /1 and signed a label attached to them.[11]

After he had finished and the Paras had dispersed, John Wood drove back to Belfast sometime after 2.00am to deliver photocopies of the statements to HQ Northern Ireland and to brief his superiors and the watchkeepers there. There the written statements would be typed out and the names expurgated using Tippex to protect anonymity. When his name was removed and replaced with a cipher, Ian McKay, for the purposes of all future proceedings and official inquiries relating to Bloody Sunday, became Soldier 'T'.[12]

The apparently straightforward and matter-of-fact narrative which characterized Ian's initial statement taken by John Wood in the immediate aftermath of the events of Bloody Sunday, represented but a glimpse of the events which unfolded in the Bogside that late January afternoon in 1972. It is just one person's perspective, a soldier's perspective, amongst many, both military and civilian; the merest sliver of personal experience. The reality and complexity of internal security operations in Northern Ireland rarely reflected the sequenced order of dates, times and events committed at a later date to a statement, a unit log or narrative of operations when in fact, and more often than not during military operations, confusion and chaos is the order of the day.

The Bloody Sunday Inquiry chaired by Lord Saville, the most recent attempt to find out exactly what happened, gathered its evidence over a period of two years from its inception and began its formal hearings in March 2000. All official records and documents were requested, unearthed and harvested and many witnesses were called to give evidence in an attempt to piece together those many slivers of experience and develop a coherent account of what actually happened on Bloody Sunday.

Despite their formal nature, the official documents produced at the time, such as Ian's statement, battalion logs and messages and signals – both sent and received – do provide an immediacy which is invaluable in trying to piece together, and thus attempt an understanding of, what actually happened in Londonderry that day. To find out more about the detail of Ian's involvement we have to go back to the moment when he entered the city with the rest of the Mortar Platoon during the early afternoon of Sunday, 30 January 1972. According to the battalion log all units were in position by 12.50pm after driving from Drumahoe.

The Mortar Platoon had parked up in its 'pigs', in Queen Street, which some soldiers remembered as a well-to-do area, well north of the containment line which enclosed the Bogside. By that time, Lieutenant Colonel Wilford had already begun the task of deploying some of his men for Operation Forecast as soldiers of the Royal Green Jackets and 22/LAD set about erecting and manning their knife-rest barricades on the streets leading to Guildhall Square.

From their assembly area on Queen Street, Support Company, under the command of Major Edward Loden, was ordered into position around the Presbyterian church and the grounds of the GPO Sorting Office, both of which stood on Great James Street, a road north of the Bogside which made up the northern side of a rough rectangle some 2,000m sq consisting of buildings interspersed with vacant plots of derelict ground, bounded to the west by Lower Road, to the East by Little James Street and William Street to the south. If rioting broke out and the order to begin the arrest operation was given by Brigadier MacLellan, Lieutenant Colonel Wilford intended to get Support Company south and into William Street at speed at the same time as he sent C Company in from the west through Barrier 14 so that they could catch rioters at Aggro Corner in a pincer movement and make arrests quickly. The problem was that a substantial wall, some nine feet high, blocked the gap between the Presbyterian Church and the GPO Sorting Office, and there was another to the south of the sorting office car park. Neither was shown on the battalion's maps and both were in the intended path of Support Company and severely limited access to William Street.

Part of the plan had called for one of the two 'pigs' of Mortar Platoon, that under the command of Sergeant O who had been with Ian in Cyprus, to be used as a siege engine to ram the high wall between the Presbyterian church and the GPO Sorting Office, knock it down using its large metal bars known as 'cow catchers' and then race across the wasteground beyond and turn left on to William Street to get in behind any rioters. But a recce had revealed that there was a substantial drop on the other side of the Presbyterian Church wall into an area of rubble and dirt which would only have grounded the 'pig'.

Lieutenant Colonel Wilford now had to re-think his options. Major Loden was ordered to send one of his platoons forward to a derelict building which had at various times been a bakery and had last been used as the offices of a taxi firm called Abbey Taxis. At 3.40pm Major Loden sent the Machine-Gun Platoon forward from its assembly positions in Queen Street to occupy the derelict shell of the Abbey Taxis building. As they moved forward Lieutenant 'N' commanding the Mortar Platoon sent men scrambling up to the top of the wall to the east side of the Presbyterian Church to cut some wire on top and, at the same time, sent more men onto the flat roof of the GPO Sorting Office to cover the wire-cutting party. Two more men were hoisted on to an oil tank next to the Presbyterian Church to look out for snipers. Ian McKay was one of those sent up on to the rooftops.

In his Treasury Solicitor's (TSOL) Statement to the Widgery Inquiry taken by M.R. Hirst of the TSOL Department in the presence of Colonel H.C.B. Overbury at County Hall, Coleraine on 5 March 1972, Ian stated that:

> On the afternoon of 30 January 1972 I was on duty in Londonderry. My platoon arrived in our vehicles in Queen Street at about 3.30 and we debussed and crossed over to the Presbyterian Church in Great James Street. I had already been told to take up a position on a roof behind the GPO Sorting Office to keep an eye out for sniper fire from the direction of William Street whilst chicken wire fencing at the end of the wall behind the Presbyterian Church over which our platoon was to cross [was cut]. My platoon sergeant had told me that the exercise was to go into the area of William Street and Little James Street to arrest rioters. From the position I was in I could see youths throwing stones, bottles and other missiles into the car park by Little James Street and also at the barricade. I also saw about two distinct waves of CS gas coming from that direction and in accordance with what I had been told I warned those members of my platoon who were standing by the Presbyterian Church to put on gas masks. I put on a gas mask also.

From his vantage point Ian could see that marchers intent on causing trouble had reached the junction of William Street and Rossville Street and even those soldiers waiting for the word to go below him could hear the noises of bottles smashing and stones thumping against riot shields and striking metal somewhere off to the east of their position. The head of the NICRA march, which had assembled at Bishop's Field in the Creggan Estate at 2.00 pm had, by about 3.30 pm, reached William Street and was approaching Aggro Corner. The sight of the men in red berets in the Abbey Taxis building had attracted a barrage of missiles and abuse from members of the DYH in the van of the march and others vented their spleen on members of the Mortar Platoon reconnoitring the wall to the east of the church, and began shouting and jeering at them. Stones were thrown but at that time there was no response from the Paras.

Even though its organizers had, late in the day, agreed that the march should be diverted, and march stewards had begun the process of shepherding the procession south towards Free Derry Corner, they lost control of a hardcore of the DYH who broke loose and steamed straight on down William Street to confront the soldiers at Barrier 14 with bricks, bottles and spittle. As the rioting at Barrier 14 got into full swing, similar stand-offs between rioters and soldiers broke out further back down the route as gangs of, mostly, youths splintered from the main body of the march to head north and charge Barriers 12 and 13 blocking Little James Street and Sackville Street respectively.

Baton rounds and CS Gas were fired by the army in retaliation at Barrier 12 in Little James Street and it was this gas which had drifted across the ground towards Ian on top of the roof behind the GPO Sorting Office. At Barrier 14 a water cannon was brought up which sprayed the rioters with purple dye in an attempt to disperse and mark them.

Lieutenant Colonel Wilford had set up an observation post on the south side of the top floor of the three-storey building northeast of the Presbyterian Church and at 3.55pm, after some twenty-five minutes of rioting, he radioed Brigadier MacLellan at 8 Brigade Headquarters at Ebrington Barracks. Worried that time was moving on and that the light would start to fade by about 4.20 pm, he could sense that the opportunity to move in and arrest the ringleaders was slipping away. He suggested to the brigadier that he send C Company immediately through Barrier 14 into the area of William Street and Little James Street around Aggro Corner, reasoning that by doing so he might be able to arrest a number of rioters. Brigadier MacLellan did not respond immediately – his delay prompted by a desire to ensure the separation of peaceful marchers from the rioters before sending the Paras in to scoop up the latter.

What happened next is perhaps the kernel of the controversy which raged for almost four decades since 30 January 1972 as to the single most important incident which sparked Bloody Sunday. Shots were fired from both sides within minutes of each other but for 38 years until 2010 the question remained unanswered: who fired first, the Paras or one of the two wings of the IRA? The Saville Inquiry concluded that the responsibility for firing the first shots on Bloody Sunday lay with two soldiers of the Machine-Gun Platoon of Support Company who fired a total of five shots between them from the Abbey Taxis building and in so doing wounded 15-year-old apprentice engineer Damien 'Bubbles' Donaghey in the right thigh, and drapery store manager John Johnston, 59, in the right leg, left shoulder and hand. Although Donaghey had taken part in rioting previously he was not adjudged to be carrying any form of weapon when he was shot. Johnston was merely cutting across wasteground to visit a friend.

These shots were quickly followed, a minute or so later, by a single rifle shot fired at soldiers of the Mortar Platoon on top of the wall near the Presbyterian Church from the flats known as Columbcille Court in the Bogside by a member of the Official IRA. The shot fired by the sniper cracked over Ian's head, missed other Paras on the rooftops and on the high wall, and slammed into a drainpipe running down the side of the Presbyterian Church. Ian recalled that, a short time after he had seen the CS gas rolling across the wasteground in front of him he had also heard a 'single high velocity shot which hit the Presbyterian Church behind me but I cannot be sure of the exact direction in which the shot came although it would have been in the direction in which I was looking. I was on the roof for altogether approximately twenty to twenty-five minutes. During this time I also heard 7.62 SLR fire from the direction of Little James Street and also baton fire.'

According to Sergeant O, after the shot hit the drainpipe the mood in the churchyard became more serious. To the Paras the briefings and talk about possible IRA snipers using high buildings such as the Rossville Flats as sniper nests had just become a reality. 'We knew that there was someone in there or around there with a gun and we realized the warning given in the briefing may well be right… This shot had a significant effect on the operation… As we now knew there were gunmen operating in the area, most of the men carried SLRs. I want to emphasize, however, that the mood had not changed to "we're going in to shoot this lot" and indeed this attitude was never there at any time. The idea was still the same, for us to get into the crowd and make arrests. The men were carrying the rifles so that they could protect themselves if they came under fire – a baton is no use when someone is shooting at you.'[13]

As the minutes ticked by, with Lieutenant Colonel Wilford kicking his heels impatiently, still awaiting a reply from Brigadier MacLellan, he jettisoned his plan to send Support Company south on foot into William Street direct from Great James Street. Instead, if and when the order came for 1 Para to go in, Support Company was warned, at about 4.00pm, to get ready to push through Barrier 12 in Little James Street in their vehicles and drive down Rossville Street in pursuit of the rioters. The order he was waiting for came in at 4.07pm but with the caveat – and this is quite clearly stated at Serial 30 in the battalion log, timed at 4.10pm – that there were to be no running battles down Rossville Street to reduce the risk of peaceful protestors being scooped up along with rioters.

Lieutenant Colonel Wilford had written three words down in his notes when he had briefed his company commanders the day before to remind them that, in order to be effective when the time came, they would have to move quickly. Now he used them again – 'Move, Move, Move!' Corporal Tom remembers the urgency of that moment; the shouts and calls for men to get down from the roof and the barked order to 'mount up, mount up'. Ian recalled what happened next in his statement of March 1972:

> We were ordered back to our vehicles… the soldiers had been shouting that it was impracticable to get over the chicken wire fence so it had been decided to move back to the vehicles and move off although I did not know at that time in exactly what direction. I had with me an SLR with 20 rounds. I should have got 50 rounds but having just returned from Cyprus I was unable to obtain more than 20.

Ian leaped into the back of one of Mortar Platoon's two 'pigs' – hard to drive, difficult to see out of and uncomfortable to ride in – with another six men, whilst his platoon sergeant got into the front passenger seat next to the driver. More men piled into the back of another 'pig' under the command of Lieutenant 'N' the platoon commander. As the engines growled into life and the 'pigs' lurched forward – Lieutenant N's leading the way – Sergeant O heard the sound of SLRs being cocked behind him in the rear of his 'pig'. Two tons of metal were now on the move towards Barrier 12, the vanguard of the rest of Support Company's vehicles which followed behind. Ian recalled that 'our vehicles drove round to what I now realise was just behind the barricade in Little James Street where we stopped for about ten seconds…We drove through the barricade about ten seconds later'.

Pushing through the barrier Ian's 'pig' snagged some barbed wire and dragged a soldier along the road for a few yards before he could free himself. The heavy Humber 'pigs' picked up speed as they rolled straight on at Aggro Corner and barrelled down Rossville Street at about 25mph. What had been envisaged as a scoop up operation around Aggro Corner had now turned into an incursion into the no-go area of the Bogside.

As soon as they heard and saw the armoured vehicles roaring down Rossville Street towards them the crowd – several hundred strong, including many civilians making their way across a patch of wasteground that had once been Eden Place – panicked and began to scatter; many of them heading for what they must have thought was the relative sanctuary of the car park of the Rossville Flats.

Seeing the crowds ahead, Lieutenant N's 'pig' turned left onto Pilot Row and immediately hooked north to come to a halt on the wasteground at Eden Place whilst Ian's 'pig' went further. Stopping momentarily to allow six soldiers to get out Sergeant O ordered it to turn left after a few more yards into the access road leading to the car park of the Rossville Flats. As it lumbered in it struck two people, Alana Burke and Thomas Harkin.

Ian's 'pig' had gone about 220m beyond Barrier 12 and the two vehicles had hemmed in some 200 fleeing people on the 50m or so of wasteground which lay between them. People were screaming and shouting, running and stumbling in all directions in their attempts to escape. As the 'pig' came to a halt in the car park, Ian and Sergeant O, the only two Paras left in it apart from the driver, jumped out to begin making arrests.

> My vehicle, which was the second in the convoy, drove down what I now know to be Rossville Street and across the wasteground between Pilot Row and Rossville Street and eventually took up position at the entrance to the forecourt of Rossville Flats. I would estimate that it took us no more than about five minutes to get from the Presbyterian Church to the point where we debussed finally. When we debussed there was a large crowd behind us on the open ground which appeared to be trying to get through the forecourt but our vehicles had cut them off. A lot of arrests were being made. Those who had succeeded in getting passed (sic) our vehicles into the forecourt, some of whom had appeared to have equipped themselves with stones… started to throw stones and other missiles at our vehicles. At about this time I also heard a burst of low velocity fire which was either automatic or very rapid single shots but I could not see where the firing was coming from or in which direction it was going. I also at this time covered my platoon sergeant who had made one arrest and he was also escorting another person who had been arrested.[14]

Firing had indeed already started. Fifty metres behind Ian, Lieutenant N had fired three shots above the heads of a crowd in Chamberlain Street, which he thought was about to rush him. In the Rossville Flats car park there were other soldiers, including Ian's platoon sergeant, who were convinced that shots were being fired at them. Thinking that they had been engaged the Paras sought out potential threats and Ian's eyes scanned the balconies of the flats above:

After I had heard the gunfire I took cover behind my armoured vehicle. I was watching the windows of the flats on the right hand side of me [Block 1] to keep a lookout for anybody who would intend to shoot at us. Bottles started to be thrown from this part of the flats, one of which I noticed in particular containing liquid which I thought at the time was a petrol bomb. However it did not explode. After a few more bottles had been thrown in my direction I sensed a distinctive smell which I knew from my previous experience in the Falls Road, Belfast to be acid. Up until this time I did not actually see any of the people who were throwing bottles containing acid... After this my Platoon Sergeant O who was behind me, told me to open fire if I saw anybody throwing acid from the flats. At this time a bottle broke very close to me and it splashed my trousers up to the waist. I was definitely sure from where the bottle had come. It came from one of the verandahs [sic] of one of the flats about three storeys up.

As he had made clear in his original RMP statement Ian claimed he saw the man who had thrown it go back into the flats and kept his eyes on the spot waiting for him to reappear. The man duly re-emerged, came quickly up to the wall of the balcony and, according to Ian who knew a thing or two about throwing, being successful during his time at Rotherham Grammar School in throwing the cricket ball, discus and shot, threw another bottle with 'a sideways movement of the arm rather than overarm'. According to his evidence Ian reacted instinctively and 'fired one aimed shot at this man in fact before the bottle... hit the ground'. The shot missed and, either undeterred or simply unaware that he was under fire, the man peered around from behind a pillar, apparently waiting to see where the bottle would land. Ian raised his SLR to his shoulder again and 'fired the second aimed shot at him which hit the wall a few feet above his head. As a result of this he disappeared'.

Neither of Ian's shots had hit his intended target but the bottle thrown at him landed and smashed very close to Ian at the back of his 'pig' and again splashed him with acid. He soon began to feel a tingling sensation on his leg. 'Dick', who had travelled down Rossville Street in Lieutenant N's 'pig' and had moved towards the Rossville Flats car park from the Eden Place wasteground after the firing had died down, remembered that he 'came across Mac, over towards [Sergeant] O's side very agitated saying that he'd been acid bombed from the balconies above. I remember shouting to [Sergeant] O whether he wanted me to put a few rounds up on to the balcony to stop them throwing stuff off the balcony but he said "no". I looked at Mac's legs and saw the acid splash. I thought it was bleach. It didn't seem that bad. Mac said it had gone into his boot'.

It was clear that Ian wanted to get his army khaki denims off quickly and it seemed a sensible solution to cut his bootlaces to speed up the process. Dick offered to perform the operation but Ian took exception to it. He said they were the only bootlaces he had!

As the immediate threat from above seemed to have diminished Ian moved to get water from one of the 'pigs' to soak his trousers and dilute the acid – a water supply was carried on the 'pigs' especially for that purpose. He also claimed to have changed his trousers in the back of the 'pig'. These were the trousers he passed to WO1 John Wood in the early hours of the next morning.

Ian admitted that during the time he had been engaging what he believed to be an acid bomber he had 'heard a lot of shooting in the area of all types' and after the shooting had died down the vehicles of Mortar Platoon were moved to the north end of the Rossville Flats where there was an ammunition check. Ian had fired two rounds. These were the only shots fired by Ian McKay on Bloody Sunday during the time the Mortar Platoon was in and around the area of Eden Place and the Rossville Flats car park but they were just two of 108 rounds of 7.62mm ammunition and 64 rubber bullets fired by Support Company in the forty minutes or so that had elapsed between Lieutenant Colonel Wilford's order to 'Move, Move Move!' a little after 4.07pm and the time the battalion log records 'all firm', with a further reference to 1 Para casualties – '1 hurt back… 2 minor acid burns – remaining with coys, 2 hurt by rocks'. By that time, and in contrast to 1 Para's casualties, thirteen men lay dead at various locations in the Bogside with a similar number of men and one woman wounded as a result of the fire of Support Company.

In the time it took for Ian to aim and fire the two shots towards the balcony of Block 1 of the Rossville Flats – actions which must only have taken a matter of minutes – other members of the Mortar Platoon had opened fire in the vicinity of the car park, mortally wounding one – Jackie Duddy, 17 – and wounding Margaret Deery, 38, Michael Bridge, 25, and Michael Bradley, 22. It is now also believed that Pius McCarron, 30, and Patrick McDaid, 24, suffered injuries from flying debris as a result of the fire. Patrick Brolly, 40, who was in Block 1 of the Rossville Flats, was also injured with cuts to his face, probably as a result of flying glass.

All units of 1 Para were back in the temporary barracks at Drumahoe by 11.40pm and by that time John Wood had already begun interviewing soldiers of other units. 1 Para's log for 30 January reveals that the number of dead (13) and wounded (14) was known to senior officers by 10.30pm – even if there was an erroneous reference to one of those being a woman 'reported trampled to death'. And yet despite those figures, Ian's platoon sergeant, who in his evidence to the Saville Inquiry remained firmly convinced that Support Company had come under fire, recalled in an interview with Peter Taylor that 'the mood between the blokes was, not elation, but at the same time, it was a job well done… if somebody's firing at you and you fire back and you kill him, you've stopped him killing you.'[15]

John Wood remembered that the troops were relaxed. I remember the late evening ITV [news] had early reports and comments and we broke off to watch. Every time Paras appeared, the men in the room cheered, with 'boos' when the civilians appeared.

And a little after 1.30am on the morning of Monday 31 January 1972, when he began to interview what he would describe as the 'fresh-faced' private from the Mortar Platoon in an attempt to get an initial statement of his part in what had happened, even the blacking of his face with cam cream could not disguise the fact that Ian McKay was one of the youngest members of the battalion. The significance of those deaths and woundings recorded in the battalion log and the far reaching implications of what had happened just a few hours earlier had not sunk in. But the time for reckoning would come soon enough. As John Wood, one of the most experienced members of SIB then serving in Northern Ireland was later to concede: 'I do not think that at that stage anyone realised what a significant event Bloody Sunday was to become'.[16]

CHAPTER SIX

Inquiry

The day after Bloody Sunday the then Prime Minister, Edward Heath, met Lord Widgery, the Lord Chief Justice of England, at Downing Street to discuss the setting up of an inquiry into the shootings. On the Tuesday, resolutions were passed in both Houses of Parliament of the United Kingdom Government in Westminster and the Parliament of Northern Ireland, to set up a formal Tribunal of Inquiry to investigate 'the events on Sunday, 30th January which led to loss of life in connection with the procession in Londonderry on that day', and Lord Widgery was appointed as the sole member of the tribunal.

Based at Coleraine County Hall, thirty miles from Londonderry, Lord Widgery opened his inquiry with a preliminary hearing on St Valentine's Day 1972 and held seventeen sessions of substantive hearings there between 21 February and 14 March, during which 114 witnesses gave evidence and were cross-examined. Three further sessions were held in the Royal Courts of Justice in London on 16, 17 and 20 March to hear the closing speeches of counsel for the relatives of the deceased, for the army and for the tribunal. What has became known as The Widgery Report was subsequently presented to Parliament on 19 April 1972.

Ian McKay gave oral evidence to the Widgery Inquiry under the anonymous title of Soldier T at County Hall, Coleraine on 8 March 1972, three days after giving his written statement to the Treasury Solicitor.

On the day itself Ian had to wait until Soldier 'R' had taken the stand. The latter, who was roughly the same age as Ian, had also been in the same 'pig' and present in the car park of the Rossville Flats when Ian had fired his two aimed shots at a man he had believed to be an acid bomber on the third floor balcony of Block 1. Soldier R had been the other man who had complained of being burnt by acid, as was recorded in the battalion log for 30 January 1972.

While Ian awaited his turn to give evidence, the last question put to Soldier R was whether he had gone to see the medical officer the following day to get treatment for his acid burns. Soldier R replied that he had but by that time it was already too late, claiming that he had lost quite a lot of hair on his legs which had 'just fallen out'. As Soldier R left the room Mr Michael Underhill, Counsel for the Ministry of Defence, rose to his feet and requested the next witness with the official words, 'I call Soldier T'.

We cannot know now what Ian was thinking or feeling as he made his way to the door but, even though he must have been 'prepped' by counsel for the MoD, it would have been a daunting prospect for a young soldier of 18 years and 9 months to know that he was going into a room to be faced by a battery of experienced inquisitors consisting of QCs and other legal representatives, under oath, in front of the Lord Chief Justice of England. Ian entered the room and was sworn in.

Michael Underhill opened his questioning by establishing Ian's rank, his time of arrival in Londonderry on 30 January 1972 and his initial role in Operation Forecast and Ian's subsequent answers to Mr Underhill's questions – delivered clearly, concisely and politely, with frequent use of the word 'sir' – followed exactly the written statements he had given to both John Wood of the SIB of the RMP on 31 January and the Treasury Solicitor on 5 March.

Lord Widgery interrupted Ian's evidence twice to obtain clarification, the first time when Ian told the inquiry that he had been ordered with another soldier onto the roof top 'just behind the Post Office Sorting Office to keep an eye out for snipers'. At that point Lord Widgery interjected: 'To do what?' Ian repeated his words: 'Keep an eye out for snipers.'

The Law Lord's second interruption of Ian's evidence came when he was describing which 'pig' he had been travelling in as Support Company had driven down Rossville Street:

LORD WIDGERY: Which pig was he in? I missed it.
Mr UNDERHILL: In the second one.
LORD WIDGERY: In the Platoon Sergeant's?
Mr UNDERHILL: Yes.[1]

Michael Underhill then turned to Ian: 'Just tell my Lord, as far as you can recall, where it halted?' 'Right there, in the entrance.' At that point Ian pointed to a map of the area created so that the positions of those involved could be identified and as Michael Underhill continued his examination and Ian went on to recount his experiences up to the point where he claimed he saw, 'quite a lot of rubbish coming out of the window – stones bottles, anything that could be thrown'. The exchange which followed included a reference to a less pressurized, more carefree period in Ian's life in the not too distant past:

Q. After that had been going on for some while did you notice something else which attracted your attention?
A. A bottle landed very close to me just on the other side of an armoured door, and after a time I could smell an acidic smell.
Q. Had you ever smelt that smell before?
A. Yes, quite a few times.
Q. Where?
A. At school quite a lot, and when I have found acid bombs before.
Q. That would be in Belfast?
A. That would be in Belfast.
Q. Did you at any stage see any of the people who were throwing these things down?
A. No, not at the time.
Q. About this time, after the acid bomb had come down, did your Platoon Sergeant give you an order?
A. Yes, he noticed this smell as well, and I pointed it out to him that it had come from the flats, and he said that if anyone else threw any acid bombs at us I was to shoot at him.'

Questioned about the shots he had fired Ian confirmed that he had discharged one round at a man who had already thrown a bottle.

Q. Were you kneeling or standing?
A. I was standing.
Q. Was it an aimed shot?
A. It was, sir.
Q. As far as you could tell, did it strike him?
A. No.
Q. So what did you do?
A. When I saw the first one did not hit him I fired another one. The first one must have alarmed him, because he stepped back, and I saw the round hit the roof of the building.
Q. Afterwards did you see him come out again?
A. No.[2]

Ian was then handed a photograph and asked by Mr Underhill whether it indicated 'where you fired the rounds that you have told my Lord about?' Ian confirmed that it did. The aerial photograph in question showed the Rossville Flats car park; it was one of a series which had been created the previous month at the request of Lord Widgery to illustrate the trajectories of the shots of every soldier who acknowledged that he had fired his rifle on Bloody Sunday. Each photograph had been marked to show the positions of individual soldiers and of his target (as the soldier had described them), the line of fire between those positions and, in some cases, the number of shots that the soldier claimed to have fired. Such a trajectory photograph was created for Ian.[3]

As Michael Underhill concluded his questioning and sat down, Ian's evidence came under the scrutiny of Mr Hill, Counsel for the next of kin of twelve of the deceased and for those who had been injured. He began his cross-examination by picking up on Ian's answers regarding the throwing of what he had been certain were acid bombs. Mr Hill was intent on establishing how exactly Ian could have been so certain that the missiles being thrown were in fact acid bombs. He pressed Ian hard:

Q. You had instructions to fire at anyone throwing an acid bomb?
A. That is true.
Q. How were you going to determine whether a bottle was an acid bomb or just a bottle?
A. You can see most bottles coming down: they are all empty. This one contained the same liquid as what the others did.
Q. What sort of liquid was that?
A. At that time it was the green-ish coloured liquid in the bottle.
Q. How did you know it was not another bottle of a window-cleaning substance or something like that?
A. People in the area were not-throwing liquid window cleaner.
Q. We have heard that they were throwing Windolene. Did you not see any liquid of this nature?

A. No.

Q. Did you not see missiles being thrown from these windows other than acid bombs?

A. Yes.

Q. A person may very well have been shot dead by you for throwing a bottle?

A. No, sir.

Q. Containing anything?

A. No, sir.

Q. How would you take precautions against that?

A. I did not fire at anyone the first time the acid bombs were thrown out of the window. I waited for orders from the Platoon Sergeant.

Q. You say that you have seen acid bombs before?

A. Yes.

Q. In Belfast?

A. Yes.

Q. Were they thrown or found?

A. No, we found them lying in a crate.

Q. Where was this?

A. At the Lower Falls area.

Q. What sort of bottles, were they?

A. These were in large cider bottles.

Q. What colour was the substance?

A. This is the same colour.

Q. Is that the same colour as the substance you saw at school?

A. Yes, they had a different colour of acid.

Q. Green was it?

A. It is not very pure. They add different things in.

Q. Would you have considered yourself seriously injured as a result of that?

A. No, sir.[4]

Mr Hill dug deeper and Ian had to concede that, from his position at least, he had not seen anyone firing at the troops or throwing a nail bomb, although when pressed as to whether he had heard a nail bomb Ian replied, 'I did not hear anything which I could discern was a nail bomb.' Mr Hill asked if Ian had heard nail bombs before to which he responded that he had, in Belfast, but when it was put to him that the sound of a nail bomb was 'quite unmistakeable' a streak of northern stubbornness surfaced and Ian countered 'that is not true'. Mr Hill appeared taken aback:

Q. You would not agree that it was unmistakeable?

A. No, Sir.

Q. Would you agree that it is a very loud noise?

A. Yes.

Q. Would you agree that it is a noise which can be heard particularly well if you are close to it?

A. Sometimes, sir, and sometimes not.

Q. You would not fail to notice it if it was close to you, would you?
A. No, sir.
Q. Even on occasions if one is far away from a nail bomb one can hear it quite clearly? Is that not so?
A. It depends on the conditions, sir.
Q. In certain conditions one could hear it perhaps a mile away?
A. That is right, sir.

Mr Hill left it at that and Mr Brian Gibbens QC representing the MoD had just a few more questions for Ian in an attempt to establish that he had indeed come into contact with acid bombs in the past and could identify them as such. Ian's response to the final question was a classic example of South Yorkshire understatement:

Q. What would you do with the acid that you found inside the bottles, and how did you know it was acid?
A. We could not leave them where they were, and we could not take them away; so we disposed of them on some wasteground on some iron railings.
Q. What effect did it have on the iron railings?
A. It did not do them any good, sir.[5]

Ian never told his parents about his role in Bloody Sunday or his part in the Widgery Inquiry. Freda saw copies of his statements but had no knowledge of the reddening and irritation to his thighs which the acid had caused although his youngest brother Neal was clearly aware of it, recalling in 1988 that Ian had received burns to his thigh and foot.[6]

In a letter to the Saville Inquiry dated 16 March 2000, the MoD stated that the medical records for Private T contained nothing that related to or documents any injury sustained on Bloody Sunday but as we know from the battalion log the two acid casualties, Ian and Soldier R, remained with their units for the duration of the operation and, unlike Soldier R, Ian never sought treatment for his burns.[7]

A letter written by his father Ken and posted on 17 February 1972 reveals nothing about Ian's role in what was then the impending inquiry; his father apparently keen to avoid the subject by talking about the country's continuing economic woes, frequent power cuts and the three-day week. He told Ian that he had been to the Wingfield Social Club where the members had sat in the dark for nearly an hour without any beer and without heating. He also kept him abreast of Ian's beloved game of football, relaying the latest news on the much anticipated evening match at Hillsborough between Sheffield Wednesday and Brazilian club side Santos, scheduled for Wednesday, 23 February 1972 and featuring none other than the greatest exponent of the 'beautiful game' the world has ever produced – Pelé. Ian was informed that the match was now in doubt as 'all evening matches are banned unless the club can hire a generator. Needless to say it would be easier to get the crown jewels'.

The game was eventually played but kicked off at 2.30pm meaning that many workplaces and classrooms for miles around were denuded as fathers and their children skipped work and lessons for a glimpse of the incomparable genius of the great man in action.[8]

In the same envelope as Ken's letter, however, was a letter from Freda which, without mentioning the subject of Bloody Sunday directly, hinted at the gloom which had been cast over the McKay household, a gloom which she evidently did not wish to transmit to her son at what was undoubtedly a stressful time.

> I am letting your dad do the letter writing at the moment. I think my letters would be too maudlin and mushy which I am sure you don't want... But I just want you to know we love you and are thinking about you all the time and can't wait until you get home on leave. Till I hear from you. All my love. Mum XXX.

Ian's appearance in front of the Widgery Tribunal was his first and last and, as outlined previously, Lord Widgery published his report just over a month after Ian's appeared before him. The final report summarized Ian's written and oral evidence along with that of other army witnesses and a representative sample of civilian evidence in the narrative of events under a section headed 'The activities of Mortar Platoon in the courtyard of the Rossville Flats'.

> Private T heard a burst of fire, possibly from a semi-automatic rifle being fired very quickly, about 30–45 seconds after dismounting from his vehicle. It came from somewhere inside the area of the Rossville Flats. He was splashed on the legs by acid from an acid bomb and noticed a person throwing acid bombs about three storeys up in the flats. On the orders of his sergeant he fired two rounds at the acid-bomb thrower. He thought he did not score a hit.[9]

For those who sought to apportion responsibility for the events of Bloody Sunday in 1972 Lord Widgery felt that the question of 'who fired first?' in the car park of the Rossville Flats was vital. In answering that question he pointed the finger squarely at unidentified civilian gunmen, stating that he was 'entirely satisfied that the first firing in the courtyard was directed at the soldiers'. In the prevailing noise and confusion which followed the Lord Chief Justice maintained it was 'not practicable for officers or NCOs always to control the fire of individual soldiers' and thereby 'no breach of discipline was...involved'. He went on to conclude that in his view:

> ...the initial firing by civilians in the courtyard of Rossville Flats was not heavy; but the immediate response of the soldiers produced a brisk and noisy engagement which must have had its effect on troops and civilians in Rossville Street. Civilian, as well as Army, evidence made it clear that there was a substantial number of civilians in the area who were armed with firearms. I would not be surprised if in the relevant half hour as many rounds were fired at the troops as were fired by them. The soldiers escaped injury by reason of their superior field-craft and training. When the shooting began every soldier was looking for a gunman and he was his own judge of whether he had identified one or not. I have the explanation on oath of every soldier who fired for every round for

which he was required to account... Those accustomed to listening to witnesses could not fail to be impressed by the demeanour of the soldiers of 1 Para. They gave their evidence with confidence and without hesitation or prevarication and withstood a rigorous cross-examination without contradicting themselves or each other. With one or two exceptions I accept that they were telling the truth as they remembered it... in general the accounts given by the soldiers of the circumstances in which they fired and the reasons why they did so were, in my opinion, truthful.[10]

Nevertheless, and as referred to earlier, Lord Widgery also stated that some of the firing had been excessive and had bordered on the reckless. He also pointed out that, as he saw it, there had been infringements' of the Yellow Card – the booklet issued to every soldier serving in Northern Ireland containing a series of instructions which aimed to govern and clarify the circumstances under which lethal force could be employed. According to Lord Widgery Ian had been amongst those who had infringed the general rules of the Yellow Card when he had, 'on the authority of Sergeant O, fired at a person whom he believed to be throwing acid bombs without first giving a prior warning'. Acid bombs were not technically classified as firearms in the Yellow Card.

Despite his comments on these apparent infringements Lord Widgery concluded that the standing orders contained in the Yellow Card were satisfactory, noting that any further restriction on opening fire would 'inhibit soldiers from taking proper steps for his own safety and that of his comrades and unduly hamper the engagement of gunmen'. He found that there was no evidence to suggest that any of those killed or wounded had been shot in the act of handling a firearm or bomb and that some were wholly innocent of such a claim but there was a strong suspicion that others had been firing weapons or handling bombs during the course of the afternoon and that yet others had been closely supporting them.

As for the Paras he found that there had been no general breakdown in discipline and that for the most part the soldiers acted as they did because they thought their orders required it. The Nationalist community was incensed. As far as they were concerned the report heaped salt into a gaping wound. Widgery's report, they claimed, was nothing more than an establishment cover-up; just another piece of pro-government propaganda which exonerated the Paras. In the immediate aftermath of Bloody Sunday the IRA had been the principal beneficiary of the pent-up rage felt in Londonderry against the British Army and its government and young men had volunteered eagerly to join its ranks. The publication of the Widgery Report only served to shepherd any waverers into the fold.

When, after the emergence of new material in the intervening years since 1972, the second inquiry into Bloody Sunday began its deliberations in 1998 under Lord Saville, Ian had been dead for almost sixteen years. Nevertheless, the evidence he had given in 1972 was considered afresh alongside that of civilian and military witnesses, some of whom had not given evidence to Widgery originally, and some who were giving written and oral evidence for the second time.

Ian's actions and the circumstances in which he took them on that day were examined in detail by the Saville Inquiry and the findings were published in

Volume 3 Chapter 51 of the final report under the sub-heading 'Private T and acid bombs'. The Saville Inquiry found that Ian had been the only soldier of Mortar Platoon who had claimed to have fired at a bomber up in Block 1 of the Rossville Flats; his position and that of his intended target corresponding roughly with his accounts given to the RMP and the Treasury Solicitor, his RMP map and the trajectory photograph created for him in 1972.

Sergeant O, Ian's platoon sergeant, gave written and oral evidence to the Saville Inquiry and was questioned specifically as to whether he accepted that Ian's firing was not in accordance with the instructions as laid down in the Yellow Card. Sergeant O responded by saying that he took full responsibility for having ordered Ian to fire that afternoon, and that as far as he was concerned Ian had had to fire because his life was in danger.

The final report of the Saville Inquiry makes it clear that the tribunal was 'sure that a number of bottles (it is not clear how many) containing some form of acid or other corrosive liquid were thrown down from a balcony of Block 1 of the Rossville Flats' and that when the bottles broke on landing 'some of the liquid… splashed Private T and Private R on their trousers, which were slightly damaged. As was reported that afternoon to Brigade HQ, these soldiers sustained minor acid burns. Neither was in serious pain though one had some physical discomfort, according to Lieutenant N. Both had water poured over the splashes to counteract the effect of the liquid and changed their trousers'.[11]

The tribunal was also sure that Ian had fired 'two shots at the man he believed (in our view correctly) was responsible for throwing the bottles'. They were not persuaded that he had hit the man with either shot and found no evidence to suggest that he did. They were certain that Ian had fired only after being told by Sergeant O to fire if another acid bomb was thrown.[12]

Despite being sure that Ian had fired in the certain belief that he was targeting an acid bomber, the tribunal was nevertheless critical of Ian's actions in doing so. Whereas Widgery had referred to Ian's firing as an infringement of the Yellow Card, by the summer of 2010 the Saville Inquiry had revised the terminology so that the two shots constituted a 'breach' of the instructions and of Rules 6 and 13 specifically. Rule 6 stipulated that a warning had to be given before opening fire except in circumstances which were described and set out in Rule 13, which dealt with situations where soldiers could open fire without warning at a person either using or carrying a firearm. Recognising, as Widgery had, that the term 'firearm' had been defined as including a grenade, nail bomb or gelignite-type bomb, but not acid bombs the tribunal reasoned that Private T, in firing without warning, was in breach of the Yellow Card. Neither did the tribunal accept Sergeant O's argument that Ian was in danger of his life and thus entitled to shoot the man in question. In their view the failure to give a warning was not a mere technicality.

The terms of Rules 13… of the Yellow Card suggest that firing without warning was permitted only in certain situations in which to give a warning was either impracticable, or undesirable, because the soldier was facing an imminent attack with a firearm or explosive device and thus any delay could lead to death or serious injury. Those considerations do not apply to a threat from a falling object which can be dodged. It is not unrealistic to think that a warning might have been an effective deterrent, the more so where the threat was less dangerous than gunfire, so that the assailant might not have realised unless warned that he was exposing himself to a danger of being killed. In our view there was a real possibility of ending the threat by giving a warning, so that it was a serious matter for Private T, without warning, to try to kill the man instead. Furthermore, we are not persuaded that Private T had no other way of protecting himself, by putting on his helmet (if he was not already wearing it), or moving to a safer position, or seeking to dodge any falling bottles. In these circumstances we do not accept that Sergeant O was entitled to assume that the condition stated in Rule 12 would be met and thus that Private T would be justified in firing. On Private T's evidence, he fired his first shot either as the man released the bottle, or just after he had released it. He then fired a second shot at the man. Quite apart from the failure to give a warning… that second shot was in our view unjustified, since there was, once the acid bomb had been thrown, no further immediate danger from the man.[13]

The Saville Report had yet more to say regarding Ian's involvement in Bloody Sunday; material which was never mentioned in the Widgery Report of 1972. Such had been the extensive trawl for witnesses and evidence that amongst the names of those who were wounded and injured the name of Patrick Brolly came up. Patrick Brolly, who died in January 2002, was 40 years old at the time of Bloody Sunday and lived with his wife and children on the Creggan Estate. He had taken part in the march that Sunday and, according to Saville, had been one of the men at the front of the crowd when it had reached Barrier 14. When Support Company had rolled into the Bogside a little after 4.07pm he had made his way south and had ducked into Block 1 of the Rossville Flats where Kathleen Cunningham, his brother-in-law's sister lived at 3, Garvan Place, on the first floor.

Even with numerous witness statements relating to the incident, both contemporaneous and of more recent vintage – several of which are confused and contradictory – what happened next is unclear but what is certain is that Patrick Brolly went to look out of a window. As he did so the window pane exploded and his face was cut by flying glass. It is known that he received treatment at Altnagelvin Hospital but was discharged the same day. Some witnesses claim it was a live round which shattered the window and lodged itself in the top of a wardrobe; others are certain it was a rubber bullet. Given the circumstances of the incident, and taking into account the evidence given to the inquiry, the Saville Report offered the following comment in a section specific to the injuries sustained by Patrick Brolly:

… it is not possible to be certain whether a live round or a rubber bullet caused Patrick Brolly's injuries. In the end we have concluded that it was probably a live round. If it had been a rubber bullet, it would have been found without difficulty, whereas a bullet lodged in a wardrobe in another room could well have escaped immediate notice… The only soldier who admitted firing live rounds into the south-east side of Block 1 of the Rossville Flats was Private T… In the end, it is our view that it was probably one of Private T's shots that went through the bedroom window of the flat and caused Patrick Brolly's injury. If we are wrong about this and the injury was caused by a rubber bullet, then in our view this is likely to have been fired by Private 013.[14]

However, in the section dealing with the Saville Report's principle conclusions and overall assessment the following passage appears:

> Private T was probably responsible for the shot that directly or indirectly injured Patrick Brolly, who was in Block 1 of the Rossville Flats, though it is possible that Private S was responsible. The soldier concerned did not aim at Patrick Brolly, neither was he on a balcony and nor was he the man at whom Private T fired. If it was a shot by Private S (who fired 12 shots in the area of the Rossville Flats car park) we are sure that it was fired for no good reason and without any regard to the risk to people in the flats. If it was Private T, it was one of two shots that this soldier fired at a man on a balcony of Block 1 of the Rossville Flats, who had thrown down at the soldiers below a bottle or bottles containing acid or a similar corrosive substance, which had caused minor injuries to Private T and Private R. These shots were fired without a previous warning and thus in our view contravened the instructions given to the soldiers as to when they could open fire, contained in the Yellow Card. Sergeant O had told Private T to shoot if the man sought to throw another bottle. Both he and Private T believed that the person concerned was posing a threat of causing serious injury. The second shot was fired after the man had thrown a further bottle and thus at a time when he was posing no threat to the soldiers. Both shots missed the intended target.[15]

So was it a round from an army SLR or a baton gun which was fired through the window of Kathleen Cunningham's flat and was it Ian, Private S or Private 013 who was ultimately responsible for the shot which shattered the glass and caused Patrick Brolly's injuries? If the Saville Report cannot be sure who was responsible then, after the passage of forty years, perhaps no-one will ever really know.

What is known is that after thirty-eight years the Saville Report turned the Widgery Report on its head. Where Widgery had once exonerated the Paras, now Saville exonerated the dead and wounded of Londonderry.

At 3.30pm on 15 June 2010 it fell to the recently-elected Conservative Prime Minister David Cameron, in a statement to the United Kingdom Parliament, to finish what Labour's Tony Blair had started twelve years earlier. As he spoke he made his and his government's position on Saville's conclusions crystal clear:

> I am deeply patriotic; I never want to believe anything bad about our country; I never want to call into question the behaviour of our soldiers and our Army, which I believe to be the finest in the world. And I have seen for myself the very difficult and dangerous circumstances in which we ask our soldiers to serve. But the conclusions of this report are absolutely clear: there is no doubt; there is

nothing equivocal; there are no ambiguities. What happened on Bloody Sunday was both unjustified and unjustifiable. It – was – wrong.[16]

He went on to itemize Lord Saville's key conclusions in the words used in the report, namely:

…that the soldiers of Support Company who went into the Bogside 'did so as a result of an order… which should have not been given' by their commander. He finds that 'on balance the first shot in the vicinity of the march was fired by the British Army' and that 'none of the casualties shot by soldiers of Support Company was armed with a firearm'. He also finds that 'there was some firing by republican paramilitaries… but… none of this firing provided any justification for the shooting of civilian casualties', and that 'in no case was any warning given before soldiers opened fire'.

Lord Saville also finds that Support Company 'reacted by losing their self-control… forgetting or ignoring their instructions and training' and acted with 'a serious and widespread loss of fire discipline'. He finds that 'despite the contrary evidence given by the soldiers… none of them fired in response to attacks or threatened attacks by nail or petrol bombers' and that many of the soldiers 'knowingly put forward false accounts in order to seek to justify their firing'. What is more, Lord Saville says that some of those killed or injured were clearly fleeing or going to the assistance of others who were dying… .For those looking for statements of innocence, Saville says: 'The immediate responsibility for the deaths and injuries on Bloody Sunday lies with those members of Support Company whose unjustifiable firing was the cause of those deaths and injuries', and, crucially, that 'none of the casualties was posing a threat of causing death or serious injury, or indeed was doing anything else that could on any view justify their shooting'.[17]

On a sunny summer's afternoon in Londonderry, the supporters of the families of those who had been killed or wounded who had gathered outside the Guildhall in Derry to watch David Cameron deliver his statement live on a large screen were ecstatic. When they at last heard him utter the words '…on behalf of the government – indeed, on behalf of our country – I am deeply sorry', justice, they claimed, had at last been seen to be done.

For some commentators in the UK press the publication of the report was proof positive that 'the innocent became guilty and the guilty innocent'.[18] *The Irish News* used two words, 'Proved Innocent' to sum up the verdict on the cover of a special edition, whilst inside it claimed 'Widgery torn to shreds' accompanied by an image of the relatives tearing copies of the Widgery Report in half. For the *Derry Journal*, just one word was enough: 'INNOCENT'.[19]

Some sections of the press chose to ignore Saville's inconclusive findings on Provisional IRA leader Martin McGuinness' role on the day due to a lack of certainty over his movements, concluding that whilst he had ben engaged in paramilitary activity during Bloody Sunday and had probably been armed with a Thompson sub-machine gun, there was insufficient evidence to make any finding other than that they were 'sure that he did not engage in any activity that provided any of the soldiers with any justification for opening fire'.[20]

Other elements of the British Press sought the views of Paras who had been present in Londonderry on Bloody Sunday in the interests of balance. One of them, an NCO who claimed that he had not fired any shots, was unsurprised by the reports findings:

> I knew we were going to get a kicking and that is what has happened... What Saville has concluded is one-sided and does not give the whole picture, but I suppose people will say we, the Paras, are bound to say that. I am not going to say that some innocent people were not killed that day – and I am truly sorry for their deaths, as, I am sure, a lot of other soldiers are as well. But to say that we went into the Bogside on that day to kill civvies cannot be further from the truth... I cannot pretend that I remember all the details of what happened that day... What I do recall is that there was firing on several occasions and it seemed to be directed towards us from the south and our guys were firing back... The firing did not go on for long, I would say about 15 minutes or so, we knew people had gone down, we did not know at the time how many had been killed or injured – that only came later. When we did find out everyone was a bit quiet, but we did think at the time that the people killed were IRA... I feel sorry for people who died if they were innocent... And I am sorry we were in Derry on that sodding day.[21]

Corporal Tom was more succinct: 'There will always be those who are not entirely convinced but even those who were there did not see or hear all that went on and after thirty-four years, when asked to recall what happened, well, that was in itself asking for a miracle. Not even Law Lords know everything and they are experts at getting things wrong.'

In Prime Minister Cameron's statement he had said that 'none of the casualties was posing a threat of causing death or serious injury, or indeed was doing anything else that could on any view justify their shooting' and he certainly never mentioned any NCOs or privates of 1 Para by name. Did he then, and by logical extension Lord Saville, mean that every man of Support Company who opened fire that day shouldered an equal share of the responsibility for what happened on Bloody Sunday?

Although the Saville Report concluded that Ian had breached the rules of the Yellow Card a closer examination of Chapter 3 reveals that, on several occasions, Lord Saville was at pains to single out Private T by name in distancing him from the actions of other soldiers at key points in his findings. It is worth reproducing the relevant passages here in the words of Lord Saville as they appeared in the report:

> It was submitted on behalf of many of the represented soldiers that it was possible that some of the casualties were accidental, in the sense that the soldier concerned fired at someone posing a threat of causing death or serious injury, but missed and hit a bystander instead. It was also submitted that soldiers fired at and killed or injured other people who were posing such a threat, but that the existence of these casualties had been kept secret by those civilians who knew

that this had happened, in order to deprive the soldiers of evidence that their firing was justified. Apart from the firing by Private T, we have found no substance in either of these submissions…

As to Patrick Brolly, if Private T was responsible for the shot that injured this casualty, this was one of the two shots that Private T fired at a man who had been throwing down bottles containing acid or a similar corrosive substance from the Rossville Flats. Such conduct *probably did pose a threat of causing serious injury* (author's emphasis). Private T (if he was responsible) neither intended to hit Patrick Brolly nor fired his rifle indiscriminately at people.

Apart from Private T (who claimed to have fired at someone throwing down acid bombs from the Rossville Flats), all the soldiers who in our view were responsible for the casualties on Bloody Sunday sought to justify their shooting on the grounds that they were sure when they fired that they had targeted and hit someone who was armed with a firearm or a nail or petrol bomb and who was posing or about to pose a threat of causing death or serious injury. In other words, all the soldiers (apart from Private T) who were in our view responsible for the casualties insisted that they had shot at gunmen or bombers, which they had not, and (with the possible exception of Lance Corporal F's belated admission with regard to Michael Kelly) did not accept that they had shot the known casualties, which they had. To our minds it inevitably followed that this materially undermined the credibility of the accounts given by the soldiers who fired…

In the course of the report we have considered in detail the accounts of the soldiers whose firing caused the casualties, in the light of much other evidence. We have concluded… that apart from Private T many of these soldiers have knowingly put forward false accounts in order to seek to justify their firing. However, we have also borne in mind that the fact that a soldier afterwards lied about what had happened does not necessarily entail that he fired without believing that he had identified a person posing a threat of causing death or serious injury, since it is possible that he was at the time convinced that he was justified in firing, but later invented details in an attempt to bolster his account and make it more credible to others. We have borne this possibility in mind when seeking to decide whether or not each of the soldiers of Support Company who fired and whose shots killed or injured civilians believed, when he did so, that he was justified in firing.[22]

Given the significance of these findings and forever in search of a possible angle, it was not long before journalists picked up on Lord Saville's comments and within hours Private T had made the pages of the national press and media services online.

On the evening of the publication of the report the news pages of the BBC Foyle and West website in Northern Ireland mentioned Ian twice in quotes taken from the report and informed those who had logged on that the actions of Private T had somehow been set apart from those of others: 'With the exception of Private T [and another soldier in one specific incident], none of the firing by the soldiers of Support Company was aimed at people posing a threat of causing death or serious injury.'

'We have concluded, for the reasons we give, that apart from Private T many of these soldiers have knowingly put forward false accounts in order to seek to justify their firing.'[23]

The following day *The Guardian* told its readers that, 'Lord Saville said that apart from the soldier identified as Private T, all the paratroopers involved "knowingly put forward false accounts in order to seek to justify their firing"'.[24]

The *Daily Mail* went much further on its website as it sought to focus on the deaths in action of two young soldiers – Private Jonathan Monk and Lance Corporal Andrew Breeze – in Afghanistan, on the same day the Saville Report was published. Echoing David Cameron's opening remarks in his statement to Parliament the *Mail*'s journalists opined that: 'On the day that the Bloody Sunday inquiry left an indelible stain on the reputation of the British Army, the bravery of these two young men stands as a potent reminder of the true face of our Forces.' According to the *Daily Mail* it was the sacrifice of these men and many other men and women like them, which would be remembered as the army's real legacy and not what it described as an 'out of control shooting spree in Derry on January 30, 1972'.

Ian – as Soldier T – appeared in another article on the website by journalist Tim Shipman who wrote that 'The Paras… came under attack from Nationalists in the area of the Rossville Flats. A soldier named Private T "fired at a man who had been throwing down bottles containing acid or a similar corrosive substance. Two of the soldiers were hurt. Such conduct probably did pose a threat of causing serious injury," Lord Saville concluded. Patrick Brolly was shot in the Rossville Flats at that time. Lord Saville *exonerated* (author's emphasis) Private T.'[25]

Twenty-eight years after he had first appeared in the national newspapers following his death in action at the height of the Falklands War and the awarding of his VC in the autumn of 1982, Ian McKay, although he may not have been front page news as he had been then, was nonetheless back in the press at another watershed moment in post-war British history. But this time, as the anonymous Private T, nobody, except perhaps for a very small group of those with whom he had served in Northern Ireland, had any idea it was him.

CHAPTER SEVEN

Professional Soldier, Sensitive Man

After the tragedy of Bloody Sunday 1 Para still had ten weeks of its scheduled residential tour left to run. Ian's service record reveals that his last day in Northern Ireland on that particular tour was 11 April 1972 and subsequently Ian returned to Aldershot with his battalion which now rejoined 16 Parachute Brigade.

When he arrived in Aldershot the garrison town was still on a high state of alert and recovering from the death and destruction wrought by the detonation of a large car bomb outside the Officers' Mess at Montgomery Lines, the base of 16 Parachute Brigade, on 22 February 1972. The Official IRA had wasted no time in exacting its revenge for Bloody Sunday in an attack planned to tear the heart out of the Parachute Regiment whose soldiers, they claimed, bore responsibility for the deaths in Londonderry. Even today it is possible for civilians to drive along the roads which weave through the Aldershot garrison and in 1972 senior officers admitted that its open plan made it difficult to defend. Early on the morning of 22 February members of the Official IRA drove a light blue Ford Cortina packed with explosive into the Officers' Mess car park and left it there. The bomb, when it went off at lunchtime that day, destroyed the Officers' Mess and several buildings round about and rocked the centre of Aldershot a mile away. Seven people died – five female kitchen staff, a 58-year-old gardener and a Roman Catholic army chaplain – not one of them a serving soldier.

Back from Belfast six weeks after the blast, even given the increased security, it must have appeared to Ian that not even his regimental home was absolutely safe but he was a professional soldier and his work had to continue.

Apart from a short time at home in March 1971 Ian had spent more than a year on duty in Northern Ireland concentrating in the main on urban, internal security operations. During that period he had had precious little time to devote to the type of training which was the more usual lot of the parachute soldier. Now was the time for him to pay attention to this important aspect of his profession whilst at the same time keeping an eye out for courses which would develop and enhance his skills as he went in search of promotion.

By mid-summer 1972 Ian had applied for and had secured a place on the Junior Non-Commissioned Officers' (JNCO) Course No. 31 at the Parachute Regiment Battle School and Tactical Wing at Dering Lines, Brecon in Wales. This course was designed to develop the skills, knowledge and understanding of the tactical handling of sections of eight or so men under very demanding simulated battle conditions for those seeking promotion to lance corporal and corporal. The JNCOs course was, according to 'Tom', one of Ian's contemporaries, 'a very hard course; set up by Paras, run by Paras, to Para standards'. Such was the demand for the quality of instruction and the final outcome that other units could and did bid for places.

Towards the end of June Freda wrote Ian a letter in which she hinted at his taxing programme of training in the high summer season, an imminent leave and Ian's penchant for certain home comforts. The mention of the latter was perhaps linked to a reference to his weight, a topic which also surfaced again. She admitted that she could not wait for the weekend and hoped nothing had changed:

'Love it seems years since we last saw you… Peter (snackbar) is stocking up on his mustard… .If the weather has been the same down there as it has been up here you will have sweated another couple of stone off I should think. It's no weather for hikes like you have to do.'

Having completed JNCO Course 31 successfully Ian then had to bide his time until he could enrol on to a section commander's course, which would place him in a good position for promotion when his superiors felt the time was right to give him more responsibility.

But Ian's sojourn in the UK in the summer of 1972 was to be all too brief. By 29 July 1972 Ian had once more crossed the Irish Sea and was back in Belfast with 1 Para which had been posted on a four-month emergency tour of the province. This time he was not stationed in the relative comfort of Palace Barracks in the loughside suburb of Holywood but in various disused mills, school buildings and police stations. In a letter to Ian addressed simply 'Support Coy, 1st Bat Parachute Regiment, BFPO 801' and posted a little over two weeks after he had returned to Northern Ireland his mother, who had been to Bridlington with all the family for a day trip to book accommodation for their summer holiday wrote: 'Mrs Dench asked about you straightaway and when we told her there was a possibility that you would be able to join us for a few days she said that was perfectly alright as the room the boys will be in is really for four people so there will be a bed for you. So we are keeping our fingers, toes and everything crossed that you will be able to get over… hoping for the 28th (August).'

Ian never did get leave to join his family by the seaside in the late summer of 1972. He and his battalion were too heavily involved in supporting the British Army's latest operation to undermine the position of the IRA in its heartlands following the detonation of twenty-two bombs in little more than an hour in Belfast on Friday, 21 July 1972 – instantly dubbed 'Bloody Friday' – which killed nine, including five Protestants, two Catholics and two soldiers. More than 100 were injured.

Bloody Friday was just the catalyst the army had been waiting for to mount a large scale operation to smash the barriers which bounded the no-go areas of both Belfast and Londonderry, move in and occupy previously inviolate IRA safe havens, over which it had exerted its influence. It was to be a massive show of strength intended to swamp the no-go areas and perhaps force the IRA into 'fight or flight'. In this way it was hoped the authority of the security forces could be re-established throughout Northern Ireland without alienating the majority of the local populace. Ian's 1 Para was part of a significant and rapid influx of troops from the UK and the British Army of the Rhine (BAOR) which, by midnight on 30 July 1972, brought the number of troops in Northern Ireland to 28,000; the largest concentration of troops in Ireland since the end of the Second World War.[1]

At 4.00am on 31 July 1972, two days after Ian had set foot in the province for his second tour of Northern Ireland, Operation Motorman roared into life. The residents of the no-go areas of Belfast and Free Derry were woken by the growling of AVREs (armoured bulldozers), armoured cars and armoured personnel carriers rattling and rolling towards them and smashing their way through the barricades behind which they lived, closely followed by 12,000 soldiers swarming in behind to occupy the streets. It was seen by many as an invasion but there was no pitched battle between the IRA and the army; the operation was simply too large to contest and the IRA trickled away, stowing their weapons into cars and vans to fight another day.[2]

Ian did not take part in the initial phase of Operation Motorman, although the operation was not officially terminated until 1 December 1972 and by then 1 Para and Ian had left Northern Ireland. For the first few days of the tour 1 Para was not even billeted on dry land, being instead accommodated aboard HMS *Maidstone*, a former submarine depot ship which had been converted into a floating barracks and moored at the Harland and Wolff shipyard in Belfast. Ten years later Ian would find another berth on another, much larger ship in more opulent surroundings which would boast a good deal more comfort for a long voyage south.

Within a week of his arrival, however, Ian was on the move again as his battalion was deployed into Belfast itself and into areas whose names had an all too familiar ring – the Shankill Road, Woodvale and the Catholic area of Ligoniel. Lieutenant Colonel Wilford set up his Battalion Tactical Headquarters at the police station in Tennent Street, halfway between the Crumlin Road and the Shankill, whilst the companies were divided between the Flax Street Mill, which was shared with the 1st Battalion, The Light Infantry (1/LI), and at Ligoniel Mill.

Half way through the four-month tour 1 Para took on the responsibility for a wider area which included New Barnsley, Whiterock and Beechmount, and yet again the men were relocated and took up residence in unoccupied school buildings in New Barnsley and Beechmount. For Wortley-born Ian and some of the other 'Toms' who hailed from the villages, towns and cities of South Yorkshire, this move must have seemed somewhat ironic. They had perhaps joined the army to widen their horizons beyond places close to home like Barnsley only to find that they were now temporary residents of a New Barnsley.

Ian did, however, take part in patrolling and checkpoint duties similar to those he had been part of during his previous tour. This round of duties invariably meant having to endure his fair share of boredom and he had told his father as much as Ken wrote back to him, 'Nice to hear that you are OK even though bored, could it be any worse?' The hours of boredom were, however, interspersed with bouts of frenetic activity, of which there were three major incidents of note.

The first occurred when a school bus was hijacked and shots were fired at soldiers of 1 Para who were guarding the bus route between the children's homes and their schools. Trouble simmered and the incident escalated over the next two days, triggered by the arrest of a number of youths who were taken to the battalion's tactical HQ at Tennent Street police station for questioning. A riot developed outside the police station and CS gas grenades were thrown into the station courtyard.

Shortly afterwards, one of the battalion's vehicles was attacked and one of the Paras was wounded by a small-calibre weapon, the others being injured by stones and bottles which were thrown at them. A number of women then stopped another vehicle and one of them tried to wrestle a rifle from one of the men inside. During the ensuing melee several women were injured and subsequently the members of the patrol were accused of brutality and of having beaten the women with rifle butts.

The following night a patrol was ambushed in an area near Berlin Street. Shots were fired and two civilians were killed. It was later alleged by the battalion that the patrol's assailants were members of the Loyalist Ulster Defence Association.

In the final incident of note an armoured ambulance was ambushed in the area of Woodvale, following which a mob gathered and serious disorder ensued.[3]

Echoes of the seemingly endless cycle of violence which characterized the Troubles were even being heard in Rotherham. In a letter posted on 4 October Freda enclosed two newspaper cuttings; the first, a pleasant item, was a photograph of her – a volunteer helper – with staff and pupils of the Newman School in a mini-bus about to set out on a week's holiday in Bridlington. The second had more serious content but still Freda thought Ian 'might be interested in this item of news in today's Star'.

Audience Walk out of Ulster Play in Rotherham
by Staff Reporter
Members of the first-night audience at Rotherham Civic Theatre walked out last night at the portrayal of British Army interrogation methods in Northern Ireland performed by a touring theatre company. The brutal ending of the play 'The Ballygombeen Bequest' by John Arden and Margaretta D'Arcy shocked several members of the audience which included old-age pensioners on reduced ticket prices. The play performed by the 7.84 Theatre Company gave no previous hint of the brutal nature of the last 15 minutes when lights were switched off for a scene in which the interrogation took place.

'Harrowing'
Civic manager Mr Alan Hawke said today: 'I knew the interrogation scene would be of a harrowing nature but until the theatre has certificates like films, it is very difficult to know what is in a play. With this kind of play I try to indicate the nature of it by putting 'for the discerning theatregoer' in the publicity. If we were to put exactly what it was like we might have nobody coming except those of a sadistic nature. I think that the scene was all the more harrowing because it was well done.'

The 7.84 Company is described in its publicity as 'United by their attitude to society and to the role of theatre in society; an attitude informed by a Socialist awareness.' Mr. Hawke said they were recommended to the Civic Theatre by the Arts Council.

In the accompanying letter Freda noted that: 'It seems like years since I heard from you although it's just over a week. I have really missed you love… I was really proud you got that Major's recommendation. It must have been an awful situation to have been in. I hope things have calmed down a little now… Take great care of yourself love. Everyone here sends their very best wishes… I swopped your photograph round the other month and put that coloured one in that you took. But you don't look very happy on it. Get one of the lads to take another one of you when you are laughing for me…. Keep your pecker up love, not long now till the end of November. All my love Mum xxxxx.'

Towards late October Freda, with the end of the tour in sight at last, wrote, 'I feel so sorry for you love. The conditions you are existing in seem dreadful. Let's hope the next five weeks go quickly and then you can start enjoying some of that hard-earned cash.' Ian was planning to buy a car. The difficulty was that his provisional driving licence had expired and he needed to take lessons to learn how to drive.

His mother organized the form filling and had already sent him a form which he had signed and sent back. 'I have got your form all filled in properly and am taking it in this morning so as soon as I have the licence I will go and make some enquiries about some lessons for you.'

The emergency tour of 1 Para came to an end on 24 November 1972 and Ian returned once more to Aldershot where the battalion again assumed its role in 16 Parachute Brigade. Ian would never see Northern Ireland again, although 1 Para would go back – seven further tours up to September 2005. He did, however, now have something to show for his seventeen months of service in the province. On 10 November, two weeks before the end of the Operation Motorman tour, he received his first medal, awarded for a minimum of 30 days service in Northern Ireland. This was the General Service Medal 1962, made of silver and sporting the clasp 'Northern Ireland'; the obverse displaying a crowned bust of Queen Elizabeth II with the reverse depicting an oak wreath enclosing a crown and the words 'FOR CAMPIGN SERVICE', the whole suspended on a ribbon of deep purple edged with dark green. Instituted in October 1964 for award to the personnel of all services who had served in what were deemed to be minor campaigns and operations since 1962, it swept away the need for separate medals for General Service in the British Army and RAF (1918–1962) and in the Royal Navy (1915–1962).[4] Tens of thousands of service personnel would be eligible to wear a medal identical to Ian's first; it would be the award of his second which would place him in more exclusive company.

For the rest of 1972 and the first half of 1973 Ian applied himself to his soldiering. He attended and successfully completed the Section Commanders' Course on 20 July 1973 and was promoted to acting lance corporal – letters from home at least were addressed to 'L/Cpl McKay' – but it was not a substantive rank. In mid-September 1973 Ian once more lugged his kit down to the Parachute Regiment Battle School and NCO Tactical Wing at Brecon; this time to become part of what was called the Demo Platoon.

Always striving to be the best in whatever activity he was involved in he was eager to learn and quick to grasp new concepts and at Brecon Ian was part of a platoon of men who had been selected and brought together to act as a model of good practice for candidates on the various courses run by the regimental instructors. As the term suggests, the platoon was used as a demonstration unit. Observers would watch Ian and his comrades in action during attack simulations, the clear message being 'this is how it should be done and this is what we expect'. The observers would then try to replicate the well-oiled manoeuvrings of the Demo Platoon when their turn came to take the field. His selection was an indication of how well his career was progressing and how his performance was being noted by his superiors.

His mother's letter of 11 September filled Ian in on all the latest family news and gossip – Freda's job interview, bang in the middle of the unhealthy surroundings of the Templeborough Rolling Mills, his father's recurrent stomach pain, Neal's application for a job at the Midland Bank and Graham's work experience placement, and she again referred to his plans for buying a car in addition to a comment regarding an injury: 'At last I have got down to this letter although I can hardly hear myself think. The Four Musketeers (Gray, Neal, Paddy and Willy) and your dad are trying to play cards and watch *Johnny Rondo* on TV at the same time... You should be nearly back to normal now. I hope it gets less boring and more interesting for you and gives you a chance to get some of that weight off... I didn't get all the gen about this car but if that is what it's going to cost you for insurance you had better get a bike... Hope you are keeping well love and that your hand has finally managed to heal up. Have you got your pay increase yet?'

Ian was still attached to the Demo Platoon two months later when he received another letter which had been posted in Rotherham on 10 November 1973 in response to a relatively rare one from him. Ian had followed this up with a 'phone call during which he had told them that he had, for a second time, been the victim of theft and that he had at last purchased a car. His mother could not resist a word of warning with her son determined take to the road: 'It was marvellous to get your letter and then to hear from you at the weekend. We are all dying to see the car but for goodness sake be careful. Have you had much chance to drive it yet? ... Don't forget if someone will come up with you we will always make room for them for the weekend or so... Very upset to hear about your loss in the bar the other weekend but as you say without proof there is nothing you can do... Anyway love, take great care of yourself and don't forget, 20 mph and watch out for the other silly drivers on the road. Hope we can see you soon.

All my love, Mum xxx'

During this period, Ian did manage to get home for the odd weekend here and there and his youngest brother's recollections of how he chose to spend his time on leave reveals something of the self-contained, self-sufficient and family-oriented man he was to become; demonstrating little desire to mix with masses of friends and sophisticated company of his own age. Neither, it appeared as he approached his twenties, had he developed a particularly keen interest in the opposite sex, a point which had also been noted by Philip Leeson when the two had been at Rotherham Grammar School together during their early adolescent years. Neal McKay recalled that: 'The [Wingfield] Club was one of Ian's favourite places; he enjoyed a few drinks, playing snooker, cards and the company of friends and relatives. In particular these nights gave him a chance to catch up with Stuart, Keith and Susan – uncles and [an] aunt who had been very good, close relatives for as long as I can remember – and people who Ian had a special affection for; together with [family] friends like the Willets and Bruces and Fishers. Mostly though these were people of my mum and dad's generation and although Ian could get on with anyone regardless of age when he came home, he never really kept in touch with old friends from school or college days. If he did ever take a girlfriend out when he came home then none of us ever knew about it.[5]

It was also at this time that Ian started to refine his skills of instruction which would become such an asset to the recruits at the Parachute Regiment Depot several years later.

Roy Butler had joined 1 Para in Northern Ireland as a raw recruit straight from the Depot in February 1972 in the immediate aftermath of Bloody Sunday. He remembered running down the ramp off the cargo deck of the ferry at Belfast Docks and the scene which greeted him was 'just like something out of Rorke's Drift' with 'two 4-ton Bedford trucks sitting there, back end all stripped down and sandbagged – and a colour sergeant from the quarter master's stores with a box of ammunition slapping a five round clip in your hand to charge your magazine in your SLR.'

Posted to B Company initially, by late 1973 Roy Butler he was keen to progress his career. One day he read a circular which was doing the rounds of the battalion with the result that he came into direct contact with Ian: 'I read that they were looking for volunteers to go to Support Company. I thought I'd done my time in B Company so I volunteered for the Mortar Platoon and got accepted and did all my training. Ian McKay used to be one of my instructors. I must say he was one of the best instructors I ever came across. I went on to be an instructor myself and I took a lot away from the way Ian used to instruct; not being bullish or out of order. If you didn't know something he'd keep you behind and then explain it all to you again and I took that away from him – not just what he said but the way he instructed. He was such a good teacher.'[6]

As the lengthening days, better weather and budding flowers heralded the onset of the spring of 1974 so Ian's career began to blossom. His promotion to lance corporal may have been announced on 1 April, All Fool's Day, but anyone who knew him and knew how seriously he took his career would be well aware that he was anything but.

Four months later, towards the end of July 1974, news filtered through to the men that the battalion was being posted to another divided city in another divided country. This time, however, the people on the streets would not be British citizens and English would not be the mother tongue. They would be travelling further afield, to the mainland of continental Europe in fact and beyond the Iron Curtain; destination Berlin. Having served on the streets in a 'hot' war against paramilitaries on both sides of the sectarian divide in Northern Ireland, Ian McKay was now all set to serve in a different kind of war. He would become a warrior in the 'Cold War'.

At the end of the Second World War what remained of pre-war Germany had been divided into four zones of occupation, each controlled by one of the victorious allied powers, namely Britain, the United States (US), France and the Soviet Union. As the capital of Germany, Berlin was sub-divided in the same fashion, although geographically this famous city was located wholly within the Soviet zone behind what Churchill had famously described as the 'Iron Curtain'. As for Berlin itself, to the west the city was divided between Britain, the US and France whilst the east was firmly under Soviet control. What's more that division had, since mid-August 1961 become set in stone – or in concrete at least – for that was the time when the government of the German Democratic Republic of East Germany, backed by the Soviet Union, had begun the construction of two parallel barriers of high concrete blocks, complete with guard towers, on either side of a wide ribbon of flat, open ground set with anti-vehicle traps and trenches. This barrier became famous, or infamous, as the Berlin Wall; a wall which completely severed West Berlin from East Berlin and the rest of East Germany which surrounded it, save for tightly controlled access via the heavily guarded checkpoints which studded its length and a rail corridor which ran through to Brunswick in West Germany.

The Berlin Wall became one of the most visual and potent symbols of Soviet domination of the Eastern Bloc during the 1960s and 1970s and was, arguably, the distillation of everything the Cold War came to stand for, at least in the eyes of popular culture. Images of euphoric Berliners clambering all over the wall and chipping pieces off the concrete slabs as souvenirs, unmolested by Russian guards in late 1989 became the abiding symbol of the end of the Cold War.

In 1974, however, the Berlin Wall was still very much intact and was the physical embodiment of the political mistrust and tension in Europe at the time and provided the backdrop to the deployment of 1 Para when the battalion arrived in the British sector of Berlin on 12 August for its two-year tour. The battalion became part of the British Berlin Infantry Brigade, consisting of three regular battalions of infantry and an armoured squadron drawn from 4th Royal Tank Regiment, plus supporting units – approximately 3,000 men – which shared the responsibility for the security and protection of West Berlin with the US Army Berlin Brigade and their French counterparts, the *Forces Françaises á Berlin*.[7]

The Berlin Infantry Brigade was accommodated in five barracks with associated quarters for married personnel. Three of the barracks – Brooke, Wavell and Montgomery – housed the three infantry battalions which came in at different points on a two-year rotation, whilst Smuts Barracks became the home of the armoured squadron, with stores and administration units in Alexander Barracks.

Both Brooke and Wavell Barracks were co-located on Wilhelm Strasse in the suburb of Spandau; close to the legendary prison which then still held the former high-ranking Nazi, Rudolf Hess, as its solitary inmate.

Montgomery Barracks was six miles further southwest in the suburb of Kladow, four miles northeast of Potsdam which was in Soviet-controlled East Germany. The border butted up against the southwest face of the Montgomery Barracks complex and even cut across part of the compound. It fell to 1 Para to take up residence in Montgomery Barracks which had so recently been vacated by 1st Battalion, The Worcestershire and Sherwood Foresters, and Ian did his fair share of unloading some of the many heavy packing cases, one of which had been allocated to every soldier.

Once settled in, 1 Para completed the triumvirate of the battalions of the Berlin Brigade by joining 1st Battalion, The Coldstream Guards and 1st Battalion, The King's Own Scottish Borderers.

Some of the Paras certainly felt that they had had a raw deal in terms of their deployment history and were convinced that part of the 'deal' agreed with the Russians was that 'shock troops' could not be stationed near the sensitive border areas. As the Paras considered themselves shock troops they complained that they never, ever got a posting to the BAOR. So when the Berlin posting became a reality some of the more experienced men like Tom, who had spent almost half of the previous five years serving in Northern Ireland, professed that it seemed like paradise. 'When we went to

Berlin it was something brand new to the Paras. A posting like Berlin was like, "phew" and we suddenly realized what the rest of the army had been doing for years and years in the BAOR.'

Ian told his family that he particularly enjoyed serving in Berlin which was his first extended period outside the United Kingdom. Berlin brought a wealth of new experiences in an environment completely different from anything he had known previously and it is no exaggeration to say that the Berlin posting would, quite literally, change his life.

Roy Butler recalls how the battalion spent its time in Berlin and outlined some of the duties Ian was involved in: 'Our job was to hold the British quarter there. We went out on exercises and training and we used to mount guard on the train that ran along the corridor through Russian-held East Germany to Berlin. Once a year the whole battalion – Land Rovers and all the equipment – used have to get on the train, go out down through the corridor and then come back again. If you left West Berlin to go down through the corridor you got checked at the Russian checkpoint as you left Berlin and then again at the checkpoint where West and East Germany met. The Russians used to time us. If we arrived too early they said we'd been speeding; if we arrived late they accused us of spying. It was all the diplomatic side of soldiering. We also used to guard Rudolf Hess in Spandau.'[8]

The latter, the formal guarding of former high-ranking Nazi, Rudolf Hess, now a deluded and lonely old man and the sole inmate of Spandau Prison, was a bizarre duty, yet nonetheless it was one in which Ian definitely took part.

Rudolf Hess had been a faithful deputy and close confidant of Adolf Hitler and from early 1939 had been second in line to assume the role of Chancellor behind Hermann Göring. He had been imprisoned several times before, the first being in 1923 along with Hitler after the failed Munich Putsch, but his influence on his Führer had waned after the Nazis had come to power in 1933, even though he had become a minister in the government. In May 1941 he evaded both German and British fighter planes and flew to Britain on a fantastical and, it is claimed, unilateral mission to make contact with what the Nazis believed was an aristocratic 'Peace Party' in Britain, either to make peace or to persuade them to become an ally of Germany against the Soviet Union. After Hess' capture and interrogation, Prime Minister Churchilll made sure that he was kept well out of the way. He was imprisoned at various locations throughout Britain, including the Tower of London and ironically, given the locations associated with both Ian McKay's life and death, Mytchett Place near Aldershot. After the war he was tried at Nuremberg, found guilty on the counts of 'conspiracy to commit crimes' and 'crimes against peace' and sentenced to life imprisonment. His place of incarceration was Spandau. In 1966, with the release of Albert Speer and Baldur von Schirach he became the last prisoner of Spandau.[9] As the Soviets refused to countenance his release, the intricately choreographed and diplomatically sensitive changing and mounting of the guard under Hess's Four Power imprisonment had to go on; each of the four powers taking it in turns to guard their prisoner.

Corporal Tom remembers that when 1 Para made up the guard they used a 'big, red-brick house just outside the prison where we did all our cooking, cleaning and sleeping'.

The Russians handed over to the Americans, the Americans handed over to the French, the French handed over to the British and the British handed over to the Russians again. The Russians didn't use the big house we did; they just used a big gate house and another open room inside the prison itself. They were escorted all the way from Checkpoint Charlie to Spandau and then they stayed put. I was guard commander at times and the Russians had a trick when they took over. In the towers there were big metal doors and as soon as the outgoing guard commander left and shut the prison gates [the Russians] used to drop these large metal doors one after the other in quick succession – bang, bang, bang, bang, bang – even at 3 o'clock in the morning. Mac took part in the guard duties according to the rota.[10]

According to Roy Butler Spandau was an amazing place:

Changing the guards in the watch towers was a real performance. All the guards used to troop into the guard room, the gates would shut and then you'd begin the process of changing the guards in the guard towers. We'd march into the courtyard and at each tower you'd stop. The old guard comes down, the new guard goes up; old guard joins the end of the column. One day Rudolf was out tending his vegetable garden and we were halfway round these towers and he stopped gardening and joined the column so that I had Rudolf Hess marching behind me. We stop. I go up [the tower], the old guard comes down and the column moves on but Hess stops at the bottom of my tower and I've got him all day long staring up at me giving me the spookiest looks.[11]

Spooky or not, the enigmatic Nazi Rudolf Hess does not appear to have perturbed the down-to-earth, football loving South Yorkshireman, Ian McKay in the slightest, as he regaled his family with possibly embellished tales of how he had spent some of his time on guard duties at Spandau playing cards with Hess. If they did play what games and the eventual outcomes are lost forever but given the hours and hours he had had to practise on an upturned riot shield in Northern Ireland one wonders whether Hitler's Deputy – who had seen his Reich both dominate and lose most of Europe between 1939–1945 – could ever have stood a chance of emerging victorious against Lance Corporal McKay.[12]

Berlin was a place where Ian's sense of humour came to the fore. There was no question that he took his soldiering seriously but at still only 21-years-old he also knew how to have fun. Some men remember him as a 'character' who could be very funny. Roy Butler remembers Ian impersonating the padre in the bar, but only ever before the padre turned up and on one occasion Ian was involved in the liberation of alcohol intended for the Support Company bar. Roy Butler tells the story:

In Berlin the bottom of the camp was about 30m from the border. Support Company was furthest away from the top end of the camp so we were right next to the [border] wall; that's where our stores and everything were. Every company had their own bar and every now and again you used to get the bar replenished;

go up to the NAAFI with a Land Rover and pick up all the beer and whatever. We used to back [the Land Rover] up to the back of the mortar stores because we had this staircase that went up to the company bar. Ian was there when we were unloading, and we sometimes used the system, 'that's two for them and one for us'.[13]

Out on exercise Ian could be relied upon to try and raise a smile. At least two photographs exist of the Mortar Platoon at the time – a 'mortar concentration' was the way the Paras described it. In one – a fairly formal pose being struck by most of the men, some of whom sport the Berlin Brigade flash of a red disc surrounding a black circle on their left upper sleeve – Ian, in forage cap as opposed to his red beret, is the only one lying on the ground in front of the group. Raising his torso off the ground on his left elbow and with his other hand resting on his hip, he strikes the pose of a man modelling swimwear on a beach rather than a soldier in uniform on a mortar fire exercise. In the other photograph of the same group, Ian stands to the extreme left, left arm resting casually on the shoulder of a comrade, whilst his right hand lifts his parachute smock up at the front, just enough to reveal the open flies of his olive green (OG) denims. Risqué? Perhaps, immature? Possibly, but for a young man in the company of many other young men in a male-dominated culture it demonstrates how relaxed Ian felt with those he had worked with for more than three years.

For many of the men their time in Berlin was like being part of one big family and that sense of belonging was perhaps felt even more keenly amongst those of the specialist soldiers of the Mortar Platoon. Tom's view was that the Mortar Platoon of that vintage was a strong unit which was 'rich in characters and personalities who were fairly fit and robust; good at their job, very good at [mortar] concentrations and our reports were fantastic.' Tom continued:

There was Mac and me and 'Stumpy' and Bill Coffey; we were all very good friends. Although Bill Coffey was mortars at the time, he had been in the Patrols Company and they again considered themselves elite, just as Support Company did. It was something special to be in there so we had a close link. We were all sort of the same year and Bill would have been a full 'screw' [corporal] about the same time as me and the same time as 'Stumpy', so we were all fairly close. When we were in Berlin we all used to be in the corporal's mess together. We'd always be more or less a group. In fact Mac used to babysit for a lot of people in Berlin. He certainly babysat for me and for 'Stumpy' and his wife.[14]

The friendships which had been forged between the men extended to their wives and, being army wives, they all knew each other, got on and mixed together whenever mess events took place. They were, according to Tom, all very talkative and very friendly. Bill Coffey and his wife Marica were another couple Ian babysat for, looking after their young son, Donald – Donny – when they went out.

The idea of young soldiers babysitting for their more senior colleagues is not as unusual as it may sound to those from an exclusively civilian background. In the army, when units are accommodated in barrack blocks with married quarters close by, young, single soldiers make up a large pool of babysitters; many of whom are 'on tap' and available to look after the offspring of more senior NCOs and JNCOs when they go out for the evening with their wives. Young soldiers have been used for years as babysitters and the custom was certainly 'standard operating procedure' across the Parachute Regiment at the time.

For Ian McKay, however, what had started out as merely babysitting for Bill and Marica Coffey, developed into something more at some point during the latter part of 1975. The more Ian, now aged 22, got to know Marica, almost five years his senior, the more his feelings for her deepened and he began to fall in love. For her part Marica reciprocated. She has conceded that she and Bill Coffey weren't happy and this at a time when Ian came into her life. 'We met, and we knew. Simple as that', was how Marica described their feelings for each other to a national newspaper in 1982, 'we could talk about anything. We were the sort of people who went out to dinner and never noticed anyone else in the restaurant.'[15]

Four years later she described to journalist Jean Carr how she and Ian had met and explained her feelings at the time:

> Nothing in my life has ever felt so right as the day I married Ian in December, 1976. We had met the year before in Berlin where I was stationed with my husband Bill Coffey, a sergeant in the Paras, and our 9-year-old son Donny. Ian was a lance corporal and when we were introduced at a mess social, I thought: 'What a nice person'. We met a couple of times after that, and he babysat Donny for us once or twice, but I don't remember when we first realized what was happening between us. It is very difficult in a small community like an army base, with everyone living on top of each other, for a single man to ask out a married woman, never mind be seen with her. But our relationship reached the stage that, when Ian was posted back to Aldershot in April 1976, I left Bill in Berlin and followed Ian back with Donny. Being in love can be very painful, insecure and uncomfortable, but from the start I felt very comfortable with Ian. There were no great highs and lows, just a steady relationship, and the happiest times were just being quietly together. I never once felt restless when I was with him, or fancied anyone else. I had no romantic illusions about marriage but with Ian I would never have done anything to jeopardize what we had, and had he lived I think it would have lasted. When we met Ian was 23 and I was 27 and his first serious girlfriend.[16]

As Marica was married to a fellow soldier who was also a close working colleague of Ian, then their relationship had the potential to cause significant difficulties in both the tight-unit Mortar Platoon and the wider 'family' of the battalion. If their relationship continued and they decided to go public there would be consequences for all parties concerned. Having once embarked on their chosen path their journey into the future together was anything but certain.

Marica Coffey was no stranger to army life and the demands it placed on families with its attendant and regular upheavals, relocations and long periods of separation, often looking after small children on foreign postings whilst serving husbands were away for long periods on exercises or manoeuvres.

Marica had been born into an army family. She had lived with her parents in such far-flung colonial outposts as Aden during the 1950s and had been educated at a boarding school on the George Cross island of Malta. She had already turned 17 when she set foot in the UK for the first time and moved to Aldershot where she had trained as a nurse in the Queen Alexandra's Royal Army Nursing Corps.[17] 'When I first went to Aldershot as a young girl we were always warned about the Paras. "Oh, you mustn't go near any of them", people used to say. But of course we did.'[18] She met, fell for and subsequently married Bill Coffey – one of those Paras – with whom she had a son, Donny, in 1967.

Tom remembers Bill Coffey as 'a good looking lad [who] had a few close friends who he used to go out with. Many of the girls would have been attracted to Bill, he was that sort of bloke; fit, a good soldier; knew what he was doing; always good looking and always well dressed but I can't say I saw him with any other women.'

When Ian and Marica's relationship finally became common knowledge several of his comrades were surprised. Tom recalled that when he found out about the relationship he was 'gobsmacked':

You'd never have put Mac down for anything like that. I couldn't believe it; could not believe it. I was so surprised I thought to myself, 'there's going to be a right bust up here' but to be honest Bill took it quite well [and] kept it to himself in the main. I thought that there was obviously going to be a bust up at some time – in some people's eyes Mac had done the 'dirty deed' and I think people thought that the best thing was to separate them. Bill Coffey took it very well. We were all surprised that there wasn't a big bust up and of course there wasn't. Then Mac got posted and it seemed to everybody that the best thing that could have been done was to keep them separate. We all thought Mac had just got out of the way but it was Mac and Marica who stayed together and then she and Bill split up and it seemed to some of us that it was very amicable.

Arrangements were obviously worked out amicably between all parties later as Bill Coffey saw his son Donny regularly after he and Marica separated and she has gone on record as saying that Bill Coffey proved to be 'a tower of strength' after Ian's death – albeit that Marica married Ian the day after they divorced. At that time, 1988, they did not maintain regular contact but Marica made it clear that Bill Coffey was 'there if I need him – as I would be for him'.

In 1976, however, it was far from clear as to how the delicately balanced situation between Ian, Marica and Bill might develop but what was clear to the two men's superiors in 1 Para was that the smooth functioning of the battalion had to be the priority. The regiment still had the best part of five months to serve with the British Berlin Brigade and quite simply Ian and Bill Coffey could not remain in the same sub-unit of the battalion. It was not even a question of easing one of them from the Mortar Platoon into another platoon or company; one of them would have to leave the battalion entirely and it was Ian who would have to go. The decision was taken to transfer him back to the UK. Packing his kit again and saying goodbye to many good friends, some of whom he had known for more than five years, he left 1 Para on 17 March 1976, five years and fifteen days after he had first joined them in Northern Ireland and was back in the UK the same day. He never went back.

'Tom' was oblivious to the decisions which had been taken at a higher level:

> I don't necessarily think it would have just been Colonel Wilford's decision but, and although I don't know for sure, I think the Families Officer would have been involved with the OC and the Adjutant as to what was going to happen next. We never got a 'whiff' that Mac was going to leave until it happened. [In the army] that's not unusual. When things happen like that you are there one day and gone the next. Civilians wouldn't think that things could happen so quickly but in the army they can, or at least they could then. By then of course I was a 'full screw' (corporal), married and living out in married quarters and people weren't going to confide in me too much as I was Bill Coffey's mate. So if one of the Toms has been seeing Bill Coffey's Mrs they're not going to tell!

Ian was posted back to the Parachute Regiment and Airborne Forces Depot at Aldershot where the regiment could begin to utilize his burgeoning skills as a gifted instructor in the training of young recruits to the full. Marica initially went back to the family home in Surrey whilst divorce proceedings got underway and plans were made to find a home in Aldershot in which the couple could begin their new life together. It had been decided that they would marry when Marica's divorce was finalized.

Throughout the entire period of the developing relationship the McKay family in Rotherham was completely unaware of the emotional and political machinations of what had been happening in Berlin. Freda McKay recalled that they received a phone call out of the blue one day in which Ian told them that 'he'd been transferred and he was coming home but that he was coming home with Marica and her nine-year-old son'. Neal McKay remembered that, 'The telephone rang one night, it was Ian again, only this time he was calling not with just the latest news but to tell us that he was going to get married! Up to that moment none of us had heard the name Marica ever mentioned before.'

Marica recounted what had happened in the summer of 1976.

> I asked Bill for a divorce. He divorced me for adultery and it was finalised on November 30 – the day before I married Ian at Aldershot register office. If there was anyone to blame for my first marriage not working it was more likely to be me. Bill has always been honourable about everything. He is a good father to Donny, taking him to visit his family and going on holidays with him. At first there was all the hurt, but in the end we all got on. He and Ian liked each other and Bill was one of the first round to see me when he was killed.[19]

Ian and Marica were married in a quiet ceremony for family and friends at Aldershot Register Office on 1 December 1976. There were no top hats or morning suits for the men nor huge dresses and a plethora of fascinators for the women. A lounge suit, shirt and tie sufficed for the groom. After the ceremony the wedding party retired to Marica's mother's house for a private celebration. It was a 'very quiet, low-key celebration but a very happy occasion for the few of us close family who were there,' recalled his brother Neal.

Married life for Ian and Marica began in earnest when they moved into married quarters on Salerno Crescent, the main spine road of the Talavera Park Estate – built in 1964 on the site of old Talavera Barracks – which housed a further 297 military families. Ian became Marica's 'best friend' and 'greatest companion' in what she still cherishes as 'a good marriage'. She found him very easy to get on with and, like countless other newlyweds before and since, they did almost everything together. Ian even persuaded her to take up cards – a favoured pursuit for him – and the game of Backgammon, although she admitted to previously having little patience for such pastimes.

For the whole of 1977 and the first eight months of 1978 Ian served on the instructing staff at the Depot, first as a lance corporal and, from 1 September 1977, as a 'full screw' with his promotion to corporal. Laurie Bland, who as a corporal served with Ian both at the Depot and in the 3rd Battalion of the Parachute Regiment (3 Para) maintains that Ian would have noticed the material benefits of that promotion in his pay packet which would have been a welcome addition to the domestic finances of the newly married couple. '[Promotion] from lance corporal to corporal is the biggest jump in pay; something like £6 a day' according to Laurie Bland, 'equivalent to the local overseas allowance in Germany' for those like Ian who had served abroad. Ian also continued to develop his military qualifications and on 16 December 1977 he attended a Unit Nuclear Biological and Chemical Weapons (NBC) NCOs course and became a specialist NBC instructor with the grade A-1.

Lieutenant General Sir Hew Pike, who as a major in the late 1970s would be Ian's company commander and later as a Lieutenant Colonel in command of 3 Para would be Ian's commanding officer during the Falklands War in 1982, has no doubt that training recruits was, and remains, a standard part of the training for up and coming NCOs. 'Recruit training absolutely needs corporals at its heart as one needs their experience and their input to make [it] work.'

Ian had experienced a great enrichment of his personal life through his marriage to Marica in 1976 and the fact that he had become a loving and respected stepfather to Donny but in the summer of 1977 his life was enriched further with the birth of a daughter – his own flesh and blood – born on 4 August in Aldershot. Ian and Marica named her Melanie.

Ian's parents were on holiday in Falmouth in Devon and Ian rang them up at the hotel to tell them the joyful news. He was so excited he was 'absolutely over the moon', according to Freda.

Fatherhood suited Ian McKay and he brought the same dedication and energy to his new role that he had applied to other aspects of his life so far. The concept of family – both in his personal and professional life – had always been very important to him. He had eschewed materialism and many of the passing fads of the late 1960s and early 1970s and now, with the birth of Melanie and the increase in size of his own family, so came increased responsibilities. They were responsibilities he took just as seriously as those he had in the army. He revelled in his enhanced role of being the father of a new baby and the wonder did not subside as the months progressed. 'He was a good husband and a fantastic father. You don't get many men like Ian,' Marica revealed in 1988. More than ten years later, in 2009, in conversation with the author, she vividly recalled a vignette of their family life during which Melanie had skipped ahead of Ian and Marica one day whilst they were out walking. Ian had been playing with Melanie, chasing her around and making her giggle with excitement and on his return to Marica's side he had exclaimed 'That's what life is all about, that little girl'.[20]

Neal McKay attempted to sum up his thoughts on his eldest brother's role as a father when he came to set them down in 1988:

> I must admit I'd never really thought of Ian in the role of father and family man, but over the following years whenever Ian was up here [Rotherham] with Marica, Melanie and Donny (Ian's step-son) or we visited them in Aldershot, he seemed to be just as happy and suited to this role of father, cook – he could make some really good curries that were usually on the hotter side of mild – nappy-changer, cleaner, storyteller and all the other tasks and joys that come with a family, as he ever was on the sports field or (I presume) on the army training ground. When Melanie was first born it was a special sight to see her almost cradled in just one of Ian's fairly huge hands (he's the only man I've ever known who could hold two pint pots in one hand and not by the rim either!). One of the sad ironies of his death was that he'd virtually made his mind up to leave the Forces a while before the Falklands in order to spend more time with his family. I recall him saying that he felt he had missed out so much on Melanie's early years and that this was upsetting him. It was on the occasions when he visited us or vice versa that he showed a side of his nature I'd never seen – a genuine tenderness and gentleness with Melanie in her first years.[21]

Like many marriages, the relationship was not without its ups and downs and disagreements but Ian's devotion to his young daughter was unshakeable. He loved his daughter and Marica witnessed at first hand how, by turns, he was 'good and gentle and strong'. She sometime used to think that even if he ever felt like he wanted to leave her after what she called one of their 'ding-dongs', that he could never bring himself to leave Melanie.

The Parachute Regiment, however, was not about to let Corporal Ian McKay become too comfortable instructing recruits at the Depot in Aldershot by day and clocking off and retreating home into the bosom of his young family by night. No matter how good an instructor he was becoming, if he wished to progress his career and accrue experience he needed to keep his own training up to date and this could only be done by being an active member of a fully functioning battalion. What's more the Cold War still had more than a decade to run and the British Army had a crucial role to play in facing off the Soviets across the German Inner Border on the North German Plain.

And so, on 6 September 1978, a little more than a year after Melanie's birth, Ian learned that he would again be returning to Germany; this time to join 3 Para which had recently returned from a four-month emergency tour of Northern Ireland and was being deployed to Osnabrück in Lower Saxony as part of the recently-formed 5th Field Force in the BAOR.

Ian's name was placed on the roll of 3 Para's A Company under the command of the then Major Hew Pike, a man whom Ian would come to know well – both at peace and in war – and with whom he would strike up a personal and professional relationship based on mutual respect and trust. Hew Pike recalled that Ian had 'originally been a 1 Para soldier and he had married Marica who had previously been married to another man in 1 Para. Because of this it was judged sensible for McKay to be posted to the Depot and then to a different battalion.' It was obvious to a man as astute as Hew Pike, who would later go on to achieve high office in the army, that Ian McKay was an up-and-coming star of the regiment; a man who came to 3 Para with a 'growing reputation as a superb instructor, a strong leader and a fine sportsman'.

He came to me in A Company from being a recruit platoon corporal at the Depot in Aldershot. I commanded A Coy, more or less, with a 6 month interval and then commanded the Battalion immediately after that. He was a corporal in A Company of 3 Para first then he was promoted to Sergeant and, unusually, stayed in the same company. That's when I really knew him best when he was in my company. I knew him very well. We used to play tennis together and he was a very good and stylish tennis player, one of the best in the Battalion, along with one of our RAF Parachute Jumping Instructors. He also played squash and was a very keen footballer, I remember him playing football and being very keen and actually at the time of the Falklands campaign he had an ankle injury which I think was from football or of course it could have been from parachuting, which was interfering with his footballing but was potentially worrying in terms of his overall military fitness. He was quite stout – very strongly built – he was the sort of guy who could have put on weight if he didn't watch it and he was quite chunky. I remember talking to him about the injury – a month or two before the Falklands war when he said he was very worried about this ankle injury. I always remember him as being an incredibly nice guy; a very easy man to get on with. Incredibly keen and committed and as I recall he had been on a NBC course and it was everybody's least favourite subject; a ghastly business. You had to put on respirators and dress up in this NBC kit and it's pretty hot and uncomfortable soldiering. He came back from this course and, typically, with the light of battle in his eyes as if he'd undergone a Road to Damascus conversion to the cause of NBC, we were all given a hard time as to how inadequate our NBC skills were. But that was what he was like. He was an extremely good instructor. Very, very enthusiastic and passionate about what he was doing but not in an overbearing way, in an engaging way. He was a very bright guy. He always struck me as well-educated. I think that Marica felt that he should perhaps have been an officer and he probably would have ended up with a commission after going down the Warrant Officer route by becoming a Regimental Sergeant Major first but he gave me the impression that he was knowledgeable, interested in everything: a very good person to have a conversation with. As a company commander you know your 100 or so men intimately and if you don't you're not doing your job very well and certainly you should know your NCOs. You're very much in the business of being the person looking at them in terms of their promotion prospects; who's going to go from private soldier to lance corporal – the most difficult promotion step in the army of course – and who has the potential to progress. The well-being of the regiment is just as important a part of the job as training people. It's no good having good officers and useless NCOs; far better to have it the other way round – good NCOs and useless officers. [Good] NCOs are crucial and McKay – and I say this in all sincerity and not just because he was killed in action in very gallant circumstances – was a very bright and promising guy.[22]

Ian struck Hew Pike at once as a man of great energy and considerable intelligence whilst noticing several significant personality traits which marked him out as someone who had a bright future in the regiment.

His manner was outgoing, self-confident and extremely enthusiastic yet he was also clearly a thinker, a man with ideas, who was always looking for a better, more professional way of tackling a problem. He was, like other top-grade NCOs of the Parachute Regiment, completely dedicated to his job, which he took very seriously indeed. He would argue equally passionately on a point of tactics or policy, with other NCOs or with the CO... As a leader he was strong but compassionate – a man greatly respected and trusted by his soldiers, because of his obvious professional competence, his infectious confidence and his utter sincerity. There was no messing about and his men knew it. He was not above himself, or arrogant – simply a sincere and highly motivated NCO who had the courage of his convictions and the ability to express them very clearly. My best memories are from those 'A' Company days in Osnabrück. My abiding image is of a man brimming with enthusiasm, energy and quickness of mind, whose outgoing and confident personality won him the friendship and respect of many. I count myself lucky to have known him so well.[23]

A month after his arrival in West Germany Ian attended another course and gained another specialist qualification, this time as a Landing Point Marshalling Team Commander on 11 October 1978. It was all grist to his mill.

Rising star and thinker of the regiment he may have been but that did not put him beyond criticism by those of his superiors who felt he may have stepped out of line. Laurie Bland was a fellow corporal in A Company when Ian arrived and he recalls one incident whilst the battalion were engaged on a Cold War exercise on the North German Plain in West Germany:

We were on a recce (reconnaissance) patrol drill and we had a simulated enemy – The Devon and Dorsets I think it was – we called them the 'Devon and Donuts'. The drill was to locate them and gain information. Well we did what we had to do and found them at a certain location and there was nobody there – just their tracked APCs all 'harboured up' – but there was no sign of any troops, no-one there. So we crept up and opened the back of one of these APCs and inside were some rifles. Ian took a night sight from one of the rifles – left the rifle and took the night sight. We carried on with the patrol and when we got back we had our de-brief back in the cookhouse at Osnabrück. [The then]

Major Simon Brewis, who was then in charge of [battalion] training outlined the good points and the bad points first and of course Ian was asked where he had got the night sight. He said that it belonged to the 'Devon and Donuts' and, well, the 'shit hit the fan' about that. [Brewis] gave Ian McKay a public bollocking – he singled him out. He was pointing out the main points about what A Company had done and B Company had done and he said 'apart from Corporal McKay who thought it was clever to steal an IWS [individual weapon sight]'. You could see Ian boiling and everybody else was raging because if it had been any other company they would have done the same. It was a public embarrassment. Ian was angry but he didn't respond and he got an apology from Major Brewis afterwards. Apparently he shouldn't have done it but from our point of view he was entitled to do so as [the other battalion] should have been guarding their vehicles. If you think about it in operational terms he was just being a professional soldier even then. He did then what he thought was right. At that time there was one night sight per section; take that away and you've captured 30 per cent of a platoon's night viewing aids and reduced their night vision capability by a third! They obviously got it back the next day but it was the embarrassment factor more than anything which stung them. Their officers would have been furious and embarrassed by the fact that they had lost such an important piece of kit and someone would have had to go and tell an exercise umpire that they had lost an IWS and ask them, "please can you go and ask [the Paras] if we can have our IWS back?". [24]

Marica, Donny and Melanie had accompanied Ian to Osnabrück and they settled into a life similar to many other families whose menfolk were part of the British Army of the Rhine. Marica recalled that they had always had a very good social life in the army and especially so when Ian was stationed in Osnabrück. The McKay's found that the mess life was very good with lots of friends and always something going on in terms of events. Ian was away a good deal, that was after all the nature of his profession, but Marica got used to it and in any case she always knew that her husband would return again before very long.

After almost six months in West Germany Ian was back at the Parachute Regiment Depot in the UK by 28 February 1979 and there now followed a period of just over three years when Ian's life alternated between postings at the Depot and 3 Para in West Germany. In this his latest tour of duty at the Depot he spent just over two months as an instructor at the Weapons Training Wing and continued to carve out a career as an excellent trainer and leader of men. The Parachute Regiment makes many demands on its members and sets high standards in terms of performance. The same is true of its instructors. For those, like Roy Butler, who had had the good fortune to come under his wing Ian McKay had a way with the young recruits. As a colleague in A Company and also someone who spent time at the Depot as a corporal instructor, Laurie Bland witnessed Ian in action with many young soldiers.

One of his greatest skills was that when he was debriefing recruits and soldiers he could engage with them and get his message across but then when he was talking

Older brother. The McKay boys in the garden of their Rotherham home in the summer of 1958, the year following the birth of Ian's youngest brother Neal. Left to right: Neal, Ian and Graham. (*Freda McKay*)

The earliest known photograph of Ian McKay taken in Sunderland on 17 September 1953 during a visit to his great grandfather Arthur Housam. Ian's mother Freda had a photograph taken at the same photographer's in the same chair. (*Freda McKay*)

A happy child. Giggling for the camera aged 5. Ian's capacity to smile and be cheerful earned him the nickname 'Sunshine' when he joined the army. (*Freda McKay*)

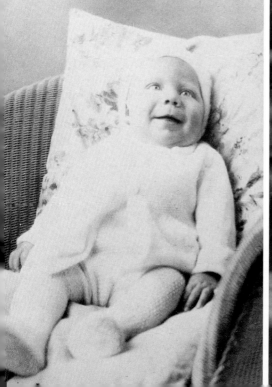

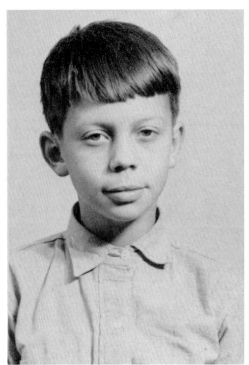
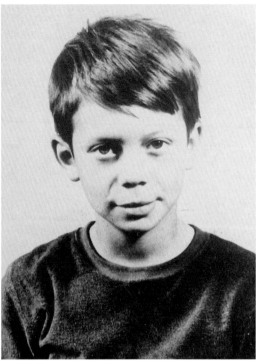

Two more serious studies of Ian aged 7, (left) and 9 (right) during his days as a pupil at Roughwood Junior School, Kimberworth Park, Rotherham. (*Freda McKay*)

The Roughwood Junior School cricket XI of 1963-64. Ian is seated front row, extreme right. Although cricket was not Ian's main sport his love of all ball games and athletic activities secured him a place in many school teams. (*Freda McKay*)

Ian's first formal form photograph at Rotherham Grammar School in the academic year 1964-65. Ian (seated, third from left) passed the 11+ examination and started school in September 1964 much to the dismay of his junior school headteacher who felt he would have been happier being a 'big fish in a small pond'. Ian's great boyhood friend Philip Leeson is seated third from right. (*Freda McKay*)

Rotherham Grammar School, renamed Thomas Rotherham College in 1969, provided many opportunities for Ian to take part in a wider variety of organised sports. As a fifth-form student, (back row, left) he proudly wears the old gold and black strip of the First XI football team. (*Freda McKay*)

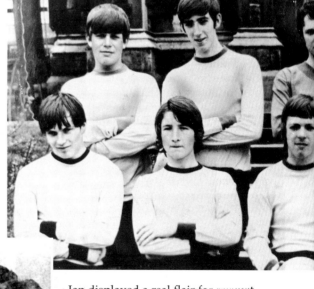

Ian displayed a real flair for racquet sports whilst at school and here he shows his certificate, awarded for reaching the finals of the Rotherham and District Inter-Schools Badminton Competition, to other competitors in 1968. Ian and partner Stuart Forrest won the doubles title in 1968 and 1969 and represented Rotherham and District in its first ever inter-association badminton fixture in October 1968. (*Freda McKay*)

Mortar Concentration. Ian shows his lighter side and indulges in a little horseplay as the Mortar Platoon of 1 Para let off steam on exercise in Germany 1974-75. (*Freda McKay*)

Ian left 1 Para when he met and fell in love with Marica who was then still married to another 1 Para soldier. He and Marica, seen here at a Sergeants' Mess Christmas function, returned to England with Marica's son Donald and they were married in Aldershot on 1 December 1976. (*Freda McKay*)

Family man. Ian's daughter Melanie was born in August 1977 and he assumed a new role as a devoted father. Here Melanie rushes towards Ian as he is snapped in front of his parents' house in Rotherham in 1980. (*Freda McKay*)

As the platoon sergeant, (centre right) of 477 Recruit Platoon, Ian worked with Capt Alan Coulson to keep an entire platoon of ex-Junior Parachute Company recruits on the straight and narrow and won them over with his calm, reasoned and supportive approach. 477 Platoon passed out in February 1982. Two of Ian's young charges, Steve Tuffen, (back row, centre) and Julian Barrett, (to Tuffen's left) would be posted to 2 and 3 Para respectively and would be seriously wounded in the Falklands. (*Freda McKay*)

Professional soldier. Ian alternated between serving in the 3rd Battalion The Parachute Regiment (3 Para) and as an instructor at the Parachute Regiment and Airborne Forces Depot at Aldershot between 1978 and 1980. He was universally respected as a skilled and patient teacher and communicator. Photographed instructing on the 'Trainasium' aerial confidence course.

In his element, out in the field in a trench on exercise. (*Freda McKay left & right*)

4 Platoon, B Company 3 Para on board the *Canberra* during 3 Para's voyage to the Falkland Islands in May 1982. As Platoon Sergeant Ian sits to the left of Platoon Commander Lieutenant Andrew Bickerdike at the heart of the group. Directly behind Ian stands 17-year-old Jason Burt who was killed at the start of Ian's charge on Mount Longdon. Ian Scrivens, aged 17 (front, extreme left) and Neil Grose, (back row, third from left) 18 on the day of the battle for Mount Longdon – were also killed. (*Andrew Bickerdike*)

3 Para broke its journey at Ascension Island on the way to the South Atlantic giving the men time to get ashore and do some training at English Bay. Cpl John 'Taff' Hedges takes cover behind a rock as Ian moves behind in a photograph taken by Kevin Capon, a member of 6 Platoon of B Company on 1 May 1982. (*Freda McKay/Kevin Capon*)

The last man to see Ian McKay alive. Cpl Ian Bailey, a section commander in 5 Platoon of B Company, 3 Para, pictured here at Teal Inlet just two weeks before the battle for Mount Longdon. (*Rod and Jan Hutchings*)

In the late 1990s Ian Bailey returned to Mount Longdon and stood on the spot where his dog tags were found by Royal Engineers clearing the battlefield in 1983. The Argentine heavy machine gun Ian McKay's party intended to attack was on the rocks above Bailey to the left with another machine-gun post above and to his right and rifle pits at the base of the rocks behind him. (*Ian Bailey*)

The Argentine .50-calibre heavy machine gun which was a thorn in the side of 4 and 5 Platoons of B Company, 3 Para during the attack on Mount Longdon. Protected by additional machine guns and rifles it was at the heart of a formidable weapons complex. Photographed in situ by Capt Bob Darby on 16 June 1982 it had been turned to fire on the pyramidal rock outcrop of Full Back – the final objective of 3 Para during the battle. Port Stanley is just visible in the distance centre left. (*Bob Darby*)

'The hardest part of war… these were names I knew'. 3 Para dead in grey body bags being loaded aboard a Royal Navy Wessex at the evacuation base under Capt Bob Darby for the twenty mile flight to the temporary mortuary at Teal Inlet on the morning of 12 June 1982. (*Bob Darby*)

The memorial at Teal Inlet constructed as a labour of love by Rod Hutchings as a symbol of remembrance to mark the original burial place at Teal Inlet. It still stands today. (*Rod Hutchings*)

The temporary burial site on the headland at Teal Inlet. Ian was buried here in a mass grave on 14 June 1982 along with twenty of his 3 Para comrades who had died on Mount Longdon. Teal settlement handyman Rod Hutchings made wooden crosses for each of the dead and cared for the plot. Ian's grave marker cross is eighteenth from the right. (*Rod Hutchings*)

'The bestest medal in the world'. Marica McKay with daughter Melanie and son Donny – now known as Don – display Ian's Victoria Cross in its Hancock's Jewellers presentation box outside Buckingham Palace on the day of the investiture; 9 November 1982. The Queen had intended to bring some of the metal used to fashion the VCs to show Melanie but she had been unable to find it. (*Freda McKay*)

Grief and Pride. Ken and Freda McKay with their son's Victoria Cross. 9 November 1982. (*Freda McKay*)

Ian McKay's Victoria Cross displayed with his General Service Medal 1962 - Northern Ireland Clasp - and the South Atlantic Medal. The medals were sold to Lord Ashcroft by Marica McKay in a private treaty sale on 24 November 1989 and are now on display in the Ashcroft Gallery at the Imperial War Museum. (*Freda McKay*)

Ian's body is reinterred at Aldershot Military Cemetery on 26 November 1982 along with fifteen other paratroopers of 2 and 3 Para. His beret, bayonet and medals including the VC are on top of the coffin which is carried by men he knew well or were with him in his final moments; left to right, Cpl John Hedges, Cpl Ian Bailey and Sgt Des Fuller. Bearers on the far side and not visible here were, from front to back, Colour Sgt Brian Faulkner, Colour Sgt Tony Dunne and L Cpl Lenny Carver. CSM John Weeks, in tears when he carried Ian's body from Longdon, provides the escort to the rear. (*Freda McKay*)

Union Flags drape the coffins of the sixteen paratroopers interred at Aldershot Military Cemetery on 26 November 1982. Ian's coffin and bearer party are on the extreme right. (*Freda McKay*)

Mount Longdon 2007. Falkland Islanders Vernon Steen (left) and Tony Smith stand near a rough circle of stones in the foreground which marks the Argentine sangar where Ian McKay died. Steen saw Ian just a few minutes before his attack on the Argentine positions. Ian's party broke cover from the rocks behind Steen and Smith thirty metres away and charged across the open towards the camera. (*Author*)

The rough circle of stones still marks the location of the commanding Argentine machine-gun post which Ian destroyed and where he lost his life. His body was found next morning by Sgt Sammy Dougherty and Pte Tony Bojko slumped across the near lip of the position with three Argentine dead and the debris of battle all around.

In Memoriam. Memorials to Ian McKay include portraits commissioned by the regiment and Rotherham Council, cottages in Barnsley and dedicated drill halls and army buildings.

(Left) The War Memorial at what was Rotherham Grammar School, now Thomas Rotherham College. (*Freda McKay*)

(Above) The Liberation Memorial in Port Stanley, Falkland Islands. (*Author*)

McKay Road, Port Stanley, Falkland Islands. There is also a McKay Close in Aldershot, leading off South Atlantic Drive. (*Freda McKay*)

(Above) 'To the World a soldier, to us the World'; Ian's headstone in Aldershot Military Cemetery. (*Author*)

New memorial. Ian's name is inscribed on the fountain pool, inaugurated on 5 October 2011, in memory of Rotherham's three VC heroes in Clifton Park Memorial Gardens. Freda McKay lays a wreath in memory of her son. Ian's life and actions will not be forgotten. (*Chris Lawton/Yorkshire Post Newspapers*)

The McKay VC Trophy. Commissioned in 1983 in Ian's memory the silver trophy is awarded every year – when operational commitments allow - to the winners of 3 Para's inter-platoon military skills competition encapsulating the 'outstanding selflessness, perseverance and courage' exhibited by Ian during the Battle for Mount Longdon. (*Freda McKay*)

to a bunch of officers, including staff officers, he could raise it to their level. Also he would never patronise and he wouldn't be patronised either. He was his own man and he wouldn't allow people to speak down to him.[25]

On 11 May 1979 Ian heard that he had successfully passed his platoon sergeant's course, a date which, according to his service record, coincided with the first day of his second stint of duty with 3 Para in West Germany. It was whilst serving in West Germany for the second time that he was promoted to the rank of acting sergeant with effect from 1 November 1979, seven months after completing the course. This second posting to 3 Para would last eleven months before he bounced back to the UK again for the last time on 10 April 1980, almost exactly two years prior to the day when he would sail from Southampton for the Falklands on board the requisitioned cruise liner the SS *Canberra*.

During his posting in West Germany Ian had been able to indulge in many sports – tennis and squash with his company commander being amongst them – but football was his first love and he played as much as he could. Laurie Bland ran the A Company football team in Germany and he played with Ian both for the company and when they represented the battalion. Laurie Bland remembers his physique and his commitment:

A lot of people have the impression that Ian was tall but he wasn't –only about 5ft 6in or 5ft 7in but he had huge thighs and a huge heart – that was never in any doubt. We used to play the midfield together for the battalion and of course with his size, Ian had a kick on him like a mule. If Ian picked up a ball about 35 yards out you knew what was going to happen – he was going to have a 'poke'. He could conjure a goal from nothing from 30–35 yards and because he wasn't the thinnest of blokes you could see some of the opposition looking him up and down and thinking 'we'll be able to roast him' and then Ian picks [the ball] up and 'bang', next thing the ball would be in the back of the net and they'd be stunned. They'd just been 'Ian McKaye'. I remember one year we drew 2 Para in the Army Cup at football. They were in Berlin so we went to Berlin and then they left and were replaced by the Irish Rangers. Coincidentally the following year, 1979, we drew the Irish Rangers in the inter-battalion infantry cup. Because battalions [stationed] in Berlin are not allowed to leave, it meant another three day trip to Berlin for us. We had to go to Berlin by the British military train which ran through the corridor through East Germany and there's thousands of Russian tanks on both sides of the track, all 'mothballed'. But because it's the 'corridor' it's so meticulous who's allowed on it. Places had to be allocated so there were about fourteen footballers plus a few sponge men and helpers. We had to have brand new ID cards made. We had our battalion ties on and were under orders to be on best behaviour. So we went to Berlin and played the Irish Rangers and we drew and as we drew we said we'd have to stay another night and replay the game next day. Well they'd already laid on a session – a party – in the NAAFI after the game so rather than it go to waste they decided they'd hold it anyway [in spite of the replay] and if both teams got drunk at least they'd both be as bad the next morning! Ian had already been in Berlin with 1 Para so Ian's in the NAAFI with us [drinking] and it was getting to be 'game on'. One of the Sergeant Majors was a guy called Thor Caithness, an immense bloke who used to play in goal for us and he and some of the senior NCOs had arranged a trip to see the Berlin Wall. Thor came in and said 'right fellas we're going to see the Wall now' and we junior ranks – all the 'diehards' [who wanted to carry on drinking] said, 'well when you've seen one wall you've seen 'em all'. Thor Caithness then turned to Ian and said, 'Come on Ian you might as well come' and Ian said, 'It's alright sir, I've seen it before when I was here with 1 Para'. He was angling to stay with us. At that point Thor Caithness – who was not only a senior Sergeant but had been Ian's Company Sergeant Major for a time – looked Ian straight in the eyes and said, 'Sergeant McKay – The Wall'. It was like an order. He couldn't get out of it. As Ian got up to leave, we were all sniggering, 'Sergeant McKay, have a good trip won't you?'[26]

The remainder of 1980 and the whole of 1981 was spent in the UK and Ian moved in what appeared to be a hectic round of postings between the Depot and the companies of 3 Para. As the nation prepared to welcome in a new year at the end of 1981, the McKay household had more reason than most to celebrate New Year's Eve. Unlike most of the rest of the population of Britain, which saw the dawning of 1982 as reason enough to let their hair down, Ian had heard, that very day, some good news which would further enhance his career.

Although Ian's statement of service reveals that he had successfully completed his specialist qualification as a platoon sergeant on 11 May 1979, some two and a half years earlier, it also shows that he did not achieve the substantive rank of sergeant until 31 December 1981. However, he had been an acting sergeant long before that date. References in Pegasus, the Parachute Regiment journal, for 1980 and the early part of 1981 clearly show that he was known as 'Sergeant' McKay well before he gained his substantive rank a sure sign of an up and coming NCO with potential.

The round up of comings and goings for B Company of 3 Para in the April 1980 issue proclaimed that: 'B Company starts 1980 with new faces: Sgts Ian McKay and Steve Robbins, Cpls Al Stewart and John Ross. We also say good-bye to some old faithfuls: S/Sgt Brian Faulkner, Sgt Merriman, Cpl Norman Duggan and Pte David Maxwell.'[27]

'B Company [3 Para] has lost a few and gained a few since the last issue... Sgt McKay flashed in from A Company and then rushed off to the Depot.'[28]

An entry for April 1982 includes a gentle but good natured dig at Ian's constant need to train hard to 'fight the flab'. 'Depot the Parachute Regiment & Airborne Forces – Recruit Company. Sgt Andy Gow departed to 3 Para after two years of excellent work and Sgt Ian McKay from the Weapon Training Wing stepped into his waistline.'[29]

Ian had been given the acting rank of sergeant with effect from 1 November 1979, just over half way through what turned out to be his final posting to Germany and, as the entries in Pegasus show, he was being posted with some frequency both between companies of 3 Para and the Weapon Training Wing and Recruit Company at the Depot. This type of fluidity was, is, not uncommon for Junior NCOs wishing to advance their careers and hoping to become Senior NCOs. Men with aspirations to advance their army careers are not usually allowed to remain with the unit or sub-unit in which they have served on their promotion in the interests of gaining experience and developing their skills and qualities of leadership with an entirely different group of individuals. Postings to work with young recruits or as an instructor at the Depot also demonstrated that an individual possessed a particular set of skills, talents and qualities which the army was keen to foster. Instructing others and working with very young soldiers is not for everyone but there was little doubt that Ian had what the army was looking for.

Ian was busy working with the recruits at Brecon when the annual Past and Present SNCOs dinner was held at Aldershot. All serving SNCOs were required to attend but of course Ian could not. On his return Ian was presented with a bill for payment to the Sergeants Mess account – the bills being paid in bulk from Mess funds – which represented his share of the total cost of the dinner. Stung by what he saw as the sheer injustice of this scattergun approach to covering costs Ian went to see Ron Lewis, his old Company Sergeant Major from his days in Northern Ireland. Ron Lewis knew Ian McKay well and knew how to handle him:

> Sergeant McKay presented himself to my office with the claim that he was being unfairly treated as, at the time of the dinner he had been with his recruit platoon at the Battle School at Brecon and because of the tight training schedule was unable to attend. He was at pains to emphasize that it was not the cost but the principle that was at stake. I deliberated for several minutes, not wanting to create a precedent, and deciding that Sergeant McKay had a genuine grievance advised him to claim a refund from the Club Secretary WO1 Tony Walker.
>
> Alas the accounts for the 1981 dinner had been closed and audited. How should I refund Sergeant McKay? He was sent for and marched smartly into my office.
>
> I looked at him. 'Sergeant McKay, the accounts for the Past and Present Dinner are closed.' A look of disdain flashed momentarily across his face. He suspected a double cross. 'However, what I will do is leave your subscriptions in credit for the outstanding £8.00 and you won't have to pay next year. No comments? Good. Fall out.' And he was gone. It is now general knowledge why Sergeant Ian McKay was unable to attend the 1982 Past and Present Dinner and the club still owes him a meal. Maybe one day in that place where all Airborne Warriors go to 'Regroup' we'll meet and even if I can't buy him a meal at least I'll assure him the £8.00 had gone to a good cause helping to provide the reception drinks for his Senior NCO compatriots who returned from the Falklands in 1982.[30]

By the end of 1981 Ian had gained a wealth of experience and his promotion to substantive sergeant was most certainly a cause for celebration. Within weeks there were further good reports about the way in which Ian was working with and developing the young, eager and still impressionable soldiers in the Recruit Company at the Depot. The January 1982 issue of *Pegasus* included the following report, referring particularly to the Recruit Company: 'It is rare that a whole platoon is made up of juniors from Junior Parachute Company (JPC) but 477 Platoon has that distinction. Captain Alan Coulson and Sgt McKay are still dispelling any pre-conditioned thoughts the soldiers may have gained in Junior Company but the platoon is proving to be of a high standard.'[31]

Private Julian 'Baz' Barrett was one of those who had been an original member of the JPC, Junior Para, and now found himself under the tutelage of Ian McKay and it appeared that Ian had his work cut out:

> When we left 'Juniors' the cohort was split into two groups. People like Jason Thomas, Neil Grose, Ian Scrivens and Jason Burt went to 476 Platoon and their platoon commander was Neil Young who had been our Junior Para platoon commander.[32] The rest of them, which was more or less an entire Junior platoon, went to 477 under Andy Coulson and Ian McKay. There were a couple who had been 'back-squadded' [kept behind from a previous cohort for reason of sub-standard performance, misdemeanour or injury] but by and large it was a new approach whereby they took the remnants of 1, 2 and 3 Platoons of Junior Company, who had joined in September 1980 and passed out in August 1981, and put them into the Recruit Company en masse as 477 Platoon. I think it was experimental and I don't know whether they ever did it again. To be quite honest we weren't like the recruits who had just come in off the streets and thereby were more compliant, we'd learned the ropes a bit and Juniors, being the age they are, tend to be a bit cocky so there were a few problems. I know the platoon staff were certainly moaning about how cocky and arrogant we were.[33]

Laurie Bland had by then followed Ian back to the Depot and was a corporal instructor running a section in 476 Recruit Platoon at the same time:

> A corporal runs a section in a recruit platoon; the platoon commander and platoon sergeant run the platoon. The platoon sergeant, like Ian, is responsible for the administration but they invariably got involved in training as they had had so much experience. Ian had '477' and was the first sergeant in Recruit Company to have a full platoon of all junior soldiers and this was something relatively new. Of course [the Juniors] had some bad habits but they also had some knowledge as they had had a year's experience. Some of the Depot staff didn't like it as they thought that the Juniors came across as knowing it all. I used to love having junior soldiers in the recruit platoons at the depot because what it meant was that if I had them doing drill and one or two of them couldn't grasp it I would say to a couple [of ex-Juniors] 'get hold of those two clowns tonight and I want them up to standard in the morning', so they were more a help than a hindrance. Well, Ian had a full platoon of them. I wasn't with Ian but you see each other enough to pick up what other people are doing. The Depot was the best thing that happened to me. You start to become much more professional and start caring about people.[34]

Bob Hilton was a young paratrooper who found himself lumped together with the ex-Junior Para young guns like Baz Barrett in Ian McKay's 477 Platoon.

I did not pass 'P' Company (Pre-Parachute Selection Course) with 476 Platoon in the autumn of 1981. Although I had completed all events, I did not perform well enough nor gain the required points to pass. I was therefore 'back-squadded' to '477', the next platoon in training. This platoon was run by Captain Alan Coulson and Sergeant Ian McKay. It was entirely made up, originally, of ex-Junior Soldiers. As adult soldiers we would refer to them as the 'Red Imps' or the 'Hitler Youth'! The Platoon Commander, Lieutenant Coulson came across to us, as recruits, as utterly bonkers. He was forever swearing at recruits if they lagged behind on a run, or chasing them up the range if we were doing an 'advance to contact' shoot. Conversely, the Platoon Sergeant, Ian McKay, was a very 'steady character'. I never once heard him shout unnecessarily at a recruit or lose his temper. To my eyes, and most of the recruits, he typified the upright, fit and steady Senior NCO that we had all come to expect of the Senior Staff in the Depot. 477 Platoon proved to be a bit of a problem platoon. Having joined Recruit Company 'en masse' they went a bit wild and got into trouble in Guildford one Saturday night. They were paraded on the balloon square, several of them sporting black eyes, cuts and abrasions, and given a right 'royal' tongue lashing by Sergeant Major Sean Lucey. Several of them were 'back-squadded' at that point and ended up in 478 Platoon.[35]

Even as a Junior and before he had joined Ian McKay's 477 Platoon, Baz Barrett remembered looking across the barrack square at Aldershot from his billet and assessing the performance of the instructors – mentally noting those he hoped he would get as well as those he hoped he wouldn't:

When I was in [Junior Para] I was in Browning Barracks and it was organised so that there were two blocks full of Juniors and two blocks full of recruits. I used to look across at the platoon staff as we were very interested in what platoon staff we were going to get. Obviously they were going to be your mentors and you'd be working with them on a daily basis. You'd see a lot of ferocious, noisy and overtly aggressive section commanders and platoon sergeants always rollicking and battering their platoons into shape and quite frequently you'd look over and think, 'I hope we don't get him' but with Ian McKay, not once when he was out on the square with his platoon did you hear him raise his voice. He did not have an ascetic and overtly aggressive manner to him like an awful lot of them did. I was very pleased that we were going to go to his platoon. I didn't know him from Adam really at that time, only by sight, but he gave me that impression from afar that he wasn't as aggressive as other staff and when I got to the recruit platoon that was the case. He was far calmer, logical and would address the platoon as a group in a far more understanding way. He wasn't a 'barker', in fact his voice, with his South Yorkshire accent to it, had quite a soothing, calming effect and you never felt you were being bollocked by Ian McKay. He was a reasonable guy. He would always give a reason as to why we should do something. He was deadly serious about what he wanted to do and he was extremely encouraging. We, as a Junior platoon, led them a merry dance and the section commanders were always getting a grip of us but obviously within the platoon structure Ian McKay and Alan Coulson were very, very mindful of the job that they were undertaking. We were always in a lot of trouble being Juniors; always up to something but if he found any of the incidents genuinely funny he would, if not be lenient, share part of the joke and have a chuckle with it. As a platoon sergeant I found him easy going both in the Recruit Platoon and, later in 6 Platoon [of B Company 3 Para]. You would appreciate it but not overstep the mark.[36]

Ian's approach to discipline was also studied and thoughtful and designed for maximum impact as Baz Barrett testified:

I don't want to give the impression that he wasn't capable of giving punishment because he was more than capable of dishing out the discipline but what he would do was to serve it cold rather than being hot-headed. He could and did give bollockings if they were needed of course but it was far more thoughtful. In many ways when his discipline came it was more effective rather than him ranting and raving about it. The other thing was that in administering discipline in the way he did, the recruit or soldier couldn't get angry so there could be no animosity towards McKay and consequently they would feel the full weight of the punishment. He wanted us to think about it. He didn't want a hot-headed scene where there was lots of noise, lots of shouting and screaming, lots of bollockings and at the end of the day the lesson wasn't learned. That wasn't his approach. His approach consistently and without deviation was, 'look, shit happens, let's learn from it and take it forward'. It is only my opinion – a personal point of view of course – but I always thought Ian McKay was a sensitive sort of fellow.[37]

Private Steve Tuffen, 18, was another member of 477 Platoon who had been one of the Junior Para originals, like Baz Barrett:

I had been a boy soldier as member of Junior Parachute Company along with others, some only 17-years-old, who were finally posted to B Company of 3 Para like Jason Burt, Neil Grose, Ian Scrivens, Mark Thomas and 'Baz' Barrett. Jason, Neil, Ian and Mark went into 446 Recruit Platoon but I was 'back squadded' because I injured myself during jump training at Brize Norton so I joined 477 Recruit Platoon. They had already done a lot of training and had already done what the Parachute Regiment calls 'Advanced Brecon' – training on the Brecon Beacons. 477 Platoon was very unusual in that we had a Captain, Captain Alan Coulson, as our platoon commander. Recruit platoons usually had a lieutenant in command. I remember Ian McKay as a very 'genteel' platoon sergeant. It seems odd to say that of a Para sergeant but that's exactly the right word to describe him. Back then 'beasting' – physical bullying – was still part and parcel of army life. I'd been punched and gripped by the throat, usually by a corporal, by the time I joined Ian McKay's recruit platoon. As a young 'crow' in the Paras you didn't like being 'beasted' but it was something that you accepted in order to achieve what you wanted to achieve and that was to earn the red beret and become a real Para. But Ian McKay was different. He achieved his goals by example rather than resorting to beating the crap out of you. His attitude was 'if you want to earn the red beret, then it's up to you'. He was always prepared to do more for us youngsters. He nurtured us and brought us on that way. That's not to say that he was soft. He could be very firm but he was always very fair. Take room inspections for example. If Captain Coulson had had to have a word that one of the rooms wasn't up to standard, Sergeant McKay would let us know in no uncertain terms that he wanted this, this and this done but there was never any physical side to it. He got on and did the job and he got us to do it as well. I really looked up to him. He was a brilliant platoon sergeant. It's strange but in one way, when I heard what he eventually did in the Falklands I couldn't see it as the action of such a quiet man but in another way I wasn't surprised at all because that was exactly what he would have done – leading his boys by example, urging them to get on and do their jobs. I still think of the man with the utmost affection and you don't do that with men who 'beasted you'. He really was the quiet hero.[38]

Steve Tuffen passed out from 477 Recruit Platoon in early 1982 and was posted to Lieutenant Coe's 2 Platoon, A Company of 2 Para. During his battalion's attack on Darwin/Goose Green on 28 May 1982, Steve was shot in the head – a fist-sized hole is how he described it to the author – and seriously wounded within 50m of where his commanding officer, Lieutenant Colonel 'H' Jones, would, a short time later, charge an Argentine trench only to be cut down by a single bullet from another. Jones would have had to have run within feet of Tuffen's wounded body on his approach to the Argentine trench he had set his mind on eliminating. Tuffen had already served as a recruit with one man whose actions during the Falklands War would earn him a posthumous VC and, as he lay unattended for some four hours on the lower slopes of Darwin Hill, drifting in and out of consciousness, the body of another would lay lifeless, just metres away on the steep bank of a narrow re-entrant.

Baz Barrett passed out at the same time as Steve Tuffen and was posted to 6 Platoon, B Company of 3 Para and found himself at Candahar Barracks in Tidworth towards the end of February 1982. Now part of a battalion at last his training began in earnest and he was delighted to see that Ian had also been posted from the Depot to be the platoon sergeant of 6 Platoon in B Company of 3 Para.

We had him from the beginning of March 1982 and went down to Hythe and Lydd to do our Northern Ireland training and Ian was the 6 Platoon Sergeant at that point. I don't know why as Pete Gray had been the Platoon Sergeant in January 1982. Maybe he went on a course or something but Ian McKay took over and he was with us for about 3 or 4 weeks at the most then Pete Gray came back into 6 Platoon and Ian was moved to 4 Platoon. Ian was certainly with us for March and halfway through our Hythe and Lydd training. There we were on one of the ranges and we had to give radio checks about 'contacts' as if we were on the streets in Northern Ireland. I was with a number of lads who were a bit older than me and were a little more experienced and of course on the other end of the line there were SNCOs like Sammy Dougherty and Ian McKay. None of the other lads wanted to give them the specific radio 'contact' because it's a very rule-bound thing and you can get rollocked for it if it's not given properly. Anyway I got the radio shoved under my nose and sent a basic radio message back about the 'contact' that we had had and I heard Ian McKay distinctly saying to Sammy 'Doc' 'he's one of mine, he's one of mine'. He patted me on the back afterwards. He wanted to know why the others weren't confident about giving the radio check so we had a little debrief about that and he told us not to worry too much about the rules but to make sure we got the message across. Now it wasn't anything brilliant that I'd done, it was just the fact that I had done what was required and to me that highlighted how seriously he took his job in training up the blokes to get into the 'Reg'. He was always encouraging and took pride in the successes of the people he had trained. With Ian he always seemed more sensitive. He was always happy to hand out praise, however low key that might be, and he was always encouraging when something went right. So he was a sensitive bloke, very conscientious about the training of his troops and the standards of troops under his command.[39]

So for Ian McKay, hugely respected by subordinates and superiors alike and demonstrably successful in a range of roles within the Parachute Regiment, 1982 had appeared to get off to a flying start and indeed held the promise of further success to come. But at the age of 28 the year of 1982 would be his last. Just a few weeks later, on 19 March and even as Ian had been congratulating Baz Barrett on his modest achievements on the south coast of England, a group of forty-one Argentine scrap metal merchants, led by Senor Constantino Sergio Davidoff, strode ashore at Leith on the island of South Georgia, a British dependency in the South Atlantic Ocean, some 8,000 miles away, ostensibly to fulfil a contract to dismantle the rusting whaling station there. It was their second visit and on both occasions they had pointedly breached formal entry procedures by thumbing their noses at the need to have their entry visas stamped at the small British base at Grytviken, thirty miles away to the southeast. At Leith they raised and saluted the Argentine flag and discharged weapons in an act of brazen provocation, although Davidoff later claimed that the shots had been fired at a reindeer.

South Georgia was half a world away from Ian's life as a sergeant instructor at the Depot, half a world away from his cherished family life in the Married Quarters, now at Salamanca Park, half a world away from his games of squash, tennis and football, but the presence of Davidoff's Argentines was the spark which lit the fuse for Britain to become embroiled in its first major conflict since the end of the Korean War.

Despite the fact that most of Davidoff's team of scrap metal merchants re-embarked on 21 March, a dozen stayed put. Exasperated by Davidoff's actions, the British Government had already ordered Captain Nick Barker of HMS *Endurance*, the Antarctic Protection vessel and Falkland Islands guard ship, to make for South Georgia and, if necessary, evict the rump of Davidoff's party.

Barker arrived at Grytviken on 24 March and landed twenty-two Royal Marines almost at the same time as another Argentine vessel docked at Leith and disgorged more than 100 Marines and supplies under the command of Lieutenant Commander Alfredo Astiz. The Argentine Navy had also responded with alacrity and deployed warships in what appeared to be turning into some colossal game of maritime chess, in order to 'protect their citizens'. Captain Barker, an old South Atlantic hand – who had reported to the Admiralty as early as 25 January that, 'the Argies were up to something' – wisely stayed offshore and on 26 March began playing cat and mouse with two Argentine frigates deep in the watery wastes of the Southern Ocean. The clock was running.

Back in Whitehall, the British Government was not really prepared for a war. Despite hard intelligence that the Argentine Navy's only carrier and submarines were at sea, despite reports that Argentine aircraft were on alert, that a Marine battalion was embarked and a SEAL team were bearing down on Port Stanley the Falkland Islands capital, Whitehall's Latin American Current Intelligence Group blithely advised Margaret Thatcher that the Argentines were only sabre rattling and that no invasion was imminent. It was a miscalculation of breathtaking proportions.

On 2 April 1982, Argentine Marine Infantry, supported by Marines of the Amphibious Commando Group, poured ashore near Port Stanley shortly after 6.00 am and after a brief skirmish captured the tiny Royal Marine garrison which was outnumbered ten to one and without any fire support. The Falkland Islands Governor, Sir Rex Hunt, formally surrendered Government House at 9.30am. The images of the surrendered British Royal Marines, face down in the dirt on Ross Road with black balaclava-clad Argentine Commandos pointing rifles at them, sent shock waves round the world and shook the foundations of the Palace of Westminster.

But it was not just the British who had miscalculated. Faced by an angry House of Commons baying for blood, Prime Minister Margaret Thatcher did the only thing she could to ensure her government's survival. Buoyed up by the counsel of the First Sea Lord, Sir Henry Leach – who, cynics said, seized a chance to save his beloved Royal Navy from Defence Secretary John Nott's defence cuts – the 'Iron Lady' elected to make a fight of it. Within a week a Task Force had sailed, with orders to regain the Falklands for the British Crown, by force if necessary.

As a dedicated, highly trained and professional paratrooper with more than ten years of experience behind him, Ian McKay would have been well aware of the force that could be applied should his battalion ever be called upon to go into action. As a servant of the state, he had undertaken to defend and protect the sovereignty of Britain and its subjects and, if required, to fight in order to do so. In August 1914 the men of the British Army had been sent to war over 'a scrap of paper', in April 1982, their descendents would be sent to war over an incident concerning 'scrap metal'. It would be a war in which Ian McKay, the professional soldier and mild-mannered, quietly spoken, family man from South Yorkshire, would perform an act of calculated bravery and self-sacrifice for which his name would be remembered for ever.

CHAPTER EIGHT

'Whatever Our Destination May Be'

In a calculated show of strength, which had more to do with press and PR considerations than the hard facts of military reality, the first ships of the British Task Force – the aircraft carriers *Hermes* and *Invincible* – sailed from Portsmouth just three days after the Argentine capture of Port Stanley, against a backdrop of feverish diplomatic activity. Primarily a naval effort at that stage, the Task Force was cobbled together without any real staff appreciation of the force levels, resources and logistics required to undertake the mission at hand and see it through to a successful completion.

Indeed, few actually envisaged a real shooting war. The swift and undoubtedly rushed departure of the carriers was meant as an unequivocal signal that Britannia could still, and indeed would, brandish her Trident. Primarily intended for the *Junta* in Buenos Aires, but also aimed at any of Britain's array of protagonists who might be vying for a place at the top table of international relations, the message was clear: Britain would respond and respond with force.

Within a week of the high visibility departure of Britain's aircraft carriers, the first units of the land-based element of the Task Force sailed from Southampton. Naval and air power were essential to the mission but barring a diplomatic settlement or an Argentine withdrawal the British would eventually have to get 'boots ashore' in order to retake, clear and consolidate the islands. That would necessitate an amphibious assault the like of which had not been attempted by Britain, acting unilaterally, since the Second World War. Given the nature of the task ahead, 3 Commando Brigade Royal Marines, (40, 42 and 45 Commandos) under Brigadier Julian Thompson were at the core of the land element. Two battalions of the Parachute Regiment, the 2nd Battalion (2 Para), then on five days notice to move, and its sister unit, 3 Para, then acting in the role of 'Spearhead' and ready for swift deployment, were extracted from the newly-formed 5 Brigade and attached to 3 Commando Brigade. These five units, along with the Special Air Service (SAS) and Special Boat Squadron (SBS) were, in 1982, probably the most highly trained, efficient and physically conditioned troops in the British Army. Their reputation as tough, professional, highly motivated and experienced troops – almost all the men, with a few notable exceptions, had, like Ian McKay, seen active service in Northern Ireland – was recognized and respected worldwide.

Having assumed the role of the Parachute Regiment's Spearhead battalion in late March, 3 Para had been expecting a posting to Northern Ireland over the Easter period. It came as some surprise, therefore, that at 5.00pm on 2 April a phone call from Brigadier Ayrey of UK Land Forces to Lieutenant Colonel Pike – taken by Major

Stratton, his then Second in Command during his absence on leave – asked whether the battalion was 'absolutely ready to go?' Major Stratton said it was, even though many men had taken advantage of a period of leave before the expected posting and had managed to get away. In fact the battalion strength stood at a little over 50 per cent. The exchange convinced Adjutant, Captain Kevin McGimpsey, that the battalion was due to become involved in something far bigger than anything it had been involved in for a generation and determined to record it for posterity. On that day, on his own initiative, he started to write up the Commander's War Diary.

Contact was made with Lieutenant Colonel Pike and just over an hour later he gave the order to initiate Exercise Fastball – the recall of the battalion to standby for deployment to the Falkland Islands as part of Operation Corporate, 'forming one body of many individuals'.[1]

Within minutes Fastball was living up to its name as the pace of events began to accelerate. Major Mike Argue, Officer Commanding (OC) B Company, the battalion's lead element, had already been told to keep his men fully informed, while the Intelligence Officer, Lieutenant Giles Orpen-Smellie, hurriedly began to compile a Falkland Islands brief. Major Martin Osborne, then OC HQ Company but shortly to become OC C Company, was ordered to contact British Rail Police to display recall chalk boards at all major main line stations. Eager to do their bit in the nation's hour of need, instead of erecting simple blackboards emblazoned with the single code word 'Candahar', the Transport Police hit upon the idea of using the very public station tannoy systems to inform any members of 3 Para loitering on station platforms to return to camp with the consequence that by 9.00pm a journalist from the Daily Mail was on the phone asking what 3 Para was up to? Three minutes later the Tidworth Garrison switchboard became jammed with the number of outgoing calls recalling members of the battalion and the harassed operators had to call upon the services of a member of the signals platoon to help out. Some of the men took the recall so seriously that they went to extreme lengths in their efforts to get back to Tidworth. Private Early of A Company heard the news while relaxing into his seat on the London to Edinburgh express and responded by pulling the communication cord to stop the train, while Private Burns flagged down and commandeered a police patrol car![2] At the Intelligence Centre in Ashford, Kent, two Parachute Regiment sergeants on a selection course to transfer to the Intelligence Corps simply drove away and rejoined the Parachute Depot, only to be told by a slightly embarrassed adjutant that technically they were guilty of desertion!

Company Sergeant Major (CSM) John Weeks of B Company and his two para passengers were blithely unaware of all the commotion Fastball was causing as they drove home to Aldershot from Candahar Barracks that evening. All three were members of the Sergeant's Mess and since Ian McKay and the other man also lived in Aldershot, it had seemed sensible for John Weeks to offer Ian and his fellow sergeant a lift home. Ian had only returned to the battalion a few weeks previously, his arrival being noted by 3 Para's RSM Lawrie Ashbridge.

As I remember Ian he was a bit of footballer. I did watch him play a few times. I remember I saw him playing for 1 Para [against 3 Para] and he was pretty good.

That irked me somewhat because I'm a football fanatic. I believe Ian was one of the shortfall guys who came to us just before we went. When Ian McKay turned up from the Depot and came in late – and remember he wasn't one of ours originally so I hadn't had that much to do with him – still, in the dealings I had had with him, it was clear he knew exactly where I was coming from. He quickly knitted in and I knew he was a guy I could talk to. There were quite a few like that in his platoon. Hedges was one and Goreing another.'[3]

Corporal Ian Bailey, a young and intelligent section commander in Lieutenant Mark Cox's 5 Platoon, and a man who would become integral to piecing together Ian's last moments on Mount Longdon, also recalled that 4 Platoon had some very seasoned junior NCOs, men from whom Ian would have to earn respect.

In the early days, when you went away from the battalion you came back to it. There were no inter-battalion postings. Then they began to open up the experience, more so after the Falklands but it happened a little before then with the odd move, like Ian moving across from 1 Para to 3 Para. During these moves the men would take some time to settle because of the inter-battalion rivalry. Ian was in 4 Platoon and again the hierarchy was very much Officers' Mess, Sergeants' Mess, Corporals' Mess, the Toms, that's how it was and Ian came into 4 Platoon with some very strong corporals; Brian Milne, 'Ned' Kelly and John Lewis, all good soldiers – long serving 3 Para soldiers – who didn't give him a hard time but could have because all the people there were staunch 3 Para people. They were 26, 27, 28, nearly the same age as Ian and certainly 'Ned' was looking for promotion himself. After the Falklands there were more inter-battalion postings as people moved around to spread the experience. I served in all three battalions for example. After I left 3 Para in 1995 I never went back but I'd spent fifteen years with them. A lot didn't like that because they wanted to go back into their own niche. So when Ian came in he came in as an outsider. Also remember that B Company had just been away for over a month to Oman on Exercise Rocky Lance so the company had gelled and Ian had missed that. He came to us as we went to Thetford on exercise and then we came back to Tidworth waiting for Easter leave and, in my case, waiting to go on my education course for sergeant but then, of course, we got the call.

Now, as CSM John Weeks drove home from Tidworth all three sergeants were a little weary. While many of their 3 Para comrades had been on leave it had fallen to B Company, as the battalion lead element, to be on duty acting as the rear party at Tidworth. As the men chatted and passed the time on the journey all were looking forward to their turn of fourteen days leave and to seeing their families after a week kicking their heels in barracks while the rest of the battalion had been off enjoying themselves. Arriving in Aldershot, John pulled up outside Ian and Marica's house at 5, Salamanca Park. It was built on the site of the old Salamanca Central Infantry Barracks, erected between 1856 and 1859 and demolished in 1961 to make way for the new married quarters which, in turn, have now disappeared to be replaced by new housing. John Weeks had often driven past the Salamanca Park area and caught sight of Ian out playing football or some other game with Donny and Melanie, running around and enjoying himself just like one of the children.

Ian got his kit out of the boot and said his goodbyes and John drove off to go home. He remembers vividly what happened next.

> I got out of the car, slung my bergan on my back and began walking down the path. I heard the phone ringing before I even got to the door but I got in, dropped my bergan on the floor and answered it and the voice on the other end just said, 'Candahar' – nothing else – and put the phone down. That was the code word that meant we had been recalled. I rang Ian immediately and said, 'I hope you haven't unpacked your bag. Have you had the phone call?' He said his wife had just picked it up and was shouting at him. I told him I'd be round to pick him up in five minutes. He complained a bit and said we'd only just got back and could we at least have an hour or two before we set off but I told him we had to go. I just picked my bergan up off the floor, went straight out and threw it in the boot of the car again. I never even saw my wife, she was out at work. Ian rang the other guy who had come back with us and I picked them both up and we drove all the way back to Candahar Barracks. I'd just done ten days as duty warrant officer and I was really peed off at going back as I hadn't been home at all but I think we were all cheesed off.[4]

Marica's obvious frustration at Ian's enforced and speedy departure was perhaps understandable given that she would have been looking forward to having her husband at home to spend some quality time together as a family. 'In the army there are no explanations just orders,' she commented later, 'and that rule applies to the families too. The Argentines had invaded, the men were sent to sort it out, and there was never any time to explain why.[5] He came in and went out' Marica told me. 'I put his dinner in a Tupperware container and he went straight away. He just said "I've got to go." I never saw him again.'

Even the most cursory perusal of Lieutenant Colonel Pike's Battalion Commander's War Diary for the next seven days reveals a head-spinning litany of orders, signals, 'phone calls in and out and requests for essential equipment, sufficient ammunition and rations as 3 Para prepared for war. It was perhaps politic that the view of UK Land Forces as conveyed to and recorded by the Adjutant, Captain Kevin McGimpsey that, '3 Para is presently "peanuts" and that we are right at the bottom of the list of priorities', was not widely broadcast to the rank and file.

The 637 men of 3 Para (a dozen or so other 3 Para men found berths aboard the *Elk*) and most of the rest of 3 Commando Brigade eventually sailed from Southampton on board the 45,000 ton requisitioned cruise liner *Canberra* – to become known affectionately as The Great White Whale – on Good Friday, 9 April, amidst emotional scenes on the quaysides not witnessed for decades. Two hundred men of 3 Para dressed in 'beret, smock, belt and shoes' lined the ship along the games deck stretching from aft near the Lido swimming pool along the port side, while the band of 3 Para and Band of the Royal Marines played a rendition of what has now become a Rod Stewart classic as the *Canberra* slipped her cables at 9.00pm. It was always bound to be an emotionally charged moment and the men had great support from their loved ones; particularly some of the wives who had travelled from Tidworth to see them off. Marica was not present, not because she did not want to go but because the swift departure took her by surprise. 'I didn't realize he would go so quickly,' she later conceded.

Alf Walton, Chairman of the Southampton branch of the Parachute Regiment Association (PRA), had also been travelling down to 106 Berth of the Western Docks since 7 April to meet some of the Paras as a practical demonstration of his branch's support for their coming trials. He was there again on the evening of 9 April as the *Canberra* prepared to set sail. 'I'm sure that most of 3 Para thought that once they were on the transport for Southampton Docks it would be a long time before they were to see their families again,' he recalled. 'I was glad that some of them had the opportunity to see their wives and children again for a short time in the passenger reception at 106 Berth where the bars were open for a beer until they were ordered on board at around 17.30. Many more of the troops did not get this chance but I know that they were glad that some of their mates had this last opportunity to hug and kiss their wives and kids before they sailed away to who knows what… The combined bands of the Parachute Regiment and Royal Marines played on the quay for some time… The crowds on the quay waving their Union Jacks and slogans of all kinds telling Argentina what to do with their corned beef! Just as it was beginning to get dark the great white ship slipped away from the quay to the tune *We Are Sailing* and the cheers and tears from the crowd stopped for a few minutes and it was almost silent. Then once again came the cheers from the crowds that lined the quays on Southampton Docks and all along the shores of Southampton Water, many more than were sailing away, all sending their love and hopes and best wishes for a safe return to those being taken away. In their hearts the unanswered question, will I see him again?'[6]

Whole blocks of flats flashed their lights in unison as the ship eased away from the docks and police cars, lights flashing, kept pace with the ship all along Southampton Water while ships sounded their sirens to be answered by *Canberra*'s deep throated roar.

Ian had the good fortune to be allocated a cabin with Colour Sergeant Brian Faulkner, a man whom he had known for many years and with whom he got on well. Brian had already been aboard the *Canberra* for several days and therefore knew the ropes. Brian had, in fact, joined the *Canberra* – then at Gibraltar and filled with paying customers on the last leg of their cruising holiday – as early as 4 April, along with Air Adjutant Captain Bob Darby after an order had come in from 3 Commando Brigade HQ to send an officer and senior NCO to reconnoitre the ship. Brian Faulkner's feet did not touch terra firma again until he hit the beach at San Carlos on East Falkland almost seven weeks later.

As Assistant Air Adjutant to Captain Bob Darby – our role in the battalion was the acquisition and planning of any airborne operation, we had to liaise with the RAF for example, to make sure we had enough aircraft to lift the men involved – we left Tidworth in early April to commandeer the *Canberra* along with Royal

Marines Major Bob Ward and two Royal Marine Commando Colour Sergeants, Surgeon Commander Rick Jolly and the Deputy Captain of the *Canberra*, 'Sam' Bradford.

> Although we weren't going by air our job was still to requisition the transport. During the interim period we were put into the Rock Hotel on Gibraltar and told to shut up, keep quiet and not come out of our rooms except for eating. During the dark hours that evening we went down to the docks and were taken out on a small boat into the middle of the Mediterranean where we saw this rather large ship with all the lights glittering, a city in the middle of the ocean – a fantastic sight – and then we scrambled up the nets through the hull and were taken to the captain's cabin where we formally issued him with the letter of requisition.[7]

The requisition party's task was to make sure the accommodation on *Canberra* was prepared ready for the embarkation of the troops, with a further plan that she be turned into a hospital ship once the troops had left. 'We sailed back for three or four days on the final part of *Canberra's* world cruise. We couldn't divulge who we were even though the passengers had been on it for ninety-eight days or so and suddenly six new faces appeared all dressed in 'civvies'. The only stage that the passengers knew that there were troops on board was at breakfast on the morning we landed in Southampton when we turned out in smock and denims and the commando lads were in their gear, only then the people on board realised who we were.'

The comedian Tom O'Connor had been doing shows as part of the cabaret on board and Brian remembered he had made a joke one night about the fact that they had made this unscheduled stop and that the people who had been taken on board were Special Forces coming to requisition the ship for the troops to go south. At that time no-one except the captain knew anything of the future plans for the liner and the irony of O'Connor's unscripted joke was not lost on Faulkner. Even so, it put the wind up the experienced colour sergeant at the time who fretted over the fact that the word might have got out.

Brian Faulkner and Ian McKay were friends. Both were Yorkshiremen who had been born and brought up in the old West Riding just thirteen miles away from each other as the crow flies and in very similar surroundings. Ian, a Rotherham man raised in an area dominated by the coal and steel industries and Brian, a native of South Elmsall, one of a string of tight-knit mining communities in the heart of the Yorkshire coalfield, had an affinity with each other:

> I first met Ian when I was on a posting from 3 Para down to the Para Depot at Browning Barracks, Aldershot as a weapon training instructor during the first half of 1976. At that time Ian was officially in the 1st Battalion and he had been posted to Depot Para as a lance corporal along with me to go to one of the recruit platoons. That was where I got to know him in the respect that he had to bring the young recruits to the training wing where several of us then delivered the weapon training – SLR, SMG, GPMG, 84s, 66s and pistols – the whole thing, as we had all qualified as instructors at Warminster. Ian and other instructors

trained the recruits on the physical side, while we did the weapons. I knew of his history as a footballer and he was an outstanding footballer, having represented 1 Para. We became friends from then on. Then in 1977 I was promoted and posted back to 3 Para then stationed in Osnabrück in Germany. Ian joined us out there as a senior rank himself and came out with his wife and family. Being in the Mess we got on together because we knew each other from our time at the Depot.[8]

Brian then lost contact with Ian due to various postings until their paths crossed again at Tidworth just before 3 Para left for the Falklands. By then Ian had been posted back to 3 Para and had taken on a platoon sergeant's role in Lieutenant Andrew Bickerdike's 4 Platoon; the first of three platoons in Major Mike Argue's B Company.

Ian and Brian lugged their gear into Cabin D17 on *Canberra*'s D Deck, a three-berth, inside cabin with no porthole or window but which at least boasted its own shower and toilet. It was Brian Faulkner's second cabin. Unfortunately the one he had chosen initially had itself been requisitioned by higher authorities and the only perk of his being part of the requisition party had slipped through his fingers. 'I had chosen a nice room for myself initially and thought it was out of the way but eventually people started to ask why a colour sergeant had a nice room up at the front on his own and told me that the room had to go to a Sergeant Major or an officer, so myself, Ian and a chap called Ray Butters, who was the Physical Training Instructor from the Army Physical Training Corps, were put into a cabin together and we shared it up until a week before we transferred across to the Assault Landing Ship *Intrepid* prior to the landings on the Falklands.'[9]

The addition of Harrogate-born Sergeant Ray Butters, a committed athlete and member of the outstanding 3 Para running team which, by the end of March 1982, had become the first Army Major Unit to hold the coveted top three army running trophies, brought the number of Yorkshiremen in cabin D 17 to three. Attached to battalion headquarters, Ray Butters would be Lieutenant Colonel Hew Pike's personal runner during the coming campaign.

Ian's initial impressions of the jewel in P&O's crown were not positive. In his first message from the *Canberra*, hastily penned on the back of a colour picture postcard of the ship and sent to his family but addressed to his mother and father at their then family home at 87, Briery Walk, Munsborough in Rotherham, Ian wrote:

MUM, DAD, NEAL, GRAHAM & SUE
Externally she looks nice enough but it's quite grotty under the white paint & fitted carpets. I certainly wouldn't pay to feel hot all day in slightly cramped, uncomfortable surroundings. Mind you the cabin I am in would cost £5,000 per person for 90 days & the food is different to that I am used to. If only we could stop working so hard I could spend a little time enjoying the benefits. All my love, Ian.[10]

There is evidence to suggest that that first postcard from the *Canberra* was written in haste to get it in the post in time for a helicopter mail lift at midday the day following the departure from Southampton. 'Grotty' might have been an apt word given that an infestation of cockroaches had already been reported to Adjutant Captain Kevin McGimpsey and RSM Lawrie Ashbridge at a ship's administration meeting held in the Crystal Room prior to the ship sailing. It was imperative, they were told, that the ship be kept clean.

By the time the helicopter had whisked Ian's postcard off the ship and back to England *Canberra* was already forty miles of the coast of Brittany and making steady progress towards the Bay of Biscay. And by that time, as Ian had intimated, 3 Para were already hard at work training for war.

Lieutenant Andrew Bickerdike was the 4 Platoon OC and the man Ian answered to as his immediate superior. It would be up to these two men, in concert with their experienced junior NCOs, to bring the platoon up to a high degree of efficiency, a task which would be rendered much more difficult in the coming weeks due to the constraints of going to war on a cruise liner.

It is fair to say that Ian and Andrew Bickerdike did not know each other extremely well. Both men were relative latecomers to B Company and particularly to 4 Platoon, although Ian had, of course, served with 3 Para previously. That said, they were both professional soldiers, both committed paratroopers and ultimately their relationship was rooted in the planning for and execution of a serious job of work as *Canberra* steamed steadily southward. As they buckled down and began to establish their respective roles neither could know that their fates were to become forever fused in the heat of battle on an inhospitable mountainside 8,000 miles from home just a few weeks later.

Ian's platoon commander had always wanted to join the Parachute Regiment but had been advised whilst still at school to join a county regiment due to rumours of force reductions. After attending the Royal Military Academy at Sandhurst, at which establishment he had been sponsored jointly by The Queen's Regiment and the Parachute Regiment, Andrew Bickerdike had been commissioned into the Queen's. He went on to serve with 1/Queen's in Germany for two years before returning to the Depot. Whilst he was at the Depot Andrew Bickerdike decided he had done three years and that the time was right to request a secondment to the Paras. He recalled that at that time, 'secondments were really only meant for non-infantry attachment – REME, Military Police whatever – so people could be attached to a parachute battalion for six months having done their wings and all the rest of it, just to get their infantry experience. So I was being a bit unusual in that I was already infantry trained – I was wanting a bit more than that. We managed to wangle it because my company commander at the Depot was a very good friend of the Parachute Regimental Adjutant at the time. So in 1981 I went off and did 'P' Company – managed to injure myself first time by smashing my leg up, hobbled through a second time but passed – did my Para course at Brize Norton in November '81 and at the beginning of January [1982] was posted to 3 Para.'[11]

At the time there was a little juggling going on amongst the officers as men were posted out and others came in to take their place.

When I arrived, Hew Pike was CO and I was posted as 2i/c A Company, whose company commander then was a chap called Tony Clarke. Tony Clarke was out on posting around March and his replacement was to be David Collett and there was a gap between Tony Clarke leaving on his next posting and Dave Collett arriving so I was actually OC A Company for something daft like a week and did the hand over to Dave Collett when he arrived. Then I was his 2i/c for the month of March. Then when the Falklands thing blew up Hew Pike could begin to get his battalion up to establishment as we were fairly thin on the ground what with postings and courses and all the usual palaver and of course the rank structure wasn't quite right. So Adrian Freer was posted back in on return to the battalion as a senior captain to be 2i/c A Company under Dave Collett and I was moved to B Company to take command of 4 Platoon. So I arrived in B Company with Mike Argue as OC, Captain Logan as 2i/c with Johnny Weeks as CSM. Ian McKay was Platoon Sergeant of 4 Platoon. I had had no time with the platoon prior to the 'balloon going up' so I really got to know the platoon and Sergeant McKay – who was acting platoon commander at the time I think, having only recently come back to the battalion from the Depot – and we were all thrown together on board *Canberra* on the way down after the Argentines had invaded. It was a real 'workup' trying to get to know all these new personalities. All the way down it was work and it was a case of Sergeant McKay and myself getting to know each other.[12]

Andrew Bickerdike was in no doubt that he had acquired the best kind of soldier to be his second-in-command and right-hand man. 'He was what I'd call a typical Para sergeant. He was a good disciplinarian; tough – he had done Depot time – and had accrued quite a lot of experience by then. At the age of 28, he'd already had about twelve years in the regiment so he was a very experienced paratrooper with tours in Northern Ireland and was very good at pulling the platoon together. The men respected him. They recognized he had the seniority, that he was not a two-minute wonder. He was a good, solid para.'

Ian also proved to be very supportive of Andrew Bickerdike, in so far as any relationship between platoon commanders and platoon sergeants went. 'He'd always say that it was *his* platoon – officers are just thrown in for a bit of light relief – a change of scene! The usual form! But I knew that if there was anything to be done and I asked him to do it, then it was done. It was also very fortunate for us all that he had three very good section commanders as well in Corporal Brian Milne – 1 Section, Corporal 'Ned' Kelly – 2 Section and Corporal John Lewis in charge of 3 Section.'

Captain Bob Darby remembered Ian as a pleasant lad.

He had the respect of the men. He was a blue-eyed boy and was going to progress; there was no question about that. He was competent, very competent and he got on well with everybody. He was the sort of guy that people like John Weeks, his sergeant major respected, as did Mike Argue his commanding officer in B Company. He was that type of an individual. I did come across him on the ranges a few times and I found him very easy going. A platoon sergeant like Ian McKay would command an integral unit of three sections within the platoon. He had an officer as platoon commander, in Ian's case Lieutenant Andrew Bickerdike, but often sergeants led the platoon, generally 30–35 men if you were up to strength, so it was a sizeable command. Firepower in those days would have been three GPMGs and his riflemen, so Andrew Bickerdike and Ian would have had a significant amount of influence on what was going on in a battle. And as we were soon to find out, a platoon sergeant is there to step in if the platoon commander is put out of action. In the army there is always somebody to take your place and McKay would have been an important cog in the wheel as a platoon sergeant, no question about it.[13]

The mantra imbued in Lieutenant Bickerdike from his days as a cadet at Sandhurst almost counted for nought when he finally found himself ensconced with his platoon on the *Canberra*.

As a young officer you go through your training at Sandhurst and you are taught that you will have your platoon, you will bond with them, you will go out on exercises with them and you will train them. You will have your platoon sergeant as your right-hand man. He will look after everything for you. You will have your experienced section commanders etc etc. You work together as a team to prepare for every eventuality. Well, when we got on *Canberra* I was on one deck – I was in cabin B69 with Lieutenant Mark Cox [OC 5 Platoon] up on B deck – Sergeant McKay was with the other senior B Company NCOs on another deck, the corporals were somewhere else and then the Toms were right down in the belly of the ship and about once a week, if we were lucky, we got the whole platoon together. It was absolute bloody chaos.[14] Here we were on a ruddy great ship, three battalions on board – two RM Commandos and us – all trying to get ready for whatever was coming, trying to find out where the hell the Falklands were and the thing we spent a hell of a lot of our time doing was sorting our kit out.

The thing that the Parachute Regiment was, is, good at, is that we trained for war whereas a lot of the British Army train because it's training. When it came to things like carrying a bomb load, the lads were all used to doing it on exercise where you are carrying blank ammunition. But you take the difference between carrying a 200-link belt of blank 7.62mm ammunition to carrying live ball 7.62mm ammunition and there is one hell of a difference in weight. We were bombing up for real operations so the lads on the *Canberra* were carrying, say, five magazines for the SLR, everyone was carrying a couple of grenades – white phosphorous, L2 – some smoke, some 'illum', a couple of 66s each, then on top of that possibly a couple of 81mm mortar bombs. When you then try to put that into the webbing that we had – the old '57 pattern stuff – the webbing couldn't take the weight. The webbing was actually falling apart. We had metal clips on the belt and we had so much weight in the pouches that the metal was bending. If you ran, for example doing a Tab round the deck on the *Canberra*, you'd have pouches falling off and it wasn't because the lads had put it together wrong it was because it was under so much strain that the metal just wasn't up to it.

We were also trying to keep some fitness training going. We broke up the promenade deck! It was a paved surface but of course with a company of boots going 'stomp, stomp stomp', it literally broke up. Remember there were three battalions on board all trying to do the same. We had timed slots when we could use the promenade deck, the top decks, a bit of an open area where you could do a bit of rifle PT or whatever. Then there were a few classrooms set up where you could do lectures and that sort of thing. Weapons training was done in the corridors, it was done in the cabins and to be quite honest for that type of training the responsibility was devolved down to section commanders and Sergeant McKay and I would just go round and visit them. But just finding the troops and getting them together was the bloody hardest part. It was chaos.[15]

Brian Faulkner found that he very rarely saw Ian McKay once the ship was under way as 4 Platoon tried to get down to work. Although they shared a room, the three senior sergeants had no real, fixed routine for organizing their living space. Army men are used to sharing – working as a team – but the three senior sergeants had such widely differing tasks with different sub-units of 3 Para that apart from sleeping in the same room their paths rarely crossed.

Ian was with a rifle company, I was the Air Adjutant working with Captain Bob Darby and all we seemed to do was administration all day making sure everybody was happy and such as you always had people coming on board. I had the occasional lecture or lesson to do on say, helicopter routine, but apart from that I had more spare time than Ian. Ray Butters was responsible for the physical welfare of the battalion on board. So technically, although we lived together in the cabin we all went our separate ways. Ian was more of a field soldier, an outdoor soldier rather than a barrack room soldier. He liked the fresh air and he liked to be out. That's why in the mornings and in the evenings he'd be out, he'd be with his guys on the sundeck doing training or running and most of his time other than that was taken up with eating and writing his letters. Often I would go up into the Meridian Room at the end of the day to have a few drinks, watch a film and have a bit of banter with the guys and usually when I came back at about 10.30pm, Ian had finished his letters and nine times out of ten he was in his bunk reading a book. Quite comfortable.'[16]

Ian's second message to his mother and father, this time a lengthier affair written on a standard thin, blue British Forces air mail letter, mentioned his accommodation and hinted at how hard he was working with 4 Platoon. It also reveals that the troops were at least aware of the high-level negotiations taking place – US Secretary of State Al Haig had already embarked on a round of frenetic 'shuttle diplomacy' and had met with General Leopoldo Galtieri in Buenos Aires – in an attempt to avert a real shooting war as they headed ever southward.

Although the British position was one of seeking to resolve the crisis through negotiation, Prime Minister Margaret Thatcher had made it crystal clear that the Falkland Islands would be retaken by force if all peaceful channels dried up. In reality once the ships of the Task Force had set sail the dictates of the military operation effectively set the pace. At his Orders Group meeting, convened at 4.30pm on 12 April, Lieutenant Colonel Pike remarked that many 3 Para soldiers had been asking him about what was going to happen. The CO was in no doubt that 'the general impression was that we would soon do a 'U' turn.' But he was keen to dispel these rumours and to emphasize to all that this was far from the truth. From what he had gathered the *Canberra* would be calling into Freetown and would get as far at least to Ascension Island. Although that destination was a mystery to many 3 Para Toms, some men of Ian's company were obviously ahead of the game. 'We're off to the Extension Islands,' one wag was heard to quip, 'They're open all the time.'[17]

RSM Ashbridge, however, harboured little doubt as to what the future held. Lawrie Ashbridge was the top soldier in 3 Para and if he had been a stick of rock, 'Gungy 3' would have run right through him. He had been cock-a-hoop on learning, years before in Berlin, of his elevation to the position of RSM and since then he had taken 3 Para on active service in Northern Ireland and recently had faced the ultimate challenge for a professional soldier, preparation for and taking his battalion to war.

'Going down on the *Canberra*, I always knew we were going to war. I just knew and I think if you could have talked to most private soldiers – not the hierarchy, the private soldiers – they also knew they were going. They just felt it. And I knew all the time that they would give 120 per cent. What was the strangest thing for me was going to war on a bloody ship. The thought of airborne soldiers doing lookout on the bridge! That I just could not get my head around.'[18]

That second letter of Ian's is postmarked 19 April, the same day as the earlier postcard. The first line of the recipient's address is scribbled out to be followed by his parents' address on the line below. Clearly decipherable beneath the scribble is, '5 SALAMANCA', Ian's home address. An obvious slip of the pen for a man whom Brian Faulkner remembers could usually be found on his bunk, during what few precious minutes of down-time he had in the evenings, writing letters to his family rather than regularly frequenting the Sergeants' Mess.

MUM & DAD

I'm sorry about the delay in dropping you a line but when the helicopter lifted our mail off two days out of Southampton we were not given much notice to get letters ready to post. This one will probably be posted when we reach Simonstown, (sic) Sierra Leone. I think that is going to be our first stop over on our route south.

You should get the postcard about now. The ship isn't really as plush as it looks and it's rumoured that it was due for scrapping... so it looks as if P&O will make a profit out of this trip. It's £100,000 per day to hire the ship, that's without food costing. We could probably have halved the time it's taken to get here as the *Canberra* is capable of quite a fast speed. The fact that it's taken so long may indicate that the government is hoping for a settlement before we get on the scene.

We are working very hard on board ship and will get our first day off on Sunday when we leave Simonstown (sic). All our running around the promenade deck is having its effect & the deck is beginning to break up in places. This will probably mean we will have to stop running on it for a while. A stoppage I personally will not oppose. The cabin I'm in takes 3 people but is quite large and has its own toilet and shower. Some of the 4-man rooms in the bottom levels of the ship are quite cramped and I wouldn't fancy living there. Still as a troopship I suppose we are a long way from complaining. The food is really quite good but not on a par with the normal meals served to the paying customers. Still, I am having to run a couple of times a day to run off the excess. You know how quickly I can clap on the weight when I get some home-cooking inside me.

We will probably reach the Ascension Isles middle of next week and have not been given any instructions further than that. I believe we will wait there until something definite has been worked out. I will get another letter off to you from there and then a lot will depend on orders received there. Give my love to everyone at home. You are always in my thoughts.

All my love.

Ian xxx[19]

Ian's letter was written after a meeting attended by Lieutenant Colonel Pike on the day *Canberra* sailed, at which it had been reported that Brigadier Julian Thompson, the Commanding Officer of 3 Commando Brigade, was 'concerned that we may eat and drink too much.' A cruise liner complete with restaurants, bars, a cinema and a swimming pool, packed with almost 3,000 calorie-burning and permanently ravenous elite troops on board, was not perhaps the Brigadier's ideal mode of transporting his brigade into a looming conflict. Ian's comments would only have served to fuel Brigadier Thompson's fears if he had been able to read the letter.

As a result of his propensity to make the most of good food while it was on offer, Ian soon realized he would have to work doubly hard to maintain his fitness levels above and beyond the regulation two periods of PT per company per day. It was the view of one or two of the young 3 Para Toms who had been under Ian's tutelage in his last recruit platoon before rejoining 3 Para, that he was not as fit as they were when it came to distance running. That may have been the case when stomping around the promenade deck but those who knew him well recognized that Ian's 'fitness' and his ability to take on and succeed at demanding physical challenges went beyond mere cardiovascular endurance.

Brian Faulkner: 'The thing that intrigued me about Ian was his fitness. He had what I would call a 'puppy face', a very young face, and he looked a lot younger than his actual age. But even though he carried a little bit of 'puppy fat', when he took everything off it was solid muscle and his fitness was astounding in terms of his capacity to take anything on. He played cricket and football – he never took rugby up which was one of my fortes – and he was exceptionally good at squash, so his capacity for doing physical training was quite outstanding.'

So outstanding in fact that as soon as he could, around seven o'clock in the morning, or in the evenings after all his training and physical sessions with his platoon or company and his own 'admin' were completed and most of his men were watching a film or relaxing in the rest rooms, Ian would then go off alone to pound the decks again. Not the tidiest of people on board *Canberra*, when he returned from his day's exertions Ian's kit would be thrown on his bed, his trainers dispatched with a kick into the darkest recesses of the cabin and there the whole assemblage would fester until either taken away to the laundry or dried out.

What with Ian doing at least three sessions per day, athlete Ray Butters racking up the miles according to his own training schedule and Brian Faulkner attending to his own timetabled PT, the cabin soon became littered with heaps of steaming, slowly ripening kit and discarded malodorous training shoes. Clearly Ian and the other occupants of cabin D 17 were doing all they could to maintain the battalion's proud traditions and uphold 3 Para's unofficial title of the Gungy 3rd!

By breakfast time on 14 April the *Canberra* was approaching the Canary Islands. The weather was improving, the decks were warming up and the sea was taking on a blue hue rather than the slate grey of the Bay of Biscay. Forty-eight hours later she was riding off Freetown, the capital of Sierra Leone. Although the original plan had been for *Canberra* to stay offshore it was decided at 9.00am to take her into harbour to refuel. She docked forty-five minutes later. Even so there was to be no shore leave. No matter, now that the weather was improving most members of B Company were already making the most of every opportunity to improve their tans built up during their recent company exercise – Rocky Lance – in Oman.

Major Mike Argue's company boasted more than its fair share of comedians in its ranks. On arriving alongside the oiling station, hard-pressed shore workers began to haul out great black pipes and proceeded to insert them into the hull of the Great White Whale. Suddenly a voice rang out, '40,000 gallons of four star… and make it quick', to be followed almost instantly by another, 'and don't forget the stamps'.[20]

But the refuelling was not all the Toms could see as they lined the decks to get a glimpse of the Sierra Leone capital or posed for photographs using the dusty town as a backdrop. Ian recorded what he saw at Freetown as well as the sights he had seen so far during the voyage in his next letter; a letter that was actually written whilst the *Canberra* rode at anchor off Ascension Island and which displays his confidence in the use of written English to conjure up images of the voyage for his parents at home in Rotherham. Although upbeat in the main, his introductory paragraph also reveals he was grappling with the difficulties of coming up with something original to say in the frequent letters he was writing home.

Dear Mum and Dad,

Well I suppose this is a bit belated but as you have gathered over the last few years it gets harder for me to write to anyone as the time goes by. I think the greatest problem is putting the thoughts I have into actual words. After writing to Marica & Donny, (now Melanie wants pictorial letters) I really find myself tongue tied. I've finally [got round] to something I should have done long [ago and] written to Grandma but I don't know her address so I hope you will pass it on for me.

Since I last wrote we crossed the Bay of Biscay, which wasn't as rough as I thought it would be, but at the same time gave quite a few soldiers a rough trip. We spotted a few whales and even a large shark not far from the ship as we closed with the N. African coast. The highlight was undoubtedly being chased by a school of porpoise. There must have been several hundred leaping out of the water & chasing alongside & in our wake until they fell behind. They are really beautiful creatures and create a huge impression on the vast number of soldiers who crowded the rails to see them. Hopefully a good omen. Freetown was a little disappointing but tremendously hot & humid. As soon as we docked the bum boats came alongside to trade but a lot of their stuff was rubbish. Someone tried to buy a monkey but it wouldn't be caught & put in the basket to be hauled on board. We did however get a good reception from the handful of Europeans waiting on the quay.[21]

This was also the first letter to his parents on which he had written his full return postal address for the campaign, '24210031 Sgt McKay, B Coy 3 Para BFPO 666'. The irony of being allotted that particular number had not been lost on the Toms. A great many had seen the film *The Omen* – a horror film released just six years earlier with a star-studded cast headed by Gregory Peck – and regarded their allotted BFPO post code with a fair degree of hilarity. In other more religious and devout quarters of the ship, however, the number was greeted with consternation, for 666 was the Biblical 'mark of the beast' from the Book of Revelation; its underlying message being the less than perfect nature of the human condition. Ian had hoped for 'a good omen' in his letter. Was he to be disappointed?[22]

Re-fuelled, the *Canberra* departed Freetown at ten o'clock that night and pressed on south into the Doldrums towards Ascension as the weather deteriorated. She crossed the equator at 5.00am on 19 April and the following day reached Ascension to join several other ships which lay at anchor in Georgetown Roads. Ian McKay had completed the first half of his odyssey to the Falklands.

The British overseas territory of Ascension Island was not the most appealing of islands. Covering an area of just thirty-five square miles, it appeared a rather barren spot, covered with centuries-old basalt lava flows and cinder cones from long-dormant volcanoes. The main feature, Green Mountain, was the 2,817ft high cone of one such volcano, the largest of the forty-four distinct volcanic cones on the island, sporting names like the Devil's Cauldron or the Devil's Riding School. The only vegetation grew on the upper slopes of Green Mountain.

What it lacked in natural beauty, however, it more than made up for in terms of its strategic importance. Situated on the Mid-Atlantic Ridge in the northern wastes of the South Atlantic, the US had built an airfield – Wideawake – on Ascension in 1943 which had become a key US base. A little over halfway between the British Isles and the Falklands, Ascension also provided Britain and the US with a footprint and a staging post in the South Atlantic Ocean between the continents of South America and Africa. With the backing of the US in terms of logistics support, it was the perfect location for the elements of the Task Force to stop and take stock of progress thus far. Here the Task Force would assemble, stores and loads would be augmented and redistributed, and a chain of command would be established. And here 3 Para would go ashore for a '24-hour package' designed to practise simultaneous landings via landing craft and helicopter, shake off their sea legs by doing some drills and training, and take part in live fire exercises.

Ian's initial observations of his latest destination were less than enthusiastic but he had packed a few extras in the hope of indulging in one of his favourite pastimes of his youth to keep himself occupied between his duties.

The trip to Ascension was uneventful and the island itself is very unimpressive. It looks like volcanic reminders of an age gone by, only vegetated on the higher slopes of the central area. The sea is infested with sharks, mainly of the Hammerhead variety & a beautiful black–blue fish with a white and blue stripe through it. I have caught quite a few, "splodging" from the back of the ship with a length of line & some hooks I have with me. They try to bite you when removing the hook & a soldier who fell in the sea off a boat received some nasty bites from a shoal of the little devils. Well I will try & write more while we are at Ascension & will definitely write before we leave, whatever our destination may be.

Give my love to everyone especially Neal, Graham and Sue.

All my love, Ian.[23]

He had already mentioned that he had at last managed to get a letter off to 'Jamjar', the McKay family nickname for Ian's maternal grandmother. Jamjar was Mrs Winnie Hargreaves, Freda's mother, who had at one time, with Freda's father Len, run The Alma public house at Mosborough on the Derbyshire/South Yorkshire border. At the age of 75, Mrs Hargreaves had not received many communications from her busy, globetrotting paratrooper grandson and had, in the past, been known to shed a few tears on hearing news of him but she was thrilled when Freda took his letter, postmarked 26 April, round to her house.

Dear Grandma,

Well isn't it an unfortunate situation we find ourselves in? I suppose this is the first time I have written to you since I joined the army. That's a terrible state of affairs considering the length of time I've been away from home. The longer I spend in the army the more I get used to be being away in strange places and the more difficult it gets to write home. I have more difficulty in putting my thoughts into words now than when I left school.

We are anchored off Ascension Isle at the moment waiting for Maggie Thatcher and the Corn Beef Cowboys to make their minds up one way or another. We haven't had too bad a trip up to now and our surroundings are helping to make the trip a little more interesting. Since we left Freetown in SIERRA LEONE it has been very hot and we have all had to be careful of sunburn. I suppose that's something far from your thoughts in England at the moment. Since arriving here we have English radio and news piped on board from a radio station ashore. This has helped tremendously to keep us in touch with home and relatives back in the UK.

Well I hope to see you as soon as the situation allows. We should get some leave when we eventually get back to England. Take care of yourself and leave a place on the sideboard in case I manage to get a souvenir from the Falklands.

Give my love to everyone at home when you see them, as I won't be able to write to everyone I should do.

All my love, Ian.[24]

After ten frustrating days of orders and changed plans the battalion finally got its chance to go ashore for an extended period. It took three hours between 5.00am and 8.30am on Saturday, 1 May to get all the men ashore and once there they stayed on the island all day. Lieutenant Andrew Bickerdike recalled how 4 Platoon's time ashore was organized.

We anchored in the Ascension Bay anchorage and went ashore by helicopter. We flew into Wideawake airfield on the Sea Kings to practise a heliborne assault and from there we tabbed across to English Bay which is about a ten kilometre tab. Within the company structure the move across was a platoon effort; organized as the sections and Platoon HQ. That meant one half of Platoon HQ, that is the Platoon Commander's Tac [Tactical] Group consisting of myself, my runner Private Barlow – an army cross-country runner – and my radio operator Private Cullen, was forward. The other half of the platoon HQ, which was just behind, was led by Sergeant McKay, who had the light, 2in mortar man [Private Balmer] and the 84 team of Privates Parry and Playle with him. I don't think we deployed the 2in mortar because we didn't have the ammunition for it. The 84 was the Carl Gustav anti-tank weapon, a rocket launcher and a bloody, great humping nuisance! We'd been stuck on ship for 2–3 weeks by that stage and then to come off onto dry land and do a ten-mile bash in hot weather – well we were in 'rag order' when we arrived at English Bay. Everyone's feet suffered. Even though we'd been doing PT and had had our boots on, a ten-mile bash across Ascension was fun and games. But we had the ranges set up there so we did a lot of zeroing [of weapons] and shooting. It was a company effort so Mike Argue got us together as platoon commanders and said, 'right, we've got to do this and this'. If I remember rightly we had a round robin. We'd go on to rifles first and 5 platoon would go on GPMG with 6 Platoon doing something else and we rotated around. That's after we had done our company bash from Wideawake airfield to English Bay. Basically we did the 'shake down' on Ascension, how to move as a platoon, live firing and a bit of dry training – platoon attack drills and so forth – and then we got back onto the LCUs and went back to the *Canberra* by boat.[25]

Corporal Ian Bailey, then leading a section in 5 Platoon, remembered how their feet hurt:

We all had the chance to get onto the island and in good para style we marched round it, problem was we had not had our boots on in weeks and a lot of people had blisters. On the boat we had not been allowed to wear our boots because we damaged the carpets. We did a lot of boat drills. The Mortars and Anti-Tanks got to fire their weapons.[26]

The Wombat gun teams of the Anti-Tank Platoon fired 37½ years' worth of High Explosive Squash Head training ammunition that day – even though the Wombats would never be used in the coming campaign – while the Milan teams scored a success with two of their highly expensive High Explosive Anti-Tank rounds.

There is a famous photograph taken that day on Ascension which includes an image of Ian McKay. In the image, taken by Kevin Capon, a keen amateur photographer and member of 6 Platoon, Ian can be seen, SLR held raised, barrel up in his left hand, moving left to right on the sand behind Lance Corporal John 'Taff' Hedges, second in command of Corporal 'Ned' Kelly's 2 Section, who is also caught on camera, crouching in a defensive position just in front of Capon's lens.[27]

Whilst at Ascension Ian received a letter from Neal, his younger brother, then working as a Clerk of the Court in the Magistrates' Department on Moorgate Street, Rotherham. It was a rare occurrence for either Neal or middle brother Graham to write – Ian later hinted as much in a letter to his parents – communications between the brothers were usually done via telephone. As revealed earlier, there had been a fair amount of sibling rivalry between Ian and his younger brother during their upbringing in the 1960s, although there was no doubt that as the brothers had matured and as Ian had spent so much time away in the army, any rivalries between them had long since given way to mutual respect.

Neal had also revealed how, despite Ian's extensive travels in the army, the East Yorkshire coast seaside town of Bridlington had always had a special place in his heart. Ian resurrected memories of those happy and carefree days as he composed his reply to Neal and any man who has ever had younger brothers born within a year or two of themselves will recognize the gently teasing tone that Ian adopted, albeit concluding with a serious final paragraph.

Dear Neal,

Well after that literary masterpiece here I am replying with a simple aerogramme (sic). It's mainly as I can post these free & it costs me a fortune otherwise. It was really great to hear from you and after I got into the habit of handling the big words I quite got into the swing of the letter. I am afraid with some of the soldiers I have you don't often use words of more than two syllables.

Well you would have really appreciated the trip so far. Plenty of Marine Life & the Ascensions would keep you happy for a while. It's just a large volcano surrounded by smaller versions which have erupted at various intervals. The earth itself is non existent & is largely cooled volcanic rock & ash which has formed incredible shapes in places. Sharks & whales, Rays and Turtles, Flying fish and porpoise we have seen them all. The fish we were catching were some kind of sea piranna (sic) and when landed were not averse to taking a lump out of a finger or leg as a few anglers found to their cost. I wasn't too impressed with your reference to my splodging abilities especially as I always came out on top in Brid harbour. DIDN'T I?

There is a fair size convoy assembled here now & quite a variety too. Cruise ships and Channel Ferries. Tankers and supply ships, and finally our escort of Assault ships and Frigates.

I hope our actual assault capability is as good as we imagine. It would be embarrassing to be dumped on the Island & not produce the goods. Still we are extremely confident & to be quite honest would rather have an end to the waiting.

All the best Neal – again many thanks for the letter & hope to see you soon.

Ian.'[28]

The letter is also interesting in that it includes a passage which reveals that the brothers were aware of, and openly discussing, tensions which they knew already existed within their parents' relationship. The family had bought Ken a dog as a surprise for Christmas but he had refused to have it in the house, a state of affairs which had generated much friction between all members of the family still in and around Rotherham. Neal's original letter to Ian – now sadly lost – had obviously included references to this and the home situation and Ian's candid comments, which put the seal of approval on any action Neal may have, or was thinking of taking, are still those of an elder brother, albeit one who has been away from the family home for twelve years and at that particular point was several thousand miles away, possibly on his way to war and thus unwilling to rock the boat himself.

'I am glad someone is keeping an eye on the situation at home and as you say someone has got to put an oar in every now and again otherwise Mum just gives more and more ground and Dad becomes more introvert and grumpy. I'm afraid that this business with the dog has carried on for too long and someone needs to be put in the picture. Even at the cost of family relations.'

The *Canberra* left Ascension Island at 5.05pm on 6 May; the eve of Ian's twenty-ninth birthday, and steamed south to rendezvous with other elements of the Task Force. The Task Group built around the two aircraft carriers *Hermes* and *Invincible*, along with their escorts and supply ships, were already stationed within the 200-mile exclusion zone off the Falklands. By the time Ian's birthday came around on 7 May he found himself inundated with messages and cards but it was a bitter sweet milestone in many ways both personally and for the British force, of which Ian was a part. First and foremost he was acutely aware that his daughter was growing up quickly and that he was away from home during some key landmarks in Melanie's young life. Secondly, news had by now filtered through that the British submarine, *HMS Conqueror* had sunk the ageing Argentine ship the *General Belgrano* – which, in a previous incarnation as the *USS Phoenix*, had escaped destruction at the hands of the Japanese at Pearl Harbor in December 1941 – with the loss of 368 men on the evening of 2 May.

The Task Force had been finally committed to battle the day before as the last few drops of Al Haig's diplomatic elixir had trickled into the sand. The failure to dislodge the Argentines from the Falklands led the British to impose a 200-mile Total Exclusion Zone around the islands in order to blockade them on their ill-gotten gains. That said, the *Belgrano*, the southern prong of the Argentine Navy's pincer threat to the Task Force, had been sunk outside the Exclusion Zone. As a result, in the north the ageing Argentine carrier *Vienticinco de Mayo* fled back to harbour. British supremacy at sea thus seemed assured but the air threat remained and the Argentine response, when it came, was swift, sure and deadly.

Even as Ian set about replying to his pile of correspondence, news had already reached the *Canberra* of a dreadful loss for the British fleet – a loss which was uncomfortably close to home for Ian. On 4 May, just forty-eight hours after the attack on the *Belgrano*, the Type 42 destroyer HMS *Sheffield* had been struck by an Exocet missile launched from an Argentine Super Etendard aircraft, crippling the ship and sending shock waves reverberating throughout the Royal Navy. Suddenly the Task

Force looked very vulnerable indeed. Years of cuts and Treasury penny pinching were exposed in that one fatal strike, putting every ship afloat at risk as fire boiled through the belly of the *Sheffield*'s flimsy hull, feeding off cheap plastic electrical trunking and melting sailors' acrylic trousers into their very flesh. Twenty men lost their lives and more were seriously injured as the inferno raged, eventually leading her captain to abandon ship. Six days later the *Sheffield* went down.

This was now a real shooting war. Lives were being lost at sea; some in the most horrific of circumstances and the rest of the ships in the Task Force were seen as fair game for the Argentine fighter pilots. In truth, as a strategic deployment to create the conditions for an amphibious landing, the Task Force had not fully realized its aim – 3 Para and the rest of Brigadier Thompson's 3 Commando Brigade were not ashore and were not certain of air superiority. The skilled and courageous Argentine pilots remained with their aircraft intact, formidable and dangerous.

Ian must have been aware that his family would be extremely anxious on hearing the news of the loss of the *Sheffield*, for he mentioned her fate in his next two letters home. The first, to his mother and father, is tinged with longing whilst trying to sound an upbeat note to ease any worries his parents may have had as their son moved ever closer to the war zone. The second, another to his grandmother and postmarked 26 May 1982, five days after 3 Para landed on the Falklands, confronts the issue of the *Sheffield* but steers clear of any hints of sentimentality.

Dear MUM & DAD,

Well what a job I have had these last few nights. So many people have written, especially birthday cards, and replies are getting harder to pen. I find myself repeating things which sounds strange to me but probably not to you. I feel there must have been some writing classes held to get Neal and Graham to put pen to paper. Mind you since the innovation of the Aldershot telephone system we haven't written much either. I reckon with calls to Bahrain & back the next bill will be horrific but I don't suppose I can blame her [Marica]…

We were all shattered by the loss of the *Sheffield* and I felt the loss the more so because of the home tie. We are within a few days of meeting up with the main fleet & will certainly be with them when you get this letter. I don't suppose we will hang about as we will be extremely vulnerable at that time & in all honesty we should be safer on the Island. The *Canberra* is a large target & must be high on the list of Argentine attack plans. After all this waiting and the seas starting to get up it will be a relief to get off the ship & stretch out. We will probably find ourselves rocking about for a bit until we get our land legs back again, having spent so long rolling in time to the ship.

I have some pictures on my wall that Melanie drew for me & even some writing she put on a letter Marica sent. I must admit I have missed them terribly, especially another landmark in Melanie's life, that of starting school. Donny wrote me a letter, probably his first ever, mostly about his work with the cadets. He seems to enjoy creeping about the woods & hills much the same as I did. I think Marica is making the most of her new found freedom, especially as Melanie is off her hands for longer during the day. I suppose it will cost her a fortune to keep her happy when we return. I hope to write another note to 'Jamjar' & keep her happy. I only hope it provides her with some amusement & doesn't result in the usual floods of tears. I understand my flowers are blooming and plants coming on. I hope Dad didn't do any damage when he was there. Mind you I don't expect my beloved [Marica] has done much to improve its looks. I hope the Guards and Ghurkhas relieve us when they arrive so we can return and get some leave. We will be up to see you as soon as we can.

All my love for ever. Ian.[29]

Dear Grandma,

Well there is a first time for everything and I don't suppose I have written so many letters to you for some years. I suppose if the truth were told my ability to remember birthdays and anniversaries ranks only with that of my brothers. I suppose it was fate that I would eventually marry a woman with the memory of an elephant, or is it that these are all things women remember, I know my Mum knows them all.

We have been plodding along now for over five weeks and really haven't had a chance to enjoy much of it. The weather up until a few days ago was very good but we still managed to put in a hard day's work. In fact there have been days when I haven't actually been able to get up on a top deck in the fresh air. When you are down in the depths of the ship with only port holes to look through you could be in any building anywhere. If only it wasn't for the unending rolling from side to side. The loss of the *Sheffield* hit us all hard but I expect those of you at home felt it just as much. It is difficult not to associate yourselves with a ship and men that bear the name of your home town. Still we have seen that since that action the navy has buckled down to its job and is now starting to fight back in earnest. I have pictures that Melanie has sent me on the wall and she is forever pestering me to draw pictures and send them home. I didn't know what I was starting when I drew a small cartoon on my first letter home. She hasn't stopped asking for more.

I hope you are all well and that the weather is brightening up for you. As we get further south the seas get heavier and greyer and the wind gets stronger and colder. We can't be far off the Arctic Circle now. I am half expecting to see an iceberg in the water.

Well I will finish now as I still have a few more to write and beginning to get writer's cramp. Something I haven't had since school.

Hope you are well. Give my love to the Bennetts and the Levine clan as I can't possibly write to all the people I really ought to.

All my love Grandma, Ian.[30]

Ian had always enjoyed a reputation as a quiet man, not easily ruffled but perhaps the marking of his birthday and the associated sense of separation coupled with the news of the loss of the *Sheffield* created certain stresses within him; stresses which had begun to surface during the next leg of the voyage south. His friend Brian Faulkner was treated to an uncharacteristic outburst which was the result of an incident regarding the focus of Ian's life – his family.

I know that Ian was extremely devoted to his wife Marica and his young daughter Melanie. His wife had been previously married to a man in 1 Para so it was her second marriage – Ian's first – and he was particularly devoted to his young daughter. I always noted during our time at the Depot that once the day had finished and he was happy that everything was squared away, dusted away, he liked to get home to see Melanie as quickly as he could.

Now on the ship, one of the things we never got to grips with was this naval term 'rounds'. This was when the Captain or an officer of the ship came round every evening, checking cabins to make sure everything was stowed away. You weren't supposed to have any items that were loose in case they flew around if the ship was hit. We used to leave photographs of our families on the sides. Ian had the bottom bunk on the left while I had the top bunk above Ian and Ray Butters had the bed on the right-hand side. Ian used to have a collection of photographs and pictures of his wife Marica, Melanie and his step-son Donny arranged around his bunk area.

During the Captain's rounds Ian was never in the cabin – being a platoon sergeant he was always with his platoon to make sure things were going well there. For some unknown reason I always seemed to be in the cabin when the rounds were carried out. As Colour Sergeant – the others were both sergeants – I had seniority so I was responsible. The Captain used to come in and say, 'That's all got to go away. I don't want those pictures up there, I don't want this and I don't want that.' I wasn't used to it. So one evening before he came round I grabbed all of Ian's pictures and things and put them under his pillow nice and neat. I remember Ian coming in and he really 'threw a track', he went potty. 'Brian,' he said, 'I don't want you ever to take my pictures or my photographs of my family down or put them up. They're mine, my private property and I'll do it.'

I fully understood Ian's point of view but unfortunately the RSM, Lawrie Ashbridge, was extremely strict on his discipline and if you didn't follow the format as a senior NCO you found yourself in front of him. But I couldn't seem to make Ian understand that if his things weren't put away I, as senior NCO in the cabin, would go in front of the RSM for not conforming to ship's regulations. Ian knew all about the rules and regulations of course but he just insisted that if the photographs had to be moved then he would move them and nobody else.[31]

A raw nerve had been touched. Ian's keen sense of justice had been bruised and he had displayed that streak of righteous indignation and stubbornness that he had revealed around the home as a child, on the sports fields of his youth and to the more experienced men of 1 Para when he had joined them as a young soldier in the early 1970s, and on throughout the rest of his army career. Ian's actions spoke louder than a thousand words ever could and the message came over clearly to Brian Faulkner: These are mine; this is my family; I love them. Leave them alone.

And there were other developments which surprised even the most experienced of men. With his wealth of experience, his resolute, no-nonsense approach to soldiering and his background as an army boxer, B Company Sergeant Major John Weeks could be relied upon to ensure that his charges were doing exactly what they were supposed to. He made no bones about the fact that if he had to exercise his authority then he would do so and someone might well get their backside kicked as a result. On the other hand a wink and a sharp but friendly jerk of the baton in the ribs of a private or lance corporal during kit inspections in the barracks was a clear signal that if you were doing things right then the CSM was on your side. Some of the junior NCOs in B Company, men like Corporal Ian Bailey, had, as young soldiers, acted as babysitters for their CSM. John Weeks was a man hugely respected throughout the company, a man used to people coming to him for advice but when Ian McKay stopped him one day out on the deck, what he had to say almost threw the usually unflappable Warrant Officer.

We'd been doing a lot of training and one day Ian came up to me and said 'Can I have a word Sergeant Major?' I said 'Yes. Here?' and he said 'No, in private.' So we got down to my bunk and sat down and I said to him 'What's the matter?' and he said, 'I won't be coming back from this.' I said 'What do you mean?', and he said again, 'I won't be coming back.' So I tried to reason with him and said, 'How can you know that Ian. We aren't even there, so how do you know you aren't coming back?' And he said, 'I've just got this feeling and I want to up my ADAT [Army Dependents' Assurance Trust] from two units to ten units.' I had five units at the time and told him that that could be arranged, that that wasn't an issue and we could get the paperwork but that I was more concerned about his state of mind. He didn't say any more and that was the end of it really. Of course I kept an eye on him after that but it didn't seem to affect him in any way. As far as I could see he was doing what he was supposed to be doing as a platoon sergeant – perhaps doing more and better than some of the others.[32]

Sergeant Major Sammy Dougherty was another Senior NCO in whom Ian confided on the long voyage south. Dougherty, a sergeant major in HQ Company, was another in the mould of John Weeks. A down to earth Ulsterman, he had also tasted success in the boxing ring, having represented teams from Ireland Select, Ulster, the Army and Combined Services as well as the battalion.

Dougherty recalled that Ian, on the occasions when he did make his way to the bar for a beer, had joined his drinking group, a group consisting of himself, CSM Weeks, Sergeant John Ross and Colour Sergeant Tony Dunn and admitted to finding it a little strange that the platoon sergeant came and sat with them. Ian also had his meals at the same table. 'He was a nice lad,' remembered Dougherty, who was not one for believing in such ephemeral concepts as fate, but one conversation with Ian made Sammy Dougherty think twice. 'One night in the bar I was talking to Ian and I said, "I've no intention of taking any risks and getting killed in this. If I do get killed then it will be to protect my men, to save lives," and he looked at me and said, "I'm not going to make it. I'm going to get killed."' What surprised Sammy Dougherty more was that Ian's words were delivered almost as a statement of fact in tones of resignation and acceptance. There was neither fear nor panic in Ian's voice nor were his words taken as a play for sympathy, something which would have been completely out of character and dismissed by his experienced comrades.[33]

A few weeks later, on the night of 11 June, CSM Weeks would see Ian again, this time with para helmet on, face darkened with cam cream, SLR in hand, festooned with ammunition and with pouches bulging with grenades. 'Just before we crossed the Murrell River, before the battle for Mount Longdon, he came up to me and he said again, "I'm not going to come back from this." That was maybe an hour before we crossed the river and got into our formations for the battle. And sure enough he did not come back.'

As Ian had predicted, the *Canberra* rendezvoused with some of Britain's burgeoning fleet – the *Ardent*, *Argonaut*, *Atlantic Conveyor*, the RFA *Stromness* carrying 45 Commando and the ferry *Norland* carrying sister battalion 2 Para – during the evening of 10 May.[34] On the same day platoon sergeants like Ian were given the job of locating and recovering the 1,100 spoons which had apparently vanished from the Atlantic Restaurant and which caused longer queues to form at meal times, thus eating into valuable training time. This might have been just one of those jobs that Ian grumbled about but got on and did to the best of his ability.

Passing Tristan de Cunha, by Thursday 13 May the *Canberra* had but 1,000 miles of its 8,000 mile epic to complete. As she cruised inexorably towards more operational waters, and with the fate of HMS *Sheffield* – the first British warship to be lost to hostile action since 1945 – so recently etched into everyone's consciousness, emergency drills took on a more urgent and utilitarian purpose. A total blackout was to be observed on board during the hours of darkness while smocks and lifejackets were to be worn at all times. An information film, *Cold can Kill*, was made available to 3 Para by the ship's adjutant. That same day Lieutenant Colonel Pike went aboard Brigadier Julian Thompson's command ship, the Assault Landing Ship HMS *Fearless* to receive his orders for the coming amphibious operation.

Ian had hinted in his letter to Neal that he felt vulnerable on board ship, a sentiment echoed by many of his comrades. These men of action; men who jumped out of aeroplanes and Tabbed for miles on foot during training exercises as a matter of course, had now been cooped up at sea on board ship for the best part of five weeks, with, for most of them, only a day ashore in all that time. Discipline had held, morale was high and training had gone well under the circumstances but in the final analysis, if the men had wanted to sail the high seas they would have joined the Royal Marines. These men were paratroopers and they were becoming increasingly restless on board; itching to get ashore to do the job they had trained for. That job would be spelled out by Lieutenant Colonel Pike at his Orders Group meeting to his officers at 2.00pm the following day and by then D-Day for Ian McKay and 3 Para would be just one week away.

CHAPTER NINE

TAB

In London, at Joint Headquarters Northwood and afloat in the carrier HMS *Hermes*, the war planners' options had run out. As the navy's demonstration of force had failed to frighten the Argentines off the islands, it seemed that only a full-blooded amphibious assault and land campaign could clinch a decisive victory, and that meant committing the Marines and the Paras.

For 3 Para the long weeks at sea had been time well spent on improving fitness, briefing, planning and training – both on weapons and essential first aid. There had also been some sunbathing and a good deal of waiting. Now, at last, it seemed the waiting was over. But there were hitches. After practising assault loading techniques from the *Canberra* into landing craft there were last minute changes. Perhaps Margaret Thatcher and her War Cabinet had gazed into their crystal ball and had observed the chilling spectacle of wave after wave of Argentine aircraft dodging the Royal Navy's air defences and hurling themselves at a gigantic, white and stationary target disgorging three battalions of Britain's finest fighting troops. They had, after all, succeeded in crippling the *Sheffield* and, indeed, would do so again, with devastating results on the day of the landings in the cases of the *Ardent* and *Argonaut*.

The 'what if' implications for the land campaign, not to mention on public opinion back home, of the Great White Whale, engulfed in a fireball whilst still packed to the gunwales with almost 3,000 of Britain's elite, was too awful to contemplate. That particularly horrific vision of the future would indeed come to pass but it would not involve the *Canberra*. It would instead, and for evermore, bear the name of *Sir Galahad*.

Now it was decided that there was to be only one unit per ship and that meant 3 Para would be on the move; cross-decking to the Assault Landing Ship HMS *Intrepid* – sister ship of Brigadier Julian Thompson's command ship *Fearless* – on D-2, 19 May, thirty-six hours before the landing, scheduled for 21 May.

Regimental Sergeant Major Lawrie Ashbridge and Adjutant Captain Kevin McGimpsey were the first men of 3 Para aboard the *Intrepid* – described by Hew Pike as a rabbit warren in which even a section commander 'had difficulty accounting for his little flock' – at 7.00am to organize the transfer, and the first of the men began to be ferried across from 2.00pm onward.

It is interesting to note here that as the tempo of operations began to increase, so the timings for operational purposes changed from local Stanley Standard time to ZULU Time, so that the various elements of the Task Force could co-ordinate its movements not only in theatre but with Headquarters at Northwood in the UK.[1]

But before the day was out, some of 3 Para were to witness a tragedy of enormous significance. Also scheduled to cross-deck to the *Intrepid* that day were men of 22 SAS,

TAB • 153

many of whom were already combat veterans of the Falklands War, having taken part in actions on South Georgia and on the successful raid on the Argentine airfield on Pebble Island. Theirs was to be the last scheduled lift of the day, cross-decking not by landing craft but by helicopter from HMS *Hermes* in readiness for further operations.

It should have been a routine flight; a short hop by Sea King, taking just minutes from launch to landing. At about 7.10pm, in fading light but with only gentle winds and a mild sea swell running, the Sea King took off from *Hermes* and headed towards the *Intrepid*. The helicopter carried two pilots, a crewman and twenty-seven men from 22 SAS, including two attached personnel and a large amount of equipment. Although slightly over the maximum payload, as it was to be a short flight the pilot reportedly reduced the fuel load to reduce the overall weight. The helicopter climbed and then, at about 300 feet, started its descent towards the *Intrepid* from astern.

What happened next has baffled investigators for twenty-five years. From somewhere up above came a flat, distinct thump, followed by another from the engine housing, directly overhead. The Sea King dipped once and then, pitching forward at a dizzying angle, nosedived towards the ocean's surface. It was all over in four seconds. The great, flailing hulk of machinery crashed into the water with incredible force, killing some of the occupants instantly. Others were knocked senseless but, by some miracle, nine men, including the two pilots, managed to scramble out of the side door, fortunately kept open during the short flight more by instinct than intent.

The Sea King sank like a stone. Eighteen SAS men, their attached RAF Forward Air Controller, his signaller, and a Royal Marine helicopter crewman were lost. The Regiment had not lost so many men at once since the loss of thirty-five during Operation Bulbasket in France in 1944. The cause of the tragic accident has never been fully explained; some accounts indicate a bird strike, possibly that most potent symbol of ill luck at sea – the albatross – whilst others cite overloading and crew fatigue.[2]

If all had gone to plan, by about 10.00pm the SAS men would have been competing for a 'doss' space in the gangways of the cramped Assault Landing Ship as increasing numbers of 3 Para, hauling their ammunition and equipment, were being shoehorned aboard. As the men shuffled along, a wry smile would have crossed Ian's lips on learning that the name of one of *Intrepid*'s bars was called the Ohio – a reminder of the title of the Olivia Newton John song that had brought him so much ribbing at the hands of his 1 Para mates in the back of the 'Pig' parked up in street in Northern Ireland in late 1971.[3]

Packed with more than 1,800 men – way over *Intrepid*'s design limits – it was difficult for so many bodies to settle in but one by one they began to stake their claim to a few feet of floor space in a bar, a corridor or passageway – some finding a home in the engine room and one even squeezing onto a cupboard shelf – as news of the crash began to filter through. The bare bones of the tragedy, as recorded in the 3 Para War Diary, are stripped of emotion: '2200. Sea King en route from *Hermes* goes down with number of SAS', but RSM Lawrie Ashbridge recalled the real impact it had on him and his soldiers.

When we cross-decked, the adjutant and I went across to the *Intrepid* half a day earlier than the rest to suss out where we were going. It was that night that the penny really dropped, because that was the night – before most of the battalion were across – that the helicopter with 22 SAS came down. To see the reaction on a naval ship is quite astounding, everything was just cleared away and we, being army, were just pushed to one side – we didn't understand what they were doing; we just let them get on with it. To see one body come out of the water completely blue, that really brings it home to people. I had been in confrontations throughout my career and had seen bodies before but this was different. I just knew it was different. That was when the penny dropped. This is it![4]

News of the loss of the *Sheffield* had hit Ian McKay particularly hard – he had after all mentioned it in two letters home – and now more priceless lives had been lost within a 100m of where he and his men were huddled. The war was creeping ever closer.

Ian McKay's DMS boots first hit the beach near Port San Carlos on East Falkland on 21 May 1982 – D-Day – in what was, with hindsight, an extraordinarily bold, three-phase operation. Brigadier Julian Thompson's design for the initial assault involved a silent attack by landing craft during the hours of darkness with all the surrounding high ground being secured by dawn. The role of 3 Para called for its members to be loaded onto a variety of landing craft from the *Intrepid* and landed ashore near Sand Bay and Settlement Bay – codenamed Green Beaches One and Two respectively – during the second phase of Brigadier Thompson's operation to secure Port San Carlos Settlement and the high ground to north and south. Led by B Company, packed into four Landing Craft Vehicle and Personnel (LCVP) and tasked with securing the beach head on Green Beach One at Sand Bay, the rest of the battalion were to follow them in then push through; A Company heading for Port San Carlos Settlement whilst C Company moved up to dig in on the reverse slopes of the dominating heights of Settlement Rocks and Windy Gap. Scimitar and Scorpion Light tanks of 4 Troop, the Blues and Royals were to accompany them to soften up any Argentine resistance. Once the beachhead and high ground had been taken B Company were then to move up on receiving the code word Musketeer – the signal for the start of the next phase of 3 Para's assault and also the name given to the operation in which the Parachute Regiment had taken part in Suez in 1956. They were to sit astride Windy Gap to augment the defensive perimeter and act as protection for the Rapier anti-aircraft missile systems which would follow them ashore.

Everyone tried to snatch a little sleep from 9.00pm ZULU on the evening of 20 May but with sky-high doses of adrenalin pumping butterflies around the stomach, sleep, if it came at all, was fitful at best. It almost came as a relief when everybody was put on Action Stations at 1.30am on 21 May and units began rousing themselves to move down through the decks into the galley, which also served as the muster area. Breakfast, served from 4.00am ZULU onwards with the entire battalion rotating through *Intrepid's* galley, came as a welcome break from the tension for some but nerves were taught. As a platoon sergeant, Ian had specific tasks to perform and so his mind would have been focussed on making sure the Toms of 4 Platoon were up and about and concentrating on the job they had been trained to do.

TAB • 155

In order to counteract any complacency on the part of his men, Lieutenant Colonel Hew Pike had already warned that the landing might have more than a whiff of the ill-fated assault on the beaches of Gallipoli 67 years earlier. Now he came on the *Intrepid's* 'pipes' and paraphrased the words of Brigadier James Hill, Commander of 3 Parachute Brigade, who had addressed his men on the eve of the British airborne landings in Normandy on 6 June 1944: 'Gentlemen, despite your excellent training and briefing, do not be daunted if chaos reigns, because it undoubtedly will.'[5] And although the chaos predicted by Hew Pike never quite materialized, nevertheless, as events began to unfold so the potential for disaster increased.

If everything had gone according to plan all 671 men of 3 Para, including a forty-man attachment of 9 (Parachute) Squadron RE, would have been loaded onto the landing craft by 4.15am local time and ashore by 6.00am under the cloak of darkness, but the move out by 45 Commando Royal Marines went more slowly than anticipated. An unopposed landing was by no means a certainty and now 3 Para would be going into battle late. With sunrise at about 7.40am local time – 11.40am ZULU – this meant the battalion would now go ashore with the breaking of the dawn, in daylight.

Ian had been shuttled across to the *Intrepid* with 4 Platoon HQ along with Andrew Bickerdike and at 8.30am ZULU was called forward from the galley to make his way towards the landing craft with the rest of B Company. After a short delay he made his way out onto the flight deck where he mustered with his men opposite the assault boats. Andrew Bickerdike remembers:

We went through the orders process on *Canberra* and then we were cross-decked about 36 hours before we landed. Again when we got onto *Intrepid* everybody disappeared in different directions. With a whole battalion boarding the ship you'd got people absolutely everywhere. Once we'd cross-decked, the next time we saw each other again as a platoon was when we were called forward to the galley. We were piped up: 'B Company proceed to other ranks galley'. We all met up there and that was where I saw Sergeant McKay issuing L2 and white phosphorous grenades. That was a platoon sergeant's role, looking after the administration of the platoon, making sure everyone was carrying what he was supposed to. Everyone was already 'ammoed' up but at that point we were also getting bombed up with grenades. Then we were priming them and getting onto the LCVPs. Because we were getting onto the LCVPs we were up and going out through the sides and into the boats which went down into the water. Next thing, we were heading for Green Beach, B Company leading the way. It should have been Jon [Shaw, 6 Platoon] and myself as the first two boats in followed by Mark Cox [5 Platoon] and Company Headquarters.[6]

As the convoy of assault ships had nosed into San Carlos Water the sound of a firefight could be heard off to their left from the direction of high ground at Fanning Head, accompanied by naval gunfire support from HMS *Antrim*. Here a patrol of 3 Special Boat Squadron (SBS), which had been airlifted ashore earlier, were engaging an Argentine combat team known as 'The Fanning Head Mob', in order to secure the approaches to San Carlos Water. Another Argentine combat team – 'Eagle' – had also been in the area of Port San Carlos and although, in the event, the landings were unopposed, as the Argentines withdrew to the north, the small force of forty-one men could have caused mayhem on Green Beaches 1 and 2. This point was demonstrated to lethal effect a short time after the landings as that same Argentine combat team, moving away from Port San Carlos, fired on a Sea King and two Gazelle helicopters with tragic results.[7]

But as his battalion butted its way through the waters of San Carlos Bay towards Green Beaches One and Two, Hew Pike could not know that the Argentines around Port San Carlos had withdrawn. His concern now was that the landing craft carrying B Company, his initial assault unit, were falling behind his own Battalion Headquarters and the rest of his battalion and that his entire force, each man burdened with something nearing 140lbs of equipment and ammunition, was vulnerable on the water. With clear blue skies above and no sea fret to conceal their approach, 3 Para was now a very visible target for the far from vanquished Argentine air threat which occasionally zoomed overhead.

Twenty years later the CO recorded his thoughts on the niggling anxiety which characterized the run in to the beach and the landings.

The …landing at Port San Carlos is endlessly delayed while the darkness so badly needed gives way to a calm, clear dawn – perfect conditions for enemy pilots. At last the landing craft manoeuvre back into *Intrepid*'s flooded dock, we load up and are under way, less one company for which we can't risk a further wait. Everything seems to be taking so much longer than we expected or hoped. The bigger landing craft, with more displacement, hit the sea bed well out from the beach – and it's too deep to wade. So the smaller craft, having emptied B Company ashore, must manoeuvre alongside for another unscheduled cross-decking. It's just as well we are unopposed – or are we? As we advance towards the settlement a Sea King and two Gazelle helicopters – 'What are they doing here anyway?' we are asking ourselves – take avoiding action ahead of A Company's leading elements. Both Gazelles are hit by enemy small-arms fire and crash, one into the water, one into the hillside. Three of the four crewmen die.[8]

At last 3 Para were ashore but their troubles were only just beginning. Eight thousand miles from home, with limited logistics and ammunition stocks and without air superiority, the assault from the sea was at risk from the moment it was launched. Most of all it was at risk from the air. Hew Pike continued: 'As we move up to try and establish what has happened and why, an enemy Pucara ground-attack aircraft whines slowly over the scattered houses of the settlement machine-gunning indiscriminately as it goes. Emerging from behind a protective pile of drying peat, just as the body of one of the Gazelle pilots is loaded into a local farm Land Rover, the realities of our situation begin to press in on us.'[9]

In one of the HQ Company landing craft several grenades leapt out of their box as the small vessel smacked hard against a rogue wave and rolled around on the floor to the consternation of the craft's occupants. Even though B Company had eventually

TAB • 157

overtaken the rest of the battalion to go in first, theirs was not a dry landing. The landing craft were just four or five feet short of the waterline when they 'hit', but the water was deep. With the Royal Marines manning the covering GPMGs yelling at them to get out quickly most men still got wet boots having to wade waist deep in the chilled waters of the Sound. And that was not all they got wet. Many remember a sharp intake of breath accompanied by an involuntary flinch and voices raised by an octave as the icy water lapped around their nether regions for the first time.

Ian McKay and Andrew Bickerdike emerged from their landing craft with 4 Platoon HQ having been told that Special Forces would be marking the beach.

SBS were obviously doing the beach patrol because we had Argentines at Fanning Head off to our left flank which they were suppressing. We had been told that the SBS would have people there to let us know that the beach was clear and to guide us in and as we came off the boat this head pops up out of the bushes with white tape wrapped around his bush hat and the cry went up, 'hey look there's an umpire!' And off we went up the beach. Now our job was to pass straight through Port San Carlos and up onto the top of the ridgeline which was known as Windy Gap. So we skirted round the buildings of the settlement, which was very small anyway and then headed straight up the hill. As we were about to go up the hill some mortar rounds started to go off on top and we thought, 'What's going off here?' It was the Mortar Platoon under Julian James bedding in the mortars. Julian James was determined to be the first person to fire a bloody mortar on the Falklands. Hew Pike gave him permission and he bedded in the mortars somewhere down on the beach area. Everybody knew what to do. Orders had been given and so we headed off up to Windy Gap and dug in. But it's a joint effort to run the platoon. He [McKay] looked after the administration – making sure everybody was doing their jobs – and I would run round doing orders and the like, which are a platoon commander's and a platoon sergeant's duties.[10]

Eventually Port San Carlos Settlement was secured and thirty-five relieved and thankful adults and seven bemused children were liberated, some of whom were pictured giving RSM Lawrie Ashbridge a mug of Liberator's Tea in one of the iconic images from the Falklands War. Lawrie Ashbridge knew that to hit the beach at Port San Carlos would be 'the moment the ball would really start to roll' and from the very first minute he knew he wouldn't have a problem with the men.

What was amazing for me as the RSM was that I didn't have to tell them to dig in. Historically, on exercises, a soldier doesn't like to dig in because he knows that somebody, sometime, is going to tell him to fill his hole in again which is a demoralizing thing. But some of the trenches I saw at Port San Carlos were unbelievable. The overhead cover that they put on, you would have thought that there were T54 tanks coming through the following morning. You didn't have to tell them, they knew. I remember speaking to a couple of soldiers from A Company and I said, 'Good trench that, what are you worried about?' and they said, 'did you see that Pucara this morning sir? You could count the flipping rivets underneath its fuselage'. It says in the 'good book', 18in of overhead cover, packed hard in case a tank goes over it. Pah! I saw three feet of overhead cover and they were doing it within hours. Their training kicked in.[11]

It was Lawrie Asbridge's fervent belief that one of the functions of an effective RSM was to gauge the mood of the battalion, to maintain good order and discipline and keep it on the straight and narrow. He made it his business to get to know what the soldiers were feeling and report on the state of the battalion back to the CO. Such information was invaluable in planning operations. And now, with the battalion ashore and their backsides in the air busily putting the finishing touches to their trenches, he was keen to get around to find out what the men were thinking. One of his first stops was a trip up to Windy Gap to visit B Company.

After we landed I wanted to know how 4 Platoon were getting on with Sergeant McKay and I remember speaking to Corporal Balmer and I asked him, 'How's your Platoon Sergeant doing then pal?' and Balmer being Balmer – he could be a little bit on edge when I was talking to him – said, 'Alright Sir'. So I asked him again, 'Come on, how's he doing?' 'He's great Sir'. So I pressed him a bit harder, 'Is that fact or fiction?' 'Fact Sir'. Now some people might say I was wrong to do that, but just by getting the odd word from a Junior NCO or a private soldier you quickly suss out that they are trying to tell you something. I spoke to young Ian Scrivens about McKay as well. 'He's only got one frigging problem Sir,' he said. 'And what's that Scrivens?' 'He's 1 Para isn't he?' Although he [Scrivens] was just a lad, that tells you a lot about the rivalry between the three Para battalions – Bullshit 1 or the Runners, The Jock Battalion or Shiny 2nd and us, Gungy 3. The strangest thing was that when I went into Scrivens' trench at San Carlos and we were passing the time of day, Ian McKay came across towards us. He didn't realize I was in the trench with Scrivens and another guy having a brew. Then he noticed me and I said something like, 'They've just given you a tick in the box Sergeant McKay, so you're alright pal.' And I always remember him saying, 'Well that's great then isn't it?' and walked on. But it was the lovely way he said, 'That's great then' and walked on and I thought, 'Good on you pal.' After he'd gone the lads in the trench turned to me and said, 'Really helped us there Sir, didn't you?' That was a rapport you'd got to have with soldiers. I always tried to create a bit of competition, a bit of something so that they would talk to each other. That was outside Port San Carlos and that incident always sticks in my mind.[12]

Their ability to dig stood 3 Para in good stead in the crucial hours after the landings for the Argentine counter attack was swift in coming. Flying at suicidally low altitudes to attack the targets anchored in the sound, the Argentine pilots hurled themselves against the ships offshore. Despite a blizzard of anti-aircraft fire the young pilots pushed home their attacks with great bravery. Many were shot down, but to the Paras ashore trying to build up their positions, the vital shipping in San Carlos Water seemed to be being badly mauled. As with so many air battles however, the decisive fighting

TAB • 159

was taking place well away from the surface observers and in reality RAF and RN Harrier pilots were catching many of the Argentine attackers both inbound and outbound from their bombing runs on the ships.

The Harrier, like its feathered namesake, was turning out to be a deadly close quarters aerial killer. The British pilots were using new American Sidewinder missiles, although one pilot shot down a Skyhawk with his cannons at a range of less than 100yds, and the air kills ratio was firmly in the British favour. By the end of the first day the Argentines had lost sixteen attacking aircraft: an unsustainable loss. For the next three days, as 3 Para brewed up and made good their holes or patrolled the area around Port San Carlos, the air assault continued with marauding Pucaras and Skyhawks over-flying their positions. But gradually it began to ebb away. By 25 May there was even talk in London of having beaten the air threat.

Such over optimistic words were to ring hollow by the time Brigadier Thompson had briefed his battalion commanders that evening, for 25 May was Argentina's National Day and her talented pilots had vowed to mark it with a crushing blow. It fell to Julian Thompson to relay the dreadful news that had come in which would later lead him to record the date as a black day. At first the British thought that they had defeated the early waves of attacking aircraft. Then the Argentine pilots delivered a decisive and crippling double blow to the Task Force, sinking another Type 42, HMS *Coventry*, and, much more ominously, the most important supply ship afloat, the 13,000 ton *Atlantic Conveyor*, which was lost, taking with it six Wessex and three heavy lift Chinook helicopters. The British strategy was now in serious jeopardy and from that heavy lift most serious of military factors: logistics.

The war now became a race against time. The follow on troops of 5 Brigade were not due until 30 May and to launch an offensive with the units then available, without air superiority, appeared folly. Nevertheless, in London, enormous pressure was building for the commanders ashore to do something. Fears of a UN imposed ceasefire with the Task Force still sitting on the beachhead and public clamour for results after the navy's heavy shipping losses, forced Brigadier Thompson and his commander, Jeremy Moore, against all their instincts and training, to embark on a series of rushed and poorly supported ground operations. This entailed 2 Para being ordered to mount what was first mooted as a battalion raid but which would develop into a full-scale battle, on the Argentine defenders of the settlements of Darwin/Goose Green, while the rest of his force embarked on the first stage of the 'investment' of the capital, Port Stanley, on the other side of the East Falkland.

The break-out would soon be under way. But with the loss of most of his helicopter transport Julian Thompson's original plan to airlift the majority of his brigade forward was now in tatters. There was now only one way to get the rest of 3 Commando Brigade forward and for 3 Para that would mean 'Tabbing' it – walking every step of the way carrying everything you needed. Even so, they were more than ready for a change of scene.

Some of the younger Toms in B Company felt that the longer they stayed around Port San Carlos the more momentum they would lose. 'We had to start moving on,' said Nick Rose, a 20-year old private in 6 Platoon. 'It just felt that we'd been there a while. The Argentines knew we were in this position, they knew where we were deployed so it did start to feel like we'd been there too long, so let's get on and start the advance.' Graham Colbeck, one of Ian McKay's fellow sergeants but serving with the Milan section of the Anti-Tank platoon, concluded his diary entry for 26 May with a sentence which echoed the sentiments in Ian's later letters from the *Canberra* – 'Everyone here just wants to get to Stanley and finish it off.'[13]

At 9.00pm ZULU on 26 May – D+5 – Lieutenant Colonel Pike finally received a warning order on Operation Sutton for future tasks. Instead of waiting for 5 Brigade to land and 'move up through our area', as everyone had been expecting, 3 Para were now told to advance and capture the settlement at Teal Inlet, some twenty miles east of their present positions. Before the Argentine invasion Teal Inlet was, by Falklands standards, a sizeable and self-contained settlement of twenty-three souls living in seven houses and the cookhouse nestling, with associated cow and sheep shearing sheds, on the edge of the water under the shadow of Evelyn Hill to the south, with the imposing 2,000ft high Mount Simon beyond. It had been a working concern, dedicated to sheep rearing and the harvesting of fleeces bound for the woollen mills of West Yorkshire, and even after Argentine forces had moved into the outbuildings three weeks after the invasion, the inhabitants tried as best they could to continue with work and life as normal.

Teal had been earmarked as a forward logistics base for the final phase of operations to capture Port Stanley and had been thoroughly reconnoitred for almost a week. Indeed, so assiduously had the reconnaissance patrols of Royal Marines Mountain and Arctic Warfare Cadre been 'eyeballing' movements at Teal from the surrounding hills, one of the men later told Jan Hutchings, wife of Teal handyman Rod, the contents of her washing line a few days previously.

Brigadier Julian Thompson's chosen axis of advance lay north of the spine of high ground that ran across East Falkland from San Carlos Water in the west almost to the outskirts of Stanley in the east. Moving out of their beachhead on the other side of San Carlos Water, 2 Para had already embarked on the first leg of their fateful journey to Darwin/Goose Green. Now it was the turn of Gungy 3. Shortly after dawn, 45 Commando set out to 'yomp' north east along a recognized track making one side of a rough triangle, to Douglas settlement via New House. They were to be followed shortly afterwards by 3 Para who were to 'make best speed all in light order' – no bergans, no sleeping bags, no tripods for the sustained fire role GPMGs – in their wake as far as Douglas, before passing through to take the lead and turning southeast along another side of the triangle to Teal.

But by then Lieutenant Colonel Pike had gained some interesting local knowledge. There was intense rivalry between the Royal Marine Commandos and the Paras and Alan Miller, the civilian manager of the Port San Carlos settlement, whose dining room had been turned over to Hew Pike for his use as a conference room, had told the CO of another, more difficult, yet more direct route which cut along the base of the intended triangular march and which did not follow recognised tracks – 3 Para would follow no-one and would cut straight across to Teal. Even so, they would have to rely on the now tenuous logistics support to 'chopper' their kit forward to pre-arranged locations.[14]

And so it fell to 460 men of 3 Para to blaze the trail. In the event, although D Company remained behind on perimeter duties and some of the mortar section

TAB • 161

managed to hitch a lift on Mr Miller's two tractors, one of them driven by his son Philip, the rest of the battalion were destined to walk every step of the way from Port San Carlos into battle and, for the survivors, all the way to Stanley itself.

The TAB, which began at 1.15pm ZULU, was a supreme test of 3 Para's physical and mental stamina. Covering more than twenty miles across some of the most featureless and spirit-sapping terrain the men had experienced, it was completed in just two gruelling marches in what some men would later describe as bizarre climatic conditions. Marching by day and lying up during the night in an attempt to rest and, most important, stay dry, men called on inner reserves of personal pride and networks of mutual support within their platoons and sections. Horizontal rain and driving winds one hour, sunburnt faces the next, they drew heavily from personal wells of endurance, lessons learned during their tough training regime and their regimental *esprit de corps*, as the weather threw everything at them over mile after endless mile of stumbling over tussocks of long, pale grass and foot-snagging vegetation, whilst carrying the equivalent of a ten-stone man on their backs.

Neither was the TAB a respecter of previous achievement. Men seen as some of the fittest in the battalion, due to their scores in the British Army's conditioning tests, became exhausted. Fifteen cases of exposure were documented and these men had to be evacuated by helicopter, and there were several who turned their ankles as sodden socks slid around in the universally loathed and equally soaked DMS ankle boots.

Trench foot, a condition well known to the men of the British Army of 1914–18, now beckoned to these men of 1982. According to Andrew Bickerdike, 4 Platoon, 'lost one bloke with trench foot at Estancia, a week prior to Longdon and he was the only one we lost as a casualty to the weather. After the war there were complaints about the DMS boots and the puttees but we did it and we did it wearing some 1945 type kit in the 1980s.'[15]

Andrew Bickerdike also recalled the TAB and, keen to set the record straight, how 4 Platoon had led the battalion on the first leg of their journey to Teal. He also revealed how he and Ian had had used lifesaving procedures learned on field exercises in extreme conditions on the Brecon Beacons in order to maintain health and morale.[16]

In some book I read, somebody said they thought it was Jon Shaw who led the company across. Well it bloody well wasn't, it was 4 Platoon. I had the great honour of navigating for the battalion across to Teal Inlet and it was bloody cold, bloody wet and pretty bloody miserable but the boys were good. When we stopped we were in assault order, we didn't have sleeping bags, we didn't have bergans and we didn't have shelters, so our routine was to use survival tactics. We would get one of those large, black polythene bags, stuff it with 'diddle-dee' [*empetrum rubrum* – a native, low level plant a little like heather], and then climb into the bag with it. That created quite a wet but warm, windproof environment.

So we would do our Tab, stop, take our waterproofs off, put on our quilts – the old Chinese Cooley suit, a superb arctic suit – zip the trousers on, put the jacket on, put our waterproofs back on top of that then get inside the poly bag with the diddle-dee. We would then 'buddy buddy' and get close to each other and literally lie down with three or four blokes together and cuddle up as a mass to keep warm. The end man would be on sentry – he would be the coldest anyway and he would then wake his neighbour up and they would swap places until everyone had had a turn on sentry. We did that as a platoon HQ. Sergeant McKay and I would be doing that at opposite ends of the line and then we had our three section groups out around us. If anyone could have seen us we looked like a bunch of tramps! We were continually soaked, continually cold.

We couldn't carry enough rations. The ration supply was not particularly regular; we'd maybe get three ration packs at once and then not see another re-supply for three or four days. Well, having three boxes of rations, we had to carry them somewhere. The boys were stuffing them in the front of their jackets, they were stuffing them in their pockets; they were so laden down. You didn't want to abandon them because you never knew when you would next get fed, so by the time we had mortar rounds and 66s and then the bomb load there was real fun and games carrying the kit. The lads were basically pack-horses but they did a cracking job.[17]

RSM Lawrie Ashbridge remembers bumping into Ian on the TAB to Teal. The exchange that ensued revealed something of Ian's self-belief. 'We'd just called a halt and I spoke to him. I asked him how he was doing and he said he was alright. Then I said, "How's the platoon?" and he said, "Not a problem". I said "You'd tell me wouldn't you?" and there was a pregnant pause – "I think so, Sir." I think he was fishing; seeing how I would react. I got the feeling that he was intimating in some way that he knew I had been asking about him, about his performance and was referring back to my conversation with Ian Scrivens in that trench at San Carlos. There's nothing wrong with that at all. I don't want a soldier to revere me as RSM, I want a soldier to live and if I am giving him some kind of identity to communicate with me, have a rapport with me, that's what a Regimental Sergeant Major in wartime is all about.'[18]

News of 2 Para's hard won victory at Darwin/Goose Green and the heavy price they had paid in gaining it – 15 dead, including their Commanding Officer Lieutenant Colonel 'H' Jones, and 32 wounded – came in while the battalion pressed ever onward. Their struggle for Goose Green, the first set-piece battle of the Falklands War, has been called 'the most studied and analyzed battalion-sized action in military history.'[19] This fact is probably undeniable as is its significance. Politically and strategically it brought the scramble for a peaceful compromise to a halt with a bloody jolt and cast the first shadow of defeat over the Argentine effort both in Buenos Aires and at their HQ in Port Stanley. For the rest of the British forces on the ground the victory at Darwin/Goose Green set a morale-boosting precedent for the four battalion-sized battles to come and, soaked and ankle deep in diddle-dee on a miserable and spirit-sapping journey, the news of their sister battalion's success filled the men of 3 Para with pride and sadness in equal measure. Pride in the achievements of the Parachute Regiment and sadness for those killed in action.

Adjutant Kevin McGimpsey logged that Brigade had informed him of the deaths of 'H' Jones and his Adjutant, Captain David Wood, at 6.00pm ZULU on 28 May. No one knew it at the time but 'H' Jones' deed that day would lead to a citation for the award of the Victoria Cross.

TAB • 163

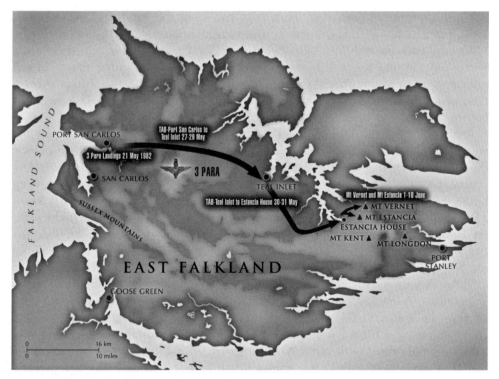

3 Para's TAB across East Falkland.

Ian heard the news of 2 Para's fight and the loss of its commanding officer as he trudged east towards the crossing of the Pedro River. It certainly made an impression on him as he would later refer to it in a letter to his parents. He knew some of the 2 Para men personally. It had fallen to Ian and the walrus-moustached Captain Alan Coulson, 2 Para's intelligence officer, to work together to keep 477 Recruit Platoon on the straight and narrow whilst serving together on the staff at Depot Para.

Stories of Argentines firing on and killing 2 Para men whilst walking in the open under a flag of truce had, quite understandably, angered the men of 3 Para. That said, there was also a grim determination abroad that when their time came to prove themselves on the battlefield, 3 Para could, indeed would, emulate the deeds of the Shiny 2nd. And their time would come, just two weeks later but on a battlefield very different from the undulating yet open ground and gorse gulleys of Darwin/Goose Green; 3 Para's battlefield would be in and among the long, frost-shattered spines of rock which stab the air from the summit of a 600ft high peak which formed the northern most bastion of the outer ring of the Port Stanley defences. The battle, when it came, would secure a place alongside Darwin/Goose Green in the illustrious history of the regiment, for it was a battle which would test the discipline, comradeship and professionalism of 3 Para to the limit, a battle which would turn out to be the bloodiest battle of the Falklands campaign, a battle which would witness another posthumous Para VC.

Northamptonshire-born Rod Hutchings had been the handyman at Teal since 1980. He and his wife Jan, lured by the rugged beauty and rare birdlife of the Falklands, had packed all their belongings in crates, picked up their then 7-year-old son and flown half way around the world to live their dream of self sufficiency in an ornithological paradise. On the night of 28 May, they had put young Gavin, by now turned 9, to bed and then, at about 11.00pm, they stoked up their peat burning stove before turning in themselves.

Rod had spent the evening marking homework as he had also taken on the voluntary role of Teal schoolteacher after the Argentine invasion, not only to occupy the Teal children but also those who had been evacuated from Stanley for safety reasons. That night, looking forward to being tucked up in a warm bed in a glowing house, they felt a little more cheered than they had done for several weeks. They knew a British Task Force was on its way, they had heard the news on their two metre radio set before the Argentines had confiscated them and it now appeared that the Argentines had finally gone. The small garrison, sleeping out in the hay barns, had not caused too much trouble, but their behaviour had become increasingly menacing as each day they toured the houses demanding food and drink whilst brandishing pistols and grenades. A few had even become brazen enough to barge into houses so the sight of the last soldier to leave, demanding food and a bottle of wine before commandeering a Land Rover and careering crazily off towards Stanley that very afternoon, had caused some relief. Now the generator had ground to a halt and as the first sleet showers of a Falklands winter began to bite outside, indoors a peaceful silence of sorts, had descended on the dwellings of Teal.

After extinguishing the candles downstairs, Rod paused on the darkened landing to remove the blackout curtain and started. There, out in the pitch darkness, he could make out five darting pin pricks of light over towards the manager's house. Rod hissed to Jan and she joined him, crouching at the window, both now shivering in their night clothes from anxiety rather than cold as the pin pricks of light increased in size as they danced towards the Hutchings' front gate. Apprehension grew as behind the lights they made out the murky shapes of five soldiers advancing up the path to their front door followed by a heavy knocking.

Rod was downhearted. 'I said to Jan, "Oh, I bet it's those blooming Argentines again. I'll bet they're after more food," and Jan said, "Yes and they'll want to come into the house for the warmth. Don't let them in or we'll never get rid of them." So we waited and waited and the banging continued and eventually I thought I'd have to go and let them in or they would knock the door down. So I put some clothes on and went back to the window and stuck my head out and saw these tiny beams of light from the little torches they had. I turned back to Jan and whispered, "They're down here." I was just about to speak when I heard a voice in a polished English accent declare, "Well chaps, there's obviously no one here. We'd better move on to the next house." I knew the Argentine officers could speak English but not with an Oxford accent. I poked my head out of the window and cried, "Hang on, we'll be down in a minute." We rushed down and opened the door and there were these five blokes standing there, some with big moustaches and all in black and green camouflage just like Argentines. I couldn't believe it and asked them if they were British and even

TAB • 165

asked them to identify themselves. One of them, the officer, showed me his paratrooper's wings and then we let them into the warmth of our kitchen. We got the coffee on and Jan started cooking them a meal of sausages straight away. The officer introduced himself as Lieutenant Mark Cox and I asked him where they had come from. When he told me they had walked all the way from Port San Carlos I didn't believe him. That was over fifty miles away over some of the worst country in the Falklands. I'd seen sheep sink in the bogs out there. Then the rest introduced themselves. As well as Mark Cox there was Corporal Stewart McLaughlin, Corporal Graham Heaton, Sergeant John Ross and Sergeant Ian McKay.'[20]

Sitting around the farmhouse table in their cosy candlelit kitchen, their liberators drawing on steaming mugs of real coffee and thawing out courtesy of the heat blasting from the peat fired Raeburn, the Hutchings' questioned the group, eager to pick up any crumb of information. The scouse, Irish and North Country accents of Stewart McLaughlin, John Ross and Graham Heaton respectively, were music to the Hutchings' ears. Never having come into contact with Liverpudlians before, they remember being fascinated by Stewart McLaughlin's scouse volubility and accent, but they also remembered that, although very polite, Ian McKay was the quietest of the lot. 'When Ian told us his name was McKay I remember telling him we had a McKay [Rex McKay] on the settlement. I asked him if he was from Scotland as I knew there were lots of McKays around Sutherland and he just said he was from Rotherham. He didn't say much. He probably didn't want to give too much away. He sat at the back, nearest the window out onto the yard and listened. He was very alert and very wary. I remember he had big eyes and they darted around the room, almost as if he was expecting an Argentine to jump out of a cupboard at any minute.' Ian had good reason to be on his guard. He was again on active service and after all, the group had left their SLRs in the hallway, magazines pulled out for safety.

Coffee and sausages consumed, Rod tried to learn more of the group's epic journey. He told them he was astonished that five men, unfamiliar to the climatic and geographical vagaries of East Falkland, could have come all the way from Port San Carlos. His statement jolted Mark Cox into action. "'Good God", he said, "We're supposed to take you down to your schoolhouse to see one of our officers. The rest of our lads are outside." He told me that we had been watched by the Mountain and Arctic Warfare Cadre and they had told the Paras that I was the schoolteacher and that was why they had come to us first. I asked him how many of them there were and Mark Cox said "About 650". I was incredulous. I thought the five had just been an advance party and told him that he must be joking but he said he wasn't and that his Commanding Officer, Lieutenant Colonel Pike was down there with two majors, Major Martin Osborne and Major Mike Argue. He asked me if I would go down to the schoolhouse, to meet Major Osborne as it turned out. It was pitch black. My son Gavin had some white Wellington boots so he pulled them on and we all went outside. We went down towards the schoolhouse and there were just masses of bodies milling about in the darkness. I met Major Osborne and he thanked me for coming to meet him. He told me how far they had come in awful conditions; that some men were going down with exposure, trench foot and dysentery and that if I couldn't help get them under cover and get them some fresh water he was going to start losing men.

The settlement manager would not even come out to meet them. Well, Jan and I began to get the men under cover anywhere we could – the big shearing shed near the jetty, my workshop, the mechanic's workshop, stables, milking parlours, outbuildings – everywhere. It took over two hours but eventually everybody had a roof over their head. After that we started to go back up towards our house to get some sleep and Mark Cox asked if it was alright if his original small group could come back with us. I said of course it was alright, we had just assumed they were. It was at that point that Ian McKay came up and said, "My men are going to be outside in one of the barns in rough conditions and I want to be with them, is that OK?" Afterwards Mark Cox told us that that was typical of Ian, always thinking about his men. Whatever the discomfort, he wanted to be with them and so he went off and quite literally we didn't see him at close quarters again.'[21]

At daybreak, with Teal finally secured and re-invigorated by a few hours rest and hot food cooked and served in buckets by Jan Hutchings, Ian's platoon put their backs into it once more, digging trenches for protection. The lone Argentine who had commandeered the Land Rover the previous day had ditched it and returned to Teal where he was found fast asleep – despite the commotion around him – in a hay barn, and taken prisoner.

After the sleet of the night before, the first real snow of the South Atlantic winter fell whilst Ian was at Teal and the temperature dropped considerably, adding to his and his platoon's discomfort. Photographs taken at the time and just a few hours apart, show deep snow in some and then clear ground in later shots as the warmth of the sun's rays burnt it off. The battalion stayed at Teal for just twenty-four hours before embarking on the next stage of their odyssey on the afternoon of 30 May.

A few, including 3 Para Chief Clerk Dave Rowntree, stayed behind to form the administrative rear echelon and settlement protection parties until the arrival of 45 Commando. There had been unconfirmed reports that the Argentines had been throwing land mines from helicopters to the east of Teal and Rod Hutchings was asked to accompany the lead elements of the battalion along the recognized track as far as the perimeter gate on the Stanley side of the settlement. On reaching it he stopped. He was going no further but he shook hands with every single man who passed through as they set out in single file; the battalion strung out for over a mile over ground which was by now white over again with a covering of snow about two inches deep. He remembers shaking hands with Ian McKay as he followed in the tracks of the man ahead whilst a couple of Scorpion tanks began to race along the flanks of the column giving cover to the advancing troops.

The new objective was Estancia House, a tiny settlement consisting of the eponymous house itself, a barn and a few outbuildings owned by Tony and Ailsa Heathman which was reached and taken without a fight on the night of 31 May/1 June. Intelligence had warned of 200–300 Argentine troops in the area but by the time 3 Para arrived they had vanished towards Stanley. A few Argentine prisoners were picked up on the way – three cold, wet and miserable Air Force soldiers, sent out from Stanley three days earlier to observe the area. Also picked up on the way, and a most welcome addition to the ranks of 3 Para, was Terry Peck, the former Falkland Islands Chief Police Officer, member of the Falkland Islands Defence Force (FIDF) and

TAB • 167

member of its Legislative Council, vehemently opposed to any moves legitimizing Argentine sovereignty over the Islands. Peck, determined not to remain impotent in Stanley as the Argentines swarmed around his home town, escaped on a motorbike and eventually made contact with elements of 3 Para left behind at Port San Carlos after the rest of the battalion had set off for Teal Inlet. Airlifted forward he became – along with Vernon Steen, a fellow, slender and member of the FIDF – an honorary member of D Patrols Company, whose members used their intimate knowledge of East Falkland's geography to their advantage in the days ahead. It had been Terry who had warned of a possible 200 Argentine troops and minefields in the area, although in the event neither threat materialized.

The importance of securing Estancia House and the high ground of Mounts Estancia (occupied by A Company) and Vernet (C and elements of B Company), which lay to the northeast, was essential in building a seven-mile long, north-south platform of high ground. This platform included the strategically valuable and already occupied heights of Mount Kent, from which 3 Commando Brigade could launch the assault on the outer ring of the Stanley defences. The Estancia position itself was situated on the shore of one of the fingers of several inlets, which branched off southeast from Teal and which pointed towards Stanley, now only twelve and a half miles away as the shell flies.

Estancia was a vital base and staging post as it reduced the supply line from San Carlos by almost a fifth, as a round trip from Teal to 3 Para's area of operations was now only fifteen miles as opposed to 100 from San Carlos. In addition, the Estancia/Vernet position was also key in anchoring the northern axis of Brigadier Thompson's plan for a two-pronged investment of Stanley. Its importance was further enhanced as the Argentine commander, Menendez, became ever more convinced – particularly after 2 Para's victory at Goose Green – that the eventual British assault would be unleashed along the Fitzroy-Stanley track to the south.[22]

The last few miles of the Tab to Estancia had been undertaken in appalling weather conditions across some of the worst terrain the Falklands had to offer – small, steep hills covered in rocks, 'stone runs' – great rivers of big white boulders flowing across their path – trouser-tugging diddle-dee bush and ferns, and deep valleys which were mostly flooded or covered with huge, sucking bogs. Even then A and B Companies still had a little further to go, plodding on up the slopes of Mount Estancia to organize the outlying defences of the settlement whilst C Company stayed in the hen-houses to catch up on some sleep.

Lieutenant Colonel Pike also clambered to the top of a mountain to get a feel for the lie of the land to the east for himself. In the momentary lulls between bouts of bad weather and poor visibility, he and his comrades caught glimpses of the looming hulk of Mount Kent to the south with Mount Challenger beyond. Closer and to the north rose the mass of Mount Vernet, a peak upon which the CO would order an OP to be established. To the east lay Stanley, a tantalizing dozen miles distant. But in between, glowering down on his battalion from the east, barring the way to and obscuring the western outskirts of the Falklands capital, was a feature rising to just over 600ft high and about 500yds across, bristling with jagged outcrops of quartzite rock jutting out at crazy angles. It dominated the northern claw of Julian Thompson's pincer as far back as the Estancia position and even to Teal Inlet beyond. Looking at the map Hew Pike and his group checked the feature on the map. Its name… Mount Longdon. It became clear to Hew Pike that Mount Longdon would be 3 Para's objective and he was left to ponder on how best to go about cracking this tough nut on the northern flank of the Argentine defensive line. For that he would need reliable information.

A forward patrol base was to be established near the Estancia–Stanley track on some low bluffs overlooking the Murrell Bridge. Observers from 3 Para had already picked up movements on Longdon during the hours of daylight, but long distance observation was not enough. More detailed information about the strength and depth of specific positions, not least about the weaponry available to the Argentines, would have to be gathered. This meant that 3 Para would have to send out patrols – not only the nine, four-man patrols of D (Patrols) Company under Major Pat Butler but two sections of 9 Parachute Squadron RE and fighting patrols from the rifle companies – to slip undetected through the warp and weft of Argentine defences and poke and pry amongst the rugged nooks and crannies of Mount Longdon. The problem was the intervening ground. From the Mount Estancia position to Mount Longdon it is some seven miles as the shell flies but there is no high ground in between which could conceal an approach from prying eyes on Longdon or Mount Tumbledown to the south. Instead, a wide, featureless valley, covered with pale yellow grass and diddle-dee and drained by the Murrell River and Shanty Stream, opens out creating a broad west-east No Man's Land between the British and Argentine lines.

And so, just as the British had sought to dominate No Man's Land between the opposing lines of trenches on the Western Front during the First World War, with a philosophy of treating the German wire as the British front line, now Julian Thompson urged his subordinates to dominate the ground, thus retaining the initiative and maintaining momentum. Any 3 Para patrols venturing out onto the bare, bleached backdrop of the valley during daylight would have stood out like a line of black ants on freshly laid concrete. Everything would have to be done at night and that's when the local knowledge of Falkland Islanders Terry Peck and Vernon Steen came into its own.

Vernon Steen recalled how he became involved with the Patrols Company of 3 Para:

In late April 1982 my family and I took the opportunity to evacuate from Stanley to Green Patch. When the call came for people to go to the Estancia to help 3 Para in late May 1982 approximately thirty people with some ten-fifteen vehicles answered that call, arriving there the day after 3 Para following their epic TAB from Port San Carlos. We were tasked with taking soldiers and equipment to the surrounding valleys and mountains in support of their front lines, forward patrols and the gun lines, which were situated to the east of the Estancia. While talking to Terry Peck one night, shortly after returning from taking ammunition and stores to one of the units, I suggested to him that I may be better used in a role as guide to patrols pushing into the area of Mount Longdon. Next thing I knew was that I was issued with combats, rifle and equipment and tasked to contact Major Patton. During the period leading up to the final assault on

TAB • 169

Longdon I was involved with several patrols to recce potential approaches and fire positions.[23]

The knowledge of the terrain which Vernon Steen carried in his head was like gold dust to the men of Patrols Company. A quiet, unassuming and thoughtful man not prone to braggadocio or hyperbole, Vernon Steen was a 'Kelper' born and bred; the kind of man for which the words 'steady' and 'solid' might have been invented. By June 1982, Mount Longdon had been both his workplace and playground for more than three decades. He knew, from his time spent shepherding sheep on and around Mount Longdon, exactly where the folds and hollows of dead ground lay on the approaches to its craggy peaks and, on the mountain itself, the many hidden holes and cavities where the sheep would congregate to shelter from the bitter winter weather.

He had spent so much time up on the mountain during his youth and early adulthood that he knew the position of virtually every rock and every kink, twist, turn and dead-end amidst the dizzying maze of rock runnels which studded the mountain. He knew Longdon better than most people knew their own back gardens:

Mount Longdon formed part of Moody Valley Farm which at one time had been owned by the widow of the late Jimmy Miller. It was managed and operated on a part-time basis by Richard Hills (the husband of Mrs Miller's daughter). My uncle, Fred Burns worked full time on the farm for about eight years from 1950 to 1958. During my younger years I lived with my grand mother (Fred's mother) because my mother was in hospital with tuberculosis. In the early 1950s I would spend my weekends and school holidays helping my uncle at the farm with such jobs as lamb marking, shearing, dipping, eye locking, feeding animals, fencing and general farm maintenance. Much of the work around the farm was done either on foot or horseback. Luckily there was a very tame old horse there called Gilpin that I rode on gathers. The area of the farm took in Mount William, Tumbledown, to the eastern side of Mount Harriet, then north to the eastern foot of Two Sisters, extending further north to the area of Furze Bush Pass on the Murrell River. On the north side the boundary was the Murrell River and Hearnden Waters to Watt Cove. The boundary then went south to Fairy Cove then west along the coast of Stanley Harbour to the Head of the Bay. The total area of the farm would have been approximately 20,000 hectares. It had about 2,800 head of sheep, mostly ewes. The sheep were shepherded regularly for lamb marking in October, shearing from November to early February and then dipping during March and April. This would involve riding or walking around the small camps (about 4,500 acres) so I had rode and walked the peaks and rocky crags of Longdon on numerous occasions during the years up until I left school in 1959. I would hate to think how many times I was on or in the vicinity of Longdon during that time. In 1963, at the age of 17, I joined the FIDF. The area of Stanley and its environs - generally within a radius of ten miles - became my playground once again. With patrols and exercises throughout the area; under the watchful eye of Royal Marines that formed the garrison in the Falklands stationed at Moody Brook. I was active with the FIDF until 1977 with a few short breaks from 1965–67 and 1968–73. However during 1969–72 I worked for the Falkland Island Company (FIC) at Green Patch Farm as a shepherd at Estancia. To reach Stanley I had to travel cross-country either by horse or four-wheel drive vehicle passing Mount Longdon. Although the Longdon area was not part of the Green Patch Farm the telephone line that served the Estancia, Teal Inlet and Douglas Station areas ran across the southern shoulder of Mount Longdon. It was my responsibility to maintain the telephone line from Moody Brook to the Malo (Teal Inlet). I would ride this about once a month carrying out maintenance on line breaks and replacing insulators by climbing 18ft poles using a device like a stirrup with sharp spurs strapped to the inside of each leg. Easier said than done! It was tiring work and very hard on the legs. I think I spent most of the time holding on for grim death slipping down the poles! In 1973 we moved back to Stanley and I worked for the Falkland Islands Government, firstly in the Post Office and then at the Falkland Islands Government Air Service. I took up as a serving member of the FIDF again until we went to the UK in September 1977 for a time and again all training and exercises were carried out with the Royal Marines in the area west and north of Moody Brook. I also worked casually for the owner of Moody Valley Farm. All in all I had accumulated a considerable knowledge over some twenty-eight years of this area of the Falklands I would like to think that I had more than a passing acquaintance with the area.[24]

And so, with the help of Terry Peck and Vernon Steen – the 'civvies' – 48 hour patrols from D Company were ordered out as early as 1 June under Captain Matt Selfridge but the rifle companies went out too. Ian McKay was to be heavily involved in this forward patrolling activity almost as soon as 3 Para had secured the Estancia position. Setting out at night, his platoon's task was to secure the bridge over the Murrell River a few hundred yards from where the patrol base was to be established.

On arrival, it had been Hew Pike's intention for every company to get a period of at least twelve hours' rest and relaxation, a time to get dry and have a hot meal. When B Company trudged down from the mountain for their stint of R and R, Hew Pike called for Andrew Bickerdike – 4 Platoon had a job to do and they would set out to do it early on 2 June.

We moved up to Estancia and again Battalion HQ based itself around the settlement and we were pushed up onto the mountains which were beyond it. We were in a B Company group. At that point I was called back to battalion HQ and was given a task by Hew Pike. I was to take the platoon [Call Sign 21][25] forward, with a mortar fire control party in support and with a Scimitar and a Scorpion, to the bridge over the Murrell River [in reality just four planks]. I was told to hold the bridge until the rest of the battalion advanced to cross it to go up into the attack. This is where it would be quite interesting to find out what happened. Hew Pike had done his appreciation and thought, right I need to hold that bridge as it is critical to the advance, and had sent me forward, which I don't think had had complete clearance from Julian Thompson. The platoon – me,

TAB • 171

Sergeant McKay and the rest of the lads – went forward at night and moved up to the bridge. I put one section forward across the bridge and two sections and platoon HQ – me and Sergeant McKay – rear of the bridge to cover it, forming all round defence. Come first light and we found ourselves right underneath Two Sisters to our right and Mount Longdon to our left. I say 'underneath' but we were quite a distance from them – more than 2,000m. But as we looked up at Two Sisters they [Argentines] were obviously looking down on us and they decided to start firing. So they started putting 155mm rounds onto us from Stanley. By this stage we'd got pissed off digging trenches because you were just digging into peat on bedrock and couldn't go down very far. So all we could do was make a shell scrape and bank up some peat around it. Sergeant McKay had been a mortar man and I'll never forget this because as we were sitting in our little shell scrape on this low ridge, looking down on the actual bridge with one section east of it, these 155 rounds began to come in. The first landed on the ground below us and threw up lots of muck, the next one landed behind us and threw up lots of muck and McKay says, 'Next one's going to land right on top of us'. So we were sitting there wondering what was going to happen. The next one came even closer – landed just in front of us – they were creeping the rounds back and forth ranging on us. McKay, being a typical mortar man, was saying, 'If they've got it right they are going to get us next time', but then, for some inexplicable reason, it stopped.

From their perch in the shallow shell scrape on the bank above and behind the Murrell Bridge, Ian and Andrew Bickerdike also witnessed another drama unfold. On the opposite bank, a long slope ran forward of the river and headed roughly southeast towards Stanley. The slope had a ridgeline about 400m forward of where Andrew Bickerdike's Platoon HQ was sited. His chief concern, as he surveyed the terrain, was that any Argentines approaching from the east could easily get to within 400m of 4 Platoon before anyone realized they were there. Bickerdike decided to put an observation Post (OP) up on the ridge line.

I sent a small party [under Corporal 'Ned' Kelly] to set up an OP. But they'd walked up there in daylight and they'd been spotted so the Argentines started firing mortars at them. These mortar rounds were coming down fairly close to this ridge. Lance Corporal Evans got on the platoon radio net and asked for permission to move a bit because the mortars were getting a bit close. So I said, 'Yeah, move'. So this OP party got up and ran 250m to the other end of this ridgeline and the mortar rounds landed on exactly the spot they had just come from. The Argentines then started mortaring their new position, so they got up again and ran back the other way. This went on for quite a while with the Argentine mortars chasing them up and down and the OP party were getting really pissed off with running backwards and forwards along this ridge line until in the end I gave the order to withdraw as we knew by that stage we were all going to be withdrawn. So I gave Corporal Kelly orders to move back and he followed what he had learned in training, classic infantry training.

There was no cover, so how do you move? You move under cover of smoke. So he gave the orders to his section, 'prepare to throw smoke, on smoke, bug out'. Of course his lads threw their smoke, up it went and they got out of their shell scrapes to start running back. The Argentines saw this and thought, 'Ah, they're using smoke therefore they must be moving', and they opened up with .50s [.5inch calibre Heavy Machine Guns] and poured this .50 ammunition onto them and the section ran back to their shell scrapes. So Corporal Kelly said 'Sod the smoke, when I say move, bugger off'. So of course he just gave the order and they moved back no problem at all. Sergeant McKay and I were sitting up on the ridge behind the river chuckling to ourselves and watching all these antics going on and it was at that point that we had to give ourselves a reality check to say, 'Hold on, we're laughing but the Argentines are trying to kill the lads!'

To counter that we'd spotted where the Argentine OP was on top of Two Sisters and I called in a fire mission which the mortars couldn't do because we were out of range of our own battalion mortars. The Scorpion I had on my left flank had withdrawn a few hundred metres under their orders as soon as the 155mm rounds came in as it was an asset that couldn't afford to be knocked out. I gave the Scorpion commander permission to engage this Argentine OP position and with his barrel really elevated he fired a few rounds but they were dropping short. It was out of his range. Then, through our mortar radio net, we called in an artillery fire mission. Now it was either SBS or SAS who were somewhere close doing an OP job and they were actually relaying orders back to the gun line for me for this fire mission. It was a very easily identifiable Argentine position on the end of this rocky feature. I got the grid reference spot on straight away. The arty ranged very quickly. We got them to fire perhaps three rounds 'fire for effect'. I doubt we even got that because ammunition was so short. So we put rounds down on this OP and it did go quiet, in fact we saw them stretchering off a couple of people so I know we'd been effective with that fire mission.

But this is where it suddenly became a bit critical at Brigade. They were saying what the hell is going on forward, why have we got artillery being used, we need that for the big push? So I think it was at that stage that someone told Hew Pike to withdraw us and get us out. I then got orders from Hew Pike to withdraw at last light. So having sat there all day taking the odd few rounds fired at us, at last light Corporal Kelly moved back from across the river, Sergeant McKay reformed the platoon and we tabbed back about 7–8km to our old position at Estancia. The area around Mount Estancia had obviously been an old Argentine position at some stage because there was a lot of abandoned Argentine kit – bits of tentage, ammunition boxes, all sorts – and of course the rest of B Company had made themselves very comfortable thank you very much. We arrived back and there was bugger all left. We had gone all the way forward, taken all this shit down at the Murrell Bridge and then recovered all the way back to Estancia to then be pretty cold, wet and miserable and not be able to use any of this kit for shelter and such like.

Ian McKay and 4 Platoon rejoined the battalion dug into trenches a mile or so further east than those it had occupied when they had set out on 2 June and found that there

TAB • 173

had been some little excitement. Indeed even while 4 Platoon had been forward at the Murrell Bridge, the D Company patrols sent out under Matt Selfridge had returned to Estancia to be debriefed by Major Pat Butler. The resulting information had been passed to Lieutenant Colonel Pike whilst he had been advising his company commanders on his future intentions for the taking of Mount Longdon during his orders group meeting at the top of Mount Estancia on the morning of 3 June. The CO learned that Captain Selfridge's patrols had worked themselves to within 50m of the Argentine positions and according to what they had witnessed felt that Longdon was occupied by '…approximately two Companies of Infantry; an independent platoon located to the northeast of the feature; an administration area at the base of MOUNT LONGDON'S eastern end; 2 x 120mm mortar base platoon; 2 x 81mm mortar base platoon and the locations of 3 Machine Guns', in addition to areas where artillery and mortars were targeted for defensive fire.[26]

Sending the information on up the chain of command to Brigadier Thompson, Hew Pike weighed up the quality of the initial intelligence and decided that his battalion would advance to contact that same afternoon. At 4.00pm ZULU the battalion set out with A Company in the lead, followed next by B Company then C Company. A little under two and a half hours into the advance, and with the lead elements making exceptionally good ground, a message came in from Brigade HQ. Perhaps the pace of 3 Para's progress was just a little too hot for Brigade, concerned as it was with the planning for a co-ordinated assault and recalling the stiff opposition faced by 2 Para during their initial advance in daylight at Goose Green. At 6.24pm Lieutenant Colonel Pike received the following message from Julian Thompson. 'I am concerned that you are pressing on too fast. I do not want you to get into a position you cannot get out of, you are therefore to stay where you are and dig in. You can carry out your future intentions but you are not to move the whole of your C/S forward. You can patrol forward only.'[27]

The first probing patrol on Mount Longdon had also gone in on 2 June, the same day that Ian's platoon had moved forward to the Murrell Bridge, but that had run into well-placed Argentine mortar fire and was forced to pull back. Now, after the order to 'dig in'and make secure Lieutenant Colonel Pike was keen for more patrols to get out, in and around Longdon.

Over the next seven days many more patrols pushed out their feelers. It was difficult for patrols to go out, complete their tasks and get back before first light so patrols went out and stayed out for two and sometimes three nights, lying up during daylight hours and completing their tasks in darkness. Using the forward patrol base 400m north of the Murrell Bridge as a staging post meant that the distance the patrols had to travel from the Estancia position was reduced but such a position so close to Longdon also drew unwanted attention as Argentine units were also out and about in No Man's Land gathering intelligence. In fact there were so many units – both British and Argentine army and special forces units – squeezed into a comparatively small area that Major David Collett, Officer Commanding A Company complained that there were '…too many guys out front wandering around recce-ing … strategic troops operating alongside tactical troops which is not the best way of doing it.'[28]

Indeed, there were two sharp firefights on consecutive days on 6 and 7 June with Argentine Special Forces of *Compania de Commando 601* and *Compania de Fuerzas Especiales 601 de Gendarmerie Nacional*, during which 3 Para bergans and radios were left behind and never recovered. Undaunted by the contacts, patrolling continued after 7 June and the patrols did excellent work – work which Brigadier Thompson recognized as being of a very high standard indeed – and penetrated deep into the Argentine positions.[29] Little by little, the pieces of the Argentine defensive jigsaw on Longdon began to fall into place and as more information was added to that already acquired, a fuller picture of the strength of the Argentine defences and the quality of the defenders began to emerge. This was translated into a scale model of Longdon that became festooned with white tape, white markers and twigs representing Argentine minefields, bunkers and machine-gun positions respectively, as more and more information was gathered.

By the time 4 Platoon rejoined the rest of B Company, the R and R system had been re-instated. One platoon per company – except for A Company a little too far forward – were being pulled back into the barns at Estancia settlement for a change of dry clothing and to get some relief from the trying conditions on the mountainsides, while ammunition and supplies were being brought up for the next phase of the investment of Stanley.

At 7.30pm ZULU on 4 June it was 4 Platoon's turn but their period of R and R was to be cruelly interrupted and ultimately shortlived courtesy of the Argentine Air Force.

Because they thought we were cold, wet and miserable up on the mountain, the platoon would be taken down to the sheep-shearing shed or one of the big barns at Estancia House to have twenty-four hours out of the front line. Just somewhere dry, so that we could to get our boots off and dry out a bit. Well we got down there and into the barn and got ourselves as comfortable as we could. Our bergans had arrived by then so we had sleeping bags that night and so we all settled down. All of a sudden it was, 'air raid warning red'. Everybody complained, 'Awww no! Get out of it – go away', and everyone went back to sleep. I am sure it was Nobby Menzies who was running the echelon at Estancia and who was organizing the R and R bit and I think he came into the barn and yelled, 'air raid warning red, everybody out'. And everyone shouted 'go away!' We got a bollocking from him for that. Suddenly, about half an hour later there were these bloody great, 'crumph, crumph, crumphs'. It was the Argentine *Canberra* bombers doing a high level bombing mission. They had obviously spotted Estancia as a potential target and were trying to hit it with these 1,000lb [freefall] bombs. Of course, when the Argentines did try to bomb the place everyone got out pretty quickly and ran out into the open to be a bit more dispersed. It was teeming with rain and we got absolutely drenched. When we got back into the shed where our kit was we were soaking wet through so we just packed up all our kit and sloped back up on the mountain. We were much more comfortable up in the hills than stuck down at Estancia![30]

TAB • 175

Major George Brown was the Quartermaster of the Forward Echelon based at Estancia House and according to him, Nobby Menzies wasn't the only one shouting and bawling about the refusal of 4 Platoon to take the air raid warnings seriously and their reluctance to leave the seductive warmth of their sleeping bags. As the men responsible Ian McKay and his platoon commander bore the brunt of Brown's verbal diatribe.

> 3 PARA were dug in trenches on the forward hilltops while waiting to go forward to take Mount Longdon. It was Lieutenant Colonel Hew Pike's policy for each platoon in turn to go down from the trenches to where I was situated in a tin sheep-shearing shed to have a hot meal cooked for them and also give them a break from sleeping in and around trenches and also try to prevent trench foot. Sergeant Ian McKay's platoon had been down once before and because the whole battalion had been through they were sent down a second time which was to his displeasure. In the early hours of the morning we were warned of a pending air raid and because there were insufficient trenches the platoons normally went over the side of the inlet which had enough room between the bank and the water to give some protection. I woke up the entire platoon which was sleeping in the shed in sleeping bags, including Sergeant McKay and his platoon commander, and warned them of the pending raid. They made no effort to get up and go out for protection. A further five minutes went by and they still made no effort to go out and I had to physically get hold of Sergeant McKay and his platoon commander and order them to get out of the building. At that stage one felt that they thought the odds against them being hit were so high that it was not worth the trouble to get out of the warm sleeping bags and go outside. The whole platoon eventually went outside and some time later a Headquarters near our location was bombed. The following morning I got Sergeant McKay and his platoon commander to one side and gave them a dressing down and reminded them of their responsibilities as an officer and SNCO. I never saw Sergeant McKay after this and …days later …he was killed earning the VC.[31]

Suitably chastised, Ian, a little drier but feeling no less miserable than many of his 4 Platoon comrades, squelched his way east across the barren terrain back to the B Company area and settled back into his hole in the ground. On 8 June, in a break between his duties, he took a blue aerogramme and blue biro out of his pack and in an uneven hand which betrayed the discomfort and cold of his surroundings began to write a letter to his family in Rotherham.

Mum, Dad, Neal, Graham & Sue,
     Sorry this is a bit scruffy but the bottom of my hole in the ground might not be the cleanest part of the islands but it's the safest. Mind you, things are very much quieter now than for some time & finding things to occupy our time is now a problem. Some clown has put one of our artillery batteries just behind our position and as the Argentine guns try and range in on them they sometimes drop one in around our positions so life isn't dull all the time.

Mail is taking the best part of three weeks to get here so I guess the same applies vice-versa. It is quite possible we will be on the way home before this gets to you. Personally I can't wait to get back on board and on the way home as we are all completely fed up with things here now.

I have never known a more bleak, windswept and wet place in my life. We spend our life with wet feet trying to dry out and keep warm. The wind blows constantly but it is cooling rather than drying. You cannot walk fifty paces anywhere, even on the mountainsides, without walking into a bog. To be quite honest once we have given them a hammering & put them back in their place the Argentines can have the place. It really is fit for nothing. I thought the Brecon Beacons was bad but this takes the biscuit.

One of the officers I knew in the Depot was shot whilst standing under a white flag when 2 Para took GOOSE GREEN so feelings are running quite high both in 2 & 3 Para. Also the papers we get, again all well out of date, mention only Marines and Guards so if we aren't officially here we might as well come home.

Apart from that bit of grousing things aren't too bad & things should be over one way or another in a week so you will probably be reading this with hindsight. We will be home hopefully about two weeks afterwards.

If we get leave we will be up to see you as soon as possible bearing in mind the wheels need taxed (sic) and insured. Still I should have plenty of money saved after this or am I expecting too much Dad?

All my love to you all, Ian.

Folding it up, licking the gum and sealing it, he wrote out the address and again, absent mindedly, began to write '5 Salamanca', which he quickly scribbled out, wrote 'oops' beside it and then printed Freda and Ken's address. He got it in the mail and the letter went back, first to Estancia, then Teal, before continuing its long journey to Rotherham. It was to be his last letter to his parents. On the day it was postmarked – 11 June 1982 – Ian, despite his long years of experience gained on active service in Northern Ireland and on postings in Germany, was steeling himself for the first major set-piece battle of his life in his career as a soldier and by the time the letter was sliced open by Freda McKay in Rotherham two weeks later, she had already received the dread news that the struggle for Mount Longdon had consumed her son.

CHAPTER TEN

'I'll See You in Stanley'

Even as Ian was writing his letter from his hole in the ground east of the Estancia position, the planning for the battle in which he would secure his place in military history was gradually being refined. Brigadier Julian Thompson's blueprint for the investment of Stanley had begun to take shape in his mind from 6 June onwards.

Resisting pressure for an attack on a narrow front along the track between Fitzroy and Stanley, an assault which the Argentine commander General Mario Menendez had expected until as late as 24 May, Brigadier Thompson's initial strike would be a three-phase operation; each phase designed to punch a battalion-sized hole through the crust of the Argentine defences, until Stanley itself was revealed and threatened.

This entailed three battalions of 3 Commando Brigade launching a staggered assault against the 'crescent moon' formed by the peaks of Mount Longdon (3 Para) to the north, Two Sisters (45 Commando), 3km to the southwest and finally curving south down to Mount Harriet (42 Commando) a further 2km distant. If everything went well and the battalions could generate enough momentum to cause the Argentine defences to crumble, there was sufficient in-built flexibility to allow for further exploitation on to Wireless Ridge and Mount Tumbledown standing sentinel on either side of the Two Sisters track to the east.

It was, of course, important to seize and secure all three objectives but the capture of Mount Longdon was absolutely vital to the success of Brigadier Thompson's overall scheme in that artillery, ammunition and all other supplies required to support the entire operation would have to pass north of Mount Kent on their way from the forward logistics base at Teal Inlet. Equally important was securing the route for heliborne traffic in the opposite direction. Lieutenant Colonel Carlos Doglioli who, as a major, served as one of two ADCs to Military Governor General Mario Menendez, along with Military Academy and Staff College classmate, Augustin Buitrago in 1982, remains convinced of the importance of the Longdon position in the overall Argentine defensive scheme. His assessment of the organization of the Argentine defence overall was that it was 'very much ...a line with no depth'.

Because of his proximity to one of the men at the heart of the Argentine effort he knew, more than most, that the simultaneous capture of Longdon and Two Sisters would create a substantial breach and lay the foundations for a breakthrough. 'This is what we, in Argentine military jargon, call an '*ataque de rupture*', a penetration attack. If Longdon fell, all the other positions of the Argentine defence could be attacked and rolled from one of its flanks, coming down from Longdon and Two Sisters.'[1]

In Julian Thompson's mind, there was never any doubt that Longdon was the lynchpin of the Argentine defence. 'The significance of Longdon was its key position dominating the supply route to Teal Inlet. It was proved vital during the battle, and at times on the following days and nights when the low cloud on the high ground prevented helicopter casevac [casualty evacuation] to Fitzroy. My Brigade Forward Dressing Station (FDS) at Teal was the only FDS able to accept casualties – for example the Scots Guards casualties were dealt with at Teal and not by their own Brigade FDS at Fitzroy. Incidentally, the Divisional Medical Officer wanted to close Teal, but I objected and Jeremy Moore [Major General Jeremy Moore, Divisional Commander and Brigadier Thompson's immediate superior] supported my objection.'[2]

Lieutenant Colonel Pike was briefed on the plan on the afternoon of 10 June. The assault would be a night attack and was to be 'silent to contact' – that is, without the support of a preliminary bombardment to soften up the Argentine positions. Julian Thompson's reasoning for this was twofold:

I was keen for all attacks on the night 11 /12 June to be silent in order to:

a. preserve surprise as to our objectives and axes, and
b. preserve ammunition, bearing in mind the problems with bringing it forward. In the end, after the night's battle, the ammunition on the gun lines was down to a handful per gun on some battery positions. It was this that made any exploitation on to Tumbledown in daylight unwise, so I stopped 45 Commando from advancing from Two Sisters. It became even more important to have the Longdon and Two Sisters assaults silent once I had allowed the attack on Harriet to be noisy, as part of the CO of 42 Commando's deception plan, as I hoped the noise in the south would convince the enemy that our axis was along the Fitzroy-Stanley track from the southwest (which he expected), and conceal our approach from the northwest.[3]

In addition, the experiences of 2 Para at Goose Green had proved how a battle during daylight across a series of relatively low, open ridges which were incised towards Darwin with numerous re-entrants, could become stalled and ultimately costly in terms of casualties. Brigadier Thompson's faith in the abilities of his battalion commanders to carry out a night assault was unshakeable. He trusted that the possibility of confusion during a night attack, a very complex operation fraught with difficulties of command and control, would be more than offset by the skill, the discipline, the motivation and leadership of 3 Para.

Three hours after he had attended Julian Thompson's Brigade Orders Group, Lieutenant Colonel Pike called his senior commanders together in the Regimental Aid Post at Estancia House. This was the start of the process of ensuring that his orders percolated down through the battalion until everyone was aware of their role in the coming battle. Before getting down to business, however, he stressed that 3 Para were to move as far east as possible towards Stanley and stressed that the battalion was to exploit its opportunities to the full. He was also unequivocal about his unit's abilities. 'If a parachute battalion couldn't do it then nobody could,' he said. 'It was now the time to pressurize the enemy.'[4]

But what of the enemy? The Argentine defenders had been constructing their rock and peat sangars and building strongpoints on Longdon since 14 April and so had had fifty-eight days, almost two months, in which to establish themselves on its craggy fastness. Given adequate weaponry and efficient re-supply of ammunition and supplies, the mountain, with its complexities of geography, terrain and orientation, should have been a defender's dream.

Viewed at a distance from the west, Mount Longdon rises dramatically from the surrounding featureless terrain, looking for all the world like the broad, horny hump of a partially submerged alligator; still and silent with a hint of menace lurking just below the surface. Sprouting incongruously and almost vertically from the diddle dee and pale tussock grass, parallel strips of mid-grey rock resembling terraces seem to stitch its northern and southern slopes, separated as they are by a broader strip of open boulder-strewn ground between. On closer inspection the steady slope from the west soon gives way to a steeper ascent, and the approach, particularly at its northwest corner, reveals that, what at first appear as terraces from afar are actually a series of jagged corridors or channels formed by huge, steeply angled, quartzite slabs leading up to a frost-shattered summit concealing numerous nooks, crannies and rock runnels.

From the western summit the ground falls away to the east into a slight, saddle-like depression forming a relatively open, narrow ridge which levels out and runs roughly northwest-southeast, to another isolated rock outcrop and then beyond up to the almost pyramidal peak of the second of Longdon's summits at its eastern end. Rugged boulder fields, with rocks of varying grades, litter all the approaches and lie scattered at various intervals along the saddle-like ridge. From the vantage point of the western summit, two further large and distinctive outcrops of rock stand out as they rear up at a crazy angle and mark out the northern edge of the ridgeline. Significantly, these larger outcrops are breached by two narrow alleys or gaps which swoop down steeply from the confusion of boulders on the crest and slice through the rocks onto the lower reaches of the northern slopes below. The more westerly and most pronounced of these gaps forms a feature which has come to be known as 'The Bowl' or 'The Hollow', and the second breach marked the junction of the defences of the 1st and 2nd Platoons of the infantry company of the Argentine regiment holding Longdon.

Beyond this second gap, this second, more easterly crag rears up then falls away, its jagged spine gradually descending to peter out at a point where today a pronounced track, which leads from the western summit, winds down towards the northeast and eventually makes its way towards Wireless Ridge. From this point the more easterly of Longdon's two peaks – 'Full Back' – is visible, but walk along the track a little way and the ground drops away; the secondary peak disappearing behind another series of rocks interspersed with carpets of coarse yellow grass and dark green ferns. It is roughly 30m, across open ground devoid of cover, from the second crag to the snout of this seemingly innocuous rocky outcrop, in front of which stands an odd-shaped rock, a piece fractured from its base so that it resembles a face missing an eye. In 1982 two Argentine sangars sat on the rocks just above, with pup tents erected at the base of the rocks below. This area has, until now, gone largely unremarked in the history of the battle for Mount Longdon but it nevertheless became the stage upon which Ian McKay played out his final act of heroism.

Hew Pike's planning for the Longdon attack was based on the sum of his knowledge gained by the British patrols regarding the sheer physical geography of Mount Longdon and the surrounding terrain; the known strength and depth of the Argentine defences, both on Longdon itself and those on the northern flanks of other features providing mutual fire support such as Two Sisters and Mount Tumbledown, and the overall scheme involving 3 Commando Brigade. Although the 3 Para patrols had done excellent work, the intelligence was, by necessity, incomplete. For the last ten days, Hew Pike's Intelligence Officer, Captain Giles Orpen-Smellie, had tried to drop pieces of the intelligence jigsaw into place but years later he reflected on his frustration as his quest to build a detailed picture was continually thwarted by those on his own side:

There was an aura of black art that had been fostered by intelligence organizations. A large part of this was the unintended consequence of experience from years of operations in Northern Ireland and the sensitivities of intelligence agencies working in that arena. There was a problem of over-classification leading to reluctance, even refusal, to release information. A number of intelligence gathering assets were deployed to the South Atlantic but their owners would not release the information they gleaned to unit level. I cite two examples: prior to the attack on Mount Longdon I went to visit an electronic warfare (EW) detachment, probably part of 14 Signal Regiment, that was set up on Estancia Mountain. The NCO in charge was thoroughly unhelpful and took my number, rank and name because I had broken some BAOR security standing order in approaching within fifty metres of his position. I pointed out bluntly that we were at war in the South Atlantic and not on exercise on the North German Plain but despite a pointed exchange I still did not get any information. Special Forces (SF) were much the same: I was approached by SAS patrols for briefings on two occasions prior to their departure forward from our positions. I was happy to brief them but when I asked them to reciprocate the answer was a cavalier cry of, 'Sorry boss, Special Forces, can't tell you.' They would not even give their routes out and back in, or their expected areas of operation to our front so that we could deconflict their activities with our own. Their cry was, 'Don't worry boss, we'll see your blokes before they see us.' It seemed that Brigade was having similar difficulties as they were never able to answer our questions on SF activity or give us any information from SF patrol debriefs. I was saddened, but not at all surprised, when an SAS patrol clashed with an SBS patrol on 2 June resulting in the death of a Royal Marine. So, the only information about the enemy that I had was the best estimate of the Argentine order of battle that had been worked out during our time at Ascension Island together with a catalogue of the equipment that they possessed gleaned from library sources such as the IISS Military Balance and Jane's. But, while this was a start, it offered the battalion nothing about the specifics of the Argentine defences on our forthcoming objective. Almost no true intelligence was given to us by the chain of command during the campaign and so we had to discover anything and everything we wanted to know for ourselves.[5]

Inevitably there would be positions and strongpoints that had not been logged and although the final intelligence summary compiled by Giles Orpen-Smellie correctly identified the Argentine regiment then holding Mount Longdon, estimates of the strength of the garrison, as recorded in the War Diary, proved to be overly generous. By the eve of battle it was noted that there were probably three companies totalling 800 men dug in on and around Longdon with the artillery support of '3x105 guns at Moody Brook and a 155 on Sapper Hill'. In fact, by the time 3 Para were moving up for their attack there was only one company of infantry reinforced by two 'Grupos' of Marine Infantry machine gunners armed with six Browning 12.7mm (0.50-calibre) heavy machine guns (HMG) and supporting riflemen under Lieutenant Dachary (24 men in total), and a reserve platoon of Brigade engineers in position on the mountain.

Giles Orpen-Smellie believes that the estimate of the Argentine strength of 800 men on Longdon, as noted in the War Diary, requires clarification.

I suggest that facts were recorded inaccurately in the War Diary. The information presented by the CO reflected the information gained by our patrols that we had previously passed to Brigade; he brought no fresh information back from Brigade. This had suggested two companies and perhaps a little more which, rounded up to three companies, might have amounted to a figure of about 300 defenders. This would not have given us the 3:1 odds in favour of the attacker required by the tactics pamphlets but did give us a 25–30 per cent edge in our favour. Had the defence really been estimated at 800 strong, or 2:1 against, I doubt that the Brigadier would have ordered an assault by only one battalion – 2 Para was moving up into our rear as part of the Brigade reserve and I believe would, had the defence really been 800 strong, also have been committed to the assault. The figure of 800 cited in the War Diary did reflect the estimated strength of the whole of 7 Infantry Regiment but it was assumed that they had elements, at least one company, further east along Wireless Ridge, which was also now known to be part of their Tactical Area of Responsibility.[6]

Most of the men defending Longdon belonged to B Company of the *7th Regimiento de Infanteria de Mecanizado* – 7th Mechanized Infantry Regiment (7 RIMec) – of X Mechanized Infantry Brigade, which had arrived in the Falklands on 14 April. The Mechanized Infantry Regiment had been deployed to Sector Plata (Silver) north of Moody Brook, an area which included Mount Longdon and Wireless Ridge in addition to Moody Brook itself, and was part of a force of 8,500–9,000 men of six infantry, artillery, air defence, engineering, coastguard and *Gendarmeria Nacional* units that eventually faced the seven British infantry units which converged on Stanley.

Based at La Plata in the province of Buenos Aires, 7 RIMec was made up of some 700 men whose military experience ranged from that of the recalled reservists who had left the Army in November 1981 and those who, in the March of 1982 had been in either the first month of their fourteen months' compulsory '*Conscriptio*' (National Service), or those in the 'Old Class' who had already served a year. The regiment boasted a long and proud history of service to the Argentine nation, as Lieutenant Colonel Carlos Doglioli observed:

The 7th Infantry Regiment is one of our oldest infantry units. It is one of only three which has two flags, a War Regimental flag (all regiments have this) and the 'Flag of the Andes' because the 7th was part of the Army of the Andes during our War of Independence. The Army of the Andes was formed in the provinces neighbouring Chile, under General San Martin`s orders (our founding father and most highly respected national hero), and it crossed the Andes to liberate Chile and then went to Peru and Ecuador and did the same thing, so the 7th had a proud tradition. Its private soldiers, whether conscripts of volunteers, have always come from the working class neighbourhoods of Greater Buenos Aires. The soldiers are typical urban products; street wise and difficult to control but once you manage to gain their respect and spread the word they are very, very good fighters. The 7th has always managed to maintain a remarkable battle performance throughout its history. Nobody was surprised with what the 7th actually achieved on Mount Longdon. Carlos Carrizo also had an Engineer platoon from X Engineering Company. It does not exist anymore. It was always a very good Brigade Combat Engineers Company. At that time brigades had one Engineering Company, now they have a full battalion. Again, it was no surprise that they too fought well on Longdon.[7]

The rank and file of 7 RIMec were certainly not raw recruits, although a few colimbas – conscripts – would later concede to being ill-prepared on a bitter winter's night on an inhospitable mountain top on East Falkland to meet the likes of Ian McKay, a man who could bring almost twelve years of elite soldiering and experience of active service in Northern Ireland to the battlefield. That said the 7th included some tough and resilient private soldiers, NCOs and officers who believed in their cause.

The defence of Longdon was entrusted to 7 RIMec's strongest company – B Company – under Captain Lopez. Lopez was fortunate to be able to draw on the knowledge and experience of the Regiment's Second-in-Command, Major Carlos Carrizo Salvadores, who first set foot on Longdon on 17 April. The next day the three platoons of B Company really set to on the serious work of building their defences in anticipation of an attack from the north. They had the best part of the next eight weeks to dig into the peat banks and hew positions out of the unforgiving rock, covering bunkers with corrugated iron and putting stone slabs and peat turves on top, making sure that all approaches up the mountain towards the western and eastern summits were covered with interlocking arcs of fire from medium and heavy machine guns protected by rifle pits. Major Carrizo Salvadores decided to switch the axis of his defences after 24 May so that they faced west with a concentration of sangars among and around the western summit.

In 1982, I was in my third year in the role of Second-in-Command of the 7th Regiment (*Coronel Conde*) based in La Plata city in Buenos Aires Province. In the Falklands, my regiment was assigned the mission of defending the northern flank of Puerto Argentino or Port Stanley. This front was about 12km from the Camber peninsular up to Monte Longdon and it was called the Plata sector. This sector was divided into three sub-sectors. Monte Longdon was part of sub-sector

Plata 2 and so came under my command. The frontage of sub-sector Plata 2 was 4km long to the north and 4km to the west; it was almost a perfect square that could contain one brigade in a defence position. At the beginning I was assigned B Company. It consisted of three platoons of riflemen, one support group and one small Class 1 logistics squadron to prepare everyday food, all under the orders of Captain Lopez. I started organizational work of the position with this company on 17/18 April. As the days passed, I realized that the assigned strength was not sufficient to occupy and defend all the area of the sub-sector that Longdon was part of (about 16sq km). Therefore, I discussed this with my CO, Lieutenant Colonel Omar Giménez, who assigned me more men. This state of affairs continued until the end of April and into May when I was given one platoon of Combat Engineers, one platoon of Marine Infantry with six 12.7mm calibre anti-aircraft machine guns, a half platoon of heavy mortars with two 120mm mortars, a ground surveillance team with a Rasit radar, one medical team and one SAM 7 rocket launcher that was part of a donation from the Peruvian Republic. I had a final total of 278 men (officers, non-commissioned officers and soldiers) with whom I finally arrived at the night of 11/12 June 1982. Because of the terrain and because of the limited strength to occupy it, I opted for organizing a redoubt with a 360 degree defence capability. Initially I placed 1 Platoon [Lieutenant Juan Baldini] to the west, 2 Platoon [Staff Sergeant Raul González] to the north and 3 Platoon [Lieutenant Enrique Neirotti] to the east with the Combat Engineers Platoon in reserve to the south because we first expected an attack from the north (in my case, from Bahia de la Anunciación). My sub-sector was on the left flank of the northern front. I put the heavy mortars in the centre of the defence so that they had 360 degree fire capability and placed the radar between the first and second platoons on the north-west face. When it emerged that the English attack would come from the west, and considering the occupation of Monte Kent and surrounding areas, I switched 3 Platoon with the Engineering Platoon in order to have the three rifle platoons facing west and the Engineering Platoon in reserve. With this organization we fought against 3 Para that night. In some English accounts, I have read that, 'Longdon was defended by the 7 Regiment reinforced by Commando units with superb, high tech night vision equipment...' We were just 278 men to defend Longdon the best way we could with what we had and in terms of night vision equipment, we only had two optical aiming sights from the Marine Infantry. Night sights supplied by the army were used to observe the battlefield, not to aim at a target. They looked like a pirate's telescope because of their size! We therefore had two sights and one pair of goggles – or equivalent – per platoon. Also, the, devilishly accurate aiming I have read about was achieved as a result of the marksmanship training on the rifle ranges and the good aim of the riflemen, nothing more.[8]

Carlos Doglioli overflew Longdon in a helicopter on 29 April, even as Carrizo Salvadores and his men were busying themselves putting Longdon in a state of defence. From the air, he was struck by the rugged terrain and what he called the 'hedgehog design' of the mountain. He was certain that the terrain, given the weaponry and firepower then available to 7 RIMec, backed up by artillery support, would render Longdon, 'a difficult nut to crack'.

In '82, our rifle platoons – including the Combat Engineers – had two General Purpose Machine Guns (GPMGs) – we called them MAGs – in a Support Squad, as well as one 88.9mm (3.5in) rocket launcher, or, as in the case of the 7th Infantry, each rifle platoon had one 90mm M-67 recoilless rifle. It was a superb weapon – the American equivalent of the 84mm Carl Gustav which the British used. In addition, the three rifle squads in the rifle and Combat Engineers platoons also had two heavy-barrelled automatic rifles (FAP – *Fusil Automatico Pesado*) – imagine a British SLR with a heavy barrel and bipod and full automatic fire capability. With two per squad, Carrizo had twenty-four of those. For the British patrols gaining information on Mount Longdon, however, it was impossible for them to confuse the FAPs with the MAGs The FAPs fire 600 rounds per minute on fully automatic and the sound is a slow 'rat-tat-tat-tat-tat' where you can count each shot. You can adjust MAGs to fire at 600, 700, 800 and 1,000 rounds per minute and so they produce a very different rattle, depending on the chosen rate of fire. MAGs need to be kept as clean as possible in order to ensure their functioning without problems and that means cleaning the whole gas mechanism a good deal. But if, in combat, you don't have time for that and you sense that your MAG is beginning to give you trouble you go to a higher rate of fire (that is you close the gas rod) and it always works. Therefore MAGs are usually operated at their higher rate of fire and so they produce a different kind of sound – a 'brrrrrrp' – rather than the 'rat, tat, tat' coming from FAPs. Besides, firing on full auto with a FAP, you should not fire more than a three round burst because, despite the bipod, you are simply wasting ammunition. A five round burst is simply stupid and when one hears such a thing one knows that there is someone very frightened out there trying to soothe his nerves! Our machine gunners tended to fire shorter bursts than our regulations indicated for medium machine guns. Manuals say that you should fire fourteen- to thirty-round bursts, but the truth is that gunners seldom fired more than seven- or eight-round bursts for two reasons; first we have always been a relatively impoverished army and insisted on making sure that each round counted and, second, there is the need to conserve ammunition as ammunition re-supply for machine guns is never easy. I spoke with Carlos Carrizo Salvadores about the positioning of the MAGs on Longdon and he told me that this decision was left to the rifle platoon commanders who placed them according to their effectiveness in their sector.[9]

In the opinion of Carlos Doglioli, the 3 Para patrols must have managed to identify the Argentine FAPs from their MAGs in the two major probes that they carried out before the main attack. In the first probe no Argentine mortars were fired, only artillery fire support coming from 3rd Artillery Group (OTO-Melara 105mm howitzers) but during the final probe the Argentines fired their 120mm mortars, together with all the other weapons in order to repel it. As the British SLR in use at the time made a slightly different sound from the Argentine FALs (*Fusil Automatique Leger*) it was possible to distinguish who was who. Such a furious response would have given the 3 Para patrol some inkling of the weaponry available to the defenders.

In addition, there was ample provision of further weaponry. Carlos Doglioli again:

We had rifle grenades (PDEF-40, projectile double effect 40mm calibre – with a very good high explosive warhead) and PAF 62, (Projectile Anti-tank for Rifle – 62mm HEAT warhead). These rifle grenades were produced in Argentina and were completely reliable and effective. ALL our FAL rifles could launch them. Carrizo Salvadores had two 105mm recoilless rifles known as 'Czekalski' in the Argentine Army because of the Polish engineer who designed them. Each infantry company had two of these in 1982. These were equivalent to the British Wombats or the American M-40s. Besides these [Carrizo] had two 81mm mortars and half the 7 Regiment's Heavy Mortar Platoon with two Hotchkiss 120mm AM-50 heavy mortars. He also had one 'Cobra' launcher – a first generation, wire guided, anti-tank missile produced by a Franco-German consortium. As regards the number of night vision sights and goggles that Carrizo's men had that night, our navy managed to find someone in the United States who sold 100 sights and 100 pairs of goggles and they were sent to the Falkland Islands at the end of May or the beginning of June, when the fighting on land had already begun. Rear Admiral Edgardo Otero, who commanded the navy component on the islands, ordered that the Marines were to keep half of them and the other half would be distributed among army units. So, the Marine .50-calibre HMGs most likely had some of these – probably one goggle or sight per weapon – and Carrizo's B Company probably got one per platoon. These kits were Litton, very good ones. As a matter of fact, the guy who sold them to Argentina faced charges in the USA and several years later went to jail for having sold these kits. He sold them as agricultural equipment! Perhaps the goggles could have passed, as indeed they did, as being useful for tractor drivers working their fields at night, but the weapon sights? The Marine Infantry .50-calibre (12.7mm) HMGs were part of an eighteen-gun HMG company formed in Puerto Belgrano [on the Argentine mainland] with marine personnel drawn mostly from the Base Security Battalion. The Browning M-2 HMGs were taken out of mothballs at the depot and readied, cleaned and checked to be sent to war. One of company's six gun platoons was sent to reinforce the 25 Infantry at the old airport, another was sent to reinforce 5 Marine Battalion, and the third one was sent to Longdon. All the eighteen Brownings were mounted on anti-aircraft pedestals – they had nothing else – and when the company was formed the HMG was considered an auxiliary weapon in an anti-aircraft role. That was precisely the reason why one of its three platoons was sent to 25 Infantry Regiment at the old airport. So, the eighteen HMGs were mounted on anti-aircraft pedestal mounts which meant that their gunners had to fire from a standing position.[10]

It was a formidable arsenal to say the least.

Shouldering his share of the responsibility for the defence of the western summit was Private Anibal Grillo, of Lieutenant Juan Baldini's 1st Platoon. In fact his was a unique position for he counted himself as being the most easterly and therefore the very last of Baldini's men. On arrival on Longdon he had dug his initial position close into a rock wall – improvising a large, fallen slab as a ready made roof – a little way forward of the second of the re-entrants between the two distinct rock outcrops north east of Longdon's summit. It proved to be a good shelter in case of bombardment but Anibal soon realized it was prone to flooding so he had pitched a tent, again hard by the rock face but on a slope in an area with better drainage just a few metres further forward. This he shared with his comrades Jorge Altieri, Sergio Sanchez and Dario Gonzalez until Gonzalez was ordered forward before 11 June to join the Cobra team on the slopes overlooking the western approach.

A stone's throw to the south, Lance Corporal Pedro Alberto Orozco and Private Ramon Omar Quintana had constructed their rifle pit. Behind him, dug into the large rock feature on the other side of the re-entrant, were the men of the forward sections of First Sergeant González's 2nd Platoon. Sited at the junction of the two platoons and dominating the approach up the re-entrant from the north and with a field of fire which covered the ground dipping into the saddle from the western summit, was a .50-calibre HMG post under the command of Marine Privates First Class Claudio Scaglione and Sergio Giusepeti. Behind and further south was a 120mm mortar which could bring fire to bear on the summit. Rising to his front, Grillo could see another rocky crag at the base of which, and out of his direct view, Juan Baldini had established his command post. The rest of his comrades of the 3rd rifle section were distributed around Baldini's position. Some 150m further west were the forward troops of Baldini's platoon forming the front line on the western perimeter of Major Carrizo Salvadores' defence.

Armed with a 90mm gun, that would in fact later malfunction in action, Privates Luis Aparicio and Juan Andrioli peered down the boulder-strewn western slope from their lofty perch, their sangar nestling between three men manning a MAG to their left and the Rasit radar on their right. They could not see all the way down, their positions so elevated that the convex curve of the hill concealed a strip of ground at the foot of the slope. To the northeast, the jutting walls of the rock corridors marching up the hillside obscured their view of the ground beyond. Southwest and below the summit, Lance Corporal Diaz's group of riflemen were within shouting distance of others in rifle pits and pup tents dotted right and left and behind, while another .50-calibre HMG stood sentinel at the junction with Lieutenant Neirotti's 3rd Platoon continuing the line of defence along the southern slopes to the east. All told, Baldini's command covered an area some 300m deep by 200m wide at the western end of Mount Longdon. It would fall to him, his men and the attached Marine Infantry heavy machine gunners to bear the brunt of 3 Para's attack.

There has been much debate surrounding the fate of these men in the mountains of the outer defence zone. Some consider themselves the forgotten army, abandoned by their officers and left to survive on a diet of thin, lukewarm soup, pasta and *maté*, a bitter herbal tea. A few took to walking miles and risking heavy penalties to 'liberate' supplies from the supply dumps near Stanley, while others were reported to have shot and roasted sheep on old bed frames. There are others, officers and private soldiers alike, who maintain that the Argentine troops were respected and helped to make themselves as comfortable as possible under the circumstances and that their officers worked hard to raise spirits, bolster morale and maintain firm but fair discipline. Whatever the final verdict of history may be, when it came to the crunch on the night of 11/12 June, the Argentines on Mount Longdon would stand up to be counted and make a fight of it.

It was already a given that 3 Para's attack would go in during the hours of darkness and that the advance to contact would be silent but Hew Pike had other considerations as he mulled over his options for an operation the like of which had not been, 'undertaken by the battalion for a generation'.[11] Longdon, at only 612ft at its highest point on the western summit, was not a great height in itself, but nevertheless dominated the surrounding low lying and open ground for at least 2,000m in all directions, providing clear fields of fire. Meanwhile known minefields, sited in patches of dead ground to the north, west and southwest, and the presence of supporting Argentine forces on Mount Tumbledown to the southeast and Wireless Ridge to the east, effectively ruled out any possibility of a flanking attack. Longdon's geography dictated that no more than a force amounting to a single company could operate along its spine at any one time. Hew Pike thus determined to assault the mountain from its western extremity with two of his three rifle companies 'up'.

Using nicknames plucked from the sports fields on which the Rugby Union code is played to denote key features on the battlefield, A and B Companies would move up the 4km from the Estancia position in darkness and cross the 'start line' (codename Free Kick) – a fast flowing, knee-deep stream 1km west of Longdon, twisting and turning northward towards the Furze Bush Pass and very roughly at right angles to the intended line of advance – at 8.01pm local time, 12.01am ZULU. A Company (Major David Collett) was to advance on the left, northerly flank, to attack and secure a spur and rocky outcrop to the northeast (codename Wing Forward) and establish a fire base from where it could support B Company, under Major Mike Argue, fighting its way up to and through the forward, western summit of the main feature (codename Fly Half) before going on to tackle the rear, eastern summit (codename Full Back).

The remaining rifle company, C Company (Major Martin Osborne), was to remain on the line of Free Kick as battalion reserve with orders to reinforce the forward platoons should Argentine resistance evaporate and the possibility of further exploitation onto Wireless Ridge present itself. This flexibility was built into the overall plan but it was also dependent on 45 Commando taking all its first-phase objectives and pushing onto and occupying Tumbledown to the southeast. Also on the start line were the sustained fire role GPMGs – 30,000 rounds – and Milan anti-tank teams – 40 missiles with another 40 in reserve – of Support Company under Major Peter Dennison, who were also to hold on Free Kick ready to go forward when the call came. The Mortar Platoon (Captain Julian James) had also established a mortar base nearby. In charge of casualty evacuation (casevac) and ammunition re-supply by means of Volvo BV 'Bandwagon' tracked vehicles was battalion second in command, Major Roger Patton.

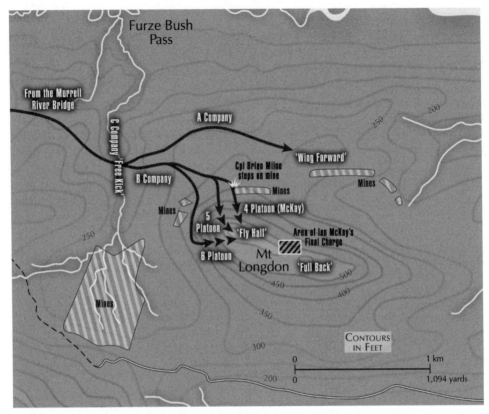

3 Para's Assault on Mount Longdon – 11/12 June 1982.

Ready, and on priority call to provide additional heavier direct support, Lieutenant Colonel Pike could draw on the services of the six, 105mm light field guns of 79 (Kirkee) Battery, 29 Commando Regiment, Royal Artillery (RA) and dedicated Naval Gun Fire Support from HMS *Avenger's* formidable 4.5in gun with a stockpile of 300 rounds, guided in by specialist Naval Gun Fire Observer, Captain Willie McCracken of 148 Battery RA.

Major Mike Argue's B Company, which would first have to ascend Longdon's western wall, seize the first summit and then engage key points of resistance along the entire length of its craggy spine, faced a daunting task. Although Hew Pike's appreciation of the narrow nature of the Longdon summit had led him to the conclusion that only one company could fight along it at any one time, there was still the possibility that that company might not have sufficient numbers to comb out all the Argentine sangars if some men were held in reserve. To counter this possible scenario, Major Argue hit upon a bold and, some would say, rather risky, model. He decided to advance all his three platoons together and use them to roll like a tide, up towards Fly Half, there to break its resistance, before driving on along the crest of Longdon, swamping the remaining Argentine positions as they went. Running from north to south Andrew Bickerdike and Ian McKay's 4 Platoon was handed the responsibility of fighting along, then up through, the gaps and alleyways between the main rock outcrops to the northwest and pushing on at a lower level, clearing the northern face and thus the northern flank of the mountain itself. Meanwhile, 5 Platoon, under Lieutenant Mark Cox and Platoon Sergeant John Ross, was to drive up higher than 4 Platoon, through a tighter series of rock channels or corridors leading to the northwest face of the summit just north of and parallel to the central approach. At the same time 6 Platoon, under Lieutenant Jon Shaw and Platoon Sergeant Pete Gray, would sweep up from the southwest and seize the rugged southern slopes on its way towards seizing the summit of Fly Half. This plan meant that Andrew Bickerdike and Ian McKay's 4 Platoon would have the responsibility of securing and sealing the left flank of B Company's assault.

It should be noted, however, that the various plans, developed both at battalion and company level, were not without their detractors. There were some – officers and senior NCOs amongst them – who felt that it was worth dispensing with the element of surprise offered by a silent night attack, in order to have secured the possible benefits of a preliminary bombardment. Longdon had, they reasoned, been subject to harassing fire from 29 Commando Regiment since 3 June. Further shelling may not have given the game away when the time came to attack. Later the thought – doubtless strengthened by Brigadier Julian Thompson's own admission in his memoir of the war, that the repeated success of D Company patrols in penetrating the Argentine defences and returning unscathed, had somehow lulled him and Lieutenant Colonel Pike into the mistaken belief that Longdon could be disposed of quickly, perhaps without any prior 'softening up' – gained ground.[12]

Strategically, however, there could have been serious consequences if HQ 3 Commando Brigade had been too prodigal of artillery ammunition during the initial phase of the final battles for Stanley. As long as Longdon remained unconquered and defiant, the supply line to Teal was unsecured and even without a preliminary bombardment, ammunition on the gun lines was, in some cases, later found to have dipped to just a handful of rounds per battery by the end of the first night's fighting. Giles Orpen Smellie, 3 Para's Intelligence Officer, remains convinced that the decision to go silent was the correct one and questions whether a preliminary barrage on Longdon could have been sustained effectively, given the length of time it actually took for 3 Para to cross the 2,500m approach from the point they started their approach march to the line of the stream marking their start line. Such a barrage would have shaken the defenders from their slumbers with extreme violence, everyone on Longdon would have been wide awake and alert and even then 3 Para would still have had more than 1,000m to go before the leading men of B Company hit the lower slopes to begin their ascent. And when the barrage finally ceased to allow B Company to begin fighting its way forward, the survivors would have been waiting, dry-mouthed, hearts pounding, adrenalin pumping and weapons ready. In such a scenario, a substantial quantity of precious artillery ammunition would have been expended with no guarantee that the Argentine defenders, taking cover in their well constructed sangars on Longdon, would have been neutralized:

The Battalion had some 2,500m of open ground to cover from the last sensible cover to the Forming up Point (FUP) and then 1,500m from the Start Line to the forward edge of the Argentine position. The ground we had to cross was such that we were not going to cover it at speed. We had proved with patrols, particularly the large fighting patrol a few days before, that the Argentines were not alert at night and that bodies of troops could get close to their positions undetected. It did not seem sensible to wake up the defenders unnecessarily. There were insufficient artillery rounds to sustain a barrage for the time required for the infantry to cross the open ground and a barrage probably would not have neutralized all the Argentine positions. Meanwhile, a number of artillery fire missions had been fired at targets on and around the mountain during the patrol phase in the days leading up to the assault. These had been marked and recorded by the gunners. Therefore, the gunners had the ability to conduct a silent fire plan, with the guns being laid on pre-recorded targets as the battalion advanced. This offered immediate fire-for-effect when it was needed.

I would suggest that these three reasons support the decision to go silent. I was not involved in taking the decision, which was presented at the time as a fait-accompli. I have heard others, notably company commanders from 2 Para, who have argued that going silent was a mistake. I have pondered upon their views and keep coming back to my opinion that it was the right decision in our particular circumstances as it allowed the battalion to achieve tactical surprise. In the event, the battalion got to the foot of the mountain undetected and the first indication that the Argentine defenders had of the assault was when Corporal Brian Milne stepped on [an] anti-personnel mine. Thereafter, the gunners and the Royal Navy provided effective artillery support, which was frequently brought in much closer than the usual danger-close distances would permit. This said, the effect of the artillery, British and Argentine, was often mitigated, either by the protection afforded by the rocks or by the smothering effect of the peat. I am still here to enjoy today because of the latter![13]

Certainly, Julian Thompson felt he had little option but to concentrate on the broader picture and conserve artillery stocks for future operations, as well as deceiving the Argentines into believing that his main thrust would come from the south with a noisy operation on Mount Harriet.

As soon as dawn broke on 11 June, men busied themselves in readiness for the coming battle. Galvanized by words of encouragement from Hew Pike, his company and platoon commanders and steadied by the old sweats like Lawrie Ashbridge, John Weeks and Ian McKay, preparations got under way. Everyone had a role and knew what to do. Their assault scales laid down exactly what had to be carried and who had to carry it, even down to the minute but potentially lifesaving details such as which pocket the spare first aid shell dressings had to be carried in so that everyone knew where they could be found in a crisis. They had done it all before in training but now this was real.

In truth – whatever their prior training, foreign postings or number of years' service – no one in 3 Para, from Hew Pike downwards, had ever experienced anything quite like this before. Thoughts of battle, of fear and uncertainty, of how one would perform, of the possibility of dead and wounded comrades, inevitably flashed through everyone's minds. These men were the heirs of a proud airborne legacy. Would they live up to expectations? Would they rise to the challenge? Some thirty-eight years on from the eve of D-Day or the drop into Arnhem in 1944, the scenes were repeated as British soldiers once more gathered around scale models of their objectives – mounds of earth representing Longdon, Two Sisters and Mount Harriet, tape and twigs indicating geographical features and objectives – to discuss opposition strong points, terrain and tactics, but this time they were 8,000 miles away from the battlefields of Normandy or the Netherlands. On the morning of 11 June Major Mike Argue strode up to the massed ranks of B Company and commenced his Airborne Brief. Andrew Bickerdike remembered it vividly:

> Orders came down through the chain of command so company commanders went and got their orders, they came back and Mike Argue gave his orders to B Company command group, essentially the platoon commanders, and we gave our orders to our platoons. Then Mike Argue got the whole company together and made quite an emotional speech because he said: 'This is it. This is the final push. We all know what we're doing. We're a band of brothers but we might not all be here tomorrow. But whatever happens, as a regiment, as a team, 3 Para are making history and we will always be remembered.' And we knew at that stage that there was going to be a punch up and chances were that there were going to be casualties. There were mixed emotions. There was elation at the fact that you have been chosen to do this job. As a young platoon commander, this was the ultimate test. You had joined the army for exactly this and everything else up to that point had been preparation for this moment. You were with the finest bunch of lads you could hope to go into action with and as a platoon commander – and I am sure it would have been the same for Ian McKay as a Senior NCO – you did not want to let yourself down, let your team down, let the regiment down, nobody. That's the driving force that binds you all together. It's the élan; knowing that you are part of a regiment that's got a fantastic history with its previous achievements and here you are ready to do your bit to make regimental history.[14]

Some of the youngest soldiers in the battalion – Neil Grose, Jason Burt and Ian Scrivens – came under the wing of their platoon sergeant Ian McKay in 4 Platoon. Andrew Bickerdike remembered how Ian ministered to his young charges:

> Ian was a very solid, reliable platoon sergeant. He looked after the lads almost like a mother hen. He looked after his lads well, helped by three very good section commanders. He was the Platoon Sergeant and yes, he looked after that platoon. But you have to remember that as young as some of the lads were, we were so committed by that stage that everyone just had to do their job. The lads were well trained; fit as butcher's dogs and you knew that whatever you asked them to do physically you wouldn't have a problem. Of course the big test for them – and for me of course – was that it would be our first experience of being under effective enemy fire. We'd all done live firing exercises over the years. Granted, some of the

lads from the Recruit Platoon at the Depot wouldn't have done it that much but they would have done their bit in terms of battle drill. The British Army's experience up to that point had really been in Northern Ireland and in Northern Ireland if you took one casualty everything ground to a halt, you set up cordons and looked after the casualty and dealt with the situation. But what was now being put across, coming down from Hew Pike through the company commanders, platoon commanders and senior NCOs and corporals, was that if we took a casualty he stayed there and our mission was to fight on, to keep the momentum going. We were in a very different situation and by this stage the lads had had nearly three weeks of living rough – cold, wet and miserable – and they were ready and keen. They wanted to get on with it.[15]

And so, too, did their commanding officer. It was well known in the battalion that during exercises, Hew Pike's favoured exhortation to his subordinates was, 'On, On', and it was clear that the key concepts now filtering down through the chain of command from the CO were, 'maintaining momentum' and 'impetus'. CSM John Weeks had been christened 'Thumper' by the men of B Company, along with a string of other names one might not always have used in polite company. Mike Argue had talked to the men as Company Commander but Weeks now felt it his responsibility as the CSM to have a word with them to reinforce the doctrine of fighting through and to prepare them for the brutal struggle which lay ahead:

We'd had our orders and then after the 'O' (Orders) Group I got the platoon sergeants together and told them that they'd heard one version of it but that now I was going to tell them how it really was. I told them that there were trenches all over the place up on Longdon and that we would have a hard fight on our hands. I told them I wanted to get everyone together to have word with the whole company before we went in. So we got the whole company together and I sat them down and gave them a brief. I said, 'You're a very young company but I'm very pleased with all the things you've done. I've been with you for two years and we've always achieved what we've needed to achieve but this will be your toughest assignment. Some of us sitting round here now are not going to come back from this battle. I believe there will be trench fighting and you will be told to fix bayonets. I know none of you have ever done it and just like me you've only ever done it with a dummy but the drill's the same – in, twist, pull out and get on to the next thing. Don't freeze; if you freeze you aren't going to pull it out and you'll be dead.' Then I said to them, 'I don't know if any of you are religious. I'm not a religious person but I'm going to go now and have ten minutes of prayer for want of a better word, because I believe that there's something up there that looks after us. I'm going to have a prayer for my family, my kids and although I can't order you to do it, I suggest you do because once we start, once the momentum of battle starts, there won't be time to think about anything. Things will be done as you go along, if you stop to think you'll be dead. You've just got to get the momentum going and keep it going. Your platoon sergeants and your section commanders will lead from the front. I'm not in a position to lead from the front but you'll hear me in my position to the rear of the platoons and I'll be bringing up ammunition and getting casualties out. I'll do whatever I need to do as CSM but all I'll say is you have to get the momentum going and keep it going. If we stop they'll swamp us.'[16]

Private Nick Rose of 6 Platoon in B Company certainly recalled that, 'What was drilled into us was the fact that you just had to keep going because if you don't the whole thing just breaks down.' Bearing in mind the premonition which Ian had shared with John Weeks on the voyage south, one can only wonder what may have passed through his mind as his CSM set out starkly that some would not survive.

Just before last light on 11 June – sunset was at 3.45pm local time, 7.54pm ZULU – Brian Faulkner, who had travelled to the Falklands in the same cabin as Ian, was on the hillside just forward of the Estancia position, preparing his load to take into battle. No longer acting as Captain Bob Darby's assistant, Brian was now fulfilling the important role of colour sergeant in the Regimental Aid Post, consisting of the battalion medical officer, Captain John Burgess RAMC, Sergeant Steve Bradley, Private Kennedy, plus a signaller and himself, and was attached to the fire support group under Captain Tony Mason and Sergeant Graham Colbeck. Each rifle company had a medic from the RAP attached to it while three, four-man teams of stretcher bearers, REME men, cooks or messmen who had become 'rifles', were attached to the RAP. He recalled that:

We were preparing everything on the hill. Everybody was sorting out their fighting order and ammunition scales. I was crouching down on the floor, tugging away and sorting out my bergan as we all were. We were sorting ammunition and medical supplies and were working out how we were going to carry it. In the RAP we carried quite a lot because we were also involved in carrying ammunition for re-supply as well as essential medical supplies and stretchers. I had my own rifle, six extra magazines, two belts of 200 rounds link for the fire support GPMGs, four grenades and all the medical equipment, as well as helping to carry a GPMG and a stretcher. In our bergans we had saline drips and medical stores – everything we thought we might need. Captain Burgess would advise us what to take and what was necessary but he let us decide how we should carry it. B Company had come on to the position and we were just to the back of the hill. The light was behind us and right in the distance, to the east, you could just see Mount Longdon. I looked up and there was Ian standing just a few yards from me silhouetted from the hill with the mountain behind him. He just sort of materialized from nowhere. There was no sun on him or anything like that; he was just standing there, smiling at me. He'd always had a struggle with his weight but he'd lost a fair bit what with all the marching and lack of real food. He'd already prepared himself and had come up with B Company ready for the advance. We just started chit-chatting and I said, 'How are you getting on, Ian? It's been a long time, nearly a month.' He agreed and I said, 'What we'll do, once we get on the mountain and then into Stanley, we'll have brew together seeing as we came all the way down together' and he said, 'We'll do that Brian. I'll see you in

Stanley.' The next time I saw Ian was a few hours later and unfortunately then I had to deal with his body. I felt it for all the other lads of course, but I'd known Ian a long time and it was very sad.[17]

The two men exchanged goodbyes and wished each other good luck then Brian watched as Ian walked over to join his platoon commander, offering quiet words of advice and encouragement to the men of his platoon as he checked and tugged at their webbing with his shovel-like hands before turning back to his own equipment.

Harassing fire from Argentine artillery had plagued the build-up all day but as the light finally faded, B and C Companies converged on A Company's location and the battalion was warned off to get into position and close up for the approach march. About thirty-five minutes later the men of 3 Para got the order to move out, shouldered their loads and set off towards the hump of rock they had seen in the east and their destiny.

CHAPTER ELEVEN

Into Battle

S ergeant Ian McKay paused at the line of white mine marker tape which had been laid by D (Patrols) Company on the eastern bank of a small stream, which flowed north to meet the Murrell River at a spot known as Furze Bush Pass on East Falkland. It was a little before 8.15pm in Port Stanley – fifteen minutes past midnight according to 3 Commando Brigade's operational ZULU time – and already into the early hours of 12 June; almost mid-winter in the South Atlantic. This was 3 Para's 'start line' – codename Free Kick – and the short halt gave the assaulting platoons of A and B Companies a last chance to gather their thoughts and draw breath as NCOs moved up and down giving their final words of encouragement.

We will never know, as he looked around the other twenty-seven men in his platoon, if Ian's thoughts lingered on his family at their homes in Aldershot or Rotherham as the season in Britain edged towards mid-summer; whether he wondered if Marica was at work or at home, still awake and watching TV, whether Melanie – way past her bedtime – and Donny, were sleeping soundly, whether his father Ken had been refereeing a snooker match at the club or whether mum Freda had had family round. Was Ian even then resigned to his fate or simply doing as he had always done and preparing for the task ahead just as assiduously as he had prepared for every other task he had ever undertaken during his service? The only evidence of his state of mind at that crucial moment is a brief conversation he had had with CSM John Weeks, which had reprised Ian's surprise statement on board the *Canberra* on the journey south. 'I remember Ian coming up to me this side of the Murrell – just before we crossed the river, before the battle for Mount Longdon and again, it's always stuck in my mind. He said, "Remember what I told you? I'm not going to come back from this." That was maybe an hour before we crossed the river and got into our formations for the battle. And sure enough he did not come back.'[1]

Premonition or not, that was for Ian alone to ponder, but now he had serious work to do. Ian McKay had always prided himself on getting the job done to the best of his ability. There was a discrete group of very young soldiers in B Company, some of whom, like 'Baz' Barrett, had been nurtured personally by Ian in 477 Recruit Platoon, and several others who had been at the Depot at the same time, who were now serving under his wing in his platoon. In the relatively short time that Ian had been his platoon sergeant 18-year-old Simon Ward, whose role was as the Number 2 on the GPMG in Corporal John Lewis's section, had developed the utmost respect for Ian's dedication. Simon later told his mother that Ian had been an inspiration and that he had 'taught him everything about soldiering'.[2]

There is no question that Ian would have felt his responsibilities very keenly. But as inexperienced as his young charges were they were nevertheless trained paratroopers;

the same age as he had been when he first stepped out on to the streets of Northern Ireland with the Mortar Platoon of 1 Para in early March 1971. Ian would have known something of what those young soldiers were thinking and feeling and would have been able to empathize with them, but it was now his job to make sure that he did everything possible to increase their chances of survival by ensuring that they fought well. He would live, and die, by that code during the next few hours. Some of those young soldiers would fight alongside him in the coming hours and several would die doing so.

Vernon Steen would also fight on Longdon that night and would come into contact with Ian McKay. He had joined Sergeant John Pettinger and Private Richard 'Dickie' Absolon of Patrols for the move forward to the start line west of Mount Longdon:

> Come last light we formed up in single file and set out. The first obstacle was to get all hands across the Murrell River without getting wet. A near impossible task under the circumstances but helped out considerably by the ingenuity of 9 Para Engineers [9 Parachute Squadron, RE] who devised a bridge from an aluminium ladder with planks of wood to place across a narrow section. This worked reasonably well and reduced the chances of a thorough soaking for most. The depth of the river would have been about two-three feet and obviously very cold, this was, after all, the middle of winter. Some snow on the ground and frost in the air was making the TAB difficult; this with the heavy loads of equipment and ammunition that Paras were carrying slowed the pace some and the deadline for crossing the start line was looking decidedly doubtful. Following the crossing of the Murrell some of the troops lost contact and drifted off to the south and east of the main column. This caused some concern and delay, however, this was resolved and the advance forward continued.[3]

'It is the hardest thing in the world,' wrote Hew Pike, 3 Para's commanding officer during the Falklands campaign, 'to write about the chaos, confusion and terrible nature of a battle. In a sense, all you can do is to tell your personal story, whether you are a young soldier in a Fire Section or the CO.'[4]

The narrative which follows is not intended to be a history of 3 Para's Battle for Mount Longdon. The battle was long and hard fought; the fighting often confused and utterly confusing for attacker and defender alike, senses heightened and driven on by a potent cocktail of adrenalin, fear and duty. The night of 11/12 June, 1982 witnessed many individual acts of courage on both sides. It is not my intention, in approaching the battle narrative as I have, to detract in any way from the experiences of those companies, sub-units and individuals whose actions helped to secure a victory for 3 Para that night, for their experiences and those of their Argentine adversaries are as valuable a part of the collective memory and history of the battle as anyone else's.

Rather the focus, quite intentionally, is on Ian McKay or at least those who came into contact with him and what narrative there is exists in an attempt to develop a coherent account leading up to and including the action for which he earned his Victoria Cross.

The night of 11 June, 1982 was bitterly cold and icy water had penetrated the boots and socks of some men who had fallen, knee deep, in the stream they had just forded. Despite the cold, the sweat – the combined result of extreme exertion during the approach march and anxiety – which had lathered their bodies on the four hour tab across country from the direction of Mount Vernet and Mount Estancia, was now doing its work; lowering body temperatures as the biting wind even began to penetrate their trusty loaned SAS windproofs. Still with about 3km to go to get to their start line on the Furze Bush stream suddenly all eyes were drawn to the east as a solitary Argentine 120mm mortar illumination shell arced high into the night sky and burst with a brilliant light, bathing the surrounding countryside in an eerie glow before slowly fading away. Bodies tensed. Silence. Vernon Steen remembered the trepidation of that moment vividly:

> Had we been spotted? Was the advance now compromised? Thankfully it appeared not and our TAB to the start line went without further incident. The position of the start line was approximately three-quarters of a mile south of Furze Bush Pass on a small stream that runs from south to north to the Murrell River. Crossing this now brought us to the final phase of the move to the assault on Mount Longdon. The move forward to the forming up position (FUP) on the northern shoulder of Mount Longdon whilst tense was text book.[5]

They had not been seen. However, B Company was now behind schedule, but not by much. Andrew Bickerdike remembers that the force moved up as a battalion snake and crossed the assault bridge [over the Murrell River] so that 'H-Hour became a slightly moveable feast because of the delays'.

The approach had gone quite well but it had been a trying experience. Each man carried a personal load in the region of 100lb which consisted of their personal stocks of rations and water, rifle, bayonet, spare magazines stuffed into every pouch of webbing and windproof pockets, 400–600 rounds of linked ammunition for the GPMGs and several fragmentation or white phosphorous grenades; a colossal weight to carry into an attack over several kilometres. Some men carried three plastic 'disposable' 66mm Light Anti-Tank Weapons (LAW) and a couple of '84s' (84mm) for the Carl Gustav Rocket Launchers. Others in Support Company carried tripods for the sustained fire role GPMGs and Milan missiles strapped below radios on their backs.

It had taken more than three and a half hours to get to the start line. The delays were due to men inching their way gingerly across the four planks augmented by a metal ladder bought from a famous hardware chain which passed for the bridge over the Murrell, compounded by the confusion resulting from the fire support teams of Support Company cutting up and separating the advancing platoons of B Company – parts of 5 and 6 Platoons became effectively lost for half an hour.

Hew Pike was keen to speed things up and so ordered A and B Companies to bypass their assembly area and begin their assault as quickly as possible. To shave precious minutes from the advance, Mike Argue had responded by ordering B Company to swing south of their intended route in order to approach Longdon more directly from the north-west rather than looping north in close proximity to A Company. It was to B Company's eternal credit that, as the seconds ticked by, they were just coming up to being fourteen minutes behind schedule. That said they still had another 1,000m or so to go to reach the lower slopes of Mount Longdon. It would soon be time.

High up in his command post towards Full Back – the eastern summit at the eastern extremity of the Argentine defences on Longdon – and unaware of the force moving inexorably towards him, Major Carrizo Salvadores and some of his HQ staff tuned their small receiver to hear the voice of Pope John Paul II celebrating Mass at the Basilica of Lujan. As the blessing began Carrizo Salvadores' three platoon commanders called in. They had nothing to report.

Roughly a kilometre away down the slopes of the mountain to the north west, just as CSM John Weeks had done a few hours earlier, so platoon sergeants and section commanders were now doing their best to invoke divine intervention by pointing their men in the direction of The Almighty, only their delivery was rather more pithy than that of the Pontiff. Corporal Trevor Wilson's brief to Private Nick Rose and the rest of 3 Section of 6 Platoon had been short and to the point; 'Say your prayers lads'.[6]

Major Carrizo-Salvadores had already ordered Sergeant Nista to switch off the *RASIT* ground surveillance radar, sited on Longdon's northwestern slopes between, as Carrizo-Salvadores revealed to the author in 2007, Lieutenant Baldini's forward 1st Platoon and Staff Sergeant González's 2nd Platoon, fearing that its signal would be picked up by the British Cymbeline mortar location system. That decision was to assist B Company during the initial stages of its advance.

It was then that CSM John Weeks shocked some men of B Company with an order which the young paras felt had been long consigned to the history books:

At just after 12 o'clock [midnight ZULU time] we hit the start line as per the plan. Then we got into battle formation. We got into extended line but then we peeled off and I can remember a bit of juggling with the approach to get 4 and 5 Platoons on the correct line; 6 Platoon went slightly further south because of the contours. It was at that stage, when we were in extended line, that I went along and told them to fix bayonets. Mike Argue, even after the event, came up to me and asked, 'Why did you ask them to fix bayonets Sergeant Major?' I told him that the briefing had said that there might be a lot of trenches and that we could expect trench warfare. The SBS and the SAS and the locals had given different briefings on different amounts of trenches, different numbers [of defenders] and John Pettinger from our own Patrols Company had been up on there and had thought there might be as much as a brigade, even though we'd been told it was a company. I'd spoken to John Pettinger back near Mount Vernet and he'd told me there were a hell of a lot of trenches up there so all I could visualize in my mind was that we were going to be involved in trench fighting. The only way you can clear trenches is by moving from trench to trench and if the trenches are close together you have to get into the first trench, clear them out of it and then get into the next trench. We didn't all have SMGs for close-quarter battle so we needed to use the bayonet. The order was passed down.

6 Platoon were to my right and I saw the first four or five lads from 6 Platoon 'clicking' and on it went down the line.[7]

Andrew Bickerdike was quite clear as regards the task he had been ordered to perform. On 8 July 1982, he wrote a report whilst still in hospital, which is now in the National Archives. In that report, one of several hand-written statements in support of the recommendation for Ian McKay's VC, he wrote that, 'On the night of 11/12 June 1982 I was commanding 4 platoon B Company 3 Para for the assault on Mount Longdon. We were left forward platoon tasked with advancing on the northern side of the rock feature to the company secondary objective.'[8]

The burden of several hundred years of British military history weighed heavily on Andrew Bickerdike at that moment as he waited to lead Ian McKay and the rest of 4 Platoon forward:

I remember clearly that as we reached the start line I ordered the lads to fix bayonets. Everyone was kneeling and I was standing in the middle of the platoon so that section commanders could look in and get their reference from me. 'Fix bayonets' was passed down the line. I remember taking my bayonet out, putting it on the end of my rifle and at that point I told myself that I was holding a Queen's Commission, I was commanding soldiers of the British Army and I was about to go into a battle as thousands and thousands of British soldiers had before me and that this was my chance to follow in their footsteps. That 'click' of the bayonet – that's when it finally came home to me what I was about to do. Everyone put their bayonets on, then there was a brief silence before the command, 'up' and they all stood up and we started advancing.[9]

'Fix bayonets'? Advancing in 'extended lines'? Surely these were concepts which belonged in books about the Western Front of France and Flanders in the Great War? Now B Company had truly reached the point of no return. As well-rehearsed as the paras were, in the booming silence before battle, the almost imperceptible sound of more than 150 bayonets clicking into place seemed to carry for miles. Would the Argentines hear? This was it.

At 8.15pm local time more than 200 men of A and B Companies and attached troops stepped over the white tape and into the unknown. As A Company headed for the rocky outcrop and the slightly elevated ground to the north, which had been code named Wing Forward to set up their fire support base, 4, 5 and 6 Platoons of B Company advanced at a steady pace and shook out into assault formation as the rising moon began to illuminate the crags and the narrow, steep-sided rock runs which seamed the lower slopes. Further up, the splintered outcrops of rock that marked the western summit of Fortress Longdon loomed above them. There was Fly Half. There was their destination. 'The start line was crossed', wrote Mike Argue later in his after action report, 'just as a good moon was rising to the east of Mount Longdon. Against the moon the jagged feature could be appreciated as well as the degree to which it dominated the surrounding area.'[10]

With the conclusion of the Pope's Mass on the radio, Carrizo Salvadores passed the order for everyone to get ready for action. He believed that 'even with the efforts that had been made to achieve peace, the enemy attack was imminent and would happen at any time'. With the order issued he got in touch with the CO [Omar Giménez] to tell him the latest developments up to that time.[11] All was quiet. The time was now about 8.30pm.

Lieutenant Jon Shaw's 6 Platoon, guided by Corporal Jerry Phillips, now detached itself from the rest of B Company and headed south in order to form up and attack the south west face of Longdon. That left 4 and 5 Platoons to advance further to the north with Sergeant Pettinger's group of guides, including Vernon Steen, positioned centrally between them – 5 Platoon to their right and 4 Platoon to the left. So far, so good.

Although Mike Argue had ordered his platoons to adopt a more direct approach from the start line, Vernon Steen nevertheless used his years of experience of the mountain and the surrounding terrain to help in shepherding 4 and 5 Platoons forward and into position using every available scrap of cover he knew. In November 2007, Vernon pointed out the same dead ground and walked me along the same route up to the point at which 4 and 5 Platoons began their final 'shake out' immediately prior to their assault. As Vernon led on, just as he had done that night when he had worked alongside men like 'Dickie Absolon of D Company to whom he had been attached, there was indeed partial cover which fell away with every step we took towards the mountain, eventually revealing it appearing to rise slowly, surely from the very ground until it towered above us; a grey, commanding, forbidding hump of rock off to our right front.

From this position the northwest-southeast axis of the mountain is slightly greater than 90 degrees to the line of the assault and even on a clear blue, sunlit South Atlantic summer morning, Longdon is immense; the huge slabs rising sheer up to the western summit of Fly Half.

Approaching from this angle, the first run of rocks is no more than 300m distant and on reaching them, which takes no more than a few minutes at a brisk walk, one is almost horizontally level with and vertically beneath the western summit; the battalion's first objective. Yet there were other significant obstacles for 4 and 5 Platoons to negotiate before they reached the rocks of Longdon.

Off to the left, ominously close and directly due north of the western summit, was a minefield which posed a significant threat to Andrew Bickerdike's left-hand section under the command of Corporal Brian Milne. Still there today the minefield is reassuringly fenced off and marked with signs bearing skulls and crossbones, but it was known to B Company before the battle as were several others – two mines had been 'lifted' during previous patrols; one of them a 25kg anti-tank mine and the other an EXPAL anti-personnel (AP) blast mine of Spanish manufacture. The men were under no illusions that if any of them tripped a mine, the rest were to keep moving on regardless. The momentum had to be maintained. Another minefield due west of Longdon – or, as it transpired later, two smaller fields which are today bracketed together – had the potential to cripple Jon Shaw's 6 Platoon.[12]

Having got 4 and 5 Platoons to the point where Mount Longdon stood sentinel in the scudding moonlight ahead of them, Vernon Steen recalled that his job was done and that, 'Major Argue stopped our move forward at about 300m from the base of the rock on the northern side of the feature. The summit was profiled against the partially moonlit sky; this I was using as a position reference. No movement was seen forward of our position and at this stage B Company shook out into battle formation. Then Sergeant Pettinger was instructed to move us to join with the Company HQ element.'

Andrew Bickerdike remembers what happened next:

We shook out into battle formation and we started to advance towards the feature. We were going in, 'two sections up, one back', in what we called half assault formation. Half assault formation is where the platoon advances with two sections 'up' or forward; in our case Corporal 'Ned' Kelly's section forward on the right and Corporal Brian Milne's section to the left. Each section was broken down into two files of three or four men each which would then shake out to either side of the section commander. I was in the centre between the two forward sections with Sergeant McKay just behind me. One half of my Platoon HQ, that is, my Tac [Tactical] Group – consisting of me, Private Cullen, my radio operator and my runner Private Barlow – was in the centre, 30m away from Kelly to my right and Milne to my left. I was followed by the other half of Platoon HQ which was Sergeant McKay's party, consisting of him, the '84' team of Privates Parry and Playle and Corporal Balmer, thirty to forty metres behind. Corporal John Lewis' section was just to the right rear of Sergeant McKay's group. The rear section came under the control of Ian McKay.[13]

Over on the right flank, 6 Platoon had already hit the forward slopes and had begun their ascent of Longdon having crossed the 1,000m or so of intervening ground in silence. Pushing on, halfway up Longdon now, 6 Platoon were beginning to penetrate the forward Argentine positions; some of the men could see the sangars and pup tents for themselves. It was a vulnerable time for the Argentines as new sentries had just been posted and Jon Shaw's men were into and through Corporal Oscar Carrizo's section of Lieutenant Neirotti's 3rd Platoon, silently slaying a number of the surprised and terrified Argentine soldiery before they had had time to react.

Over on the other side of the summit to the north, 4 and 5 Platoons were also closing with the mountain, their approach accompanied only by the rhythmic 'swish, swish' of DMS boots brushing against the tangled knots of tussock grass. Still silence. Was B Company really going to pull this off?

At about 9.30pm Major Carrizo Salvadores received a call from Giménez asking him to investigate a garbled message which had been relayed to the CO from Lieutenant Ramos, the forward artillery observation officer from his post on the southwestern slopes. In an attempt to clarify the situation Carrizo Salvadores telephoned with Lieutenant Baldini in his HQ bunker in the lee of the western summit of Longdon. It was now, according to Carrizo-Salvadores, about 10.00pm local time – 2 o'clock in the morning in the UK.

Suddenly and violently the night was ripped apart just 30m or so off to Andrew Bickerdike's left as his left forward section commander Corporal Brian Milne, stepped on an AP mine and screamed out in agony.

Brian Milne recalled that as his section had advanced they had begun to crest the gently rising ground in front of them and so he had gone forward to take a look:

We were worried about being silhouetted. I went over and had a word with [Andrew Bickerdike]. I was told to keep advancing and I went back to my section to pass the word. I put my left foot forward and did a somersault. There was an extremely loud bang and a ball of fire and the next thing I knew I was lying on my back. I had a very severe burning sensation and the ache of broken bones. I knew exactly what had happened. My immediate thoughts were about the intense pain. Everything runs through your mind at once. I had screamed, so I knew I was alive. In my own mind I knew I was going to lose that leg. When you lie down all night with injuries like that, you tend to come to terms with it.

Advancing just metres to the right of Brian Milne, the explosion threw Andrew Bickerdike off balance for a few moments, both physically and psychologically:

We'd crossed the start line, were moving on and at some point Brian Milne trod on an AP mine. We had been completely silent, there was no other noise and now to have an explosive device go off – even though it only contains 1/3 of an ounce of HE, there's enough to smash a man's leg, and make a bang and flash. For just that moment everyone stops because you think, 'What do we do now?' Then I shouted, 'on' and it was case of, 'keep moving, keep moving', and we carried on. We had to leave Brian there and carry on up the hill but then you wondered if we were all in a minefield and every time you put your foot down you wondered whether it was going to be your last. We carried on for what seemed like ages but it could only have been a minute or two at the most, before [the Argentines] had alerted themselves, woken up, got to their fire positions and opened fire on us.[14]

Only Brian Milne's section had been unlucky enough to have brushed the western extremity of the minefield to the north of Longdon, rather than the entire platoon having to stride through it and, although there were several more men off to Milne's left, it had been the section commander himself who had become the victim. It also explains why no other men became casualties of the Argentine mines apart from the man who, according to Corporal Phil Probets, came up later to assist Milne:

I was a Regimental Medical Assistant in HQ Company 3 Para (Regimental Aid Post) from April 1978 to late 1981. My latter two years were spent as B Company Medic. I transferred back to a rifle company in Late '81 in order to gain promotion and forward my career. I requested, and was posted to, 5 Platoon... I had only been in B Coy for just over four months when Argentina attacked the Falklands and I was replaced as a section commander and grouped with Company HQ so that I could provide greater medical support during the landing and assault phases. For the attack on Mount Longdon I suggested that I support 4 and 5 Platoons due to the greater number of men. The attack became noisy when there was a loud explosion. I was immediately summoned to assist a casualty; all hell broke loose as I ran toward him. When I got to the casualty I saw it was Corporal Brian Milne from 4 Platoon who had stepped on a mine. I remember thinking, 'Once I've sorted him, how will I get him out of the minefield?' I don't know how much time I spent trying to help Brian Milne, using the torch to see what I was doing did not make me very popular as I was attracting the attention of snipers. I had to switch the torch on and off, there was no alternative. I had just finished stabilizing Brian when I heard the call from my Company Sergeant Major, John Weeks, 'We need you up here, as quick as you can'. I left Brian with one of his soldiers and, with my fingers crossed, made my way out of the minefield and up the mountain to Company HQ. Brian Milne was eventually evacuated by Volvo BV Bandwagon. The BV pulled up right beside him; the driver [Lance Corporal Bassey of the Motor Transport Platoon] jumped out and stepped straight on a mine. He lost his leg as well, there but for the grace of God...[15]

The blast of the mine triggered by Brian Milne was heard up in Carrizo Salvadores' command post near Full Back and the Argentine defence was jolted into action. 'At that moment,' the Argentine commander recalled, 'an anti-personnel mine exploded to the northwest of the position and that, in practice, marked the beginning of the action which would last until the following day.'[16]

The mountain now appeared to explode into life as the Argentine bunkers and *RASIT* radar section under Sergeant Nista of Baldini's 1st Platoon came into action along with the forward sangars held by men of Staff Sergeant González's 2nd Platoon, spraying 4 and 5 Platoons on the north western slopes with fire interspersed with green tracer rounds. Frantic calls from the Argentine front line units were put in to their mortar and artillery batteries towards the rear and urgent screams of 'fire mission, fire mission' soon brought down rounds which thumped the ground over which the paras had just advanced. The battle for Longdon had been joined. Ahead lay almost ten hours of the most unimaginable and bloody, hand-to-hand gutter fighting.

For the 'civvy' Vernon Steen his first experience of being under fire came as a shock:

Following the organization of the battle formation of B Company Major Argue gave the order to advance. What seemed like moments later an explosion was heard off to our left; I now know that this was the result of Corporal Milne stepping on a mine. Next moment all hell broke loose, firing seemed to come from every nook and cranny in front of us but thankfully most of it seemed to go over our heads. I recall kneeling by the side of Corporal Absolon thinking 'what the hell is going on'. While I had been on live firing exercises, I had never been on the business end of a bullet, let alone this eruption.[17]

For Vernon Steen and the men of 4 and 5 Platoons it seemed like the Argentines had opened up simultaneously with everything they had and the ferocity of that initial fusillade took Andrew Bickerdike's mind off the dangers lurking beneath his feet and concentrated it instead on the bullets he could now hear whipping and cracking through the air, mixed with green tracer rounds spraying off rocks. Fortunately, most of the Argentine fire was indeed going high and, at that stage, Andrew Bickerdike too thought it reminiscent of the live fire exercises he had taken part in, in Wales or at Otterburn in Northumberland.

Now that the 'silent' attack had gone well and truly 'noisy', any pretence at maintaining an orderly advance was shed as 4 and 5 Platoons waddled as best they could, given the loads they carried, to make the safety of first cover of the rock line a short distance ahead. A little further southwest the men of 5 Platoon also began to scramble for the rocks. 'At this stage,' recalled Steen, 'we decided that the best course was to make for some rocks about 200m to our front. This at least gave us cover from the enemy fire, and gave us a vantage point to return it. At this stage effective fire was returned and with the momentum gained the assault continued.'

Corporal Ian Bailey was one of the three section commanders of Lieutenant Mark Cox's 5 Platoon, which had shaken out and advanced to the right of 4 Platoon. Due to the angle of approach they were further down the slope and slightly closer to the first line of rocks: 'We just heard a bang. Our two sections, mine and Graham's [Heaton's] were on the right of 5 Platoon and we heard a bang with a flash and then we just ran forward because we could see we could get into cover using the first outcrops of rocks. After that there was just shit everywhere.'[18]

Andrew Bickerdike's 4 Platoon was converging on Longdon from a position much further north and approaching at a steeper angle than previous studies of the battle have indicated. This is significant in that the consequence of such an angle of approach was to pitch 4 Platoon into the cover of rocks more than 150 horizontal metres further east along the northern face of Longdon than previously thought and, when combined with the studied testimony of those who were with Ian McKay at the time, has a direct bearing on the actual location at which Ian McKay won his Victoria Cross. After initiating their fight forward 4 Platoon would find itself in a position beneath Longdon's first summit.

Having already spent a good deal of his life building up an intimate knowledge of the geography of the mountain, Vernon Steen has no doubt as to the position in which he eventually found himself and this was well before the hard slog of the main phase of fighting had begun: 'We reached the foot of the rock face forming the side of the highest point of Mount Longdon.' Hugging the rocks for cover and arriving at this point relatively unmolested during the early stages of the battle, the men of 4 Platoon would already be in line with, albeit a good deal below, B Company's first objective and more than halfway into the Argentine 1st Platoon's positions. Further fighting, with the Argentine resistance stiffening, would carry 4 Platoon into the Argentine 2nd Platoon position to a point beyond the area which was later christened 'The Bowl', where it would be joined by the vanguard of men from 5 Platoon who had fought up and over the summit and had begun to trickle down through gaps in the rocks to the east to join it.

Such was Andrew Bickerdike's position on first reaching the rocks on the northern side of Longdon that he felt his platoon was on the receiving end of friendly fire from Lieutenant Jon Shaw's 6 Platoon, which was also continuing its advance from the southwest. With the venom of the Argentine fire directed towards the sound and light of the explosion of the AP mine triggered by Corporal Brian Milne, 6 Platoon had so far progressed virtually unmolested but the fire now unleashed towards the northwest was seen by the men on the right flank. Private Nick Rose remembered glancing across and seeing the flashes of British red and Argentine green tracer dancing up and down the hillside and thinking that 'it looked just like a two-way firing range'.

Now, however, 6 Platoon became engaged in battle on its own side of the hill. Argentine Corporal Carrizo recalled how his section was quickly engulfed:

> Outside the English were running past, screaming to each other and firing into tents and bunkers. I could hear my men being killed. They had only just woken up and now they were dying. I could hear muffled explosions followed by cries, helpless cries. I knew grenades were being thrown into the bunkers in the follow-up. The Sergeant and I discussed surrendering, but decided we'd wait until it was over. All we could do was wait. The English were all around us. They had arrived within seconds, like lightning. I prayed and prayed a grenade wouldn't come into our bunker. The sheer mental pressure exhausted me.[19]

Galvanized now by the sheer instinct to survive, the Argentine defence in 6 Platoon's area bristled into life, sweeping the western and southwestern slopes with fire from rifles, MAG and one of the six Browning 12.7mm (.50-calibre) Marine Infantry HMGs under Corporal Lamas on the right of Neirotti's position, as the first of the British shells called in by Captain Willie McCracken RA began to fall towards the secondary peak of Full Back.

On the opposite side of the summit, on the north face of Longdon, 4 Platoon's Tactical HQ followed by Platoon HQ led by Ian had, according to Andrew Bickerdike, already passed the start of the rock line and, despite the volume of fire directed towards them, their continued approach had so far been largely across dead ground which helped conceal them from the Argentines. Amidst the cacophony he and Ian came together to engage Argentine positions as 4 Platoon began to bump up against the sections on the right – northern facing – flank of Lieutenant Juan Baldini's command:

> Jon Shaw was somewhere up in the rocks to our right and there were Argentine positions in the rocks between us. So as we were advancing we suddenly started to get all this fire coming at us from the rocks on our right flank. Initially we had been talking on the radio on the platoon 'net' (network). My radio operator, Cullen, was on the B Company net. He was talking to Company HQ so if Mike [Argue] needed to speak to me I'd grab the handset. Sergeant McKay, coming a little way behind, was carrying a 350 radio. He would have been listening on the platoon net so that when I was talking to the section commanders he would also have been listening in. I was screaming on the radio, on the company net, telling Jon to stop firing at us and he was screaming back telling me that it wasn't him, that he was on the other side and it was Argentines. Of course I thought that if we fired back there was a risk of us hitting 6 Platoon. But when we got into the rocks orders and instructions were given and received by word of mouth. Sergeant McKay was telling me that he'd identified one of the [Argentine] positions from his location just behind me and he asked if he could engage it. I

gave the go ahead. They lobbed a couple of '66s' (single-shot 66mm Light Anti-Tank Weapon) into this rock and obviously hit something because it went up with a hell of a bang. So we knocked that position out and carried on up the hill, by which time the fire was starting to come down lower and although it wasn't effective because we hadn't taken any casualties at that stage it was getting very close. At that point I gave the order for the platoon to move up even closer into the rock line. We still had 6 Platoon well over to our right, further up on the hill top and 5 Platoon were starting to come up and were starting to become mingled in with us, then it became a bloody great melée and we started taking casualties.[20]

On the right flank of B Company 6 Platoon pressed on undaunted and established a precarious toehold just beneath the summit of Fly Half, but in the darkness and confusion it had bypassed a bunker holding at least seven men. Dotted elsewhere on the mountain were snipers with passive night sights. As Lance Corporal Murdoch's section toiled forward to a position roughly 50m beyond Fly Half, they veered northeast, working towards the reverse slopes of the peak and The Bowl. Crossing a strip of open ground they came within range of an Argentine sniper further east along the crest towards Full Back. James Murdoch was hit and fell. Still alive, he lay exposed in the open, being hit repeatedly and as medics frantically moved amongst the rocks trying to tend the wounded, Private Stewart 'Geordie' Laing decided that he could not leave his comrade out in the open to suffer any longer. Responding to Corporal Murdoch's cries, Laing broke cover and dashed to his rescue only to be struck himself three times in the chest. He died instantly. This level of casualties – five dead and eight wounded, almost 50 per cent of Lieutenant Shaw's command – could not be sustained. Shaw asked for and got permission from Major Mike Argue to 'go firm' – to consolidate and hold the ground taken on the southwestern slopes and immediately south of Fly Half. So, 6 Platoon had been ruled out of the equation and the ultimate outcome of the operation now rested squarely on the shoulders of the men of 4 and 5 Platoons.

Some 75m down the slope to the west from Ian McKay and the rest of 4 Platoon, Lieutenant Mark Cox's 5 Platoon was now being sucked into some hard fighting, having borne the brunt of the initial Argentine fusillade after Corporal Milne had stepped on the mine. Here, only a little further west down the slope, the configuration of the rocks was more extreme and much more complex than those which had provided initial sanctuary for 4 Platoon and consequently rendered them more difficult to negotiate. The route to the summit here is chiselled with several parallel lines of steep-sided, northwest-southeast rock outcrops which served to funnel the paras into completely separate and isolated channels. Ian Bailey remembered that once they had gained the cover of the rocks and then switched left to begin their ascent of the slope he and his men had been squeezed shoulder to shoulder at several points, almost queuing up to get through some of the narrowest gaps. Even in war, it seemed, the British formed a queue.

Meanwhile, 5 Platoon had passed through the first Argentine position unchallenged but now it faced a long and painful struggle to haul itself to the summit to join

6 Platoon. Given the micro terrain in which they now had to fight, the men's training kicked in and the platoon began to break down into smaller 'fire and movement units'; small groups working forward independently, some men drenching sangars with rifle, 66mm LAW or 84mm anti-tank rounds before others rushed forward to take it with bomb and bayonet. There would then be a pause whilst another objective was identified and the entire process would be repeated a little further up the mountain. By such means was progress made trench by trench in the dark but it is important to reflect at this point that progress for these small parties of 5 Platoon was far from uniform.

Those who worked and fought up the rock channels to the vertically higher ground to the east fought different battles to those whose route funnelled them along the sheer rock walls which eventually ran out into ground which ran below the summit. Here, one man's battle on one side of a rock wall might as well have been in a different world from the battle waged by another fighting on the opposite side.

It was painstaking and hazardous work made all the more deadly as the Argentines rolled grenades down some of the stone passageways up which the paras were obliged to advance, raining searing fragments of metal and razor-sharp stone chips down on them as the grenades exploded. Metre by metre 5 Platoon clawed its way forward and one group silenced a GPMG position which had pinned them down just below the summit. Ian Bailey remembers that much of the responsibility devolved onto the JNCOs – the section commanders and lance corporals, and small groups of individual soldiers.

We just grabbed whoever was with us and began isolating positions and taking them out as we came across them. We actually missed positions because the Argentines were hiding down in the bottom of them and we had to come back and find them later. It was just chaos. Everything was going off everywhere and people were screaming, people were getting shot and we just started to move through any way we could. That was when everybody began to get separated and platoons started to become mixed. Everybody was all over the place. People got split up going through the rock alleys. 'Stew' McLaughlin's section got caught up with half of mine and I got caught up with Graham [Heaton's] as we began to veer further north. Also, 4 Platoon were trying to get into the rocks as well to try and get as much cover as they could to identify the enemy, then move off and move through. We were going uphill, coming back down, trying to move around to the sides and [the Argentines] were throwing grenades, bouncing them down the sheer faces of the rocks on to us. We were trying to take cover and the peat was absorbing a lot of the explosions but it was going on everywhere; just utter chaos. We'd take a break then spot some enemy, then we'd organize and have talk, 'OK, you go as fire support, we'll go this way, let's try and take it out.' [The fighting] was so broken that platoon commanders, certainly on my side of 5 Platoon, did not have direct control. From the start line to the time I got shot I never saw my platoon sergeant or my platoon commander. The next time I saw my platoon sergeant was on the [hospital ship] *Uganda* when he came to visit me.

It was the corporals who were doing it because you just didn't see people in command. We were just getting in as much as we could. We knew where we had to go. You couldn't hang around and wait [for orders] you just had to get on with it. It was just me, Graham [Heaton] and 'Scouse' [McLaughlin]. We just got on with it ourselves with the people who were there, because people were mingling by that time and that included people from 4 Platoon.[21]

The confused and fragmented nature of the fighting was a distinctive feature of the Battle for Mount Longdon which was common to all and, as 4 and 5 Platoons began to converge, so Andrew Bickerdike and Ian Bailey, two men who would be involved in Ian McKay's final action, were inexorably drawn together. Andrew Bickerdike:

As we worked forward through the rocks we took positions out. I had 'Ned' Kelly's section on my right and by now Brian Milne's 2i/c, Lance Corporal Evans had taken over on the left. There was lots of small-arms fire coming in mixed in with '.5s' [.50-calibre] hitting and zinging off the rocks. Green and red tracer was going in all directions. They were certainly using FNs and there was definitely .50-calibre fire from the top of the hill, because the green tracer was bloody loud and it was bloody big – 'bump, bump, bump' – nothing like a GPMG. There was a lot of automatic fire as they had their FNs on automatic too. We were using quite a lot of white phosphorous on the trenches. We preferred to use white phos' because it was less dangerous to us when we started throwing grenades into trenches. They were not using their mortars by then because we were in among their positions, it was mostly direct-fire weapons. Most of my casualties came from small arms fire.[22]

Contrary to much of the received wisdom regarding the history of the battle, Andrew Bickerdike is adamant that '4 Platoon *did not* (his emphasis) meet 5 Platoon in what has become known as Grenade Alley; we were much further north and east by then, moving parallel to [5 Platoon] and just below the main rock outcrops until we swung south again on the rock line to find more cover. We then became mixed together – imagine two goose eggs half-overlapped, with 4 Platoon being the eastern egg. Mark Cox came forward to me to liaise, we talked and then I went forward again with Sergeant McKay and my team.'

The right-hand section of 4 Platoon under 'Ned' Kelly had fought its way into the upper reaches of the treacherous rock gullies which had diverted them into 5 Platoon's sector and now, with Kelly's group working up behind groups of 5 Platoon and joining them, these men on the left flank pushed on, eventually reaching a position forward of but below Fly Half. Vernon Steen showed me the location in 2007 and informed me that, 'we eventually found our way into the first bowl just to the east of the summit'.

It was at this point that Ian Bailey met up with 'Ned' Kelly.

By this time people from 4 Platoon were coming through and I had a chat with 'Ned'. He was involved in the assault because some of his men had an '84' and so they fired some rounds into Argentine positions because they could see there was a problem. There were positions we had taken towards the top of the hill where Graham [Heaton's] section were actually firing back into the 6 Platoon area to take out the sniper who was doing all the shooting. Somebody would go one way, somebody would go the other, somebody would come under fire so we'd all stop, get back into cover and shout, 'Right what's everybody seen?' Then we'd decide what to do. You make the decision as the corporal but you're using everybody else's eyes and ears to find out where the enemy weapons are but, remember, there may have been [weapons] which hadn't opened up.[23]

There is no doubt that after very hard fighting the now co-mingled and joint force which comprised men of 4 and 5 Platoons was strung out in and among the rocks and Argentine sangars, not only around the summit of Mount Longdon but also in some cases as much as 60ft vertically below the peak, and penetrating into Staff Sergeant González' 2nd Platoon area of responsibility beyond the northern entrance to The Bowl further east. By now however, the momentum of the assault was slowing considerably.

As casualties mounted on both sides Longdon became an inferno. In many cases it was close-quarters fighting with the paras engaging Argentine bunkers often at a range of a few metres to the accompaniment of the roar of machine guns, the bangs of grenades and anti-tank weapons, and the heavier crash of artillery and naval shells which shattered the rocks leaving livid red scars or thumped buried themselves in the peaty earth with a thump. The mountain pulsated with light from multiple explosions and it became wreathed in the thick, acrid smoke from burning sangars and the fumes from white phosphorous.

The battle had been raging now for some two hours and the Argentines were trading blow for blow with B Company. On the northern slopes Platoon Commander Andrew Bickerdike recalled that 'we'd got as far as Fly Half and pushed on' but the advance was slowing with every position the paras engaged.

Later, in July 1982, Andrew Bickerdike wrote that, 'After advancing approximately 150–200m parallel to the rock feature it became apparent that our advance was becoming impossible due to heavy fire from enemy positions in the rocks. This fire was from several FNs/GPMGs and an HMG. I ordered 4 Platoon to move to the rock feature for cover and also to regroup. When we got into cover we met the majority of 5 Platoon.'[24]

The mixed force of 4 and 5 Platoons had started to make an impression on the positions held by Staff Sergeant González' men. Anibal Grillo recalled he was the 'last soldier' – the furthest east – of Baldini's 1st Platoon and had spent time before the battle with Lance Corporal Pedro Orozco and Private Ramon Omar Quintana whose post, almost in the middle of The Bowl at the snout of González' 2nd Platoon, he could almost reach out and touch from his own. When the British finally worked their way into The Bowl he remembered that 'Orozco and Quintana both died here. Orozco was seriously wounded and died immediately, Quintana succeeded in dragging himself along to my position where he also died.' Also killed at this time, the victims of a '66' or '84' rocket according to Grillo, were Marine Privates First Class Claudio Scaglione and Sergio Giusepeti. Their deaths resulted in the silencing of a tactically significant .50-calibre HMG on rising ground just east of The Bowl.

Now 4 and 5 Platoons could look to press on. Having come this far Ian McKay and Andrew Bickerdike were now sheltering in the rock outcrops well beyond the northeastern rim of The Bowl in an attempt to identify further lines of the Argentine defences before trying to advance towards Full Back, the final objective. That next line of defence was to prove formidable. At its heart was yet another .50-calibre heavy machine gun, sited in an elevated yet well-protected position on a sheep track which ran along the flat crest of a rock wall – a weapon photographed in situ by Captain Bob Darby when he was sent back up to Longdon on a salvage operation on the morning of 16 June – augmented by two further 7.62mm MAG (GPMG) machine guns.

One of the MAGs was positioned in a well-constructed, stone-built sangar dug in under the rocks and complete with overhead cover provided by large, flat slabs of rock to the sides and roof supported by lengths of railway track salvaged from the rusting light railway of the disused rock-crushing plant at the foot of Mount Tumbledown or the even older light gauge track which used to link the naval station at the Camber with the Admiralty wireless station on Wireless Ridge. Dotted around in close proximity, numerous riflemen and snipers – some equipped with night sights – were dug into stone-built bunkers on top of the rocks above and rifle pits surrounded by tents at the base of the walls below. This position was proving to be a painful thorn in the flesh of B Company's advance.

In his statement later in 1982, Andrew Bickerdike described the situation in simple terms: 'by now [it] was getting more hazardous and required decisive action. Whilst being covered by two section GPMG, Sergeant McKay, Corporal Bailey, myself and several others moved forward to recce the enemy positions.' Ian Bailey recalled further details of that reconnaissance:

We'd flanked the summit [Fly Half], which was the first objective, although there was fighting still going on around it. In fact there was firing everywhere. I'd gone well forward with 'Boots' Meredith because we could hear this '.50' but didn't know exactly where it was. We were recceing. We found the location of the '.50' – it was above us and slightly to our right – then we moved back and that's when we bumped into Andrew's [Bickerdike] HQ including Andrew, his radio operator and Ian McKay. We moved forward again and I explained where the '.50' was. Ian was right there. We were lying down on a slope, Ian was tucked behind a little rock near me and some of his platoon – 'Ned' Kelly and some of his lads – were just around a corner of other rocks and I'd been pointing out where the machine gun was. I said to Andrew, 'Happy boss?' and he said, 'Yeah'. At that point I made to move off. I'd encroached into their area so I was going to pull back and I was just about to leave [when] a number of rounds came in and Andrew and Mick [Cullen] got shot. As Andrew moved, a round hit him – how it got him in the thigh I'll never know but it came over; probably wasn't even aimed at them but he took the round in the thigh. It threw Andrew backwards and Mick was shot in the mouth. 'Boots' Meredith started doing first aid on Andrew and Mick Cullen. Mick was the more serious. Some others – the rest of Andrew's HQ were there – Ian was there, literally next to me. Then Andrew shouted to Ian, 'Sergeant McKay, It's your platoon. Crack on'. I know that sounds very corny but it was said, because I heard it.[25]

As Andrew Bickerdike had moved forward with his recce group he had seen a shallow gulley which he knew that he would have to cross to get a look at the position of the heavy machine gun. He remembered that at that time it was pretty quiet.

There was lots of fire coming from our right but nothing coming from our front. So I took my radio operator with me and went round these rocks to have a look. We got down and it was quiet, nothing there – or so we thought. I shouted to the lads, 'Cover me, I'm going across to the next cover'. As I broke cover, that's when they opened fire from two or three positions and I'd been caught in a bit of an ambush. The bunker/trench that hit my group was less than 20m in front of us – *firing perpendicular to the rock line* – I remember it vividly as I saw the muzzle flash of the weapon that hit me! I was hit in the left thigh by a single 7.62 mm round which went straight through and I bounced backwards as if I'd been rugby tackled – a quick back somersault – and landed behind a bit of cover on a bit of a slope. I was hit by a 7.62mm high velocity round – a .50 would have taken my leg off – which passed through the triangle between the sciatic nerve, femur and femoral artery of my left thigh. The surgeons subsequently could not make out what attitude my leg had been in to avoid more serious injury and death. The round was fired on single shot – it was definitely not a burst of automatic fire – but what immediately followed was a significant volume of automatic fire from several positions. My helmet came off after I was hit. I didn't have the chinstrap fastened, and my impromptu back somersault dislodged it; however, it was still attached to me as I had a handset for my PRC349 clipped to the side of it. My head and the inside of the Kevlar were soon reunited! My interpretation of the event was that someone fired too soon – if they had held their fire for a few seconds longer, and all fired simultaneously, as in an ambush, they would have caused more casualties. You wouldn't believe it but I then came out with something that was like a scene from a comedy film. Of all the things to say I shouted, 'The bastard got me'. It was just such a classic officer's line from a corny war film and it amused quite a few of the 'Toms' around me. In the same phase of fire, Mick Cullen my radio op, took a round through his lip which took a couple of teeth out and Barlow my runner got hit in the kneecap. We all ended up in a heap. Cullen was really quiet – he was just spitting out teeth and blood and trying to talk on the radio and just dribbling blood into the handset. Barlow was making quite a bit of noise as his wound was excruciatingly painful. I lay on my back, got my knife out of my pocket, sliced the trouser leg open and just saw a tiny little trickle come out so I knew an artery hadn't been hit but I could feel it getting a bit wet and messy round the back. So I applied lots of shell dressings and got it wrapped up. I was on the company net and I spoke to Mike Argue who had come on the radio wanting a sitrep. He said, 'On, on, press on', so I said, 'I'm afraid I've been hit' and he thought I said, 'I'm afraid of being hit'. So of course he was urging me to 'Get on, keep moving', and I ended up by saying, almost matter of factly, 'Well I can't Mike because I have actually been hit'. So I'm badly wounded, I'm lying down and I've got Barlow and Cullen lying with me and we're behind a small bank of earth with a lot of fire coming into it. As I was lying there trying to get the dressings on I could feel all these thuds at the back of my head as they were pouring fire into this piece of cover. We were in a fairly exposed position and trying to slide further and further down behind this small bank although we were still trying to fire at the Argentines. We had no choice; we were in a pretty shitty position. Ian McKay had already come forward at this point and I said to him, 'Sergeant McKay, I'm down, you're now in command. The platoon's yours.' I was 'Sunray' he was 'Sunray Minor' so 'Sunray Minor' took over.[26]

The attack by 4 Platoon had been stopped dead in its tracks. The Argentine Marine Infantrymen crouching behind the heavy machine gun and the men of 7 RIMec firing the MAGs and rifles which supported it – in good cover and prepared to make a fight of it – had checked the advance with some violence. It was clear that the Argentines were not packing up and running into Stanley. They were, in the main, standing and making a fight of it.

Just two hours into the battle and with 6 Platoon already ruled out, groups of 5 Platoon being held up east of The Bowl and now the composite 4/5 Platoon group held up with casualties which needed evacuation, B Company's advance was in danger of grinding to a halt at all points.

The seriously wounded all over the western half of the mountain now needed urgent medical aid and those still fighting needed ammunition and fire support but the planned fire support base that should by now have been established by Major David Collett's A Company and Support Company under Major Dennison on the knoll called Wing Forward to the north, had not materialized. These companies had managed to reach Wing Forward but once there had come under sustained and accurate fire from several well-concealed snipers in Sergeant González' 2nd Platoon area whilst Argentine 155mm and 105mm howitzer rounds had fallen amongst them. Sheltering behind the rocky outcrops and low peat banks most of the Paras had gone to ground and were trying to engage the snipers whenever the opportunity arose but without the benefit of up to date night sights.

Both A and Support Companies were well aware of what was happening, but pinned down as they were, they were not in a position to intervene effectively. McKay's mixed party was now the furthest forward of any of B Company and well into the Argentine 2nd Platoon position from where the snipers were operating. In any event, those of A and Support Companies who were in a position to engage the Argentines on the mountain were afraid of hitting their own men fighting from right to left – west to east – across their immediate line of fire. Corporal Vincent Bramley remembered the spectacle of the firefight on the mountain and his feelings of frustration at being unable to influence the outcome. 'It was like a football match,' he remarked, 'when you want to join in and help your side.'[27]

Midnight – four o'clock in the morning in Aldershot and Rotherham – was also a time of crisis for the Argentines. Major Carrizo-Salvadores has recorded that 'the situation was critical seeing that contact with the 1st [Platoon – Baldini] had been lost. The commander of the 3rd [Platoon], Lieutenant Neirotti, was wounded and there was a struggle going on to the north, in Staff Sergeant González' 2nd [Platoon's] sector with which there was no communication either.'[28]

The struggle was becoming distilled into a bloody battle of attrition which had more than a whiff of the most savage examples of dugout fighting in the trenches of the First World War but with the added stopping power and ferocity of modern automatic weapons and rockets. In order to secure victory the men on both sides would have to dig deep and call on hidden depths of determination and the ability to endure to the end. There could be no draw on this mountain. Something extraordinary would be required if B Company was to regain the initiative.

The wounded Andrew Bickerdike had shed the reins of command of 4 Platoon and it was Ian who now picked them up and assumed command of the composite force from his own platoon and the left section of 5 Platoon under Corporal Bailey. The situation was critical; no one was giving him orders or telling him what to do next. He had no time, or means, to call for any fire support which, in the event would not have been available in any case. Ian now had several choices. He could have tried to withdraw his men into cover with the result that the wounded, who could not move and were still under intense fire, would undoubtedly have been killed and perhaps more men may have been hit. In this scenario all momentum would have been lost with only the slimmest of prospects of picking it up again. If he 'froze' at this, the moment of his greatest test as a paratroop soldier, his platoon would undoubtedly lose more dead and wounded under the tremendous weight of effective fire being brought to bear. Known by those who had worked with or who had been trained by him as calm and reasonable, intelligent, logical and a thinker, Ian's response, almost spontaneous when he realized the gravity of the situation, later surprised many people who thought of him as a man who carefully weighed his options before acting. Yet Ian would have been well aware of the probably fatal consequences of delay and inaction.

He held men's lives in his hands; they were now his responsibility and he would have been keenly aware that he had to do something. At that moment one wonders whether he recalled his own words, uttered to Sammy Dougherty in the bar on the *Canberra* one evening on the voyage south: 'I've no intention of taking any risks and getting killed [but] If I do… then it will be to protect my men, to save lives.'

In those few seconds after Andrew Bickerdike went down and he assumed command Ian chose to commit himself to an immediate attack on the machine-gun post which was causing so many casualties – the likely outcome of which would have been all too apparent to him. Perhaps this was the moment that Ian had been working towards all his professional life. It was a far cry indeed from his previous experience of active service in Northern Ireland; a far cry from Belfast and Londonderry, from the car park of the Rossville Flats and bricks or bottles filled with bleach. Some ten-and-a-half years on from Bloody Sunday Ian McKay was just moments away from winning the Victoria Cross; just moments away from the end of that life.

Ian Bailey recalled Ian coming back to assess how many men he could muster for the task ahead. It was at this point that Vernon Steen saw Ian:

When we had got into position on the eastern edge of the first Bowl stock was taken of the situation. Enemy fire had subsided a little and the opportunity was taken to move into a second and larger bowl further on. Sergeant Pettinger re-assigned me to 4 Platoon which was led at this time by Sergeant Ian McKay. I was unaware that the officer commanding 4 Platoon, Lieutenant Bickerdike, had

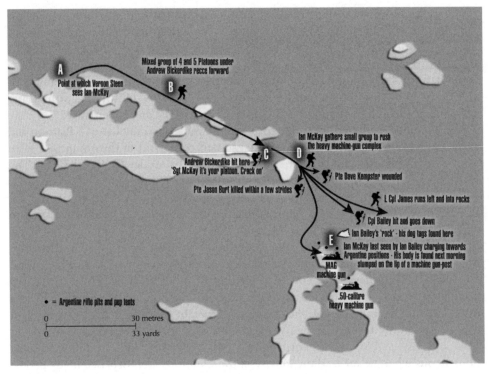

Sergeant Ian McKay's Final Charge – 12 June 1982.

been wounded just forward of the position we were in and that command had passed to Sergeant McKay. I made myself known to him. He then gave some quick order to several of the members of his platoon which was essentially to move to the left down a slope of rocks and then skirmish forward to attack Argentine machine gun positions which were hampering the progress of the advance east along Mount Longdon. These enemy positions were placed in good cover and in effect seemed almost to defy destruction despite heavy bombardment from the guns of HMS *Avenger*. The craters are still there today as evidence. Before leaving the second bowl position Sergeant McKay and the men lightened up by shedding their fighting order and carrying extra ammunition and grenades in the pockets of their combat smocks. Once prepared the group slipped off down the rocks out of sight below, this was to be the last I would see of several of them.[29]

Looking at Ian Bailey Ian said, 'You're going to stay here for the moment' and moved off declaring that he was going to 'have another look' at the situation:

He went and spoke to Ned, who was round the corner with some of his lads and told him to lay some covering fire down, then he came back and said, 'You're going to come with me.' I said 'OK' and asked him what we were going to do?

'We've got to go across here and take this .50 out, it's holding us up. Who have we got?' There was Ian, me, Lance Corporal Roger James, Dave Kempster and Jason Burt – five of us. James was from the Sergeants' Mess. He was a Tom who was attached to my section with a lad called 'Piggy' Else as the '84' team. Once they had fired all their rounds for the '84' they became riflemen. James was up there with us.[30]

From his position on the ground behind his protective bank of earth Andrew Bickerdike could see his platoon sergeant, upper body hunched forward and darting quickly backwards and forwards between and behind rocks and he could hear him clearly. 'It was at that point that McKay grabbed the people who were with him – "You, you and you, with me", gave quick orders and went for it. I saw him do it. There was no hesitation. He knew what had to be done. He knew we were in a pretty desperate position. I can hear him still, giving the instructions.[31]

From his position Ian would have looked out across an open strip of ground and noticed a well-worn sheep track which first ran gently away to his left before curling right and weaving its way back uphill through a gap in the rocks. As the track levelled out it snaked off to the left again and ran up a slight rise along the crest of a long, 3m high rock wall. The distance from his position, across the track and up the slope to the base of the far rock wall on which sat the machine guns was no more than 35m.

We can never know exactly what went through this professional soldier's mind at that point in the dark on that mountain amid the chaos of explosions, fiery bursts of tracer and the screams of the wounded. But we can conclude, from Ian McKay's character and past behaviour, that it was a mixture of stubbornness, training and belief in what he was doing, tempered by the knowledge that he was in charge and his soldiers looked to him for a lead, added to the fury that an unseen enemy was killing his boys. He knew the risk he was taking. But he also knew that he had to do something, and do it quickly.

Ian told Ian Bailey that they had to 'get across to some more rocks to make a better assessment', as Bailey later recalled:

The .50-calibre has a very pronounced sound – 'bump, bump, bump' – not like the GPMG, so we knew where the .50 was. James was out on the far left, then Jason [Burt], then [David] Kempster, then me with Ian out on the right. 'Ned' Kelly had moved around some rocks and as we moved off he fired rounds towards the .50 and used 66s to keep their heads down. We were then running across this piece of ground – 'pepper potting' as we went across – to get underneath the .50 so that we could then try and get round to it. What we didn't know was that there were [Argentines] below. As we went across we got rounds coming at us straight away. I knew somebody went down to my left – Jason was killed within about two steps – and I knew somebody else was moving further off to my left. We went on and just fired into one position as we ran past it. I could see Ian, running, in the corner of my eye to the right and we got to a position where we were taking lots of rounds. That's when I got hit. I thought I'd tripped, literally; I went to get up again and I had no movement in my right leg. I'd been hit in the right hip. I then went down again. Fell forward. I put my hand down and saw lots of blood. At that point it went quiet; then the firing started again. You see, the Argentine position that got me, which shot Jason and shot [and wounded] Kempster, was still there – a sangar with a tent around it. We just hadn't seen it. That was the one that took us out but that position did not kill Ian. It wasn't the .50, the .50 was above it. Because Ian was off on the right, he had totally avoided the sangar that got me. He had gone round it and just kept going. He had gone in front of 'Ned's' section and had run on the other side of some rocks and gone uphill, got on top of it and took out the .50. The last time I saw Ian McKay alive, he was still moving on my right. I was hit, went down, tried to get up and I never saw him again. There was firing going on, two explosions then it stopped and there was nothing. Ian died in the trench.[32]

Certainly the heavy machine gun had fallen silent but what Ian Bailey could not know as he lay wounded on the ground just a few metres away was that as the rest of the assault group had been shot or had managed to duck and dive into cover, Ian McKay had continued on alone, charging uphill across the open space to follow the line of the sheep track, bearing down on the muzzle flashes of one of the 7.62mm machine-gun posts under a blizzard of bullets. The explosions had signalled the detonation of Ian's grenades. He never reached the .50-calibre heavy machine gun but such had been the overwhelming force of his feat of arms that its team, and the team of the other MAG machine gun must have felt that a platoon was bearing down on them and, for the time being at least, had quit their posts.

Before the volume of fire had subsided entirely, however, Ian Bailey had been hit twice more as he lay helpless on the ground.

I was lying there – in a slight depression – and that was when I got shot again. They put another two rounds in – 'double tapped' – one across the back of my neck and another, a tracer round that burnt the fingers on my right hand as my hands were in front of me. I heard someone shout and heard another voice in the rocks to my left – I now know it was Lance Corporal James because I heard him talking to some of the other lads afterwards – he was trying to shout back. After about forty minutes to an hour I heard John Lewis, the other 4 Platoon section commander and I indicated to him where I was with my leg. I shouted out that in front of me, no more than 10m away, was another Argentine position. They then went in and cleared it. It was taken out by 'Sule' Alhaji with rifle grenades; I got some of the grenade shrapnel in me – then he came back. 'Lewi' was already with me and I told him I had seen somebody else go down but then I heard somebody else say, 'No, he's dead.' After that, some of the lads from my section came around me and they took over the first aid.[33]

Andrew Bickerdike recalls the blessed relief of the silence which followed Ian McKay's charge:

Within a few seconds of him going forward with his group it all went quiet again because they had obviously neutralized the immediate threat. There was a lot of fire coming our way before he went and then a lot of fire stopped. It was that quick action that saved lives and turned the events in that phase of the battle. It neutralized the immediate threat and kept the momentum going. Ian's action saved my life.

When I interviewed Andrew Bickerdike in 2006, at this point he was taking a print of the famous Peter Archer painting of Ian's VC action out of a frame to let me have a closer look. Crouching down with one knee on the floor he stopped talking and his hands became still as he turned to look me in the eyes. When he spoke again he did so in a low voice. I thought I detected a slight quavering:

> There hasn't been a day go by since then when I haven't thought of Ian McKay and what he did and how he saved my life. I've thought about him every day I've been spared. If it hadn't been for that quick action, the chances are I wouldn't have come out of there alive. I was told by people afterwards that he had attacked two positions; took the first one and neutralized it and it was the second one that got him. When it went quiet in our area – of course there was still firing elsewhere – we shouted for him but there was no response. Well, there wouldn't be. He was gone.[34]

Some 8,000 miles away in Rotherham, Freda McKay had been awake since about 2.30am in the early hours of that Saturday morning, 12 June 1982. Since the beginning of June she had been waking up like clockwork at around the same time and had found it almost impossible to get back to sleep. The nights were long in the quiet of the house with only her thoughts to occupy her for fear of disturbing the rest of her family.

Down in Aldershot her daughter-in-law was also awake. In the Day Room of Farnham Hospital all was still and quiet in the dead of night as Marica took a well-earned breather on her break from night duty. As a trained nurse Marica was working part-time as an auxiliary – just two nights a week – on the geriatric ward, which was a taxing role at the best of times and so she looked forward to her breaks when they came. Whether at work or at home she always tried to catch the 3.00am news bulletin on the BBC World Service but for the moment all was still.

As she sat alone in the silence she recalled vividly that 'something brushed my neck, then brushed against my hair so that I flicked at it'. Although she would never dismiss the experiences of others out of hand Marica McKay is not given to flights of fancy or swayed by tales of the supernatural but nevertheless she had already confided her fears for her husband's safety to one of her colleagues. 'He's not coming back', I had said. 'I just knew, in my heart of hearts, he wasn't coming back.'[35]

CHAPTER TWELVE

To the World a Soldier

The scene which greeted CSM Sammy Dougherty and Private Tony Bojko as they picked their way carefully amongst the rocks on the north face of Longdon in the cold half-light of dawn of 12 June 1982 beggared belief. A lowering mist, heavy with acrid vapours from shattered and still smouldering Argentine sangars, shrouded the rocks. Already the sickly sweet odour of blood and death – a pungent mix of rust, sweat and human excrement, had descended on the mountain. Bloodied shell dressings, ammunition boxes, spent cartridges and discarded plastic 66 rocket launchers lay strewn amongst the human detritus of war: clothing, blankets, sleeping bags, unused tubes of toothpaste and plastic disposable razors – and corpses.

Everywhere now exhausted men were moving slowly through the mist; spectral figures inspecting the debris, checking equipment, herding prisoners and attempting to restore some semblance of order after the chaos of battle.

The Battle for Mount Longdon was over – 3 Para had been victorious but it had taken ten long and bloody hours and exacted a heavy price, but what price exactly was still unclear. Although B Company CSM John Weeks and his team had been zig-zagging up and down the mountain most of the night evacuating the wounded, he and the other SNCOs like Sammy Dougherty were still trying to ascertain the precise number of casualties. The British Army loves its paperwork and even in the immediate aftermath of such a bloody contest as Longdon CSM John Weeks was required to 'account for everything and everybody' and fill in the requisite forms.[1]

During the fighting the evacuation of the wounded had been the priority, the dead were, after all, beyond saving, and it had been hazardous work retrieving men, often at the furthest extremities of the battlefield from under the noses of the Argentines and under heavy fire. The aim was to get them out of danger by the fastest means possible and back to a forward aid post in the relative safety of the area around Fly Half, of which 3 Para had taken an admittedly unsteady grip. Ian Bailey was eventually extracted from his exposed position as was Andrew Bickerdike:

Eventually Johnny Weeks came forward. He was sent up to organize and evacuate the wounded. We'd obviously knocked out a lot of Argentine positions but had taken quite a few casualties. I was wounded but I could shout and I got everyone back out and stayed there until the end until Johnny Weeks came back and picked me up and put me over his shoulder. He says I was screaming in agony – well I can't remember that bit! John Weeks must have carried me at least 150m back along the northern face of the rock features. I was laid up against the rock face with several other casualties to await stretcher bearers coming up from the RAP which was located further down the western slope of Longdon. As I was deemed only lightly wounded I remained until the last man in the group – and remember feeling very exposed and vulnerable with nobody else around, and no weapon (Mark Cox had taken my SLR). I remember VIVIDLY being with Corporal Probets, the B Coy medic, when Neil Grose died (we were laid side by side). He fought like a lion with CPR to save Grose, but to no avail… it affected him deeply, and he cried over the body. I'm sure as a medic he felt guilt if he lost a man, and I suspect he is still carrying those scars. I will certainly never forget him. He did an outstanding job as company medic and he should know that he did all he could in such extreme conditions.[2]

With the final capitulation of Major Carrizo Salvadores' command and his withdrawal of the remaining 78 of his 287 men at about 6.30am, the search for bodies could begin in earnest.

CSMs Sammy Dougherty and John Weeks had organized small parties to comb the mountain and collect all the 3 Para bodies, put them on ponchos, (mostly Argentine) and transport them to a central location near the RAP. Here they could be 'examined and the personal possessions removed by the Padre, who arranged for bodies to be placed in body bags out of the sight of the injured, prior to evacuation by Volvo'.[3] At this point personal items such as photographs and wedding rings would be logged and retained by the Rev Derek Heaver – always 'Derek the Cleric' to his airborne flock – to be sent back to relatives in the UK.

Leaving one of two identity discs or 'dog tags' on the body Colour Sergeant Brian Faulkner's team working at the RAP and fatigued beyond belief – they had received their first casualty within fifteen minutes of the start of the battle and had worked flat out all night – would then place the dead into body bags. Next they would be loaded, first for the overland journey in the tracked Volvo Bandwagon vehicles to rendezvous with choppers on the other side of the Murrel Bridge for the heli-lift to the improvised hospital and mortuary of the Dressing Station at Teal Inlet twenty-one miles (thirty-four kilometres) to the west.

Some of the men did not have the stomach for the task which Sammy Dougherty and John Weeks were asking of them. It was hardly surprising. Although some of 3 Para had witnessed the death of comrades in Northern Ireland and the sad but essential business of getting a body into a cumbersome, heavy-duty polypropylene bag, the task can never be straightforward. After a battle like that fought on Mount Longdon the difficulties were magnified. Many of the dead had suffered horrific injuries and if the body you were expected to recover happened to be that of one of your friends who had so recently been alive and full of vigour, then the experience for some could have been traumatic in the extreme.

There were a few who realized that it was a dread task which simply had to be done and those who did volunteer, Sammy Dougherty put in pairs. He grabbed Tony Bojko, a man who had fought alongside him that night on the eastern end of The Bowl. 'Armenian by birth, gungy but hard as nails and could carry lots of heavy equipment', according to Dougherty, Bojko was a man he could trust.

Dougherty remembers that they walked east, 'well forward, beyond the Stanley side of The Bowl', until they came across one particular scene of utter devastation:

We walked towards the area where the heavy machine gun was which had given us so much trouble during the night. We found a GPMG mounted on a tripod – used in a sustained fire role I guessed in a natural defensive position; a rock slab providing overhead cover, like it had fallen over and was suspended on two vertical slabs of rock. A little further along, right on the track, was a '.50-cal' on a long stand. I remember thinking that it was a funny weapon because you would have had to stand up to fire it and have been exposed.[4]

Tony Bojko describes how the GPMG was 'up in the air and there was MG stuff all over the place'. He and Sammy had seen the bodies around it but had assumed they were Argentine and were moving on when Bojko noticed something different about one of them. 'It was very cold but as we moved around the mist began to lift. We didn't notice at first – nearly walked past – then recognized that one of them had a British windproof on'.[5]

Sammy Dougherty described the scene:

Around the GPMG were the bodies of three Argentine soldiers who had been manning it. One of them lay spread-eagled towards the rear of the trench and the other two were just yards outside it. Face down, slumped over the front parapet of the bunker – half in, half out – was Ian McKay. Although he was face down I recognized him immediately. I got Bojko to help me lift him off the parapet, which was not easy.[6]

'One of his arms was sticking out,' recalls Tony Bojko, 'it was solid, so we had to cut his webbing off.'

Ian's body bore the marks of his titanic effort in attacking the Argentine positions. Tony Bojko could see that a large patch of skin had been torn from one cheek which revealed the teeth and that blue lines had already started to appear on the rest of his face, which, Tony felt, 'was just like marble'. Sammy Dougherty also noticed that:

His right hand had practically gone. He must have had a grenade in his right hand and must have been shot and killed before he could release it. In my opinion I think Ian had decided that the only way he could be sure of getting the grenade in to where it would do most damage was to hold on to it and throw himself into the sangar with it. I looked at the back of his windproof and it was full of holes. I could see the holes in his back. The Argentines must have re-occupied the area around the heavy machine gun position after Ian had attacked it and the 3 Para machine guns must have been hitting Ian's body as they tried to neutralize the [Argentine] fire.

Sammy had seen dead bodies before but rigor mortis had set in and what with the low temperatures an already heart-rending task for the no-nonsense Ulsterman became even more difficult. And so in a final act of tenderness towards a friend, Sammy Dougherty talked to Ian as if he was still alive, bringing humanity to an inhuman situation. 'I spoke to him and told him, "Oh I'm sorry Ian, I've just got to move you over here a little bit," and then I took his webbing off. I took his dog tags off and kept one and pushed the other down inside one of his boots. I had just finished when John Weeks and the adjutant [Captain Kevin McGimpsey] came along and I gave the one dog tag to him. Then we got Ian wrapped up on an Argentine poncho and we carried him down to our RAP.[7]

Tony Bojko described how John Weeks 'came over and stood by while we were wrapping him up. There were tears in his eyes as Sammy and Johnny carried him back and then down the hill.'[8]

Corporal Phil Probets who had earlier fought so hard during the battle to save Neil Grose had accompanied John Weeks. 'At first light it was the job of myself and John Weeks to walk around the mountainside to collect the dog tags of our dead, including Ian McKay's. It was an unpleasant job. I remember just placing the dog tags on a rock beside Mike Argue. We just looked at each other and then I walked off. Command is a lonely place and he must have felt like shit.'[9]

Hew Pike later recalled the words of one of British history's finest military leaders in the grim aftermath of the battle his battalion had just fought: 'There was a deep sense of grief in the battalion at our losses, all such good men, with their lives still before them. Personal memories came to mind, even in these frightful circumstances. Playing squash with the delightful, bright and highly promising Ian McKay, who had been a battalion footballer, but who had had worries over a persistent knee injury… No wonder the Duke of Wellington is reputed to have remarked that there is nothing so melancholy as a battle won – unless it be a battle lost.'[10]

The CO would never take to the squash or tennis court again with his talented sergeant. Ian had organized and led a headlong charge into a blizzard of fire; a beacon of inspiration to others who followed him to almost certain death and injury – every one of those who accompanied Ian on that final assault was either killed or wounded.

He had proved beyond doubt his courage, leadership and self-sacrifice in his attempt to silence the heavy weapon complex at the heart of the Argentine defence in order to break the deadlock at the sharp end of the fighting and save his men's lives in the process.

The morning after the battle Hew Pike was aware that his battalion's victory, to slightly misquote another of the Iron Duke's famous phrases, had been a 'near run thing'. Even after Ian's prompt and selfless action at about midnight local time had silenced a GPMG and, it must be assumed, since a period of silence followed, put the fear of God in the riflemen around it making them scatter for safety, Ian had not won the battle for his CO. As Sammy Dougherty and Tony Bojko had seen, he had not destroyed the heavy .50-calibre machine-gun position single-handedly. What he had achieved, however, by breaking the local hard core of resistance and the subsequent hiatus in the volume of Argentine fire which immediately followed his assault, was to allow the remnants of 4 and 5 Platoons to move into better cover in the rock outcrops beyond the eastern lip of The Bowl, reorganize and prepare to consolidate their tenuous grip on the western half of Longdon.

Back at B Company HQ in the minutes after midnight no one knew that Ian McKay was dead. They had heard over the company 'net' that 'Sunray 21' (Bickerdike) was down and 'Sunray Minor' (McKay) was missing. Major Mike Argue used the slight lull to send Sergeant Des Fuller forward to find Ian if he could, co-ordinate what remained of the bloodied 4 Platoon and to get word back to Argue 'by fastest possible means'. But the lull also favoured the Argentines who now, realizing that Ian's attack was not being reinforced, seeped back into the sangars around the same heavy machine-gun position he had so lately attempted to destroy.

From positions further towards the secondary summit around Carrizo-Salvadores' command post bunker at Full Back, the tempo of Argentine fire also began to increase as Carrizo-Salvadores prepared to launch a counter attack of his own. It would take another six hours after Ian's death for the Battle of Mount Longdon to run its bloody course.

Sergeant Fuller set off up the hill and negotiated the reverse slope well beyond The Bowl. His mission was to attempt to suppress the Argentine resistance in the area which Ian had attacked, not knowing what he would find when, and if, he got there. With the aid of Corporal Stewart 'Scouse' McLaughlin's section of 5 Platoon, Fuller reached the area where Ian had fallen and found the forward elements of 4 Platoon – short on numbers with several badly wounded men – in a sorry state and coming under increasing fire again from the re-occupied Argentine heavy machine-gun complex as the defenders there grew in confidence. In a series of ferocious assaults, Fuller, McLaughlin and their men tried, sangar by sangar, to work a way towards it but their initial impetus could not be maintained and these attacks too eventually ground to a halt.

Just as 6 Platoon had done more than two hours earlier Sergeant Fuller, his position now bolstered by the steady and uncompromising presence of CSM John Weeks, who had already begun to organize the evacuation of the wounded, withdrew the men back towards the relatively secure area around The Bowl west of Fly Half and 'went firm'.

Mike Argue had by now moved his HQ in amongst the rocks east of the summit of Fly Half and although the situation was far from clear, he knew enough to appreciate that his company, as it stood, was not going to get much further along the crest of the mountain. Fly Half was, for the moment, secure, but the battalion was only half way to its final objective.

It was now, as B Company had withdrawn, that Major Carrizo Salvadores seized the initiative. Ordering the forty-five men of his reserve – the 1st Platoon of the 10th Engineer Company under Lieutenant Quiroga – forward from its positions around his command post and Full Back, they moved along the crest in the darkness and did not shirk their duty as they headed towards the fighting. They did well but did not succeed in driving the paras back from their precarious perch around the summit and probably did little more than help in shoring up a buckling defence east of Fly Half, extricating the survivors of isolated bunkers in the process. This was a critical stage in the battle, the outcome of which now hung in the balance.

By about 2.30am Lieutenant Colonel Pike had managed to move up to Fly Half to assess the situation for himself. Fire from Argentine positions on Full Back had checked the frontal assault of B Company whilst A Company – still relatively intact – were still being pinned down on Wing Forward to the north east. B Company had fought magnificently and had at last secured Fly Half but he found Mike Argue's command in a perilous state. Strung out between the western summit and the furthest extent of their skirmishing, skeletally thin and isolated groups were hanging on by their fingernails with the dead and unrecovered wounded on the ground and those still fighting screaming for ammunition re-supply.

Argue's B Company had crossed the start line with six officers and 112 men, including those attached from other companies. It was well on the way to its final casualty figure of thirteen dead and twenty-seven wounded, a third of its strength, and there was no conceivable way now that it could reach and take Full Back.

> As we pushed on over the top ourselves, doing our best to exploit the protection of the rocks… we veered over to our right as I tried to link up with…Mike Argue, and then shifted left again, to find ourselves in a bowl with great rocks on its eastern side, that afforded a measure of protection from ground fire. By now the artillery and mortar fire of both sides had intensified, and as the rocks around us rang to this harsh and deafening noise, we went firm in what cover we could find at the front end of the bowl, where I could try to exercise at least a degree of control in the confusion of so much close-quarter fighting. Mike and his soldiers were having a terrible time, as they attempted to get round the flanks of well prepared enemy positions that dominated the little tracks and approaches running below the spine of the summit ridgeline. The southern slopes were impossibly dangerous as artillery fire plastered them from positions around Port Stanley, the northern approaches the only option, but well covered by enemy direct fire weapons.[11]

Under Major Osborne, C Company was still on Free Kick but would take too long to get into the battle. A radical solution would be necessary if 3 Para were to secure Full Back. Some of the fire support GPMG and Milan missile teams were already arriving in B Company positions to help in bringing fire to bear on the Argentines along the ridge line to the east, amongst them Sammy Dougherty and Tony Bojko who would fire into the area where Ian McKay's body lay.

> As I discussed the situation with Mike, three enemy corpses lying close to us in the moonlight, we concluded that his company could not continue to batter themselves in this way against such stubborn opposition, and I then talked to [Major] David Collett [OC A Company] about what he thought he could do from the north. He had already had three of his own soldiers killed by enemy fire that dominated his positions from the rocks, but we agreed that he should now try to pull back and approach on the same axis as B Company, then passing through them and continuing to press the attack home. All this took many hours – many hours in which the constant shelling and fire fights instilled in me a growing feeling of helplessness, yet a conviction that with our magnificent soldiers we must and would prevail.[12]

It was a bold scheme. As A Company made its way back to the lower northwestern slopes to begin its assault, Captain Willie McCracken called down artillery and Naval Gunfire Support from HMS *Avenger* with aplomb to within 30m of B Company's positions as Mike Argue reorganized his battered command for one final effort to break through and take the heavy machine gun which had caused so much misery to his men for so long. Moving along the same sheep track which Ian and his party had used earler, Lieutenant Mark Cox lead a composite force from 4 and 5 Platoons and fire support teams along the northern slopes in a flank attack under cover of HMS *Avenger's* 4.5 inch barrage, towards the spot where Ian had last been seen charging the Argentine weapon. Cox only managed to get his team a little way along the track but as the naval gunfire lifted to the east they ran into the same volume of fire which had previously halted B Company's advance.

This time, however, the defenders included forty-six fresh reservists of First Lieutenant Raul Fernando Castañeda's 2nd Platoon of C Company, 7 RIMec, which had recently arrived on Longdon from Wireless Ridge. They had arrived a little before 3.00am in response to Major Carrizo Salvadores' request for reinforcements at 1.30am.

Castañeda's men joined in resisting Cox's advance but the paras fought with rifle and bayonet until they too became exposed to the fire from Argentine positions clustered around Carrizo Salvadores' HQ. Numbers were now so low in B Company that Argue realized his 'numbers were now critical considering the position of the enemy and reported as much to the CO'. They could get no further.

Now A Company passed through and with fire support teams ensconced on the eastern slopes of Fly Half as a combined firebase, Major Collett deployed his men for the assault. Under a supporting barrage provided by British artillery, a light machine gun, three Milan rocket posts and five sustained fire GPMGs, which raked the Argentine positions back and forth in the very area where Ian McKay's shattered body lay slumped over the parapet of the Argentine machine-gun post, Major Collett – drawing on B Company's experiences – ordered his platoons to conduct a slow and methodical advance from sangar to sangar moving one platoon forward at a time. It was time consuming but effective as metre by metre the paras searched out and destroyed the Argentine bunkers on their relentless crawl towards Full Back and although some Argentine troops abandoned their posts many more clung on and held fast on the eastern summit and around Carrizo Salvadores' HQ. Fire from Mount Tumbledown to the south added further to the paras' difficulties.

With daybreak just a little over an hour away it looked as though Brigadier Thompson's fears of the battle spilling over into daylight hours were about to be realized but A Company's assault gathered pace and as dawn broke Major Collett's men had breached the Argentine defences around Full Back and were almost onto the battalion's second objective. Major Carrizo Salvadores' men had fought the paras all night but now, at a little after 6.30am, he finally disengaged and withdrew towards Port Stanley in the half light and mists of dawn. His men had been tenacious opponents and their resistance underestimated.

'So as the darkness began to give way to the dawn,' wrote Hew Pike, 'with David's men still crawling forward on the belly, as he put it, taking out one position after another in a systematic process of attrition, resistance was broken, and the opposing forces starting to melt away in what remained of the darkness. The mountain was ours.'

A Company had finally seized Full Back and combed out the last of the Argentine bunkers whilst 3 Platoon went beyond to secure and guard the long slope down to Wireless Ridge. During the two hours or more it had taken to reach Full Back, A Company's casualties amounted to one man – Private Coady – wounded by fragments from his own grenade.

Longdon finally belonged to 3 Para which had equalled, if not excelled, the performance of its sister battalion at Darwin/Goose Green fifteen days earlier, if only in terms of doggedly pursuing its objective against heavy odds. The battle might have been over but the battalion had paid a heavy price. Losses amounted to eighteen killed and more than forty wounded; Argentine losses were thought to be twenty-nine killed, one-hundred-and-twenty wounded and fifty taken prisoner.

But even as Sammy Dougherty and Tony Bojko set out on their journey which would eventually lead them to the body of Ian McKay, and others busied themselves with the evacuation of the wounded and the consolidation and reorganization of positions the first of the Argentine rounds from the direction of Port Stanley came crashing in amongst the rocks. The suffering of 3 Para was not over for this was merely the opening salvo of the most sustained artillery barrage suffered by any unit of the British Army since Korea in the summer of 1953.[13] It would claim the lives of five more men and wound several more, bringing the total casualty list to twenty-three dead and forty-seven wounded, and ensure that the struggle for Mount Longdon would go down in history as the bloodiest battle of the entire Falklands Campaign.

As the officer commanding HQ Company, Captain Bob Darby answered directly to 3 Para's Second-in-Command Major Roger Patton as the link between the rear echelon and the forward units, and as such shared the responsibility for ensuring the smooth re-supply of ammunition and equipment to the fighting units and the crucial evacuation of the wounded as well as the bodies of the dead.

He recalled how, after the fighting on Mount Longdon had been going on for about eight hours, he had tuned in to the radio traffic on the battalion 'net' and knew that 3 Para had taken casualties. Major Roger Patton had pushed on with Colour Sergeant Brian Faulkner and the rest of the RAP to the base of Longdon and had established a position on the western side from where he could send up the stretcher parties to bring down the casualties and the dead. It would now fall to Bob Darby to ensure that Ian's body was safely evacuated from the battle zone:

With dawn [of 12 June] approaching, our positions on Longdon were coming under increasingly intense artillery fire. I went back to a location about 2km west of the Murrel Bridge to set up a reception area for the wounded. I was told that the choppers were coming in to 'medevac' (medical evacuation) the wounded back to Teal Inlet. By now it was becoming light and the first helis were on their way from the direction of Estancia. The morning was cold and overcast, the cloud base being just above ground level. I laid out a red marker light to guide them in. The first heli to arrive – a Gazelle – came in very slowly at very low speed and no more than 30ft above the ground along the valley floor between Mount Kent and Mount Vernet. I presumed the pilot was following a fence line to our given position. The first heli to arrive only had one 'coffin' pod to carry away the stretcher cases which was not sufficient. The walking wounded sat inside. We required a larger capacity lift to get the wounded away as soon as possible. By mid-morning a naval Wessex heli arrived and we were able to get more wounded away. The BVs [Volvo Bandwagon vehicles] were still moving between Mount Longdon and my location. I decided we could casevac quicker if we could evacuate directly from the RAP. When the next pilot came in I quickly briefed him on the situation and suggested it might be quicker if we flew directly to the RAP. He agreed and, with me standing in the door with the load master, we flew up to Longdon. We landed and I saw the RAP party sheltering in the rocks below Longdon. I wanted to get out and explain that we would pick up the remaining casualties from their location. As I started to walk towards them a shell exploded not 100m away, certainly close enough to put the fear of God into the pilot. The load master called me in and we moved out at high speed towards my previous location. I remember in the early hours of the morning seeing the soldiers – the walking wounded – coming down wrapped in blankets following the BVs which carried more serious cases. They were walking down from the forward RAP back to my base on the Murrell track. There were lots of them. It quite surprised me how many there were. I remember getting into one of the BVs and seeing one of the soldiers, it could have been Brian Milne, and the tibia in his leg was pointing into the air. It was yellowy, white, completely stripped of flesh. The whole of the floor of the BV was covered in blood, it was like walking on spilt paint; sticky and it had that awful iron smell. But the walking wounded were in shock. So we got all the wounded out first followed by the dead. Brian [Faulkner] got the DCM [for his work that night]. He held the whole lot together, he really did.[14]

When I interviewed him in 2006, the shock of seeing the number of men killed in taking Longdon still had the power to move Bob Darby after twenty-four years.

What you have to remember is that we had never experienced this sort of confrontation situation before. We'd been to Northern Ireland; lost a few guys every other tour but all of a sudden we have eighteen dead in the assault and then all the wounded guys on top of that. It really hits you. Once all the wounded had been evacuated the bodies of the dead began to come down from Longdon in the early morning. This is the hardest part of war, dealing with the bodies of your friends and comrades. We didn't wait for them all to come down at once. They came down in batches and as soon as the Wessex came in we loaded them up and they went off to Teal Inlet. The dead were brought down in grey body bags. One thing that surprised me was that all the body bags were grey. I thought this was very un–military like, as I would have thought they'd have been green. I'd only seen one body bag before – a grey one – in Ireland and the 'civvies' had brought it in so naturally on the Falklands I thought that those we used were 'civvy' body bags. They were very, very durable, and obviously they had to be 'drip-proof'. The zip ran diagonally across the bag so that you could get the body in more easily. The bodies came down in the back of the BVs. Somewhere up on the mountain Johnny Weeks and his boys from B Company had cleared them all off. I recall looking at the dead laid out on the ground in their body bags. We had laid them all out ready for evacuation their names written with marker pen on each bag. These were names I knew. Some I had spoken to less than twenty-four hours before. One – Lance Corporal Scott – had talked about his passion for flying and his love for his children and how much he missed them. Now it was all gone. There were some Argentine marines taken prisoner who had been manning the .5s [Browning heavy machine guns], and without ceremony they were loading up our dead on to the helis which took all the bodies back for initial burial at Teal Inlet. They had already dug a mass grave at Teal with a dozer blade. It seems almost surreal now after twenty-four years. I actually felt quite angry. One of the press lads came up. He worked for *The Guardian* I think and he was a bit 'anti' the whole thing, and I said 'is this what you've come for?' It wasn't his fault but I was really upset about all these young men – I was angry, not weepy upset just f****** angry. Why did [the Argentines] hang around, why hadn't they just run away? All these fit, healthy young men like Ian McKay whose lives had ended and the wounded whose lives had not necessarily been ruined but had been changed.

It had been barely two weeks since Ian had shaken hands with Rod Hutchings at Teal Inlet settlement's perimeter gate as 3 Para had set out on the next leg of its epic TAB from Teal Inlet to Estancia House. He had made a favourable impression on Rod and Jan Hutchings during his first visit to their home in the dead of night and perhaps they had hoped that at some point they might see him again but now the manner of his return would bring them nothing but sadness. It would fall to Rod to perform two acts of remembrance and memorial for Ian and those other men of 3 Para who had joined him in making that solemn twenty-mile heli-lift to Teal. In many cases that journey via the evacuation chain from Longdon – poncho or stretcher off the mountain, tracked vehicle for the 6km journey to Bob Darby at the helicopter landing site and then on to Teal – took six hours.

Two weeks earlier, before Ian had arrived, Teal Inlet had been home to just twenty-three souls but after the departure of 3 Para and the arrival of 3 Commando Brigade HQ and its supporting units, the population statistics had rocketed. The settlement cookhouse near the small jetty had been turned into a field hospital and after the three battles in the mountains of 12/13 June – Longdon, Mount Harriet (42 Commando) and Two Sisters (45 Commando) – the medical services were doing a brisk business and not just with wounded British troops. Argentine casualties evacuated at the same time were being cared for with equal skill and compassion.

A shed outside had been converted into a makeshift mortuary and it was there where Ian's body would lie for almost forty-eight hours until arrangements could be made for burial.

Not all of 3 Para's personnel had left Teal when they set off for Estancia. Dave Rowntree, a warrant officer in the Battalion HQ, was also the battalion's Chief Clerk in the rear echelon and he had set up a clerk's office in a workshop. The Hutchings' had struck up a friendship with Rowntree over the previous two weeks as he called in each day to check on the progress of a couple of 3 Para men with trench feet whom the Hutchings' had agreed to take in. Rowntree loved his Bounty bars and on his daily visits he got into the habit of taking chocolate bars for the Hutchings' young son Gavin and emptying them out of his red beret on to the table. Jan Hutchings recalled that Dave Rowntree was not one to impose but on one occasion they did eventually persuade him to share a hot meal with them:

Just as he was about to tuck into a big steak there was a knock on our front door and a messenger summoned Dave to the mortuary. He was needed for the very sad duty of identifying bodies of 3 Para following heavy casualties on Mount Longdon. He asked Rod to accompany him. When he returned, Dave's face looked as if he had aged ten years – it was grey. Understandably he could not finish his meal so I made hot drinks and we talked for an hour. Being amongst friends I think helped and as he left he asked if we would attend the burial service the next day.[15]

Teal Inlet had already witnessed several burials, all in a small plot on the headland overlooking the water and now, after 2 Para's second battle of the war for Wireless Ridge, fought in the early hours of 14 June, there was to be another. On a bitterly cold day with sleet sweeping in from the water across the low headland near the jetty, and the wind blowing the robes of both Derek Heaver and David Cooper, padres of 3 and 2 Para respectively, Ian was buried along with twenty of his comrades. Only Corporal Stephen Hope and Private Richard Absolon were not interred at the same time.[16]

Jan Hutchings later wrote that:

Nothing can prepare one for such a sad event as a mass burial service, and over the next few days twenty-nine British troops were laid in a temporary grave with one Argentine in a separate grave nearby. The long line of stretchers bearing those body bags to the open grave remains one of my saddest memories. Each one we noticed had a name stencilled on the side and I felt devastated as I suddenly realized that two of the first five Paras that had arrived at our door two weeks earlier had been killed – Stewart McLaughlin, the friendly Scouse, and Sergeant Ian McKay, who was to be awarded a posthumous Victoria Cross. After the service we spoke to Rev Derek Heaver, one of the officiating army chaplains (who a few days earlier had shared tea and Welsh cakes in our home), who told us of his experiences on the battlefield. He looked shattered and we invited him home but he refused as he was returning to Longdon to tend to the wounded. The hospital was full, many of the casualties being young Argentine conscripts. As I glanced back at the burial area, I noticed the lone figure of a soldier gazing down at the open grave – his wan, anguished face remains with me still. While Rod made hot drinks, I put up the blackout curtains upstairs, weeping as I did so for those buried that day and with sorrow for their loved ones, 8,000 miles away.

Several hours earlier and, with only the news bulletins and snippets of information gleaned from letters written to the wives and partners of Ian's fellow soldiers, Monday morning 14 June for Marica McKay simply marked yet another day when her husband was away at war. She had had enough to keep her busy. Melanie had had chicken pox and was recovering and there were several mundane housekeeping tasks to perform. For a start the kettle was on the blink and she had determined to go into town to buy a new electric model. It was about 8.30am. 'I'd just gone upstairs to finish getting ready and I heard a knock at the door and sent Melanie to answer it.'

The married quarters in Salamanca Park was as safe as anywhere could be for a five-year-old to answer their front door. The neighbours were all service families after all. In fact Corporal Scott Wilson of 9 Parachute Squadron RE, who was attached to 3 Para for the Battle of Mount Longdon and was killed in action on the same day as Ian, lived at No. 47 with his wife. It was probably a friend or the wife of another soldier popping round for a chat or with the latest news. When Marica came downstairs to see who her visitor was she knew it was serious. 'It was Sue Patton, the wife of Roger Patton, the Second-in-Command of the battalion and she was standing there with Simon Brewis [the Regimental Colonel]. I remember Sue was carrying a bag and I could see a big bottle of brandy on top of it. I asked her why she'd brought it, I didn't need any brandy but she said "oh yes, you do". I asked them, "is he wounded or dead?" Sue just said, "dead".[17]

Any details of Ian's fate, relayed to Simon Brewis at Regimental HQ at a distance of 8,000 miles, would have been sketchy at best, particularly as the Argentines had yet to surrender. Hew Pike had worked well into the small hours of 14 June preparing a plan for his battalion to fight The Battle of Moody Brook at 4.00am on the morning of 15 June – a battle which, thankfully, 3 Para never had to fight.

Marica did not ask for any details in any case; 'I couldn't see the point. Ian was dead.' She concedes that, even now, she finds it difficult to remember what happened for the rest of the day – just a series of blurred recollections of people and things going on around her: her inability to tell Melanie straight away about what had happened to her father; Sue Patton using the telephone and having some difficulty trying to get in touch with both of Ian's parents in Rotherham; using the phone herself to call her sister Kay in Bahrain; a news bulletin, sometime in mid-morning, with the ironic information that there was a possibility of an Argentine surrender and the anguish in Harry Nilsson's voice coming from a radio – 'I can't live, if living is without you'. 'I went out and bought that record later,' she told me, 'but I never played it.'

Sometime about 9.30am the phone rang in the office which Ron Jackson shared with Freda McKay in the workers' welfare department at British Steel's Stainless Division in Tinsley. He was interviewing and advising someone who was just about to be made redundant and she was dealing with the details for a trip they were organizing for retired employees.

I was sitting at my desk and the phone rang. I answered it and it was Sue Patton. She said, 'I'm very, very sorry but I have to tell you that Ian was killed in action but you must know that he died very, very bravely. I'm here with Marica now and I'm sure you'll want to talk to her later but I'm very sorry that I've had to tell you this.'

I remember howling 'NO, NO, NO, NO' and Ron looking up but he just kept on talking to this other chap. My other boss Jim came out of his office a little further along the corridor and Don Prior, the security officer in the next office, came down to me straight away. He asked me to calm down and to tell him what had happened, so I'm trying to tell him all about Sue Patton who's with my daughter-in-law because Ian had been killed. He asked me what Marica's phone number was and I was in state but I remembered. He'd already sent for the two nurses from the medical centre and he went back to his office and rang Marica's number just to check it wasn't a crank call. He spoke to Sue Patton. They took me down to the medical room where they made me a strong cup of tea with lots of sugar. I'd packed up smoking at Christmas but that set me off again and I lit up. Don Prior knew Graham worked at Stocksbridge so he rang his boss; they put Graham in a car and brought him to me at 'Stainless'. I was worried because Neal had an appointment at Northern General Hospital that morning and Ken was supposed to be going with him and I didn't want Ken to get the news before we could be with him. Don Prior got the firm's car and when Graham arrived it took us straight up to outpatients. By the time we got there Neal had actually gone in to see the consultant. We went into a room and explained and the doctor came to see us and asked if we would like him to tell Neal who was in the consulting room. I said 'yes please'. We got Neal and the firm's car took us straight home. Don had asked where Ken would be and I told him he was probably at the hospital so I asked him to ring Keith, Ken's brother, just in case he hadn't gone.[18]

Ken McKay was at home. He had been due to take Neal for his appointment but he had only recently come out of hospital after a heart scare and hadn't felt well that morning. Security guard Don Prior contacted Ken's brother Keith at about 10.00am and Keith drove up to see him. Ken had the TV on, waiting for the fourth day's play of the England v India Test Match from Lord's to start. Ken had been given tablets for his heart and so Keith asked where they were. 'He asked why' recalled Keith, 'as I went to get a glass of water. "Just take one now will you?" I said and he looked at me and I sensed then that he thought something was wrong. He took one and I just told him straight out – it was pointless me hanging on. I could see he swooned a little bit. Within five minutes it seemed like everyone had turned up; the Territorial Army representative from York and others.'

Official confirmation arrived the next day on headed paper in stark black and white:

Infantry Manning and Record Office (South)
Higher Barracks
Exeter
14th June 82
Dear Mrs McKay,

It is with deep regret that I write to confirm the news given to you concerning the death of your son, Ian. May I offer my sincere condolences in your bereavement and pass to you the profound sympathy of the Army Board in your tragic loss.

With renewed sympathy,
Yours sincerely,
Colonel A G Wooldridge

This was just the first in an avalanche of cards and letters of condolence from family, friends, work colleagues and acquaintances – including local MP Stan Crowther – in the days which followed and the publication of Mark Whiting's piece in the *Rotherham Advertiser* on 18 June. The postman's bag for the round which included the McKay household would bulge even further by the year's end as Ian's actions and the announcement of the award of the VC became public knowledge and captured the imagination of complete strangers who felt compelled to write to Freda and Ken. The following short letter from a local shopkeeper serves to illustrate the memories which the announcement of Ian's death triggered.

> Dearest Freda and Ken,
>
> I am very, very sorry to read about Ian in this morning's paper. I still remember your boys coming to the shop in the mornings before school and dear Ian being so protective to his brothers, and now the brave lad gave his life in the protection of others. He was brought up to be caring by caring parents Freda dear. My heart goes out to you and your family.
>
> Fay and Wilf Tupling.

Freda spoke to Marica a little later on the day of Sue Patton's dread tidings and two days later she, 'went down to Aldershot and stayed with her [Marica] for a couple of days. I think the first thing I said was "are you all alright?" But we were just stunned really.'

After the initial shock Marica refused to let Ian's death swamp her, after all she had both Melanie and Donny to consider and she was of the opinion that if she let herself fall she would never get up again. Freda describes her daughter-in-law as possessed of a 'very strong and determined personality. I think I was the only one to see her cry when I went to stay for those few days after we had heard the news and that was only for a few minutes'.

'I think I kept it in somewhat,' Marica revealed in 2009, 'I had to cope, to keep going for the children. That's also how the army operates but it didn't mean I felt any the less for Ian or what he had done.'

Ian McKay, it seemed, had been influenced by two strong and determined women. The first he inherited by birth, the second – and the first serious relationship of his life – he married. Marica once revealed that her mother-in-law was, like her, very strong; a superwoman who, by 1982, had had to cope not only with Graham and Neal's debilitating disease but also with Ken's deteriorating heart condition. The inner strength which lay at the core of two of the three most important females in Ian McKay's life would now provide the rock on which they would anchor their grief.

After Freda left Aldershot to return home to Rotherham, Marica travelled to Suffolk to stay with her family and it was only then that she felt able to tell Melanie. How does one begin tell a five-year-old that her father has been killed in a war in a land so far away? Marica revealed to me that in the end she opted for the cushion of a white lie in the hope that it would lessen the impact. 'I told her that Daddy was very ill, that he couldn't come home and that we wouldn't be able to see him again' and although it appeared that Melanie had readily accepted this version of events, Marica later overheard her telling one of her friends, 'my Daddy's been killed in the Falklands'.

Ian's stepson Donny also had to be told. He and Ian had got on very well and Ian had treated him like his own son. Now the sad duty of breaking the news fell to his real father, Marica's ex-husband Bill Coffey. He and Marica had always maintained a civil working relationship for the sake of their son and Bill did not baulk at the prospect of travelling from London, where he was serving with 10 Para in the Territorial Army, to be with them when they needed him most. Marica's sister Kay had already flown in from Bahrain and stayed for a month to provide any support she could.

As Marica had attempted to come to terms with the news on the afternoon of 14 June, her husband had been laid to rest in the quiet earth of Teal Inlet on East Falkland along with his comrades in arms. All over Britain, from Renfrew (Lance Corporal James Murdoch) to Ross-on-Wye (Private Timothy Jenkins) and other points south and east, and even New Zealand in the case of Richard Absolon, the wives, girlfriends, children, mothers and fathers of twenty-two more families would have received the same news.

Apart from Derek Heaver there had been no senior level representation of the battalion at the burial service and with good reason – 2 Para had secured Wireless Ridge early that morning and had lost three more men in doing so. Although the Argentines had streamed off the last of the mountains back in the direction of Port Stanley in what appeared to be a headlong retreat they had not yet surrendered.

At 1.44pm UK time Hew Pike ordered C Company of 3 Para to 'get on the move directly behind 2 Para' who by now were gleefully charging after the Argentines down from Wireless Ridge towards Moody Brook, just over three miles (5.5km) from the centre of Port Stanley.

An hour and three quarters later, with word coming back that the Argentines were now beginning to show white flags, the men of 3 Para took their red berets out of their packs, put them on and made best speed off Mount Longdon across Wireless Ridge and descended into Moody Brook hard on the heels of their sister regiment. They finally pitched up on the waterfront of Port Stanley on Ross Road West, opposite the racecourse, directly behind 2 Para. As the legally binding 'Instrument of Surrender' would not be recognized until 11.59pm that night all units were to remain on full alert but by 5.00pm the battalion had taken shelter in the houses, garages and peat sheds along Ross Road.

With the surrender duly signed 3 Para spent the following day making themselves as comfortable and clean as possible and the task of administration became the main concern for everyone. CSMs began to prepare lists of who they had still with them, what kit they had missing and initiated a complete check of all weaponry. Hew Pike pulled a chair up to a table and began the time consuming but sad and serious business of writing letters to the next of kin of those who had been killed, and drafting bravery citations in longhand. This he did before writing to his wife but he finally got a letter off to her on 16 June.

Well, here we are! If you look at *The Times* of Saturday, 22 May, page two, there is a picture of Stanley – I am in a bungalow in the bottom half of the picture. We arrived in the afternoon of 14 June, and the sudden collapse was as unexpected as it was marvellous. <u>Never</u> have I been so utterly relieved and elated – even that morning after first light, artillery was still raining in on our position on Mount Longdon, and I was that morning giving out orders for an attack that night (14/15 June) on Moody Brook Camp – we would have taken it, but only at still more loss. A hailstorm was falling, and I was becoming quite concerned at the closing winter and how long the battle would continue, with more casualties in worsening weather, freezing, snowy, wet. That we would succeed I had no doubt, it was the cost that was concerning me so much... The sun came out and it was a fine, crisp afternoon, quite firm going underfoot, as we almost ran into Stanley, down the moorland – to be greeted by scenes of destruction and shambles... I'm sorry I didn't write as soon as we arrived, but I have been sitting in this bungalow writing to Next of Kin and drafting citations and still have not finished, and I do want to get them cracked now, while we pause to discover what happens next.[19]

Chief Clerk Dave Rowntree had by now moved up from Teal Inlet and, along with Corporal Worsley, the men had placed themselves at a desk, set up their typewriters and began to clatter away as fast as the CO could write. The letters to the next of kin of the dead were the priority and all citations were to be taken seriously but there was one citation in particular which Hew Pike was keen to complete and it had to be done correctly, for this was an award in a class of its own. He did not have the requisite form to hand so Rowntree typed out the details on paper following the format of the official paperwork. Personal details could always be filled in later; it was the content Hew Pike was keen to start moving up the chain of command. It read as follows:

Serial No: Thirty Eight

OP CORPORATE – HONOURS AND AWARDS

A. McKAY
B. IAN JOHN
C. SERGEANT, 24210031
D. 29, other details not available.
E. Details not available.
F. <u>VICTORIA CROSS (POSTHUMOUS)</u>

Sergeant McKay was Platoon Sergeant of 4 Platoon who were left forward platoon on the night of the attack on Mount Longdon (11/12 June). The platoon had drawn level with 5 Platoon on their right, after a short delay caused by entering an anti-personnel minefield and receiving a casualty in the right forward section.

On moving up 4 Platoon entered an area partially unobserved to any enemy on the ridge but unprotected by the crags higher up the slope. The left forward section of 4 Platoon then came under fire from heavy and medium machine guns, immediately wounding the Platoon Commander. The enemy fire was heavy indeed, raking back and forwards pinning down the platoon and preventing any further movement eastwards.

Sergeant McKay took immediate command of the platoon and quickly assessed the threat. Then, gathering some of his own men and members of the left section of 5 Platoon, he gave swift orders for the destruction of the enemy position, only some 50m to his front in a small re-entrant. McKay then led his men forward under cover of fire from a small support group, personally moving in to assault the main bunker with two other soldiers. One of these soldiers was shot dead, the other moving higher on the right, received multiple wounds from a burst of machine gun fire. Undaunted, McKay pressed home his attack with his rifle and two grenades, which entered the enemy sangar. Seconds later Sergeant McKay was himself killed, falling across the sangar wall. After this attack, enemy fire from that position was eliminated and the platoon was able to reorganize for their next task along the feature.

Sergeant McKay's example of leadership, supreme gallantry and self-sacrifice was beyond praise.

H W R PIKE
Lieutenant Colonel
Commanding Officer

17 June 1982

It is a document which has never been seen before beyond the eyes of a very small group of people, yet it was the first draft of what was to become a very famous citation indeed. Hew Pike's first draft of a hugely significant event in Britain's recent military history.

On the same day as the citation was typed up, Hew Pike, accompanied by Majors David Collett, Mike Argue, Pat Butler and Hugh Dennison, and several CSMs including John Weeks, flew out to the hospital ship *Uganda* by Wessex helicopter to visit the sick and wounded. Andrew Bickerdike and Ian Bailey were recovering along with many others of the 3 Para wounded. All seemed in good spirits. On the way back to Stanley they dropped in to Teal Inlet to visit the small cemetery and pay their respects to the dead.

They found the gravesite a mound of topsoil with turves arranged on top. Settlement handyman Rod Hutchings had been busy since the burial assiduously constructing a wooden cross for each of the twenty-one dead of 3 Para, seven others from 2 Para and Royal Marines units and the lone Argentine, Ramon Omar Quintana, who had been mortally wounded when 4 and 5 Platoons had fought their way into and beyond The Bowl five days earlier. Had the young Argentine faced the vastly more experienced Para sergeant on the night of battle? It is a question to which there is no answer. Rod and Jan had accepted responsibility to care for the cemetery and Rod took his duties very seriously. In his notebook, on alternating pink and blue pages, he wrote 'DETAILS OF MEN BURIED AT TEAL INLET FOLLOWING GT BRITAIN/ARGENTINE WAR APRIL/MAY/JUNE 1982' and listed each one by unit, name, rank number and date of death from, 'LEFT TO RIGHT ON BURIAL GROUND'. It is thanks to Rod Hutchings' attention to detail that on contemporary images of the cemetery it is possible to make out Ian's grave – the eighteenth cross from the right as one looks at them.

There was one aspect of the visit which upset Hew Pike, however, and according to the battalion War Diary disturbed him so much so that a reference to it also found its way into a letter to his wife which he wrote the following day:

> Yesterday I flew to the SS *Uganda* in Grantham Sound, to see our casualties – they are being marvellous, so brave, and all will live – but five have lost limbs, you will know who, I expect – all have sent telegrams and most have spoken on the Marisat telephone to their families – one lost eye, two can't speak at present... then on to Teal Inlet where twenty-one of our twenty-three dead are buried – Corporal Hope and Private Absolon are at Red Beach, San Carlos Bay as they died after reaching hospital there. They all have crosses and marked graves, on a nice patch, overlooking the sea – but it wasn't fenced and there was a calf blundering over one of the crosses – we've fixed that. Anyway, it looks as if all bodies may come home now. I hope so, although what a thankless task. We held a Memorial Service in Stanley Cathedral this morning. Brigadier Julian Thompson came, and I made a short address, we had three hymns (incredibly slow playing organist), prayers, a lesson and Corporal Steggles read the names of the dead, Corporal Black some prayers. It was absolutely the right thing to do although of course we will have a full one with families in Aldershot Garrison Church on return. [It was in fact held as the central event at an open air parade that October in the Aldershot Town Football Ground in the presence of the Prince of Wales, the Colonel-in-Chief].[20]

Hew Pike's reference to 'All bodies' coming home was perhaps somewhat premature. True, he had had a visit from Major Chris Keeble, Second-in-Command of 2 Para, late on the night of 15 June at which Keeble had been 'adamant that he would get the bodies of 2 PARA back to the UK'. Repeating his late CO's clever re-working of the words of Rupert Brooke's famous poem The Soldier before his death in action during the Battle of Darwin/Goose Green on 28 May 1982, Keeble had stated baldly that 'Colonel H Jones had promised his soldiers that none would be left behind "in some forgotten field"'. As in Ian's case, a citation for a posthumous VC in recognition of 'H' Jones's action on Darwin Hill on 28 May was being formulated and in life he had undoubtedly been a formidable character, yet, despite his pre-war promise to get the bodies of his men back home, could he really influence from beyond his own grave a tradition of non-repatriation of war dead which had begun during the First World War and had continued throughout the Second World War?

Certainly there were those who thought Jones had had a point. A groundswell of opinion was building behind the notion back home as next of kin, including the parents of 17-year-old Jason Burt, who had died within the first two strides of the attack on the HMG position led by Ian, began to question the Thatcher Government's insistence that those killed in battle on the Falkland Islands should be buried and remain on the Falkland Islands in the spirit of the 'fellowship of death'. The War Diary for 3 Para for 7.00pm on 18 June 1982 noted that 'The CO had heard a rumour that our own dead would be repatriated – however, Brigade had still not been given a definite answer.'[21]

A decision had still not been taken when Brigadier Julian Thompson saw his senior commanders three days later and by the afternoon of 25 June, after 3 Para had left the Falklands aboard the ferry *Norland* bound for Ascension Island and home, Hew Pike was telling his company commanders that, 'the repatriation of our dead was now doubtful'.

But faced with a barrage of letters from the next of kin, including one from Mrs Edna Wallace who had succeeded in having the body of her 17-year-old son Eddie repatriated from Aden in 1965, the lady who was 'not for turning' changed her mind.

On 8 July, 1982 she announced the government's decision in the House of Commons:

> After considering all aspects of this most difficult problem, including the practical difficulties involved, and having read the letters I have received from the next-of-kin of those killed and others, I have decided that, where next-of-kin wish, arrangements will be made for the return to the United Kingdom of the bodies of the fallen who have been given temporary burial on land in the Falkland Islands. Where next-of-kin wish the bodies to remain in the Falkland Islands they will be buried with all due ceremony at Port Stanley.[22]

Not only were the bodies of the dead now allowed to be brought back to the UK but also their next of kin were given a choice as to the type of ceremony they preferred, ranging from interment with full military honours to a private burial with no military representation. There was also a choice as to whether they wished to have a regulation Commonwealth War Graves Commission headstone or not.

On their return to the UK the 3 Para Orderly Room staff busied themselves in drawing up a handwritten grid showing the names of the twenty-three dead and the names and addresses of their next of kin who were then contacted as to their preferences. In Ian's section of the grid someone had written 'Marcia McKay' under the column 'Next of Kin' and had corrected it to 'Marica'. A handwritten note adds the information that there is a 'son – 13, Donny; daughter – 4, Melanie'. Under Ian's name are scribbled the words, 'body home – Aldershot'.

Neither Marica nor Ian's mother and father wanted his body to stay on the Falklands after the choice of repatriation was offered, amid fears for the safety of his grave if ever the Argentines were tempted to invade again. They did not relish the prospect of him lying in a war grave in a land under the possible future control of a power he had died in helping to defeat.

It was the Royal Fleet Auxiliary *Sir Bedivere* which sailed into Teal Inlet to pick up those, like Ian, who were buried in the cemetery there. Jan Hutchings witnessed its arrival. 'From out of the window one day I watched *Sir Bedivere* sail towards the settlement for the sad task of removing to their final resting places those valiant men who "for our tomorrows gave their todays". On a windswept headland overlooking the beach, where hundreds of tons of stores and ammunition had been brought ashore to support the British offensive, there now stands a memorial [bearing the names of] those brave men… who did not return to these [British] shores. My husband Rod was so honoured to be asked to build this lasting reminder, its construction being a labour of love.'

Ian's body joined that of sixty-two others on board *Sir Bedivere* for the long journey home but first *Sir Bedivere* sailed to San Carlos Water and rode at anchor offshore as fourteen men whose next of kin wished them to remain on the Falkland Islands were laid to rest in the new cemetery at Blue Beach overlooking the British landing beaches, during a ceremony on 25 October 1982. Ironically, one of those men was Lieutenant Colonel 'H' Jones who had promised his men that he would not leave them 'in some forgotten field'. His widow Sara Jones had decided that it was fitting that her husband's body should be buried near the battlefield on which he fell.

Sir Bedivere weighed anchor and turned north for the mouth of the bay as the strains of the Last Post, played by Private John Urquhart of the Queen's Own Highlanders, drifted out over San Carlos Water. Ian McKay was going home but it would be no ordinary homecoming. He was going home to a hero's welcome.

Lieutenant Colonel Hew Pike was in no doubt that Ian McKay's action was worthy of a Victoria Cross. The conditions of the award, according to Statute Thirdly of the Royal Warrant, are that the VC 'shall only be awarded for most conspicuous bravery or some daring or pre-eminent act of valour or self-sacrifice or extreme devotion to duty in the presence of the enemy'. As a guide, the standard to be applied includes a 90 per cent possibility of being killed whilst performing the deed. In the eyes of his CO Ian McKay had fulfilled all those criteria and more.

He had set the ball rolling with his original citation, which he hoped would be looked on favourably by Commander-in-Chief Fleet and overall Task Force Commander, Admiral Sir John Fieldhouse and his Land Deputy, Lieutenant General Sir Richard Trant. But his first citation, written in the bungalow on Ross Road in Port Stanley, needed to be supported by the signed statements of three independent witnesses to Ian's action.

With that in mind Hew Pike had, almost immediately on 3 Para's return to the UK, submitted an addendum to his original citation including more detail regarding the action:

It was typical of this outstanding Senior Non-Commissioned Officer that he should have taken immediate command of the platoon after his platoon commander had been wounded. This he did without any orders from his company commander and with characteristic, single-minded confidence and determination. A young sergeant of brilliant promise he then proceeded to demonstrate his high professional dedication and to apply his training with cool, exemplary skill. A plan was made, orders issued, an ad hoc force added to his own platoon, and under his leadership the plan was at once executed. All this under withering and sustained HMG fire. During the planning and execution of the attack, McKay's supreme leadership was combined with quite extraordinary courage. And in the final assault on the position, McKay inspired those around him in a manner beyond all praise. He was killed, as he had lived, at the front of his men. His example of magnificent courage combined with superb tactical skill and leadership must rate among the few paramount instances of such action in recent military campaigns. We can only reflect with awe on his matchless bravery and professional sacrifice.[23]

Major Mike Argue, as OC B Company, was tasked with obtaining the witness statements and in addition to his own, which he submitted to Hew Pike on 9 July, he obtained testimony from Andrew Bickerdike and Ian Bailey – two of the men who had been closest to Ian during the battle – and Private Logan, all three of whom were still being treated in hospitals in the UK for their wounds. The final statement was completed on 13 July and dispatched up the chain of command.

Two weeks later the recommendations for the posthumous award of the VC were put to the British Army VC Committee, setting out the final citations which Sir Richard Trant had expanded personally and which had been approved by commanding officers. There were three men on the final list – all of them from the Parachute Regiment; Lieutenant Colonel 'H' Jones and Private Stephen Illingsworth of 2 Para and Ian. Of the three, Ian and 'H' Jones were judged to be 'Priority 1', whilst Stephen Illingsworth was 'Priority 3'.

The recommendations of senior officers for the award of the VC range from a straightforward 'recommended' through 'strongly recommended' to 'very strongly recommended'. In Ian's case the following was noted:

'Sgt McKAY – 3 PARA.

(1) The citation is Very Strongly Recommended by Land Deputy C in C FLEET and Recommended by the Task Force Commander.
(2) This recommendation is given joint priority with that for Lt Col JONES and in my view it is a clear cut case of outstanding leadership, bravery and example shown by a NCO in a desperate situation.
(3) Although all those who formed the group he led were either killed or wounded the citation is corroborated by the Platoon Commander and two other wounded members of the platoon....
(4) It is recommended that Sgt McKAY is deserving of the posthumous award of the VC. The alternate award is the DCM posthumous.'[24]

It is now a matter of record that the VC Committee recommended the posthumous award of the Victoria Cross to Ian and 'H' Jones whilst Stephen Illingsworth received the posthumous award of the Distinguished Conduct Medal.

During the course of these deliberations Ian's body was, of course, still buried at Teal Inlet and would remain there until well after the official announcement of his VC which was made in the London Gazette of 11 October 1982, along with almost 600 further awards related to service or actions during Operation Corporate but the press had already been briefed.

Over the weekend of Saturday and Sunday 9 and 10 October 1982 and on into Monday there was a blizzard of coverage of the two Parachute Regiment VCs. Breathless headlines trumpeted Ian's achievement, often accompanied by that photograph of Ian – the one with Spot the dog taken by John Bates more than ten years previously, very much in evidence and splashed all over the front or inside pages of the red-topped tabloids. The following selection of headings is just an example:

'For Valour – The Para VCs' – *Daily Mail*, 9 October 1982.
'For Valour', 'Ian Gave his Life to Save Company' – *The Daily Express*, 9 October 1982.
'Two Men of Valour', 'Tears of a Widow Whose Man Won the VC – The Anguish and the Pride' – *The Daily Mirror,* 9 October 1982.
'Valour of Red Devils' – *The Sun*, 9 October 1982.
'Sergeant McKay – "Courage, Leadership and Inspiration" – The Boy Who Grew Up to Win the VC' – 'Ian McKay, The Para who died to Save his Comrades' – *The Mail on Sunday*, 10 October 1982.

Such was the feeding frenzy as the press jostled for a piece, any piece, of the two VC widows, Marica McKay and Sara Jones, that *The Sun* shamed itself by publishing an entirely fictitious 'World Exclusive', which they claimed they had secured with Marica. And they almost got away with it. The story only came to light because the sub-editor dated the story by the phrase, 'fought back her tears last night' and gave her house as 'Rotherham'. On the night in question, Marica was nowhere near Rotherham but safely ensconced in the Howard Hotel in London paid for by *The Daily Mirror* having agreed to give them an exclusive.

The sordid affair – in which it is alleged that a senior female *Sun* journalist asked questions of female employees in its offices and passed their answers off as Marica's – prompted an investigation by the Press Council which upheld a complaint against *The Sun*. In their edition of 8 August 1983, *The Sun* issued a formal apology and said 'We're Sorry'. Marica's name was also mentioned in a debate on the Right of Reply Bill in the House of Commons on 3 February 1989. One wonders how Ian McKay would have reacted to all the attention but Marica is certain she knows. 'He would have wondered what all the fuss was about. He would probably have said that he was only doing his job and that the award of the VC was not just for him but for everybody else as well.'

The investiture was held at Buckingham Palace on 9 November 1982 a little less than a month after the official announcement and was attended by Marica, Donny, then 15, 5-year-old Melanie, Ken and Freda. Lieutenant Colonel Hew Pike was present that day to receive his award of the DSO from the Queen.

Freda recalls being 'taken upstairs to the Blue Room where a man came and spoke with us and told us what to do when the Queen arrived':

Another family was in another room. Our ceremony was first, a separate ceremony before the main one in the Ballroom. The ceremony was due to begin at 10 o'clock and we were waiting for about twenty minutes before the Queen was announced. She walked in and the medals were behind her. I remember her outfit: blue dress, no gloves, no hat. We all lined up as a family group. There was no announcement or any reading of Ian's citation, she came down the line and spoke to each one of us. She spoke to Marica first [in a dress which matched exactly the shade of the VC ribbon]. She said she was very sorry but she was going to bring a small piece of one of the cannons that they make the VCs out of but she had been looking everywhere for it and couldn't find it. She mentioned Ian's bravery, only briefly, and then she presented the VC in its box.[25]

Freda remembers that Melanie was excited but behaved very well.

After we'd received the VC I saw Melanie looking over at another award, I can't remember what it was – shiny, coloured ribbon – and she kept glancing back and forth between the VC and this other medal. I could see she was thinking like a child 'if our medal is so special why isn't it as pretty as the others', but when she was asked about it later she said, 'my daddy's medal is the bestest medal in the world'.

Marica not unnaturally had mixed emotions during the investiture. She was immensely proud of Ian's achievement, just as Freda and Ken were, but this was suffused with a sadness and a yearning that some of the best years of her life, years she might have shared with her soul mate, had been snatched from her grasp. She had proved her resilience often enough in the past but she revealed that in later life she has often wondered 'what if?' 'The decision,' she says, 'had already been made that Ian would come out of the army after the Falklands. He had had enough. He had achieved what he had wanted to achieve. He was family oriented and wanted to move on. Find a different challenge.'[26]

Marica has never revealed what she and the queen discussed at the investiture, preferring to keep that to herself. It is pure speculation but perhaps they discussed the impending arrival of the ship which was carrying the remains of her husband back to British shores for Ian's homecoming was just week away.

Marchwood Military Port near Southampton is a drab, workaday place at the best of times but as dawn broke on 16 November 1982, grey and cold with rain coating the smooth tarmac of the dockside with an oily sheen, it had the capacity to lower the most optimistic of spirits. The only colour came from the huge Union Flags which were draped over the two containers holding the bodies of sixty-four of the Falklands war dead. Ian was one of them. Apart from the bold colours of the Union Flag there were no other flags, no bunting, no military band, for this was not a celebration. These men, having been buried once 8,000 miles away, were coming home to be buried again in their native soil. Their families wished it so. As *Sir Bedivere* slid into the dock, still displaying her battle scars, a few relatives and military representatives stood silently in line to greet her. Slowly and carefully, to the accompaniment of the pipes of Lance Corporal Ian MacKinnon of the 2nd Battalion The Scots Guards playing *The Flowers of the Forest,* a traditional Scottish lament dating back to the Battle of Flodden in 1513, the containers were lowered ashore. 'This is the saddest duty I have ever had,' he was later to remark. Making the short journey to the customs shed, individual coffins were transferred to black hearses for the journey to their final resting places all over Britain.

The final leg of Ian's long journey took him back to his physical and spiritual home – to Aldershot where his family lived and his beloved Parachute Regiment was based. Ten days after *Sir Bedivere* had docked at Marchwood, Ian and fifteen comrades of 2 and 3 Para, including Jason Burt who had fallen with him in his final charge for the Argentine HMG on Mount Longdon, were laid to rest with full military honours in the military cemetery at Aldershot.

The morning was bright and clear as the McKay party arrived at the regimental headquarters. There they were greeted by officers, warrant officers and NCOs of 2 and 3 Para along with the members of the other men's families and were escorted to the temporary chapel of rest in the Montgomery Gymnasium. Here, each in his coffin draped with a Union Flag, the men of 3 Para were together in death as they had been in life on Mount Longdon. Some of the relatives wept openly together and gained solace in each other's company.

Over a buffet lunch there were many meetings and mini-reunions. Marica was introduced to the friends and family of Ian Scrivens who had travelled from Yeovil and Freda chatted to the officers, including Lieutenant Colonel Hew Pike, Major Mike Argue and Padre Derek Heaver.

After lunch the majority of the 800 relatives were taken in a fleet of sixteen coaches to the Royal Garrison Church for the service which was conducted by Padre David Cooper of 2 Para, while Ian's padre, Derek Heaver, gave the address. It was the same pairing which had officiated at Ian's first burial at Teal Inlet. Another short coach journey transported the relatives to the gates of Aldershot's Military Cemetery, a beautifully maintained space with winding paths, numerous trees, spacious lawns and manicured slopes. The route for the coffins was lined by guards from both battalions; motionless with heads in red berets bowed and arms reversed, black boots gleaming.

The relatives walked slowly, quietly past the bearer parties and took their places on one of the slopes, with sixteen Union Flags below and around that sad rectangle stood the widows, the parents, the brothers, the sisters and other close relatives and friends.

As the sixteen bearer parties moved slowly forward the 3 Para band played. Clergy and service chiefs arrived and each of the fallen was recommitted individually. As the time of the ceremony approached the bright blue sky faded to grey; clouds gathered and as the first of the dead was lowered, the cold rain arrived and increased in intensity as the ceremony progressed. It was as if the very elements had conspired to bring a touch of the Falkland Islands down onto the hillsides of Aldershot as if to give the relatives a flavour of the conditions in which their sons and husbands had died. The weather did not help Neal and Graham McKay as they stood in the cold and damp as the ceremony began. In fact Neal had to be treated in an ambulance during the service.

Ian was carried by NCOs who had known him well, among them Colour Sergeant Brian Faulkner, a fellow Yorkshireman and friend, Sergeant Des Fuller who had taken over 4 Platoon for the final stages of the battle, and Corporal Ian Bailey, now sufficiently recovered from his wounds and the last man to see Ian alive. At the rear of the bearer party was CSM John Weeks. Ian's maroon beret, his medals, including the VC, and his belt and bayonet were carried on top of his coffin. Derek Heaver officiated once more at Ian's committal. Three volleys rang out for Ian from a firing party on a third slope to the east, a piper from 15 Para (Scottish Volunteers) played a lament and buglers sounded the *Last Post* and *Reveille*.

During the evening, the cemetery authorities re-turfed the graves, erected temporary wooden crosses and planted many flowers and wreaths on them, so that by the following morning the relatives could return to pay their last respects to their loved ones.

It was not until 19 July 1983, after the ground had settled, that permanent Commonwealth War Graves Commission headstones were erected. It was at that point that Marica chose a simple and fitting tribute for a man who will always be remembered – by his family and friends; by the men he taught, served and fought with; by his regiment; and, crucially by those whose lives he saved on a cold, dark, inhospitable mountain far away all those years ago. Ian McKay was, is and will always be a Falklands Hero: a man who secured his place in history as the last Victoria Cross recipient of the twentieth century.

It is fitting perhaps that the final words on Ian McKay should be those chosen by his wife Marica with the blessing of his family and which are now inscribed on his headstone. These few words, from a woman who lost her husband and best friend in a war of liberation half a world away, leaving his daughter with fleeting memories of a father she can barely remember, seem particularly appropriate and deserve to stand as Ian McKay's epitaph.

> To the World a Soldier
> To us the World
> Till we Meet Again

Explanatory Notes

Introduction

1. Winston S. Churchill, The River War, (London: Longmans, Green and Co., 1899) Vol.1, p.37.
2. Corporal Ian Bailey, interview with the author, 20 November, 2006.
3. Ian Bailey's was a fascinating account and I learned that he was still experiencing pain as the fragments of the bullet which he took in the hip in 1982 moved towards the surface occasionally. He had had to have further treatment over the years since 1982 and by 2009 the pain had become so bad that he had another major operation and had to give up work. Worse still he felt he had no choice but to put his Military Medal up for sale to fund further treatment. It was sold for the record price of £70,000 for a Military Medal group. See Postscript on p.256.
4. In the army, infantry soldiers TAB (Tactical Advance to Battle); Royal Marines.

Chapter 1: Forebears, Flour and Football

1. Freda McKay had had a quadruple heart bypass the year before Ken's death.
2. See the comprehensive Sunderland AFC Statistics site at: http://www.thestatcat. co.uk/Mplayers/MPG404.asp Accessed 9 March 2011.
3. See *Peterborough United – The First Decade – The 1930s* by Russell Plummer at http://www.theposh.com/page/History/0,,10427~79763,00.html also http://www.upthe posh.com/people/7753/career/ for Len Hargreaves' Peterborough playing record. Both sites accessed 9 March 2011.
4. A third daughter, Marie, was born in June 1944.

Chapter 2: My Scruffy Little Kid

1. Freda McKay – interview with the author 20 February 2007.
2. Peter Harper, *Sgt. Ian John McKay VC (1953–1982) – A Memoir with Recollections and Tributes from his Friends.* (NCUACS: Bath unpublished) p. 44.
3. After what Freda McKay called a 'heavy, struggling childhood' both Graham and Neal survived beyond the age of 3 and both did well at school. They went on to secure good jobs; Graham a clerical worker at British Steel Corporation and Neal as a clerk to the Magistrate's Court in Rotherham.
4. Freda McKay – interview with the author, op.cit.
5. *Sgt. Ian John McKay VC (1953–1982) – A Memoir with Recollections and Tributes from his Friends.* op.cit., pp.44–47.
6. Mrs Freda McKay – interview with the author, op.cit.
7. *Sgt. Ian John McKay VC (1953–1982) – A Memoir with Recollections and Tributes from his Friends.* op.cit., p. 47.
8. Freda McKay – interview with the author, op.cit.
9. *Sgt. Ian John McKay VC (1953–1982) – A Memoir with Recollections and Tributes from his Friends.* op.cit., pp.53–54.
10. *Sgt. Ian John McKay VC (1953–1982) – A Memoir with Recollections and Tributes from his Friends.* op.cit., p. 49.
11. Freda McKay – interview with the author, op.cit.

12. *Sgt. Ian John McKay VC (1953–1982) – A Memoir with Recollections and Tributes from his Friends.* op.cit., p. 49.

13. The three other houses at Rotherham Grammar School in 1964 were Founder's, Hoole's and Snell's.

14. *Sgt. Ian John McKay VC (1953–1982) – A Memoir with Recollections and Tributes from his Friends.* op.cit., pp.54–55.

15. *Sgt. Ian John McKay VC (1953–1982) – A Memoir with Recollections and Tributes from his Friends.* op.cit., pp. 54–55.

16. *The Rotherham Advertiser,* 31 August 1968, p.12, 30 August 1969, p.12 and 28 August 1970 p.24. With grateful thanks to Peter Bower, Rotherham Archives and Local Studies Supervisor for his assistance with this search.

17. *Sgt. Ian John McKay VC (1953–1982) – A Memoir with Recollections and Tributes from his Friends.* op.cit., p. 58.

18. The fictional William Wilson – The Wonder Athlete, also a Yorkshireman like Ian, first appeared in *The Wizard* comic in 1943. A supreme athlete he was credited with a number of extraordinary sporting and physical feats in his comic strip adventures amongst which were being the first man to conquer Mount Everest, captaining the England cricket team to Ashes victory over the Australians and breaking the world long jump record whilst running a three-minute mile!

19. *Sgt. Ian John McKay VC (1953–1982) – A Memoir with Recollections and Tributes from his Friends.* op.cit., p. 58.

20. *Sgt. Ian John McKay VC (1953–1982) – A Memoir with Recollections and Tributes from his Friends.* op.cit., pp.56–57 and email correspondence with the author 13 – 16 November 2011.

21. *Sgt. Ian John McKay VC (1953–1982) – A Memoir with Recollections and Tributes from his Friends.* op.cit., pp.56–57 and email correspondence with the author 13 – 16 November 2011.

22. *Daily Mail* 9 October 1982.

Chapter 3: Crow

1. Parachute Regiment Recruiting Brochure c. 1970, p.14. Accessed via the highly informative online database Paradata, the Living History of the Parachute Regiment and Airborne Forces commissioned by the Trustees of the Airborne Forces Museum at http://www.paradata. org.uk/media/14500?mediaSection=Documents&mediaItem=17184. Accessed 15 November 2011.

2. *Sgt. Ian John McKay VC (1953–1982) – A Memoir with Recollections and Tributes from his Friends.* op.cit., p. 49.

3. Ibid., p. 47.

4. Paradata www.paradata.org.uk/units/no-1-parachute-training-school-raf-abingdon. Accessed 15 November 2011.

5. The image is still being used today and is featured on the previously mentioned Paradata site. See www.paradata.org.uk/people/ian-j-mckay. Accessed 15 November 2011.

6. Interview with the author, 22 November 2011. Not only was Ian not in regulation uniform for this famous shot but he had also contrived to put his collar badges – known as 'dogs' – on the wrong way round. The parachute regiment collar dogs are made in 'facing pairs', one on each lapel, so that the lions which surmount the Queen's Crown above the parachute face inwards, towards each other. Studying his right collar carefully the eagle-eyed will note that the lion is facing to Ian's right when it should have been facing to his left! With thanks to Bob Hilton.

7. Peter Taylor, *Brits – The War Against the IRA*, (London: Bloomsbury 2002) pp.23–29.

Chapter 4: 1 Para

1. Peter Harclerode, *Para! Fifty Years of the Parachute Regiment* (London: Arms and Armour Press 1992) p.287.

2. *Operation Banner – An Analysis of Military Operations in Northern Ireland*, (MOD: 2006). Chapter 1, p.5.

3. Operation Banner ran for almost thirty-eight years and remains the British Army's longest continuous deployment. It finally came to an end at midnight on 31 July 2007.

4. *Para! Fifty Years of the Parachute Regiment*, op.cit., pp.283–284.

5. Ibid., p. 285.

6. *Brits – The War Against the IRA*, op.cit., p.33.

7. John Parker, *Paras – The Inside Story of Britain's Toughest* Regiment (London: Metro Books 2000) p.321.

8. Interview with the author, 18 April 2007.

9. Lieutenant Colonel Michael Dewar, *The British Army in Northern Ireland*, (London: Arms and Armour Press 1985) p.52.

10. On the same day as Gunner Curtis died two men were shot and killed by the British Army. Bernard Watt (28), a Catholic civilian was shot during street disturbances in Ardoyne, Belfast and IRA member James Saunders (22), was shot during a gun battle near the Oldpark Road in Belfast. Three days later on 9 February 1971, two BBC engineers and three construction workers were killed near a BBC transmitter on Brougher Mountain, County Tyrone by an IRA landmine which was probably intended for a British Army patrol known to have been checking the installation.

11. *Brits – The War Against the IRA*, op.cit., p. 59.

12. A memorial to the three young Scottish soldiers killed on 10 March 1971 – erected in 2010 and funded by public donations – now stands by the roadside at the spot where their bodies were found. In July 2011 it was vandalized with sectarian graffiti scrawled on the memorial stone and corner posts and the surrounding rope was broken.

13. *Hansard,* British Soldiers, Northern Ireland (Murder) 11 March 1971, Vol. 813 cc597–605. See http://hansard.millbanksystems.com/commons/1971/mar/11/british-soldiers-northern-ireland-murder#S5CV0813P0_19710311_HOC_300. Accessed 15 December 2011.

14. Ibid.

15. *Hansard,* Defence Estimate. 1971–72 (Army), Vote A. 11 March 1971 Vol. 813 cc671–742. See http://hansard.millbanksystems.com/commons/1971/mar/11/defence-estimate-1971-72-army-vote-a. Accessed 15 December 2011.

16. In defiance of a government ban, members of the Orange Order attempted to march through the mainly Catholic town of Dungiven, County Londonderry on the evening of 13 June 1971. The Orangemen broke through a Royal Ulster Constabulary (RUC) cordon and soldiers of the Royal Highland Fusiliers and 1 Para were stoned on the bridge as they attempted to hold the crowd back. Tear gas was used.

    See Martin Melaugh, University of Ulster Conflict Archive on the Internet (CAIN), *A Chronology of the Conflict 1971* at http://cain.ulst.ac.uk/othelem/chron/ch71.htm. Accessed 15 December 2011. Footage of the riot was shot by ITN news and it was shown in bulletins at 6.07 pm and 10.00 pm that evening.

17. Interview with the author, 15 January 2007.

18. Interview with the author, 15 January 2007.

19. *Brits – The War Against the IRA*, op.cit., p. 67.

20. In the week following the early morning swoop and arrest without charge of 342 republican suspects on 9 August 1971, twenty people were shot dead in the Province; sixteen by the British Army and two by the IRA. This was almost as many as had been killed in the previous six months. See *Brits – The War Against the IRA*, op.cit., p.75.

21. Ibid., p. 68.

22. Tony Geraghty, *The Irish War – The Military History of a Domestic Conflict* (London: Harper Collins 1998) p.55.

23. Email exchange with the author 3 and 4 February 2011.

Chapter 5: Bloody Sunday

1. *Brits – The War Against the IRA*, op.cit., pp. 82–83.
2. Ibid., p.84.
3. Ibid., p.92.
4. Peter Taylor, *Provos – The IRA and Sinn Fein* (London:Bloomsbury 1997) p. 117.
5. Ian McKay (Soldier 'T') – written statement taken by the Treasury Solicitor's Department for the 1972 Widgery Inquiry into Bloody Sunday in the presence of Colonel H. C. B. Overbury at County Hall Coleraine 5 March 1972, in the archive of the *Report of the Bloody Sunday Inquiry (Saville Inquiry)* at http://webarchive.nationalarchives.gov.uk/20101103103930/http://report.bloody-sunday-inquiry.org/evidence/B/B725.pdf#page=11. See also Sergeant 'O' – original oral evidence to the 1972 Widgery Inquiry into Bloody Sunday in the archive of the *Report of the Bloody Sunday Inquiry (Saville Inquiry)* at http://webarchive.national archives.gov.uk/20101103103930/http://report.bloody-sunday-inquiry.org/evidence/B/B439.pdf. Accessed 28 December 2011.
6. Transcript of interview with Sergeant 'O' conducted by John Goddard, Tony Stark and Neil Davis of Praxis Films. 14 May 1991, pp.52–53 in the archive of the *Report of the Bloody Sunday Inquiry (Saville Inquiry)* at http://webarchive.nationalarchives.gov.uk/20101103103930/http://report.bloody-sunday-inquiry.org/evidence/B/B439.pdf. Accessed 30 December 2011.
7. *Report of the Tribunal appointed to inquire into the events on Sunday, 30 January 1972*, which led to loss of life in connection with the procession in Londonderry on that day by The Rt. Hon. Lord Widgery, OBE., TD HMSO: 18 April 1972. See http://cain.ulst.ac.uk/hmso/widgery.htm#part1. Accessed 30 December 2011.
8. The SIB was the military equivalent of the CID in the civil police force. The minimum rank for an SIB officer at the time of Bloody Sunday was sergeant. Service in the SIB entailed a rigorous selection and training regime. Any sergeant wishing to join the SIB would have had to have gained at least eighteen months experience in the RMP before requesting a transfer and then undergo a lengthy period of training including an eighteen week course in England. After that he would be promoted to acting sergeant and serve a further two years on probation before final acceptance. The archive of the *Report of the Bloody Sunday Inquiry (Saville Inquiry)*, Index to Evidence. Statement Ref. CW1, p.1 at http://webarchive.nationalarchives.gov.uk/20101103103930/http://report.bloody-sunday-inquiry.org/evidence/CW/CW_0001.pdf. Accessed 30 December 2011.
9. In January 1972, 178 Provost Company was a constituent part of 1st Regiment Royal Military Police which had entered the Army's Order of Battle on 5 November 1971 being raised specifically for service in Northern Ireland. Prior to the formation of the Regiment, military police units had consisted of small, independent provost companies supporting units from brigade to army level but due to the burgeoning numbers of RMP posted to Ulster in response to the rapidly deteriorating security situation, and particularly after the introduction of internment in August 1971, it was decided that a Regiment should be formed to bring disparate units under one command. The Regiment's sub-units on formation consisted of 174 Provost Company (based in Lisburn but later Armagh), 175 Provost Company (based in Lisburn but responsible for Belfast), 176 Provost Company (based in Londonderry), 177 Provost Company (Province-wide close protection escorts) and 178 Provost Company (Investigations – Province-wide SIB support). By 30 January 1972, 179 Provost Company had joined the Regiment with responsibility for operations in Belfast with 180 and 181 Provost Companies following later that year.
10. Email correspondence with author – 3/4 February 2011.
11. The statement was written out by WO1 Wood and signed by Ian McKay. Statements were always taken with names written in, although the signature and any other references which may have led to the identification of individual soldiers were blanked out or, to use the official term at the time, 'expurgated', using Tippex. The term used by the Saville Inquiry was 'redacted'. The

author has seen a handwritten copy of the initial RMP statement which had been in the possession of Ken McKay marked 'I J McK' at the point where it mentions passing his trousers to WO1 Wood. Both the original handwritten and typed versions of the RMP statement forms indicate that the statement was dated 31 January 1972, although the time at which the statement was, 'recorded and signature witnessed' is clearly marked as 2.00am on 30 January 1972. This must be an error as the incidents to which the statement refers did not take place until the afternoon of 30 January. The Saville Inquiry makes no mention of this and assumes a date of 31 January.

12. With the exception of a number of senior Army officers who gave evidence under their own names, military witnesses who were later called to give evidence to the Widgery Inquiry were granted anonymity to protect them and their families. Their names were replaced by ciphers in the written and typed versions of the RMP statements – alphabetical for those who maintained that they had fired live rounds on Bloody Sunday (the 'lettered soldiers') and numerical for the others (the 'numbered soldiers') and these were used when giving evidence to the Widgery Inquiry. Where appropriate, the ciphers used in the Widgery Inquiry were retained and used in the Saville Inquiry with the addition of the soldier's rank at the time of Bloody Sunday. Any military witnesses who had not been designated a cipher in 1972 were identified by their rank and the prefix 'INQ' followed by a number.

13. Sergeant 'O' – Written evidence to the Bloody Sunday Inquiry (Saville Inquiry).Statement Ref. 575 p.4 in the archive of the *Report of the Bloody Sunday Inquiry (Saville Inquiry)* at http://webarchive.nationalarchives.gov.uk/20101103103930/http://report.bloody-sunday-inquiry.org/evidence/B/B439.pdf. Accessed 30 December 2011.

14. Ian McKay (Soldier 'T') – written statement taken by the Treasury Solicitor's Department for the 1972 Widgery Inquiry into Bloody Sunday in the presence of Colonel H. C. B. Overbury at County Hall Coleraine 5 March 1972, in the archive of the Report of the Bloody Sunday Inquiry (Saville Inquiry) at http://webarchive.nationalarchives.gov.uk/20101103103930/http://report.bloody-sunday-inquiry.org/evidence/B/B725.pdf#page=11

15. *Brits – The War Against the IRA*, op.cit., p.101.

16. Email correspondence with author – 3/4 February 2011.

Chapter 6: Inquiry

1. Ian McKay (Soldier 'T') – oral evidence to the 1972 Widgery Inquiry into Bloody Sunday at County Hall Coleraine 8 March 1972, p.88 in the archive of the *Report of the Bloody Sunday Inquiry (Saville Inquiry)* at http://webarchive.nationalarchives.gov.uk/20101103103930/http://report.bloody-sunday-inquiry.org/evidence/B/B725.pdf. Accessed 3 January 2012.

2. Ibid., p.90.

3. The image can be seen at http://webarchive.nationalarchives.gov.uk/20101103103930/http://report.bloody-sunday-inquiry.org/evidence/B/B725.pdf. Accessed 3 January 2012.

4. Ian McKay (Soldier 'T') – oral evidence to the 1972 Widgery Inquiry into Bloody Sunday at County Hall Coleraine 8 March 1972, p.88 in the archive of the *Report of the Bloody Sunday Inquiry (Saville Inquiry)*, op.cit.,p.92.

5. Ibid., pp.93–94.

6. *Sgt. Ian John McKay VC (1953–1982) – A Memoir with Recollections and Tributes from his Friends.* op.cit., p. 49.

7. *The Report of the Bloody Sunday Inquiry (Saville Inquiry) Vol. 3, Chapter 51 – Firing by the soldiers in Sector 2, Private T and acid bombs* at http://webarchive.nationalarchives.gov.uk/20101103103930/http://report.bloody-sunday-inquiry.org/volume03/chapter051/. Accessed 3 January 2012.

8. The author has to admit that he was one of those who played truant that day with his father in order to see Pelé grace the pitch at Hillsborough.

9. *Report of the Tribunal appointed to inquire into the events on Sunday, 30 January 1972*, which led to loss of life in connection with the procession in Londonderry on that day by The Rt. Hon. Lord

Widgery, OBE, TD HMSO: 18 April 1972. See http://cain.ulst.ac.uk/hmso/widgery. htm#part1. Op.cit.

10. Ibid.
11. *The Report of the Bloody Sunday Inquiry (Saville Inquiry) Vol. III, Chapter 51 – Firing by the soldiers in Sector 2, Private T and acid bombs.*, op.cit.
12. Ibid.
13. Ibid.
14. *The Report of the Bloody Sunday Inquiry (Saville Inquiry) Vol. IV, Chapter 5 – Sector 2: The Launch of the Arrest Operation and Events in the Area of the Rossville Flats. The Casualties in Sector 2* at http://webarchive.nationalarchives.gov.uk/20101103103930/http://report.bloody-sunday-inquiry.org/volume04/chapter055/. Accessed 3 January 2012.
15. *The Report of the Bloody Sunday Inquiry (Saville Inquiry) Vol. I, Chapter 3. – The events of the day* at http://webarchive.nationalarchives.gov.uk/20101103103930/http://report.bloody-sunday-inquiry.org/volume01/chapter003/. Accessed 3 January 2012.
16. *Hansard,* Saville Inquiry, 15 June 2010, Col. 739–740. See http://www.publications.parliament.uk/pa/cm201011/cmhansrd/cm100615/debtext/100615-0004.htm. Accessed 3 January 2011.
17. Ibid.
18. *The Independent,* 16 June 2010, p.10.
19. *The Irish News,* 16 June 2010, Cover page. *The Derry Journal,* 16 June 2010, p.1.
20. *The Report of the Bloody Sunday Inquiry (Saville Inquiry) Vol. I, Chapter 3. – The events of the day* at http://webarchive.nationalarchives.gov.uk/20101103103930/http://report.bloody-sunday-inquiry.org/volume01/chapter003/. Accessed 3 January 2012.
21. *The Independent,* 16 June 2010, op.cit., p.5.
22. *The Report of the Bloody Sunday Inquiry (Saville Inquiry) Vol. I, Chapter 3. – The events of the day* op. cit.
23. *Bloody Sunday: Key Soldiers Involved – The Soldiers Who Shot.* 15 June 2010. BBC Foyle and West website at http://www.bbc.co.uk/news/10287463. Accessed 17 January 2011.
24. *The Guardian* 16 June 2010. See http://www.guardian.co.uk/uk/2010/jun/16/bloody-sunday-soldiers-military-uk. Accessed 17 January 2011.
25. Tim Shipman, McGuiness and the Machine Gun: Provisionals' Godfather had Central Role in the Troubles Before, During and After Derry Killings, *Daily Mail* Online, Last updated 17 June 2010, at http://www.dailymail.co.uk/news/article-1286923/Bloody-Sunday—Saville-Inquiry-Soldiers-served-Ulster-died-Afghanistan.html#ixzz1jqlOoyYi Accessed 17 January 2011.

Chapter 7: Professional Soldier, Sensitive Man

1. *Operation Banner – An Analysis of Military Operations in Northern Ireland,* op.cit., Chapter 2, p. 9.
2. Ibid., Chapter 2, pp.8–11.
3. Peter Harclerode, *Para! Fifty Years of the Parachute Regiment,* op.cit., pp. 292–293.
4. Mackay and John W Mussell., *Medal Yearbook,* (Honiton: Token Publishing 2002), p.187. The General Service Medal 1962 was awarded until 2007 when it was superseded by the Operational Service Medal.
5. *Sgt. Ian John McKay VC (1953–1982) – A Memoir with Recollections and Tributes from his Friends.* op.cit., p.50.
6. Interview with the author.15 January, 2007.
7. 1 Para was one of only two battalions of the Parachute Regiment to serve in the Berlin Brigade in the entire period between January 1948 and August 1994; 2 Para being the other battalion which was part of the garrison from May 1977 to June 1979.
8. Interview with the author.15 January, 2007.
9. I C B Dear and M R D Foot, (Eds.), *The Oxford Companion to World War II,* (Oxford: Oxford University Press 2001), p.415

10. Interview with the author, 15 January, 2007.
11. Interview with the author, 15 January, 2007.
12. After Hess was found dead in a summer house with an electrical cable around his neck in August 1987 at the age of 93, Spandau prison was demolished or, as Roy Butler put it, 'as soon as he died they flattened it and built a NAAFI'.
13. Interview with the author, 15 January, 2007.
14. Interview with the author, 15 January, 2007.
15. *The Daily Mirror*, 11 October 1982, pp.14–15.
16. *The Sunday Mirror*, 2 November 1986, pp.22–23.
17. Jean Carr, *Another Story – Women and the Falklands War* (London: Hamish Hamilton, 1984), p.43.
18. *The Daily Mirror*, 11 October 1982, pp.14–15.
19. *The Sunday Mirror*, 2 November 1986, op.cit.
20. *Woman*, op.cit., and interview with the author 25 January, 2009.
21. *Sgt. Ian John McKay VC (1953–1982) – A Memoir with Recollections and Tributes from his Friends.* op.cit., pp.50–51.
22. Interview with the author. 3 April, 2006.
23. *Sgt. Ian John McKay VC (1953–1982) – A Memoir with Recollections and Tributes from his Friends.* op.cit., pp.68–69.
24. Interview with the author, 15 January, 2007.
25. Ibid.
26. Ibid.
27. *Pegasus, Journal of the Parachute Regiment and Airborne Forces.* Vol. XXXV, No. 2, April 1980, p.47.
28. Ibid. Vol. XXXV, No.3. July, 1980.
29. Ibid. Vol. XXXVI, No.2. April, 1981, p.26.
30. Sgt. Ian John McKay VC (1953–1982) – *A Memoir with Recollections and Tributes from his Friends.* op. cit., p.72.
31. Ibid. Vol. XXXVII, No.1. January, 1982, p.5. Captain Alan Coulson went on to become the Intelligence Officer of 2 Para and was present during the Battle of Darwin-Goose Green on 28 May 1982. He chose not to wear the Kevlar para helmet in use at the time of the Falklands campaign relying instead on the old style metal version.
32. Jason Burt, Neil Grose and Ian Scrivens, three 17-year-old recruits, were all posted to B Company of 3 Para. Ian McKay was not their Platoon Sergeant but they would share the same fate as the respected NCO on the night of 11/12 June 1982.
33. Interview with the author, 3 August, 2006.
34. Interview with the author, 15 January, 2007.
35. Interview with the author, November, 2011.
36. Interview with the author, 3 August, 2006.
37. Ibid.
38. Interview with the author, 8 December, 2007.
39. Interview with the author, 3 August, 2006.

Chapter 8: 'Whatever our Destination May Be'

1. *The 3rd Battalion, the Parachute Regiment. Commander's War Diary Narrative* for 3.00pm on 4 April 1982, p. 4. Courtesy of Sir Hew Pike. The War Diary was compiled by Kevin McGimpsey and many historians have had good cause to thank him for his assiduous logging of events, often in very fraught and difficult circumstances whilst on the Falkland Islands. McGimpsey went on to author the world renowned *The Story of the Golf Ball* and is a leading authority on golfing memorabilia heading the Golfing Memorabilia department of a famous auction house. See also *Pegasus*, Vol. XXXVII, No.3, July 1982 p. 40.
2. *Pegasus*, Vol. XXXVII, No.3, July 1982 p.49.
3. RSM Lawrie Ashbridge – interview with the author, 5 December 2006. NB ranks are those held at the time of the Falklands Campaign although many achieved higher rank during their subsequent careers.

4. Company Sergeant Major John Weeks, interview with the author, 22 November 2006.

5. Jean Carr, *Another Story – Women and the Falklands War* (London: Hamish Hamilton, 1984) p.15

6. Ibid., pp.47–48.

7. Colour Sergeant Brian Faulkner, interview with the author, 6 November 2006.

8. Ibid.

9. Ibid.

10. Postcard in the possession of Freda McKay and quoted with permission. It is post marked, 'London 19 April 1982' and stamped 'Maritime Mail'. See also *Sgt. Ian John McKay VC (1953–1982) – A Memoir with Recollections and Tributes from his Friends.* op.cit., p.73.

11. Lieutenant Andrew Bickerdike, interview with the author, 11 October 2006.

12. Ibid. The 3rd Battalion, the Parachute Regiment, Commander's War Diary Narrative for 11.45pm on 6 April 1982, p.13, records the following, 'Switch in Orbat – Capt Freer confirmed as 2IC A Coy, Lt B Griffiths to move from B Coy to C Coy as a platoon commander and Capt Starkey to revert back to 2IC C Coy.'

13. Captain Bob Darby, interview with the author, 26 September 2006.

14. Andrew Bickerdike jotted down important B Company cabin allocations for quick reference in his notebook. CSM John Weeks and CQMS Dunn were in D72 while the three other B Company Senior NCOs, Sergeants Gray (6 Platoon), Ross (5 Platoon) and Fuller (Company Headquarters) shared D 44. The privates of the three sections of 4 Platoon were distributed between cabins F 201, F261 and F223

15. Lieutenant Andrew Bickerdike, interview op.cit.

16. Colour Sergeant Brian Faulkner, interview op.cit.

17. *The 3rd Battalion, the Parachute Regiment, Commander's War Diary Narrative* for 16.30 hours on 12 April 1982, op.cit., p.29.

18. RSM Lawrie Ashbridge, interview with the author, op.cit.

19. Letter in the possession of Freda McKay.

20. *Pegasus,* Vol. XXXVII, No.3. op.cit., p.50.

21. Letter in the possession of Freda McKay.

22. The Book of Revelation is the final book of the New Testament. Chapter 13, verse 18 of the King James Bible states, '…Let him that hath understanding count the number of the beast: for it is the number of a man; and his number *is* Six hundred three-score *and* six'.

23. Letter in the possession of Freda McKay.

24. Letter in the possession of Freda McKay.

25. Lieutenant Andrew Bickerdike, interview, op.cit.

26. Corporal Ian Bailey, interview with the author, 20 November 2006.

27. Capon's photograph of Ian at English Bay appeared in several national newspaper articles and books but he has never been credited. He was later evacuated to the hospital ship *Uganda* with trench foot and by that time he had shot eight rolls of self-loaded film. Capon placed seven rolls in his smock which then went missing on board the *Uganda*. The McKay image was on the one roll he was able to bring home. Kevin Capon now works for the MOD as a civilian member of the Army news team. Since leaving 3 Para, he has won several prestigious awards for his photography and films including an ITV award for his filming of operations in Iraq and a tri-service award for his film of a landmines project in Africa. He has also won the Army Photographer of the Year and Defence Photographer of the Year Competitions. His image is used in the plate section of this book with permission and I am delighted to bring its creator to the attention of a wider readership.

28. Letter in the possession of Freda McKay.

29. Letter in the possession of Freda McKay.

30. Letter in the possession of Freda McKay.

31. Colour Sergeant Brian Faulkner, interview with the author, op.cit., On 11 April the Ship's Adjutant had announced that, 'there will be rounds of the ship daily at 17.30 hrs, all ranks are

responsible for cleaning their own cabins which are to be clean and tidy with all kit stowed for inspection.' *The 3rd Battalion, the Parachute Regiment, Commander's War Diary Narrative* for 3.25pm on 11 April 1982, op.cit., p.24.

32. Company Sergeant Major John Weeks, interview with the author, 22 November 2006. Army Dependents' Assurance Trust – established as a voluntary contributory scheme on 1 October 1973 and which guaranteed a tax-free monthly income for dependents in case of accident or death determined by the level at which contributions were made. It began to be phased out in February 1992.

33. Sergeant Major Sammy Dougherty, interview with author, 8 February 2007.

34. The *Ardent* and *Argonaut* were bombed in Falkland Sound on 21 May 1982, the *Ardent* being sunk. The container ship, *Atlantic Conveyor* became another victim of an Argentine Exocet on 25 May. There was grievous loss of life amongst the crews of all three whilst most of the Task Force's helicopter capability went down with the *Atlantic Conveyor*.

Chapter 9: TAB

1. The timings for 3 Para for operational purposes changed from local Stanley Standard time to ZULU Time at the same moment that the first of the men cross-decked to the *Intrepid* by landing craft. ZULU Time is equivalent to Greenwich Mean Time (GMT). Given that the UK had moved its clocks forward on to British Summer Time, that is GMT or ZULU +1 hour, local time in Stanley was GMT -4 hours by the time of the transfer to the *Intrepid* ready for D-Day. Sunrise in the Falklands on 19 May was 7.38am local, (11.38am ZULU), whilst sunset was 4.14pm, (20.14pm ZULU). Most timings in the text will be in ZULU Time as cited in operational documents but reference to local sunrise and sunset times will be made to enable readers to get a feel for the prevailing light conditions at key moments.

2. Mackay, F. and Cooksey, J., *Pebble Island – Operation Prelim* (Barnsley: Pen and Sword, 2007) p. 93.

3. Graham Colbeck, *With 3 Para to the Falklands* (London: Greenhill Books, 2002) p. 83.

4. RSM Lawrie Ashbridge – interview with the author, op.cit.

5. Graham Colbeck, op.cit., p.85. See also Julian Thompson, *No Picnic* (London: Cassell, 2001) p. 49.

6. Lieutenant Andrew Bickerdike, interview with the author, op.cit.

7. Martin Middlebrook, *The Falklands War 1982* (London: Penguin, 2001) pp.214–215, see also *The 3rd Battalion, the Parachute Regiment, Commander's War Diary Narrative* for 12.00 midday on 21 May 1982, p.104.

8. Hew Pike in Dale, Iain (ed.) *Memories of the Falklands* (London: Politico's Publishing 2002) pp.76–77.

9. Ibid.

10. Lieutenant Andrew Bickerdike, interview with the author, op.cit.

11. RSM Lawrie Ashbridge, interview with the author, op.cit.

12. Ibid. At the time of the landings Ian Scrivens was one of three 17-year-old privates in 4 Platoon of B Company along with Jason Burt and Neil Grose. All three had been together in the same 476 Recruit Platoon at the Depot where their platoon sergeant had been and had passed out in the February of 1982. All three were to die on Mount Longdon along with Ian McKay.

13. Graham Colbeck, op.cit., p. 95.

14. Middlebrook, op.cit., p. 274 –277. See also Vincent Bramley, *Excursion to Hell* (London: BCA, 1991) pp.45–46 and Christian Jennings and Adrian Weale, *Green Eyed Boys* (London: Harper Collins, 1996) p.99.

15. Lieutenant Andrew Bickerdike, interview op.cit., Vincent Bramley, op.cit., pp.45–56. Jennings and Weale, op.cit., pp.99–102.

16. It is interesting to note that of the fourteen exposure cases, ten were from C Company, with one each from A, HQ and Support Companies. The fourteenth was a Gunner attached to B Company. *The 3rd Battalion, the Parachute Regiment, Commander's War Diary Narrative* for 8.00am on 28 May 1982, p.110. As mentioned earlier Kevin Capon of B Company, the man

who had taken the picture of Ian at English Bay, suffered a serious case of trench foot at Estancia and was evacuated to the hospital ship *Uganda*.

17. Lieutenant Andrew Bickerdike, interview with the author, op.cit.
18. RSM Lawrie Ashbridge, interview with the author, op.cit.
19. Duncan Anderson, 'Let's Remember Arnhem' 2 Para and the Battle of Darwin-Goose Green, *Battlefields Review*, 19, 2002, p. 51.
20. Rod and Jan Hutchings, interview with the author, 6 March 2007.
21. Ibid.
22. Duncan Anderson, *The Falklands War 1982* (Oxford: Osprey, 2002) p. 56.
23. Vernon Steen, interview with the author on Mount Longdon, 14 November 2007 and email correspondence December 2007–June 2009.
24. Ibid.
25. C/S refers to 'call sign' and the same rules apply on any frequency on any radio network or 'net'. On the Battalion net, C/S 1 refers to A Company, C/S 2 B Coy and so on. Thus C/S13 refers to the 3rd of the three platoons of A Coy, whilst C/S 21 refers to the 1st of the three platoons of B Company which is 4 Platoon. The 'Sunray' of any call sign is the commander of that call sign and 'Sunray Minor' his Second in Command. Thus it is not only the Commanding Officer of a battalion who is a 'Sunray'. In the case of C/S 21, 'Sunray' was 4 Platoon Commander, Lieutenant Andrew Bickerdike and Ian McKay, as his Platoon Sergeant, was his 'Sunray Minor'. There is also a Company 'net 'on which 4 Platoon is C/S 1 and its three Sections become C/S11, C/S12 and C/S13. In that case Corporal Brian Milne, commanding 1 Section of 4 Platoon, was the 'Sunray' of C/S 11.
26. *The 3rd Battalion, the Parachute Regiment, Commander's War Diary Narrative* for 11.00am on 3 June 1982, p.114.
27. Ibid.
28. Jennings and Weale, op.cit., pp.110–114.
29. Julian Thompson. op.cit., p.112.
30. Lieutenant Andrew Bickerdike, interview with the author, op.cit., Four ground burst bombs fell a little under two kilometres southeast of Estancia House. No one was hurt.
31. *Sgt. Ian John McKay VC (1953–1982) – A Memoir with Recollections and Tributes from his Friends.* op.cit., pp.70–71.

Chapter 10: I'll See You in Stanley

1. Lieutenant Colonel Carlos Doglioli, correspondence with the author. December 2006–March 2007.
2. Brigadier Julian Thompson, e-mail response to author's query. January 2004. See also Nicholas van der Bijl, *Nine Battles to Stanley* (Barnsley: Leo Cooper, 1999) pp.164–165.
3. Brigadier Julian Thompson, e-mail response to author's query. January 2004.
4. *The 3rd Battalion, the Parachute Regiment, Commander's War Diary Narrative* for 7.30pm on 10 June 1982, p.117.
5. Captain Giles Orpen-Smellie – unpublished memoir. Giles Orpen-Smellie noted that the dead man was Sergeant N.I. ('Kiwi') Ford, Royal Marines. The lesson from this tragic incident, which 3 Para had already learned from their own 'blue-on-blue' incident on 22 May, was that clear control measures were needed for patrols. Shortly afterwards Major Hector Gullen, a Parachute Regiment officer serving with Headquarters 3 Commando Brigade, was appointed to be the Brigade Patrol Master. He immediately implemented inter-unit patrol boundaries and other measures to prevent a repeat of the tragedy. I am indebted to Lieutenant Colonel Smellie for the above.
6. Ibid.
7. Lieutenant Colonel Carlos Doglioli, op.cit.
8. Lieutenant Colonel Carlos Carrizo Salvadores, correspondence with the author. January, February 2007.

9. Lieutenant Colonel Carlos Doglioli, op.cit.
10. Ibid.
11. Colonel Hew Pike DSO, MBE, With Fixed Bayonets, *Elite Magazine*, Vol. 2, 20, 1985, pp. 381.
12. Graham Colbeck op.cit., pp.179–180. See also Jennings and Weale, op.cit., pp.122–123 and Julian Thompson op.cit., p.112.
13. Captain Giles Orpen-Smellie, interview and correspondence with the author, March 2007
14. Lieutenant Andrew Bickerdike, interview with the author, op.cit.
15. Ibid.
16. Company Sergeant Major John Weeks, interview with the author, op.cit.
17. Colour Sergeant Brian Faulkner, interview with the author, op.cit.

Chapter 11: Into Battle
1. Company Sergeant Major John Weeks, interview with the author, op.cit.
2. Letter to Freda McKay from Mrs Cynthia Ward, mother of Simon Ward, 3 Section, 4 Platoon, B Company, 3 Para. 12 October, 1982.
3. Vernon Steen, interview with the author on Mount Longdon, 14 November 2007 and email correspondence December 2007–June 2009.
4. Hew Pike, *From the Front Line – Family Letters & Diaries 1900 to the Falklands & Afghanistan* (Barnsley: Pen and Sword 2008) p.159.
5. Vernon Steen, interview with the author, op.cit.
6. Jon Cooksey, *3 Para Mount Longdon – The Bloodiest Battle* (Barnsley: Pen and Sword, 2004) p.62. See also Jennings and Weale, op.cit., pp.126–127. David Aldea, *Mount Longdon – The Argentine Story* (www.britains-smallwars.com/Falklands/David/Longdon) Nicholas van der Bijl, op.cit., pp. 171–172, and Max Arthur, *Above All Courage* (London: Sphere 1987), p.300.
7. Company Sergeant Major John Weeks, interview with the author, op.cit.
8. Signed witness statement of Lieutenant A J Bickerdike in support of the recommendation for the award of the Victoria Cross to Sergeant Ian McKay. Recommendations for Honours and Awards-Army (1965–1980). The National Archives, (TNA), WO/373/188.
9. Lieutenant Andrew Bickerdike, interview with the author, op.cit.
10. *The 3rd Battalion, the Parachute Regiment, Post-operational Report – Op Corporate, Annex B., 22 October 1982, p.B-1.*
11. *Teniente Coronel de Infanteria* Carlos Eduardo Carrizo Salvadores, 'El Combate en Monte Longdon', in *Coronel* Martin Antonio Balza (Ed.) *Malvinas: Relatos de Soldados*, (Buenos Aires: Biblioteca del Suboficial, Vol. 154, 1983) p.81.
12. The minefield which lay to the left of 4 Platoon is now marked on the Stanley Minefield and Area Clearance Situation map as Minefield No.76, the one to the west of Longdon being No. 77. There are a further three to the east of No. 76 which describe a rough semi-circle to the north of Mount Longdon.
13. Lieutenant Andrew Bickerdike, interview with the author, op.cit., Corporal Brian Milne's 1 section consisted of Lance Corporal Evans, a GPMG team of Private Logan (No.1) and Private Burt (No.2), and Privates, Duffy, Wynne-Jones and Thomas. Corporal Kelly's 2 section included Lance Corporal Hedges, Privates Eisler and Jelf as Nos. 1 and 2 respectively on the GPMG, and Privates Scrivens, Swain and Harrison. Corporal John Lewis had 3 Section with Lance Corporal Goreing, Privates Field and Ward as Nos.1 and 2 on the GPMG and Privates D.R. Kempster, Grose and Stone.
14. Ibid.
15. Corporal Phil Probets – email correspondence with the author. September 2008.
16. *Teniente Coronel de Infanteria* Carlos Eduardo Carrizo Salvadores, El Combate en Monte Longdon, op.cit., p.81.
17. Interview with the author on Mount Longdon, and email correspondence, op.cit.
18. Corporal Ian Bailey, interview with the author, 20 November, 2006.
19. Vincent Bramley, *Two Sides of Hell*, (London: Bloomsbury 1994). p.140.

20. Lieutenant Andrew Bickerdike, interview with the author, op.cit.
21. Corporal Ian Bailey, interview with the author, op.cit.
22. Lieutenant Andrew Bickerdike, interview with the author, op.cit.
23. Corporal Ian Bailey, interview with the author, op.cit.
24. Signed witness statement of Lieutenant A J Bickerdike in support of the recommendation for the award of the Victoria Cross to Sergeant Ian McKay, (TNA), op.cit.
25. Corporal Ian Bailey, interview with the author, op.cit.
26. Lieutenant Andrew Bickerdike, interview with the author, op.cit.
27. Vincent Bramley, *Excursion to Hell*, (London: BCA 1991) p. 90.
28. *Teniente Coronel de Infantería* Carlos Eduardo Carrizo Salvadores, El Combate en Monte Longdon, op.cit., p.82.
29. Vernon Steen, interview with the author on Mount Longdon and email correspondence, op.cit.
30. Corporal Ian Bailey, interview with the author, op.cit. Lance Corporal James appears on the nominal roll as a private in the Sergeant's Mess. His was not a permanent appointment. Companies gave up a couple of men every six months to assist in the mess which, at the time, was run by Colour Sergeant Allen. James was Allen's right-hand man, effectively helping him to run the mess efficiently acting as barman, taking the booking for functions and booking men into beds when they stayed overnight. Shrewd with money, several men interviewed said that he had 'found his niche' in the Sergeants' Mess and is remembered by many as having 'a heart of gold' but he was recalled to his company for Operation Corporate when he was needed. He was well known to and a friend of many members of the Sergeants' Mess including John Weeks and Sammy Dougherty. Ian McKay would have known him well.
31. Lieutenant Andrew Bickerdike, interview with the author, op.cit.
32. Corporal Ian Bailey, interview with the author, op.cit. On Andrew Bickerdike's handwritten list of casualties David Kempster is listed as being wounded in the 'arm' and 'face'. Out of twenty-eight men of 4 Platoon, thirteen would become casualties during the battle. In addition to Ian McKay three more were killed; Jason Burt and Ian Scrivens were both 17-years-old and Neil Grose had turned 18 on the day of the battle. They had passed out of the Parachute Regiment and Airborne Forces Depot four months earlier in February 1982.
33. Ibid. Private Suleman Alhaji was a member of the Motor Transport (MT) Platoon, and was attached to a rifle platoon – in his case 5 Platoon-for the battle. Other members were attached elsewhere. The MT Platoon lost two men killed on Mount Longdon; Private Tony 'Fester' Greenwood and Lance Corporal David Scott both whilst fighting with 6 Platoon on the southwestern slopes.
34. Lieutenant Andrew Bickerdike, interview with the author, op.cit.
35. Marica McKay, interview with the author, 25 January, 2009.

Chapter 12: To the World a Soldier

1. Each sub unit of 3 Para would later compile its own Post Operational Report so that lessons could be learned and deficiencies in procedures and equipment addressed. Every single item of clothing and kit also had to be accounted for, itemised and costed prior to replacement. Captain and Quartermaster Norman Menzies compiled such a list in September 1982. Nine L1A1 SLR rifles, one L42A1 sniper rifle and five sub-machine guns were lost with hundreds of other items of clothing and equipment. Quite apart from the enormous human cost of the campaign, the monetary cost of 3 Para's involvement was worked out to the penny. It came to a grand total of £74,049.32. *3rd Battalion, The Parachute Regiment Operation Corporate – Clothing and Equipment Losses, Annexes A-E*. 27 September 1982.
2. Lieutenant Andrew Bickerdike, interview with author, op.cit. John Weeks claimed in one source that Bickerdike defecated on him as he carried him out. Bickerdike is happy to refute this; 'I did not shit down John Weeks' back! I had Argentine shit on my clothes having crawled through

some of their mess because they 'crapped' behind rocks and mounds rather than dig proper latrines. Most of us crawled in it at some point. Mark Cox came forward to my position after I was hit and ran his hands over my leg looking for the wound. That would have been helpful – if his gloves hadn't been covered in 'Argie' shit!'

3. *3rd Battalion, The Parachute Regiment. Operation Corporate – Post Operational Report, Annex N – Medical Report*, p.4.
4. Sammy Dougherty, interview with the author 8 February 2007.
5. Tony Bojko, interview with the author 12 February 2007.
6. Sammy Dougherty, interview with the author, op.cit.
7. Ibid.
8. Tony Bojko, interview with author, op.cit.
9. Corporal Phil Probets, email correspondence with author, op.cit.
10. Hew Pike, op.cit., pp.162–163.
11. Hew Pike, op.cit., p.160
12. Ibid.
13. Duncan Anderson, *The Falklands War 1982*, (Oxford: Osprey 2002) pp.65–66.
14. Bob Darby, interview with the author, op.cit. The removal of the dead went on the next day. The Commander's War Diary for 13 June records that: 'At first light the removing of 3 Para dead continued. Stretcher bearers assisted in the following manner – coming up from C/S 9A location at the bottom of the western reverse slope, our dead were then flown back to Teal and Ajax'. These were the men who were killed by Argentine shellfire after the mountain had been secured.
15. Jan Hutchings, *Falklands Memories* (unpublished), p.7.
16. Stephen Hope was hit by a sniper on 12 June and died of wounds aboard the hospital ship *Uganda* the following day whilst 'Dickie' Absolon was mortally wounded by a shellburst on 13 June. Richard Absolon was taken to the hospital at Ajax Bay and both were buried in the burial ground at Red Beach.
17. Marica McKay, interview with the author, op.cit.
18. Freda McKay, interview with the author, op.cit.
19. Hew Pike, op.cit., pp.163–164.
20. Ibid., pp.165–166.
21. *The 3rd Battalion, the Parachute Regiment, Commander's War Diary Narrative*, op.cit., p.133.
22. Hansard Falklands Casualties (Burial), 8 July 1982 Vol. 27 c159W 159W at http://hansard.millbanksystems.com/written_answers/1982/jul/08/falklands-casualties-burial. Accessed 27 January 2012.
23. Recommendations for Honours and Awards-Army (1965–1980). The National Archives, (TNA), WO/373/188.
24. Ibid.
25. Freda McKay, interview with the author, op.cit.
26. Marica McKay, interview with author, op.cit.

Postscript

Ian McKay's Victoria Cross was initially loaned to the Parachute Regiment by his wife, Mrs Marica McKay, and it went on display at the Imperial War Museum (IWM) in London for a time. It was then removed from the IWM and became the subject of a Private Treaty Sale in which the auction house Sotheby's acted on behalf of Mrs McKay. The VC was purchased by persons acting on behalf of Lord Ashcroft on 24 November 1989 for an undisclosed sum and so passed into the Ashcroft collection. There was never any personal contact between the parties acting for both Mrs McKay and Lord Ashcroft.

Lord Ashcroft purchased the three medals awarded to Ian – the VC, the General Service Medal 1962 with clasp 'Northern Ireland', and the South Atlantic Medal. The Ashcroft Collection also holds Ian's beret and parachute 'wings'.

Although the purchase price was never disclosed and it was not sold for the highest price for a VC by the standards of the late 1980s, nevertheless it was a very substantial price and came very close to it. The price was certainly substantially higher than most other VCs coming on to the market at the time due to its rarity value – being one of only two awarded for the Falklands campaign and the last VC of the twentieth century.

Almost exactly twenty years after Ian McKay's VC was sold, the Military Medal (MM) which had been awarded to the then Corporal Ian Bailey for his actions in attacking the same heavy machine-gun complex at the same time as Ian McKay, came onto the market, along with six more medals and associated memorabilia.

Auctioned by Dix, Noonan Webb on 2 December 2009, Ian Bailey's MM group of seven was purchased by Lord Ashcroft for a hammer price of £70,000, the highest price ever paid for a MM group.

The author has it on very good authority that Lord Ashcroft was delighted to acquire Ian Bailey's medals for the Ashcroft Collection and that there must surely come a time when the medals of both Ian McKay and Ian Bailey will be displayed side-by-side in the Ashcroft Gallery at the IWM, as a tangible expression of the achievements of both men as they charged side by side towards the Argentine machine guns on Mount Longdon on 12 June 1982.

Supplement to The London Gazette of Friday, 8 October 1982.

Monday, 11 October 1982. Ministry of Defence.
Honours and Awards
Army Department

The Queen has been graciously pleased to approve the posthumous award of the VICTORIA CROSS to the undermentioned in recognition of valour during the operations in the South Atlantic:

24210031 Sergeant Ian John McKAY, The Parachute Regiment.

During the night of 11th/12th June 1982, 3rd Battalion The Parachute Regiment mounted a silent night attack on an enemy battalion position on Mount Longdon, an important objective in the battle for Port Stanley in the Falkland Islands. Sergeant McKay was platoon sergeant of 4 Platoon, B Company, which, after the initial objective had been secured, was ordered to clear the northern side of the long East/West ridge feature, held by the enemy in depth, with strong, mutually-supporting positions. By now the enemy were fully alert, and resisting fiercely. As 4 Platoon's advance continued it came under increasingly heavy fire from a number of well-sited enemy machine gun positions on the ridge, and received casualties. Realising that no further advance was possible the Platoon Commander ordered the platoon to move from its exposed position to seek shelter among the rocks of the ridge itself. Here it met up with part of 5 Platoon.

The enemy fire was still both heavy and accurate, and the position of the platoons was becoming increasingly hazardous. Taking Sergeant McKay, a Corporal and a few others, and covered by supporting machine gun fire, the Platoon Commander moved forward to reconnoitre the enemy positions but was hit by a bullet in the leg, and command devolved upon Sergeant McKay.

It was clear that instant action was needed if the advance was not to falter and increasing casualties to ensue. Sergeant McKay decided to convert this reconnaissance into an attack in order to eliminate the enemy positions. He was in no doubt of the strength and deployment of the enemy as he undertook this attack. He issued orders and, taking three men with him, broke cover and charged the enemy position.

The assault was met by a hail of fire. The Corporal was seriously wounded, a Private killed and another wounded. Despite these losses Sergeant McKay, with complete disregard for his own safety, continued to charge the enemy position alone. On reaching it he despatched the enemy with grenades, thereby relieving the position of beleagured 4 and 5 Platoons, who were now able to redeploy with relative safety. Sergeant McKay, however, was killed at the moment of victory, his body falling on the bunker.

Without doubt Sergeant McKay's action retrieved a most dangerous situation and was instrumental in ensuring the success of the attack. His was a coolly calculated act, the dangers of which must have been too apparent to him beforehand. Undeterred he performed with outstanding selflessness, perseverance and courage. With a complete disregard for his own safety, he displayed courage and leadership of the highest order, and was an inspiration to all those around him.

Letter from Lieutenant Colonel Hew Pike DSO MBE to Ken and Freda McKay

10 October 1982.

Dear Mr and Mrs McKay,

We are all so proud and delighted about the news of Ian's Victoria Cross, albeit so terribly sorry that his magnificent achievement cost him his life. We all mourn his loss deeply, and shall ever continue to do so, for he was a wonderful man.

But you must feel justly proud that your son has achieved such unique recognition for his bravery and leadership. His is the first Victoria Cross ever to be awarded to member of 3 PARA, including all our actions of World War 2. That perhaps is indication enough of his supreme self-sacrifice.

We all rejoice with you, and salute him. It was particularly touching that you should have said…that the award is the battalion's as well as Ian's – I know Ian himself would have thought this, and every soldier in the battalion feels inspired and a better man for Ian's example – we all do.

I was privileged to know your son well – he was a corporal in 'A' Company when I was the OC. He was an outstanding instructor, and an obviously up-and-coming NCO in every way – intelligent, energetic, firm and determined. He was, as you know, a talented sportsman – I myself used to play quite a lot of squash and tennis with him and often enjoyed watching him play football. Above all, perhaps, he was a person whom it was always a pleasure to have about – bright, cheerful, enthusiastic, outgoing, interesting, and utterly dedicated to his profession. Even I, not even related, feel a dreadful sense of loss – miss him terribly and I feel the whole Regiment does. Such a man cannot be replaced and the loss cannot be compensated…

It only remains to say again, how immensely proud we all are. Every soldier in the army salutes Ian's memory – indeed, I believe the whole nation does so. As for all of us in 3 PARA we feel a special sense of pride and of sadness. I shall never forget him, nor I think will any of us.

Bibliography

Official Reports

Recommendations for Honours and Awards – Army (1965–1980). The National Archives, TNA: PRO WO373/188.

3rd Battalion, The Parachute Regiment – Commander's War Diary Narrative of Operations.

3rd Battalion, The Parachute Regiment – Operation Corporate – Post Operational Report.

3rd Battalion, The Parachute Regiment – Operation Corporate – Clothing and Equipment Losses, Annexes A-E. 27 September 1982.

Secondary Sources

Mark Adkin, *The Last Eleven?*, (London, Leo Cooper, 1991).

Duncan Anderson, *The Falklands War 1982*, (Oxford, Osprey, 2002).

Michael Ashcroft, Victoria Cross Heroes (London, Headline, 2006).

Hugh Bicheno, *Razor's Edge – The Unofficial History of the Falklands War*, (London, Weidenfeld and Nicolson, 2006).

Vincent Bramley, *Excursion to Hell*, (London, BCA, 1991).

Vincent Bramley, *Two Sides of Hell*, (London, Bloomsbury, 1994).

Jean Carr, *Another Story – Women and the Falklands War*, (London, Hamish Hamilton, 1984).

Winston S. Churchill, *The River War*, (Green and Co., Longmans, London, 1899).

Graham Colbeck, *With 3 Para to the Falklands*, (London, Greenhill Books, 2002).

Jon Cooksey, *3 Para Mount Longdon – The Bloodiest Battle*, (Barnsley, Pen and Sword, 2004).

Iain Dale, (ed.) *Memories of the Falklands*, (London, Politico's Publishing, 2002).

Dear, I.C.B. and Foot, M.R.D., (Eds.), *The Oxford Companion to World War II*, (Oxford, Oxford University Press, 2001).

Colonel Michael Dewar, *The British Army in Northern Ireland,* (London, Arms and Armour Press, 1996).

Tony Geraghty, *The Irish War – The Military History of a Domestic Conflict*, (London, Harper Collins, 1998).

John, Glanfield, *Bravest of the Brave – The Story of the Victoria Cross*, (Stroud, Sutton, 2005).

Peter Harclerode, *Para! Fifty Years of the Parachute Regiment*, (London, Arms and Armour Press, 1992).

Peter Harper, *Sgt. Ian John McKay VC (1953–1982) – A Memoir with Recollections and Tributes from his Friends*, (Bath, NCUACS, 1989 – unpublished).

Max Hastings and Simon Jenkins, *The Battle for the Falklands* (London, Michael Joseph, 1983).

Jan Hutchings, *Falklands Memories*, (unpublished).

Christian Jennings and Adrian Weale, *Green Eyed Boys*, (London, Harper Collins, 1996).

Rick Jolly, *The Red and Green Life Machine*, (London, Century, 1983).

James Mackay and John W. Mussell, *Medal Yearbook*, (Honiton, Token Publishing, 2002).

John Parker, *Paras – The Inside Story of Britain's Toughest Regiment*, (London, Metro Books, 2000).

Hew Pike, *From the Front Line – Family Letters & Diaries 1900 to the Falklands & Afghanistan*, (Barnsley, Pen and Sword, 2008).

Francis Mackay and Jon Cooksey, *Pebble Island – Operation Prelim*, (Barnsley, Pen and Sword, 2007).

Martin Middlebrook, *The Falklands War 1982*, (London, Penguin, 2001).

Martin Middlebrook, *The Fight for the Malvinas – The Argentine Forces in the Falklands War*, (London, Viking, 1989).

Ministry of Defence, *Operation Banner – An Analysis of Military Operations in Northern Ireland*, (MOD, 2006).

Don Mullan, *Eyewitness Bloody Sunday*, (Dublin, Merlin Publishing, 2000).

John Percival, *For Valour*, (London, Methuen, 1985).

Peter Pringle and Philip Jacobson, *Those are Real Bullets Aren't They?* (London, Fourth Estate, 2000).

Phil Stone, Don Aldiss and Emma Edwards, *Rocks and Fossils of the Falkland Islands* (British Geological Survey for the Department of Mineral Resources, Falkland Islands Government, 2005).

Peter Taylor, *Provos – The IRA and Sinn Fein*, (London, Bloomsbury, 1997).

Peter Taylor, *Brits – The War Against the IRA*, (London, Bloomsbury, 2001).

Julian Thompson, *Ready for Anything – The Parachute Regiment at War 1940–1982*, (London, Weidenfeld and Nicolson, 1989).

Julian Thompson, *No Picnic*, (London, Cassell, 2001).

Nicholas van der Bijl, *Argentine Forces in the Falklands*, (Oxford, Osprey, 1992).

Nicholas van der Bijl, *Nine Battles to Stanley,* (Barnsley, Leo Cooper, 1999).

Periodicals and Journals

Duncan Anderson, 'Let's Remember Arnhem' – 2 Para and the Battle of Darwin/Goose Green, *Battlefields Review*, 19, 2002.

John Hughes-Wilson, The Falklands War 'How the Devil Did You Do It?' *Battlefields Review*, 18, 2002.

Colonel Hew Pike DSO MBE, With Fixed Bayonets, *The Elite*, Vol 2, 20, 1985.

The Falklands War (fourteen-part serial) Marshall Cavendish, (1983).

Pegasus, Journal of the Parachute Regiment and Airborne Forces. Vol XXXVII, No 3, July 1982 and Vol XXXVII, No 4, October 1982.

The Rotherham Advertiser.

Sheffield Star.

Woman, 28 March 1987.

Argentine sources

Teniente Coronel de Infanteria Carlos Eduardo Carrizo-Salvadores, 'El Combate en Monte Longdon', in *Coronel* Martin Antonio Balza (Ed.) *Malvinas: Relatos de Soldados*, (Buenos Aires: Biblioteca del Suboficial, Vol 154, 1983).

Informe Oficial del Ejercito Argentino – Conflicto Malvinas – Tomo II – Abreviaturas, Anexos y Fuentes Bibliograficas. Anexo 49 – Organización En Detalle de la Posición del Subsector Plata Entre Los Días 05/12 Jun 82. Anexo 50 – Ataque a la 1/B/RI 7 en Monte Longdon el 112130 Jun 82.

Websites

www.bbc.co.uk/news/10287463

www.britains-smallwars.com/Falklands/mt-longdon.htm

http://www.britains-smallwars.com/Falklands/David/Longdon.htm

www.cain.ulst.ac.uk

www.dailymail.co.uk/news/article-1286923/Bloody-Sunday—Saville-Inquiry-Soldiers-served-Ulster-died-Afghanistan.html#ixzz1jqlOoyYi

www.guardian.co.uk/uk/2010/jun/16/bloody-sunday-soldiers-military-uk

www.hansard.millbanksystems.com

www.webarchive.nationalarchives.gov.uk/20101103103930/http:/report.bloody-sunday-inquiry.org

www.paradata.org.uk

www.publications.parliament.uk

www.theposh.com

www.thestatcat.co.uk

www.uptheposh.com

Index